Security, Trust, and Regulatory Aspects of Cloud Computing in Business Environments

S. Srinivasan
Texas Southern University, USA

A volume in the Advances in Business
Information Systems and Analytics
(ABISA) Book Series

Managing Director:	Lindsay Johnston
Production Editor:	Jennifer Yoder
Development Editor:	Allyson Gard
Acquisitions Editor:	Kayla Wolfe
Typesetter:	Michael Brehm
Cover Design:	Jason Mull

Published in the United States of America by
Information Science Reference (an imprint of IGI Global)
701 E. Chocolate Avenue
Hershey PA 17033
Tel: 717-533-8845
Fax: 717-533-8661
E-mail: cust@igi-global.com
Web site: http://www.igi-global.com

Library of Congress Cataloging-in-Publication Data

Security, trust, and regulatory aspects of cloud computing in business environments / S. Srinivasan, editor.
    pages cm
 Includes bibliographical references and index.
 Summary: "This book compiles the research and views of cloud computing from various individuals around the world, detailing cloud security, regulatory and industry compliance, and trust building in the cloud"-- Provided by publisher.
 ISBN 978-1-4666-5788-5 (hardcover) -- ISBN 978-1-4666-5789-2 (ebook) -- ISBN 978-1-4666-5791-5 (print & perpetual access) 1. Information technology--Management. 2. Cloud computing. I. Srinivasan, S., 1948-
 HD30.2.S438 2014
 658.4'038028546782--dc23
                              2013050990

This book is published in the IGI Global book series Advances in Business Information Systems and Analytics (ABISA) (ISSN: 2327-3275; eISSN: 2327-3283)

British Cataloguing in Publication Data
A Cataloguing in Publication record for this book is available from the British Library.

All work contributed to this book is new, previously-unpublished material. The views expressed in this book are those of the authors, but not necessarily of the publisher.

For electronic access to this publication, please contact: eresources@igi-global.com.

Advances in Business Information Systems and Analytics (ABISA) Book Series

Madjid Tavana
La Salle University, USA

ISSN: 2327-3275
EISSN: 2327-3283

Mission

The successful development and management of information systems and business analytics is crucial to the success of an organization. New technological developments and methods for data analysis have allowed organizations to not only improve their processes and allow for greater productivity, but have also provided businesses with a venue through which to cut costs, plan for the future, and maintain competitive advantage in the information age.

The **Advances in Business Information Systems and Analytics (ABISA) Book Series** aims to present diverse and timely research in the development, deployment, and management of business information systems and business analytics for continued organizational development and improved business value.

Coverage

- Big Data
- Business Decision Making
- Business Information Security
- Business Process Management
- Business Systems Engineering
- Data Analytics
- Data Management
- Decision Support Systems
- Management Information Systems
- Performance Metrics

IGI Global is currently accepting manuscripts for publication within this series. To submit a proposal for a volume in this series, please contact our Acquisition Editors at Acquisitions@igi-global.com or visit: http://www.igi-global.com/publish/.

Titles in this Series

For a list of additional titles in this series, please visit: www.igi-global.com

Security, Trust, and Regulatory Aspects of Cloud Computing in Business Environments
S. Srinivasan (Texas Southern University, USA)
Information Science Reference • copyright 2014 • 333pp • H/C (ISBN: 9781466657885) • US $195.00 (our price)

Approaches and Processes for Managing the Economics of Information Systems
Theodosios Tsiakis (Alexander Technological Educational Institute of Thessaloniki, Greece) Theodoros Kargidis (Alexander Technological Educational Institute of Thessaloniki, Greece) and Panagiotis Katsaros (Aristotle University of Thessaloniki, Greece)
Business Science Reference • copyright 2014 • 449pp • H/C (ISBN: 9781466649835) • US $190.00 (our price)

Feral Information Systems Development Managerial Implications
Donald Vance Kerr (University of the Sunshine Coast, Australia) Kevin Burgess (Cranfield University, UK) and Luke Houghton (Griffith University, Australia)
Business Science Reference • copyright 2014 • 303pp • H/C (ISBN: 9781466650275) • US $185.00 (our price)

Uncovering Essential Software Artifacts through Business Process Archeology
Ricardo Perez-Castillo (University of Castilla-La Mancha, Spain) and Mario G. Piattini (University of Castilla - La Mancha, Spain)
Business Science Reference • copyright 2014 • 482pp • H/C (ISBN: 9781466646674) • US $195.00 (our price)

A Systemic Perspective to Managing Complexity with Enterprise Architecture
Pallab Saha (National University of Singapore, Singapore)
Business Science Reference • copyright 2014 • 554pp • H/C (ISBN: 9781466645189) • US $185.00 (our price)

Frameworks of IT Prosumption for Business Development
Małgorzata Pańkowska (University of Economics in Katowice, Poland)
Business Science Reference • copyright 2014 • 416pp • H/C (ISBN: 9781466643130) • US $185.00 (our price)

Handbook of Research on Enterprise 2.0 Technological, Social, and Organizational Dimensions
Maria Manuela Cruz-Cunha (Polytechnic Institute of Cavado and Ave, Portugal) Fernando Moreira (Portucalense University, Portugal) and João Varajão (Universidade de Trás-os-Montes e Alto Douro, Braga, Portugal)
Business Science Reference • copyright 2014 • 943pp • H/C (ISBN: 9781466643734) • US $325.00 (our price)

www.igi-global.com

701 E. Chocolate Ave., Hershey, PA 17033
Order online at www.igi-global.com or call 717-533-8845 x100
To place a standing order for titles released in this series, contact: cust@igi-global.com
Mon-Fri 8:00 am - 5:00 pm (est) or fax 24 hours a day 717-533-8661

To my family:
Lakshmi, Sowmya, Shankar, and Harish

Table of Contents

Section 1
Cloud Security

Chapter 1
Anita Lee-Post, University of Kentucky, USA
Ram Pakath, University of Kentucky, USA

Chapter 2
Amir Zeid, American University of Kuwait, Kuwait
Ahmed Shawish, Ain Shams University, Egypt
Maria Salama, British University in Egypt, Egypt

Chapter 3
Joseph M. Kizza, University of Tennessee – Chattanooga, USA
Li Yang, University of Tennessee – Chattanooga, USA

Chapter 4
M. Sundaresan, Bharathiar University, India
D. Boopathy, Bharathiar University, India

Detailed Table of Contents

Section 1
Cloud Security

Chapter 1

    Anita Lee-Post, University of Kentucky, USA
    Ram Pakath, University of Kentucky, USA

Cloud Computing refers to providing computing and communications-related services with the aid of remotely located, network-based resources without a user of such resources having to own these resources. The network in question typically, though not necessarily, is the Internet. The resources provisioned encompass a range of services including data, software, storage, security, and so on. For example, when we use a mail service such as Gmail, watch a movie on YouTube, shop at Amazon.com, or store files using DropBox, we are using cloud-based resources (The Google Chrome Team, 2010). In this chapter, the authors examine the evolution of Cloud Computing from its early roots in mainframe-based computing to the present day and also explain the different services rendered by Cloud Computing in today's business and personal computing contexts. This chapter provides a comprehensive view of the rapidly flourishing field of Cloud Computing and sets the stage for more in-depth discussions on its security, trust, and regulatory aspects elsewhere in this compendium.

Chapter 2

    Amir Zeid, American University of Kuwait, Kuwait
    Ahmed Shawish, Ain Shams University, Egypt
    Maria Salama, British University in Egypt, Egypt

Cloud Computing is the most promising computing paradigm that provides flexible resource allocation on demand with the promise of realizing elastic, Internet-accessible, computing on a pay-as-you-go basis. With the growth and expansion of the Cloud services and participation of various services providers, the description of quality parameters and measurement units start to diversify and sometime contradict.

Such ambiguity does not only result in the rise of various Quality of Service (QoS) interoperability problems but also in the distraction of the services consumers who find themselves unable to match quality requirements with the providers' offerings. Yet, employing the available QoS models that cover certain quality aspects while neglecting others drive consumers to perform their service selection based only on cost-benefit analysis and performance evaluation, without being able to perform subjective selection based on a comprehensive set of well-defined quality aspects. This chapter presents a novel QoS ontology that combines and defines all of the existing quality aspects in a unified way to efficiently overcome all existing diversities. Using such an ontology, a comprehensive broad QoS model combining all quality-related parameters of both service providers and consumers for different Cloud platforms is presented. The chapter also provides a mathematical model that formulates the Cloud Computing service provider selection optimization problem based on QoS guarantees. The validation of the provided model is addressed in the chapter through extensive simulation studies conducted on benchmark data of Content Delivery Network providers. The studies report the efficient matching of the model with the market-oriented different platform characteristics.

Chapter 3

Joseph M. Kizza, University of Tennessee – Chattanooga, USA
Li Yang, University of Tennessee – Chattanooga, USA

Cloud computing as a technology is difficult to define because it is evolving without a clear start point and no clear prediction of its future course. Even though this is the case, one can say that it is a continuous evolution of a computer network technology. It extends client-server technology that offers scalability, better utilization of hardware, on-demand applications and storage, and lower costs over the long run. It is done through the creation of virtual servers cloned from existing instances. The cloud technology seems to be in flux; hence, it may be one of the foundations of the next generation of computing. A grid of a few cloud infrastructures may provide computing for millions of users. Cloud computing technology consists of and rests on a number of sound, fundamental, and proven technologies. This includes virtualization, service-oriented architectures, distributed computing, and grid computing. Based on these fundamental and sound computing principles, one wonders whether cloud computing is the next trajectory of computing. This chapter discusses this in depth and also looks at the security issues involved.

Chapter 4

M. Sundaresan, Bharathiar University, India
D. Boopathy, Bharathiar University, India

Cloud storage systems can be considered to be a network of distributed datacenters that typically use cloud computing technology like virtualization and offer some kind of interface for storing data. To increase the availability of the data, it may be redundantly stored at different locations. Basic cloud storage is generally not designed to be accessed directly by users but rather incorporated into custom software using API. Cloud computing involves other processes besides storage. In this chapter, the authors discuss different viewpoints for cloud computing from the user, legal, security, and service provider perspectives. From the user viewpoint, the stored data creates a mirror of currently available local data. The backup feature allows users to recover any version of a previously stored data. Synchronization is the process of establishing consistency among the stored data. From the legal viewpoint, provisions regulating the user processing and storage of the data must have to be constant from when the data is stored in the cloud. The security viewpoint requires interaction with the Web application, data storage, and transmission. The service provider viewpoint requires the maximum level of cloud storage service at the minimum cost.

Chapter 5

Dipankar Dasgupta, University of Memphis, USA
Durdana Naseem, University of Memphis, USA

Many organizations are adopting cloud services to reduce their computing cost and increase the flexibility of their IT infrastructure. As cloud services are moving to the mainstream to meet major computing needs, the issues of ownership and chain of custody of customer data are becoming primary responsibilities of providers. Therefore, security requirements are essential for all service models (while the degree of defensive measures may vary) along with satisfying industry standard compliances. The authors develop an insurance framework called MEGHNAD for estimating the security coverage based on the type of cloud service and the level of security assurance required. This security coverage estimator may be useful to cloud providers (offering Security as a Service), cloud adopters, and cloud insurers who want to incorporate or market cloud security insurance. This framework allows the user/operator to choose a cloud service (such as Saas, Paas, IaaS) and other pertinent information in order to determine the appropriate level of security insurance coverage. This chapter describes an extension to the MEGHNAD (version 2.0) framework by incorporating security-related compliances. The compliance for each sector requires specific protection for online data such as transparency, respect for context, security, focused collection, accountability, access, and accuracy. The MEGHNAD tool can also generate a SLA document that can be used for monitoring by a certified Third-Party Assessment Organization (3PAO).

Chapter 6

Bina Ramamurthy, University at Buffalo, USA

In this chapter, the author examines the various approaches taken by the popular cloud providers Amazon Web Services (AWS), Google App Engine (GAE), and Windows Azure (Azure) to secure the cloud. AWS offers Infrastructure as a Service model, GAE is representative of the Software as a Service, and Azure represents the Platform as a Service model. Irrespective of the model, a cloud provider offers a variety of services from a simple large-scale storage service to a complete infrastructure for supporting the operations of a modern business. The author discusses some of the security aspects that a cloud customer must be aware of in selecting a cloud service provider for their needs. This discussion includes the major threats posed by multi-tenancy in the cloud. Another important aspect to consider in the security context is machine virtualization. Securing these services involves a whole range of measures from access-point protection at the client end to securing virtual co-tenants on the same physical machine hosted by a cloud. In this chapter, the author highlights the major offerings of the three cloud service providers mentioned above. She discusses the details of some important security challenges and solutions and illustrates them using screen shots of representative security configurations.

Section 2
Regulatory and Industry Compliance

Chapter 7

S. Srinivasan, Texas Southern University, USA

Compliance with government and industry regulations is an essential part of conducting business in several sectors. Many of the requirements revolve around financial, privacy, or security aspects. Most of the requirements are due to federal regulations in USA while some are industry requirements that are applicable globally. Even some of the federal regulations in USA apply to service providers abroad when they are providing service to entities in USA. In that sense, all of the compliance requirements discussed here apply to a global audience. In this chapter, the authors discuss in detail the scope of the Health Insurance Portability and Accountability Act, Sarbanes-Oxley Act, Federal Information Security Management Act, Gramm-Leach-Bliley Act, Payment Card Industry Requirements, and the Statement on Auditing Standards 70. These compliance requirements concern protecting the customer data stored in the cloud with respect to confidentiality and integrity. Several of these requirements have significant enforcement powers associated with them, and businesses need to take these requirements seriously and comply. The compliance aspect involves gathering and reporting appropriate information on a regular basis. The authors present details on all these aspects in this chapter.

Chapter 8

    S. Srinivasan, Texas Southern University, USA

Cloud computing is facilitated often through the open Internet, which is not designed for secure communications. From the cloud user perspective, access to the cloud through a Virtual Private Network (VPN) is a possibility, but this is not the default access method for all cloud users. Given this reality, the cloud service users must be prepared for risk management because they do not control the cloud hardware or the communication channels. Added to this uncertainty is the potential for cloud service outage for risk management planning. In this chapter, the authors discuss the various aspects of risk management from the cloud user perspective. In addition, they analyze some of the major cloud outages over the past five years that have resulted in loss of trust. This list includes the outages in Amazon Web Services, Google, Windows, and Rackspace.

Chapter 9

    Michael Losavio, University of Louisville, USA
    Pavel Pastukhov, Perm State University, Russia
    Svetlana Polyakova, Perm State University, Russia

Cloud computing allows us to solve problems of information on a global scale and of a full range of tasks. Cloud computing has many advantages, but the reliability of data protection is a major concern of provider-client, industry, and governmental regulation. These information systems must comply with existing standards and anticipate new standards of information security. The legal process must distinguish who is responsible for what within a dynamically changing infrastructure significantly different from traditional models. The authors first examine the models and substance of regulation as established by service-level agreements between cloud providers, their clients, and their clients' customers. The authors discuss industry self-regulation and government regulations regarding data protection, privacy, criminal and tort law, and intellectual property law complicated by the inherent cross-jurisdictional nature of cloud computing.

Chapter 10

    Mario A. Garcia, Texas A&M University – Corpus Christi, USA

As computer technology evolved over the last 30 years, so did the opportunity to use computers to break the law. Out of necessity, digital forensics was birthed. Computer forensics is the practice of extracting information from the digital media in order to prosecute the individuals that carried out the crime.

Forensic challenges presented by cloud computing are vast and complex. If a company becomes the target of a digital criminal investigation and they are using cloud computing, some unique challenges are faced by a digital forensics examiner. The data in the cloud only represents a "snapshot" of when it was sent to the cloud. Establishing a chain of custody for the data would become difficult or impossible if its integrity and authenticity cannot be fully determined. There are also potential forensic issues when the customer or user exits a cloud application. Items subject to forensic analysis, such as registry entries, temporary files, and other artifacts are lost, making malicious activity difficult to prove. The challenges of applying forensics to a cloud environment are tied to cloud security. This chapter discusses securing a cloud environment and how that would help with the forensic analysis.

Section 3
Trust Builders in the Cloud

Chapter 11

Bing He, Cisco Systems, Inc., USA
Tuan T. Tran, InfoBeyond Technology LLC, USA
Bin Xie, InfoBeyond Technology LLC, USA

Today, cloud-based services and applications are ubiquitous in many systems. The cloud provides undeniable potential benefits to the users by offering lower costs and simpler deployment. The users significantly reduce their system management responsibilities by outsourcing services to the cloud service providers. However, the management shift has posed significant security challenges to the cloud service providers. Security concerns are the main reasons that delay organizations from moving to the cloud. The security and efficiency of user identity management and access control in the cloud needs to be well addressed to realize the power of the cloud. In this chapter, the authors identify the key challenges and provide solutions to the authentication and identity management for secure cloud business and services. The authors first identify and discuss the challenges and requirements of the authentication and identity management system in the cloud. Several prevailing industry standards and protocols for authentication and access control in cloud environments are provided and discussed. The authors then present and discuss the latest advances in authentication and identity management in cloud, especially for mobile cloud computing and identity as a service. They further discuss how proximity-based access control can be applied for an effective and fine-grained data access control in the cloud.

Chapter 12

Haibo Wang, Texas A&M International University, USA
Da Huo, Central University of Finance and Economics, China

This chapter considers the data center site selection problem in cloud computing with extensive reviews on site selection decision models. The factors considered in the site selection include economic, environmental, and social issues. After discussing the environmental impact of data centers and its social implications, the authors present a nonlinear multiple criteria decision-making model with green computing criteria and solve the problem by using a variable neighborhood search heuristic. The proposed model and solution methodology can be applied to other site selection problems to address the environmental awareness, and the results illustrate both the robustness and attractiveness of this solution approach.

Chapter 13

Girish Suryanarayana, Siemens Corporate Research and Technologies, India
Roshan Joseph, Siemens Corporate Research and Technologies, India
Sabishaw Bhaskaran, Siemens Corporate Research and Technologies, India
Amarnath Basu, Siemens Corporate Research and Technologies, India

Cloud technology is used for a variety of purposes in order to handle large volumes of data. This chapter explores a rural healthcare project in India in which cloud technology was introduced in order to store and share large volumes of data. This project benefits from cloud technology because of the ability to store patients' full health history on the cloud and access them wherever services are provided. The impetus for this project originated with the fact that many hospitals maintained their proprietary information systems, and thus, patient history was unavailable to physicians outside of that system. The search engine used in this project is called Indexer, which can search a vast collection of records stored in the cloud and help with the diagnosis. The solution developed supports multi-tenancy of data and uses the Azure platform. The project has taken adequate precautions to protect the data. This project is not focused on privacy protection per se but on saving lives.

Chapter 14

Sathish A. Kumar, Coastal Carolina University, USA

Cloud computing is touted as the next big thing in the Information Technology (IT) industry, which is going to impact the businesses of any size. Yet, the security issue continues to pose a big threat. Lack of transparency in the infrastructure and platforms causes distrust among users, and the users are reluctant to store information on the cloud. This undermines the potential of cloud computing and has proved to be a big barrier in the realization of the potential of cloud computing and its widespread adoption. The big paradigm shifts in the technology has not been reflected on the methods used to secure the technology. When an organization builds the infrastructure for cloud computing, security and privacy controls should be kept in mind from the holistic security perspective. It is also critical that the organization monitor and adapt controls to determine the success of cloud computing in dealing with the security and reliability issues relating to the cloud. From an organizational control perspective, the authors suggest an independent governing body to mediate between the cloud provider and the user, with the control framework that they have developed to fulfill their responsibilities of protecting the cloud environment.

Foreword

It gives me great pleasure to write this Foreword for this timely book, *Security, Trust, and Regulatory Aspects of Cloud Computing in Business Environments*. The book comprises 14 chapters arranged into 3 sections. The editor has put together an excellent collection of chapters on many of the important aspects of cloud security. In Section 1, "Cloud Security," there are 6 chapters. The chapters deal with the basics of Cloud Computing and the security issues to be considered in selecting a cloud service provider. Moreover, the cloud security aspects are discussed from the perspective of the cloud user, cloud service provider, and cloud service vendor in another chapter. One of the chapters analyzes Cloud Computing from various perspectives such as trust, service-oriented architecture, virtualization, etc.

In Section 2, "Regulatory and Industry Compliance," there are 4 chapters. These chapters deal with various regulatory aspects in USA such as the Sarbanes-Oxley Act (SOX), Federal Information Security Management Act (FISMA), Health Insurance Portability and Accountability Act (HIPAA), and the Gramm-Leach-Bliley Act (GLBA). These acts significantly protect information handling. Additionally, this part describes the requirements of the Payment Card Industry (PCI), which is global in nature. There is also a chapter on Cloud Forensics, which describes how one could trace the access requirements to stored data in internal systems.

In Section 3, "Trust Builders in the Cloud," there are 4 chapters. There is a fine discussion on cloud provider selection by a potential customer based on Quality of Service criteria. Extending on this theme another chapter discusses data center site selection aspects from the perspective of green computing. The book concludes with the importance of identity management in the cloud and shows how trust aspects significantly enhance the cloud adoption.

The contributors to this compilation come from various parts of the world and bring their expertise from multiple viewpoints. The editor has selected the chapters covering a wide array of important issues in Cloud Computing. The title of the book clearly reflects the contributions contained in the book. I wish to congratulate the editor for an excellent job in assembling in one source a set of important content related to Cloud Computing in the business environment. The readers will find the content well suited for their understanding of the issues associated with security, regulatory compliance, and trust aspects of Cloud Computing.

Ravi Sandhu
University of Texas – San Antonio, USA
October 18, 2013

Ravi Sandhu *is Executive Director of the Institute for Cyber Security at the University of Texas at San Antonio, where he holds the Lutcher Brown Endowed Chair in Cyber Security. Previously, he was on the faculty at George Mason University (1989-2007) and The Ohio State University (1982-1989). He holds B.Tech. and M.Tech. degrees from IIT Bombay and Delhi, and M.S. and Ph.D. degrees from Rutgers University. He is a Fellow of IEEE, ACM, and AAAS, and has received awards from IEEE, ACM, NSA, and NIST. A prolific and highly cited author, his research has been funded by NSF, NSA, NIST, DARPA, AFOSR, ONR, AFRL, and private industry. His seminal papers on role-based access control established it as the dominant form of access control in practical systems. His numerous other models and mechanisms have also had considerable real-world impact. He is Editor-in-Chief of the IEEE Transactions on Dependable and Secure Computing, and founding General Chair of the ACM Conference on Data and Application Security and Privacy. He previously served as founding Editor-in-Chief of ACM Transactions on Information and System Security and on the editorial board for IEEE Internet Computing. He was Chairman of ACM SIGSAC, and founded the ACM Conference on Computer and Communications Security and the ACM Symposium on Access Control Models and Technologies and chaired their Steering Committees for many years. He has served as General Chair, Program Chair, and Committee Member for numerous security conferences. He has consulted for leading industry and government organizations, and has lectured all over the world. He is an inventor on 29 security technology patents. At the Institute for Cyber Security, he leads multiple teams conducting research on many aspects of cyber security, including secure information sharing, social computing security, cloud computing security, secure data provenance, and botnet analysis and detection, in collaboration with researchers all across the world. His Website is at www.profsandhu.com.*

Preface

Cloud Computing has emerged as an effective alternative to organization-based information systems. In the traditional approach, companies invested in the hardware and software and created their own Information Systems departments. Managing such a department required extensive expertise for the personnel involved. Moreover, with the rapid advancements in both hardware and software capabilities, it became very cost prohibitive for many companies to manage their own systems. Furthermore, companies needed extensive financial resources in order to build and maintain a reliable information system that would be up and running at all times because of the 24x7 need for access to information. Nearly a decade ago, the concept of Cloud Computing emerged as a way to provide an alternative for companies in having access to computing resources and at the same time not have to worry about managing their own computer systems. Over the past eight years, this technology has matured quite a bit and many new cloud service providers have emerged. Among these cloud service providers the leaders are Amazon, Google, Microsoft, Rackspace, and Salesforce.

Amazon Web Services (AWS) quickly evolved as the leader in cloud services. Its offerings such as Elastic Compute Cloud (EC2) and Amazon Simple Storage Service (S3) attracted customers globally. Today, Amazon is by far the largest cloud service provider. Their market penetration shows that they are 14 times larger than the nearest cloud service competitor. As mentioned above, Google, Microsoft, Rackspace, and Salesforce all provide specialized services that are in demand. Unlike Amazon, Google is providing its leading cloud products such as Google Docs, Skydrive, GoogleApps, and Gmail as a free service. Microsoft is trying to transform their key product, the Microsoft Office, into the new Office 365 suite as a cloud service. Microsoft is also a major player in the Software as a Service and Platform as a Service markets through their Office 365 and Windows Azure services. Rackspace specializes in Web hosting and highly reliable customer service for their cloud offerings. Salesforce has been the leader in Customer Relations Management (CRM) application via the Web for nearly 15 years. In this book, we look at the services offered by these companies and how these different service providers are trying to guarantee security of customer data both in processing as well as in storage.

Cloud computing has a significant impact on e-commerce. This service is expected to grow from a $54 billion economic impact in 2014 to $240 billion in 2020 globally according to an IDC study. Furthermore, this level of economic impact is accompanied by a significant job growth globally. The job growth projection for three years is shown in Table 1.

The reader will find in the chapters of the book the significance of keeping up this level of job and economic growth using cloud computing.

We try to highlight in the various chapters how security and trust plays a key role in customers feeling reassured about using cloud services. In spite of widespread adoption of cloud computing, many users

Table 1. Job growth projection for three years

Year	Global job growth in millions
2013	9
2014	11
2015	14

are still concerned about security of their data in the cloud. The reason for this concern is that the cloud users were accustomed to controlling their hardware and software. This gave them the confidence that their data did not fall into the wrong hands. With the popularity of cloud computing, when a cloud user places their data in the cloud they do not control the hardware or software. Furthermore, some of the major cloud service providers such as Amazon, Google, and Microsoft have had outages in their services. Except in rare cases, the data was not lost but was unavailable when needed. I wanted to assemble in one source the material that addressed many of the issues that cloud users faced regularly. That is the reason for the title of the book, Security, *Trust, and Regulatory Aspects of Cloud Computing in Business Environments*. In this book, I have assembled a collection of 14 chapters that address various aspects of cloud service use. These chapters were contributed by various people from around the globe. This global aspect further enhances the value of this collection of chapters because it shows how people around the world view the cloud services. Even though many of the cloud service providers are US-based, the end users are all over the world.

The book is organized in three sections. In Section 1 the focus is on cloud security. This section consists of six chapters that address the issues associated with cloud services from a security perspective. The content here explains the basic features of cloud computing for the uninitiated and compares the cloud service with other newer technological approaches to making computing accessible to the masses. The chapters in this section address the rationale for cloud computing and the different perspectives of cloud services. Chapter 1 gives an extended overview of all the basics of cloud computing such as the three primary service types—SaaS, PaaS, IaaS—and the four deployment models—Public cloud, Private cloud, Hybrid cloud, and Community cloud. Moreover, many security issues are also highlighted in this chapter. Chapter 2 addresses the question of Quality of Service (QoS) that can be expected from the cloud service provider. This is an important aspect and this is emphasized in multiple chapters of the book. It is important for the cloud customer to note that they may have compliance issues to address and so knowing the QoS will help significantly in meeting the compliance requirements. The analysis here is quite extensive, and there is simulation data to show that QoS aspects could be met by the cloud service provider. Chapter 3 poses the basic question "Is Cloud the Future of Computing?" In answering this question the authors clearly point out the significant strides made during the last decade in the area of high speed communications and thus facilitate the success of cloud computing. This chapter goes on to discuss in detail various security issues that the cloud customer must be aware of in making a decision about the choice of cloud service provider.

In Chapter 4, the authors discuss the different perspectives with which one could view cloud services. The viewpoints considered are from the user, legal, security, and service provider perspectives. The details in this chapter pertain to the following. When viewing cloud service from the cloud customer perspective it is important to know that the data is protected in storage and during transmission as well as its availability. The cloud customer will need to understand the data backup features of the cloud service provider. The cloud customer needs full synchronization of data in all the stored versions, as the data integrity is key to the success of any business. The legal perspective focuses on the question of liability of the organization storing the data. The cloud customer wants to be assured that the data stored did not get altered by unauthorized entities. Since the user does not physically control the stored data and the cloud service provider for operational reasons keeps multiple copies of the data, a greater level of responsibility lies with the cloud service provider in protecting the stored data. It is to be noted here that the cloud service provider will not know the sensitivity levels of various data stored in the cloud, and so it is the responsibility of the cloud customer to designate such data sensitivity so that the cloud service provider could provide adequate security. The authors discuss the security aspects from the perspective of storage, transmission, and Web applications that access the data. This chapter concludes with a discussion of the cloud service provider perspective where the goal is to provide maximum level of cloud storage at the least cost for the service provider. From the experience of Amazon Web Services, this is a significant challenge for the cloud service provider as some of the service failures occurred during the process of duplicating the data elsewhere for redundancy.

Chapter 5 focuses on security from a coverage estimation aspect. The authors here discuss the cloud security from a compliance perspective and show how the MEGHNAD model that they had developed would help in security coverage estimation. The framework developed here would allow a cloud customer to choose one of the three types cloud services (SaaS, PaaS, IaaS) and combine it with other related requirements such as data availability and decide on the level of security insurance coverage that they would need. In this chapter, the authors describe an extension of the MEGHNAD project by incorporating security related compliance aspects. The significance of this aspect is that various industries have different levels of data protection requirements such as transparency of storage policies and location, security, assurance for data integrity, access control, and accountability. The authors also show how the enhanced MEGHNAD project discussed here could be used to generate Service Level Agreements (SLAs) that could be used by a third party organization to monitor the service. It is worth noting that for security purposes the cloud industry is attracting the services of security specialists who have the expertise to monitor security aspects on behalf of a cloud customer. The reader would be well served by taking this information and contextualizing it from the results of Ponemon Institute Study in 2011 where many cloud service providers think that it is not their responsibility to protect the customer data. Results of this particular study are discussed in at least two other chapters as well.

We conclude Section 1 with a chapter focused on securing business IT in the cloud. In Chapter 6, the author focuses on three major cloud service providers – Amazon Web Services (AWS), Google App Engine, and Windows Azure. These three services account for nearly 85% of all cloud services globally. Another reason for choosing these three service providers for consideration in this chapter is because AWS is a well-known IaaS service provider, Google App Engine is a dominant SaaS service provider, and Windows Azure is a leading PaaS service provider. The security issues involved here range from access point protection at the customer end to protecting the virtualized cloud infrastructure and assuring the cloud customer of the separation of services in a multi-tenant environment. The author provides a detailed overview of the security aspects tested using screen shots so that the reader could follow the details easily.

In Section 2, the topic is Regulatory Aspects and Industry Compliance. The four chapters in this section discuss in detail various regulatory and compliance requirements for the cloud customer and how the cloud service providers could provide the necessary data and transparency for the cloud customer to meet their compliance requirements. In order for information gathered by businesses to remain secure, many governments have enacted laws. In USA, the major laws in this regard are the Sarbanes-Oxley Act (SOX), the Health Insurance Portability and Accountability Act (HIPAA), Gramm-Leach-Bliley Act (GLBA), and the USA PATRIOT Act. Besides government regulations, there are also industry standards that must be met by businesses. Foremost among these types of industry requirements is the credit card industry compliance requirements known as PCI-DSS (Payment Card Industry – Data Security Standard). Since credit card usage is global in nature, all cloud service providers must meet these industry standards. Chapter 7 focuses on the compliance requirements in general based on HIPAA, SOX, GLBA, and PCI. These compliance requirements concern protecting the customer data stored in the cloud with respect to confidentiality and integrity. Many of these laws have significant penalties associated with them for non-compliance. Foremost among them are the SOX and HIPAA laws. In order for cloud customers to meet their expectation for cloud security compliance, it would be better for the cloud service provider to have their own set of guidelines that enable the cloud service user to document their own data protection. This aspect is facilitated by a set of global auditing guidelines called SAS-70 Type II Audit. Since the Federal government in USA is a major user of technology, there are additional guidelines known as the Federal Information Security Management Act (FISMA) that must be met when dealing with federal systems. From the use of cloud services perspective it is important to note that because of its global nature, many foreign governments are concerned about the impact of USA PATRIOT Act whereby the US government could access all data stored in US territories. This is an important issue for the cloud service providers to consider when they back up the data.

Chapter 8 in the book discusses in detail the risk management issues associated with cloud service. The main issue for several cloud customers is the availability of the cloud service on a 24x7 basis. The major cloud service providers are large enough to assure a 99.99% availability of their service. The author points out that in order to provide this level of service the system outage could not exceed 53 minutes per year. However, in reality many of the service providers have experienced outages that lasted for as many as three days at a time on a repeated basis. This kind of lack of reliability poses a significant risk for several businesses because they depend on the cloud service providers for all their computing needs. This chapter shows how businesses could transfer some of their risks to the cloud service provider and make changes in others to mitigate their risk. This includes using encryption to store data. However, this is costly for most businesses. An alternative to this approach would involve protecting the data during transmission only via a Virtual Private Network (VPN). Another alternative discussed here points out the use of Virtual Private Clouds (VPCs). Only large businesses could afford to use VPCs as it provides all the benefits of a cloud service but involves higher costs than the standard public cloud. Another approach to reducing risk involves the use of hybrid cloud and community cloud. These would be applicable for only certain segments of cloud customers. The details on these are discussed in this chapter.

In Section 2, we have included two chapters on Cloud Computing Forensics so that the user will be aware of the issues with regard to security and how they could track the evidence on the cloud. Chapter 9 discusses the forensic aspects from both the US and Russian perspectives. The other chapter discusses the basic tools available for performing a forensic analysis in the event of a data breach. To begin with, the customer must be assured that the cloud infrastructure is reliable. In order to provide this kind of assurance to the cloud customer the SAS 70 Type II Audit would provide the necessary documentation. Often people are concerned with their ability to analyze any breaches in their data. The approach in this chapter is from the compliance aspects of regulations in place and the service level agreements agreed to by the cloud service provider and the cloud customer. A significant challenge to forensic examination of data in the cloud is the cross-jurisdictions involved because the cloud service providers store data in various parts of the world where the legal requirements for data privacy vary widely.

Chapter 10 on Cloud Computing Forensics discusses some of the tools available for this purpose. Typically, in forensics examinations the chain of custody for the data becomes an important factor. The chain of custody for data will be difficult to prove in a cloud environment. A forensics examiner will need access to the hardware used in committing a crime because the hardware will contain registry entries, temporary files, and other important pieces of information that could be tied to the perpetrator of the crime. In a cloud environment, the access to the hardware is ruled out because the cloud customer does not own it and so other means of proving the breach becomes essential. The challenges posed by cloud computing in this regard include establishing the responsible party in a dynamically changing infrastructure. This is vastly different from the traditional forensics approach where the forensics examiner will be able to examine the computer used to commit a crime.

We conclude the book with Section 3, titled "Trust Builders in the Cloud." This section contains four chapters. Chapter 11 addresses the question of Authentication and Identity Management in the cloud for business services. In order to realize the full potential of the cloud the cloud customers need to understand how best they could control access to their cloud resources and manage the identity of all users who access their data. First, this chapter identifies the challenges and requirements of the authentication and identity management system in the cloud environment. Then the chapter discusses the recent advances in authentication and identity management in the cloud, with special attention paid to mobile device access. This chapter concludes with a discussion on proximity-based access control for an effective and fine-grained data access control in the cloud.

The focus of Chapter 12 is Green Computing in the context of site selection for locating the data centers for cloud storage. When we look at many of the cloud outages over the past five years, we notice that many of the outages occurred in one geographic area of the world. Since the cloud service provider chooses the site for locating their data centers, the only choice the cloud customer has is in choosing their storage sites. The discussion in this chapter will help answer some of the questions for the cloud customer regarding site selection for their storage sites based on the available data centers of the cloud service provider. These factors include economic, environmental, and social issues. The authors present a nonlinear multiple criteria decision-making model with green computing requirements. This site selection model could be applied to other problems as well where environmental issues are a factor to be considered. The authors show that this approach is very robust.

In Chapter 13, the authors look at an application of the cloud computing methodology to solve a practical problem in the world. It relates to addressing the healthcare needs of rural population in India. The solutions discussed in this chapter could be applied to various parts of the world where the communications infrastructure is not adequate, but the healthcare needs are extensive. This chapter describes the practical aspects of such management from a major global corporation in a country with a very large rural population. The challenge is in making the cloud technology available in rural parts of the world. One of the important takeaways from this chapter is that the rural population in the world cares more about receiving medical care than about privacy protection. For this population, living trumps data security.

The final chapter in the book addresses the importance of organizational control related to the cloud. In Chapter 14, the authors discuss the importance of having security features as part of the original design rather than as an add-on feature. It is pointed out that without transparency in policies related to data storage customers will be reluctant to store data in the cloud. Features such as share, download, and import are risk factors for a business and so there should be better organizational control on all these aspects when the data is stored in the cloud. One of the recommendations of the authors to enhance customer trust is to have an independent third party as an intermediary to verify the security practices of the cloud service provider at each stage of the data movement through the cloud.

It is my earnest hope that this collection of chapters will spur further interest among the readers to explore the various issues raised in these chapters. For example, the security and trust aspects are very important for businesses and consumers. In fulfilling their business expectations, the businesses have to be compliant with regulations in each jurisdiction in which they are doing business. Given the global nature of cloud technology, the issues that arise span multiple jurisdictions across the globe and so there is no one single standard to be met in order to provide the cloud service. The collection of chapters in this book is but one attempt in helping people understand the issues involved with security in the cloud and how they could protect the data by diversifying their cloud usage among multiple service providers.

The contributors to this book come from USA, India, China, Russia, Kuwait, and Egypt. I want to thank all these contributors for their dedication and commitment to this project. This project took over one year to complete and all the contributors patiently waited as the review process was completed and met all the requirements of the publisher.

I have carefully edited all the chapters in the book for accuracy of content and presentation. It is very likely that some errors and omissions might have escaped my attention. In such cases, I take responsibility for such omissions, and I very much welcome your communication to set the matter straight. I will be able to keep the book error-free by updating the publisher's Website after the publication of the book.

S. Srinivasan
Texas Southern University, USA
November 4, 2013

Acknowledgment

A book project of this nature succeeds with the collective contributions of many people. First and foremost, I want to thank my family for being so understanding and supportive of the many hours that I devoted to this project. I want to express my sincere appreciation to the following people at IGI Global for their support of this book project over the past year: Ms. Kayla Wolfe, Ms. Monica Speca, Ms. Jan Travers, Ms. Christine Smith, and Ms. Allyson Gard. Ms. Allyson Gard, the Editorial Assistant, has been of great help in answering the many questions that came up as I was corresponding with the various contributors. Thank you all for guiding this project. When I started this project in August 2012, I needed to send out the Call for Chapters. This effort was ably assisted by Miss Ana Ruiz, Student Assistant at Texas A&M International University's Sanchez School of Business by creating the distribution list. When the chapter materials started coming, I needed to find a sufficient number of reviewers. In this effort, the Association for Information Systems helped me by allowing me to post the Call for Reviewers to their membership with interest in Cloud Computing.

The reviewers came from various countries. I want to thank all the reviewers for their insightful comments that helped enhance the quality of the chapters. I want to thank each of these reviewers for their timely contribution to this book project.

I want to express my deep debt of gratitude to Dr. Ravi Sandhu, Lutcher Brown Endowed Chair in Cyber Security and Executive Director of Institute for Cyber Security at the University of Texas at San Antonio, for writing the Foreword for this book.

S. Srinivasan
Texas Southern University, USA

Section 1
Cloud Security

Chapter 1
Cloud Computing:
A Comprehensive Introduction

Anita Lee-Post
University of Kentucky, USA

Ram Pakath
University of Kentucky, USA

ABSTRACT

Cloud Computing refers to providing computing and communications-related services with the aid of remotely located, network-based resources without a user of such resources having to own these resources. The network in question typically, though not necessarily, is the Internet. The resources provisioned encompass a range of services including data, software, storage, security, and so on. For example, when we use a mail service such as Gmail, watch a movie on YouTube, shop at Amazon.com, or store files using DropBox, we are using cloud-based resources (The Google Chrome Team, 2010). In this chapter, the authors examine the evolution of Cloud Computing from its early roots in mainframe-based computing to the present day and also explain the different services rendered by Cloud Computing in today's business and personal computing contexts. This chapter provides a comprehensive view of the rapidly flourishing field of Cloud Computing and sets the stage for more in-depth discussions on its security, trust, and regulatory aspects elsewhere in this compendium.

1. THE EVOLUTION OF CLOUD COMPUTING

The adjective "Cloud" in Cloud Computing refers to the network used for service provisioning. In diagrams describing cloud-based services, the cloud is often literally depicted as the outline of a hand-drawn cloud on paper. The use of cloud-like shapes in diagrams depicting networks such as the Internet dates back many years and is a staple of mainstream text books and articles on data communication networks. The term "Cloud Computing," though, is relatively new. To better comprehend this relatively nascent phenomenon, let us go back in computing history and examine earlier models of provisioning services over a communications network, i.e., the precursors of present-day Cloud Computing.

DOI: 10.4018/978-1-4666-5788-5.ch001

1.1 Time-Sharing on Mainframe Computers

The early 1950s saw the advent of commercial "mainframe" computers such as the IBM 701. These computers were single-user, non-shareable, one-job-at-a-time systems and were rented by companies for about $25,000 a month. Several programmers signed up, on a first-come-first-served basis, for "sessions" on a mainframe where each session was a block of time dedicated to processing a single "job" (i.e., a program). Each programmer took about 5 minutes to set-up his/her job including punching in at a mechanical clock, hanging a magnetic tape, loading a punched card deck, and pressing a "load" button to begin job processing (Chunawala, n.d.). Inefficiencies in the process due to excessive manual intervention resulted in much wasted processing time even as jobs were queued and often delayed.

To improve process efficiency, General Motors (GM) and North American Aviation (NAA) (today, part of Boeing) developed an operating system, the GM NAA I/O (Input/Output) system and put it into production in 1956 (Chunawala, n.d.). This heralded the advent of "batch processing" where multiple jobs could be set up at once and each run to completion without manual intervention ("Batch Processing", n.d.). Further improvements were realized with the advent of the IBM System 360 mainframe in 1964 which separated I/O tasks from the CPU (Central Processing Unit) and farmed these out to an I/O sub-system, thus freeing up the CPU to perform computations required by a second job when another job was interrupted for I/O operations. Batch processing offered several benefits: Individual jobs in a batch could be processed at different times based on resource availability, system idle time was reduced, system utilization rates were improved and, as a consequence, per-job processing costs were reduced.

With batch processing, a computer's time is considered considerably more valuable than a human's and human work is scheduled around the machine's availability. In contrast, "interactive computing," considers a human's time as being the more valuable and views a computer only as a capable "assistant." Early implementations of interactive computing include the IBM 601 that allowed a single user interactive use at a time. However, allowing one user to monopolize a scarce resource also resulted in considerable inefficiency in resource utilization. On the other hand, offering several interactive users seemingly concurrent usage would result in better use of the electronic assistant ("Interactive Computing", n.d.). In 1961 MIT introduced the world's first Time Sharing Operating System, the Compatible Time Sharing System (CTSS). In due course, IBM introduced a Time Sharing Option (TSO) in the OS 360 operating system used in the IBM System 360. Time Sharing introduced further processing efficiencies over batch processing. Rather than process a job in its entirety, time sharing would devote a short duration of time called a "time slice" to processing a job and then turns to devote similar attention to another job. The CPU so rapidly switches from job to job that it appears to each user that his/her job has the full and complete attention of the CPU -- a user experiences no noticeable delays.

A natural outgrowth of interactive computing was remote access to a computer via terminals. Several terminals were "multiplexed" over telephone lines using individual modems to connect users to a single mainframe. Shared mainframe interactive access and use via multiplexed terminals and the telephone network may be regarded the earliest Cloud Computing model although it was then referred to as Time-Sharing. In the 1960s, several vendors offered Time-Sharing "services" to businesses. These included Tymshare, National CSS, Dial Data, and BBN using equipment (mainframe and minicomputers) from IBM, DEC, HP, CDC, Univac, Burroughs, and others.

1.2 Peer-to-Peer and Client-Server Computing

The advent of commercially–viable personal computers (PCs) from Apple, Commodore, and Tandy Corp., coupled with the rising use of PCs beginning in the late 70s and well into the 80s and beyond heralded the decline of Time-Sharing with larger (mainframe and mini) computers (Scardino, 2005). Initially, PCs, apart from use for business computing using software like VisiCalc (spreadsheet) and Lazy Writer (word processing), were also used as terminals to connect to the larger machines by running terminal emulation software. Soon the market opened up to vendors like Atari, TI, NEC and others. In 1981, IBM entered the fray with its IBM PC. In due course, many users discovered that the combined processing capability of a number of networked PCs was sufficient to meet their needs. Such "clouds" began proliferating in two forms – peer-to-peer and client-server computing.

1.2.1 The Peer-to-Peer Model

In peer-to-peer (or P2P) computing, each computer in the network can act as both a service requestor and a service provider for the remaining computers in the network/cloud. This facilitated the sharing of expensive and/or scarce resources such as data files, printers, scanners, hard disks, and tape drives. There is no central authority or "master," like a mainframe in time-sharing, where each terminal acted in a subservient, "slave" role and only when the mainframe made time available for it. In a P2P network, every computer could act as master or slave at different epochs. P2P networks enabled intra- and inter-organizational networks with each additional computer added to the network bringing added capability to the system. At the same time, the network was more resilient than one with a master-slave arrangement as it did not have the vulnerability of a single point of failure – if one or a few nodes (i.e., PCs) in a P2P network were to fail, the rest of the "cloud" could continue operating.

The Internet, originally conceived as the ARPANET in the late 1960s by the US Department of Defense, was a P2P system (Minar, 2001). Its goal was to facilitate the sharing of computing resources around the U.S. using a common network architecture that would allow every host to be an equal player. Whereas early, widely-used applications like Telnet and FTP were Client-Server applications, the system as a whole was P2P as every Internet host could Telnet or FTP any other host and hosts were not associated in master-slave relationships. The widespread deployment of PCs, first in businesses and then in homes, fueled the rapid proliferation of P2P computing in the 80s and after.

1.2.2 The Client-Server Model

Personal Computers were also exploited in a different manner which may be seen as a via-media between the completely autocratic mainframe-dumb terminal model and the fully democratic P2P model. The Client-Server model was introduced by Xerox PARC (Palo Alto Research Center) in the 70s. This model assigns one of two roles, namely client (i.e., slave) or server (i.e., master) to every computer on a network. Thus, a single computer may not act as client or server like in the P2P model. At the same time, the network is not restricted to hosting multiple, weak clients (i.e., terminals) tethered to a single, powerful, server as in mainframe-terminal networks. A server makes available resources in its purview that a client seeks. Each server also deals with multiple client requests and does so in a time-shared manner as discussed earlier with mainframe computing.

The Internet, which started out as largely a P2P network, morphed over time into a largely client-server network. This transition was accelerated by the Internet boom of the mid 90s when the general public, and not just scientists, flocked to the net as a means for email exchanges, web browsing, and online shopping. This transformation has continued until the post-year 1998 re-emergence of P2P applications like Napster, Gnutella, Kazaa, and BitTorrent for music, movie, and game file-sharing. Indications are that the Internet will likely continue as a hybrid environment hosting both P2Pand Client-Server applications for the foreseeable future.

1.3 Grid Computing

Yet another paradigm in Cloud Computing's evolution is Grid Computing whose origins date back to the 90s. This paradigm was motivated by analogy to the electrical power grid that provides pervasive, dependable, and consistent access to utility power ("Grid Computing", n.d.). Grid Computing is a variant of Cluster Computing with the difference being that the computers on a grid could be heterogeneous, loosely coupled/dynamically harnessed, and geographically dispersed systems. Grid Computing also differs from conventional Distributed Computing by emphasizing large-scale resource sharing, devotion to innovative applications, and high-performance.

A Grid Computing system is also an autonomous system in that it aims to be self-configuring, self-tuning, and self-healing. Together the members of a grid form a "virtual" super-computer whose power and resources are available to a user based on resource availability, capability, performance, cost, and quality-of-service expectations. Grid Computing systems are devoted to processing complicated tasks such as the search for extraterrestrial intelligence (SETI), protein folding, drug design, molecular modeling, financial modeling, high-energy physics, brain activity analysis, earthquake and warfare simulation, and climate/weather modeling ("Grid Computing Info Center", n.d.). An especially large Grid Computing system is the WLCG (Worldwide LHC Computing Grid) spanning more than 170 computing centers in 36 countries. Its purpose is to store, distribute, and analyze the near-25 petabytes of data generated every year by the Large Hadron Collider (LHC) at CERN (Conseil Europeen pour la Recherche Nucleaire (French), or the European Council for Nuclear Research), Geneva ("Worldwide LHC Computing Grid", n.d.).

1.4 Utility Computing

The Utility Computing model was also inspired by utility services like electricity but in a manner different from Grid Computing. Utility Computing drew its inspiration from how public utility customers pay metered rates based on usage. In similar spirit, Utility Computing seeks to make available cloud-based computing resources to customers for payment based on usage. In essence, a user outsources all or part of its computing resource needs to another entity, the Utility Computing services provider (Strickland, 2008). The key distinguishing characteristic is that the fee for services is not a flat fee but is usage based. The benefits to a user are that it is absolved of owning such resources and of attendant responsibilities such as those related to acquisition, housing, installation, maintenance, troubleshooting, upgrading, securing, and usage.

Though the term "Utility Computing" was first postulated in 1961, companies like IBM with their mainframe time-sharing models were, in a sense, pioneers in Utility Computing ("Utility Computing", n.d.). Following the decline in mainframe demand and the emergence of PCs, Utility Computing resurfaced in the late 1990s and early 2000s with vendors like InSynQ, HP, Sun Microsystems and Alexa establishing Utility Computing services. Today, Utility Computing vendors include well-recognized names like IBM, Amazon, and Google. Of the various Cloud Computing-related historical milestones discussed thus far, the Utility Computing paradigm is perhaps closest in spirit to present-day Cloud Computing and also the cause for much confusion as to what distinguishes it from Cloud Computing.

1.5 Virtualization

Another concept underlying Cloud Computing is Virtualization. Virtualization refers to the simulated creation of something – a computer, an operating system, a storage device, or any other computing or communication resource (such as a wide network) – without having a physical/actual instance of it. This concept dates back many decades and was pioneered beginning in the early 1960's by entities like GE, IBM, MIT, and Bell Labs. Following a few years of experimenting with one-off, laboratory versions of the concept, the IBM CP-67 mainframe, launched in 1968 and running the CP-CMS operating system, was the first commercial computer to support Virtualization and was installed at eight customer sites (Conroy, 2011).

There are several kinds of Virtualization in the computing world. A discussion encompassing all of these kinds is beyond the present scope. Hardware or Platform Virtualization is a common instance that we describe next. In general, Hardware Virtualization results in the creation of one or more "guest" or "virtual" machines (VM) running within a "host" or "actual" machine. This may be accomplished with the aid of software generally called a Hypervisor or Virtual Machine Monitor (VMM). Examples of VMMs include Microsoft's Virtual Server, VMWare's GSX, and IBM's VM/ESA. To each of many guest users supported by a single host, it appears as if an isolated, self-contained computer is available for his/her use although each of these is a virtual machine and not an actual/physical computer. The extent of virtualization in Hardware Virtualization could also differ. There are three levels of Hardware Virtualization called Full Virtualization (near-complete hardware environment simulation to allow guest applications to run un-modified), Partial Virtualization (some hardware environment elements, but not all, are simulated permitting some applications to run un-modified), and Para Virtualization (absolutely no hardware environment simulation but guest applications run in isolated domains and must be modified).

Two common forms of Hardware Virtualization are Server Virtualization and Desktop Virtualization. Thus a single, physical (i.e., host) server could support multiple virtual servers, resulting in fewer physical server instances, energy savings, and maintenance ease. Desktop Virtualization (also called Desktop as a Service (DTaaS), Virtual Desktop, or Hosted Desktop Services) allows users to access an entire computing environment via a remote client device such as a smartphone, tablet, or laptop by running desktops as Virtual Machines on a provider's server where all desktop user environments are managed and secured. Further, DTaaS allows sharing of virtual desktops among multiple users. By outsourcing Desktop Virtualization, issues such as resource provisioning, load balancing, networking, back-end data storage, backup, security, and upgrades are handled by DTaaS providers such as Citrix.

Note that Hardware Virtualization is distinct from Time Sharing. Traditional Time Sharing devotes an entire host computer to multiple users but at different times – we do not create multiple, self-contained machines, all concurrently available to multiple users. With Virtualization (Beal, 2012), there is the potential for more efficient use of resources (i.e., fewer physical machines, better space efficiency, better energy efficiency (reduced electrical consumption and reduced cooling costs), better security (each user could be running a separate operating system and not sharing one), and increased reliability (a single user could not crash the entire system, only his/her Virtual Machine)). However, Virtualization also exacts a toll – the more VMs that are deployed, the greater the potential degradation in performance of each VM and there still are privacy and security risks to the multiple users sharing a single physical host. Even so, as we shall see subsequently in this chapter, Virtualization is being harnessed as a key enabler of modern Cloud Computing.

1.6 Service-Oriented Architecture

A further development that underlies Cloud Computing is the Service-oriented Architecture (SOA). SOA allows an application's business logic or individual functions to be modularized and presented as services for other consumer/client applications (Kodali, 2005). These service modules are "loosely coupled" in the sense that the service interface of a module is independent of its implementation. As such, application developers or system integrators can build applications by drawing upon service modules as needed without regard to their underlying implementation details. For instance, a service can be implemented either in .Net or J2EE (Java 2 Platform Enterprise Edition), and the application consuming the service could use a different platform or language. Each module offers a small range of simple services to other components. The modules can be combined and re-combined in numerous ways and comprise a highly flexible information technology (IT) applications infrastructure. Thus, SOA is an approach to building IT systems that allows a business to leverage existing assets, create new ones, and easily enable changes that businesses inevitably must accommodate over time (Hurwitz, 2013).

Note that the emphasis of SOA is on software reusability – don't "throw away" effort already put in nor spend time re-inventing the wheel as with coding each application from scratch. With the emphasis on re-using simple code modules, a company does not experience the traditional development and maintenance time and cost drawbacks commonly associated with a proliferation of expensive, monolithic systems drawing on heterogeneous technology. Each software module in SOA is something that provides a business service and these business services are invariably shared by many different applications company wide. Through software redundancy reduction or elimination, SOA provides much of the same benefits associated with software consistency, maintainability, and scalability (Hurwitz, 2013).

1.7 The Cloud Computing Paradigm

The above-discussed computing paradigms, while distinct from one another in some respects, also possess shared traits. A predominant common characteristic is that all of them involve provisioning shared resources over a networked infrastructure that we call a "cloud." Today, though, there is considerable brouhaha over the most recent paradigm in this evolutionary chain, called Cloud Computing.

What is Cloud Computing and how does it differ, if at all, from any or all of the paradigms just discussed? There is considerable confusion surrounding the term. This confusion is not restricted just to the lay person or prospective clients of the service. At Oracle OpenWorld 2008, Oracle Corp. CEO Larry Ellison famously noted (Farber, 2008):

The interesting thing about Cloud Computing is that we've redefined Cloud Computing to include everything that we already do. I can't think of anything that isn't Cloud Computing with all of these announcements. The computer industry is the only industry that is more fashion-driven than women's fashion.

Ellison also went on to observe:

We'll make Cloud Computing announcements. I'm not going to fight this thing. But I don't understand what we would do differently in the light of Cloud.

The computing community at large was (and, perhaps, is) divided … about half believed that Ellison was absolutely correct in his assessment and the other regarded him as a heretic. To us, Ellison was not arguing that Cloud Computing was a fad but that the label was a fad and that he and others had been practicing Cloud Computing in one form or another for a number of years without using the label Cloud Computing. More recently, Ellison followed through on his second observation and, as recently as September 2012, announced the launch of an Infrastructure-as-a-Service (IaaS) cloud service (Bort, 2012), one of several possible services we discuss subsequently in Section 4. Examining available literature on Cloud Computing lends credence to Ellison's viewpoint as many explanations of Cloud Computing fall short. As one example (Biswas, 2011):

Just like water from the tap in your kitchen, Cloud Computing services can be turned on or off quickly as needed. Like at the water company, there is a team of dedicated professionals making sure the service provided is safe, secure and available on a 24/7 basis. When the tap isn't on, not only are you saving water, but you aren't paying for resources you don't currently need.

This explanation begs the question, "What, then, is Utility Computing?" and adds to the confusion in an already confused client-base. On the other hand, there are other descriptions that better articulate what Cloud Computing is and why it is different.

The National Institute of Standards and Technology (NIST) defines Cloud Computing thus (Mell and Grance, 2011):

Cloud Computing is a model for enabling ubiquitous, convenient, on-demand network access to a shared pool of configurable computing resources (e.g., networks, servers, storage, applications, and services) that <u>can be rapidly provisioned and released with minimal management effort or service provider interaction.</u>

The key insight on how Cloud Computing differs from its predecessors is contained in the latter portion of this definition that we have underlined for emphasis. Perry (2008) elaborates on this aspect:

The big news is for application developers and IT operations. Done right, Cloud Computing allows them to develop, deploy and run applica-tions that can easily grow capacity (scalability), work fast (performance), and never — or at least rarely — fail (reliability), all without any concern as to the nature and location of the underlying infrastructure. .... So although they are often lumped together, the differences between Utility Computing and Cloud Computing are crucial. Utility Computing relates to the business model in which application infrastructure resources — hardware and/or software — are delivered. While Cloud Computing relates to the way we design, build, deploy and run applications that operate in a virtualized environment, sharing resources and boasting the ability to dynamically grow, shrink and self-heal.

We see that while the distinction between Cloud Computing and its predecessors (most notably, Utility Computing) might appear ambiguous from a consumer standpoint, there is a clear distinction from a provider perspective. The focus of Cloud Computing is on mitigating or eliminating problems associated with traditional application development and freeing up organizational IT units to focus on business strategy and how to best leverage cloud-based IT to support that strategy. As should become evident in our discussions that follow, Cloud Computing, depending on needs, draws upon many of the earlier paradigms such as Utility and Grid Computing, Client-Server and Peer-to-Peer Computing, Virtualization, and Service-Oriented Architecture. These earlier paradigms comprise the building blocks of present-day Cloud Computing.

2. CLOUD COMPUTING MODELS

To date, four models for Cloud Computing services deployment have been defined – Private Cloud, Public Cloud, Community Cloud, and Hybrid Cloud ("Cloud Computing", n.d.). We discuss and differentiate between these deployment models next.

2.1 Private Cloud

A Private Cloud (InfoWorld, n.d.) is cloud infrastructure established for sole use by a single organization. It is also referred to as an Internal Cloud or Corporate Cloud (Rouse, 2009a). Either the organization's corporate network and data center administrators become cloud service providers operating behind the corporate firewall or the Private Cloud is hosted by a third-party provider solely for the organization. Either way, such a cloud serves the organization's "internal" customers and no one else. If constructed in-house, establishing a private cloud requires a significant commitment to virtualizing the business environment. In essence, the organization must acquire, build, and manage such a cloud all of which calls for substantial resource investments. An outsourced Private Cloud also is more expensive than a Public Cloud. Thus, a Private Cloud usually negates the cost advantages that accrue with outsourcing IT infrastructure which is a primary goal of migrating to the cloud for many organizations. Yet some organizations have sought to establish Private Clouds for reasons other than cost savings, such as better control, security, privacy, customization flexibility, and reliability, vis-à-vis a Public Cloud service (Altnam, 2012).

Private Cloud toolkits include IBM's Web Sphere CloudBurst Appliance, HPs CloudStart, and Amazon's Virtual Private Cloud. Third-party Private Cloud vendors such as Sabre Holdings establish Private Clouds for individual airlines and Siemens has set up individual secure, virtual test centers for its partner organizations. Other examples of Private Cloud implementation include NASA's Nebula and the US Defense Information Systems Agency's Rapid Access Computing Environment (RACE) program (McKendrick, 2010). As is evident from these examples, Private Clouds tend to be deployed by large organizations with significant resources at their disposal.

2.2 Public Cloud

A Public Cloud (Rouse, 2009b) is one that is operated and managed at datacenters belonging to service providers and shared by multiple customers (multi-tenancy). As such, it does not reside behind an organization's corporate firewall nor is it meant for exclusive use. Multi-tenancy results in lower costs to each tenant. However, this cost reduction comes at a price.

A recent Trend Micro survey (Subramanian, 2011b) of 1200 organizations with at least 500 employees in 6 countries notes that 93% indicated that they were using at least one cloud service provider, 38% felt that their cloud service providers were failing to meet their IT and business needs, 43% had a security lapse in the last year, 55% were concerned about un-encrypted shared storage, and 85% chose to encrypt and also keep local copies of all files in the cloud. Apart from security-related concerns, multi-tenancy also means susceptibility to resource contention issues between tenants, reduced control, reduced infrastructure visibility/transparency, and having to cope with varied compliance/regulatory requirements as the infrastructure could potentially be located at multiple locations worldwide.

Public Cloud toolkit vendors include the Elastic Compute Cloud (EC2) from Amazon, Blue Cloud from IBM, the Azure Services Platform from Microsoft, and AppEngine from Google. Illustrative case studies of Public Cloud deployment by an automaker (Lamborghini), an education sector (Northern Ireland), an online movie rental company (Netflix), a city council (Sunderland City), a TV Channel (Channel 4), and others may be found at "Public Cloud Examples and Case Studies" (n.d.).

2.3 Hybrid Cloud

A Hybrid Cloud, sometimes called a Cloud Federation, is one that is composed of at least one Private Cloud and at least one Public Cloud

(Rouse, 2010). A Hybrid Cloud is a via-media between choosing just Public or Private Clouds given their respective strengths and weaknesses discussed above. It is an attempt by an organization to get the best of both worlds.

Some organizations deploy both types of clouds with mission-critical applications or inward-facing applications deployed on Private Clouds and other applications (including external-facing applications) deployed on Public Clouds. Another motivation for Hybrid Clouds is Cloud Bursting, where an application running on a Private Cloud is dynamically deployed on a Public Cloud during a demand surge (Subramanian, 2011a). Some suggest that the Hybrid Cloud is an intermediate stage, with organizations moving more content to Public Clouds as that environment matures but using Private Clouds for critical applications in the interim. A Hybrid Cloud makes the migration easier to achieve.

2.4 Community Cloud

We just discussed two extreme cloud types (Private and Public) and a combination type (Hybrid) that imbibes some of each of the two extreme types. A fourth approach, the Community Cloud, is also a hybrid cloud but in quite a different sense. A Community Cloud, like a Public Cloud, employs a multi-tenant infrastructure. However, all members of the community belong to a specific group with common computing concerns related to service levels, security, regulatory compliance, etc. (Rouse, 2012). These concerns are addressed to the community's satisfaction by a Community Cloud and in that sense they receive Private Cloud-like benefits. The intent is to take advantage of the benefits of the Public and Private Cloud types all within the same cloud. A Community Cloud can be co-located and governed by the participating organizations or be outsourced.

The "community" in a Community Cloud may be a specific vertical industry such as education, government, or healthcare (Butler, 2012). Thus, a Healthcare Community Cloud is one customized for members of that industry. Community Cloud toolkits include IGT Cloud from International Game Technology devoted to gaming companies, the Optum Health Cloud from United Health Group intended for the healthcare community, Creative Cloud from Adobe for creative professionals (O'Dell, 2012), and the Global Financial Services Cloud from CFN services . An example application of this strategy is the Community Cloud deployed by the Virginia Community College Systems (VCCS) to serve its 23 colleges and 40 campuses (Grush, 2011).

3. CLOUD COMPUTING SERVICES

Given our understanding of the term "Cloud Computing," its evolution, and models for deployment, we next turn to examining the different services rendered by Cloud Computing in response to customer needs. Figure 1 pictorially depicts the various Cloud Computing services and provider and customer interactions with the cloud and its services using wired and wireless devices. These services span a client's infrastructure needs, application needs, security needs, storage needs, and so forth. We discuss each, in turn, below.

According to the NIST, Infrastructure as a Service (IaaS), together with Platform as a Service (PaaS) and Software as a Service (SaaS), are the three fundamental Cloud Computing service models (Mell and Grance, 2011). These three service models follow a computer's architecture and provide services at the hardware, system, and application level respectively (Zhou, 2010). We discuss the three basic variants and sub-classes within each in the following sections as well as a few other service models namely, Data as a Service (DaaS) and Security as a Service (SECaaS).

Figure 1. A conceptual view of cloud computing

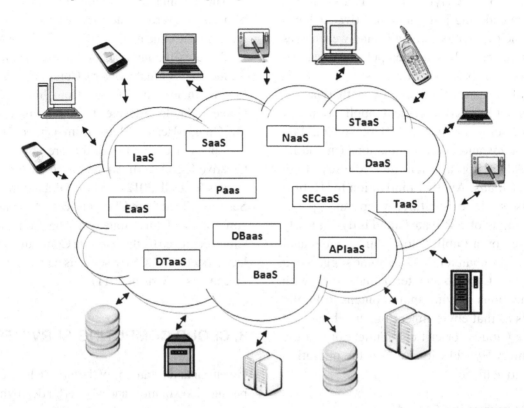

3.1 Infrastructure as a Service (IaaS)

IaaS, a hardware-level service, provides computing resources such as processing power, memory, storage, and networks for cloud users to run their applications on-demand (Stallings, 2013). This allows users to maximize the utilization of computing capacities without having to own and manage their own resources. It represents a paradigm shift from viewing infrastructure as an asset to regarding it as an outsourced service. IaaS providers (e.g., Amazon EC2, Windows Azure Virtual Machines, Google Compute Engine) host computers as Virtual Machines that are managed by low-level codes called hypervisors such as Xen or KVM to meet users' computing needs. IaaS users pay for resources allocated and consumed on a Utility Computing basis and enjoy the flexibility of dynamically scaling their computing

infrastructure up or down according to resource demands without incurring capital expenditures on these resources that are often underutilized (Hurwitz, 2012).

3.1.1 Network as a Service (NaaS)

Network as a Service (NaaS), an instance of IaaS, provides users with needed data communication capacity to accommodate bursts in data traffic during data-intensive activities such as video conferencing or large file downloads. NaaS providers (e.g., Verizon, AT&T) operate using three common service models: virtual private network (VPN), bandwidth on demand (BoD), and mobile virtual network (MVN). VPN extends a private network's functionality and policies across public networks such as the Internet. BoD dynamically allocates bandwidth to bursty traffic demands by multiple users. MVN is a mobile network that is not owned by a mobile services provider but is leased from an entity that owns the infrastructure. In essence, the lessor provides NaaS to the lessee, who in turn provides needed services to end consumers (i.e., is a reseller). By considering networking and computing resources as a whole, NaaS providers are better able to optimize these resource allocations to users with network connectivity services ("Network as a Service", n.d.).

3.1.2 Storage as a Service (STaaS)

Storage as a Service (STaaS), a form of IaaS, provides storage infrastructure on a subscription basis to users who want a low-cost and convenient way to store data, synchronize data across multiple devises, manage offsite backups, mitigate risks of disaster recovery, and preserve records for the long-term. With data growing at an annual rate of over 20%, storage capacity requirements will need to be doubled every two to three years (Marko, 2012). According to InformationWeek Analytics Public Cloud Storage Survey, archiving emails and meeting retention policies were the top reasons for storage growth (Biddick, 2011). By outsourcing storage to STaaS providers (e.g., Amazon Simple Storage Service, IBM Tivoli Storage Manager), users shift the burden of capacity management, operations, and maintenance to the provider. In addition, the growing use of mobile devices such as smartphones, laptops, and tablets to access company data will intensify the need for data consolidation and synchronization. STaaS users have access to their data anytime anywhere over the Internet. They can specify how often and what data should be backed up. They can also request a copy of the data in case of data corruption or loss. Indeed, backup, disaster recovery, file archiving and email archiving were the top reasons that organizations were considering cloud storage (Biddick, 2011). However, concerns over security, privacy, reliability, availability, performance, data loss and service disruptions, especially for industries such as healthcare, financials, and legal services, may prevent users from using STaaS to store their primary (or mission-critical) data.

3.1.3 Database as a Service (DBaaS)

Database as a Service (DBaaS), also related to IaaS, provides users with seamless mechanisms to create, store, and access databases at a host site on demand. DBaaS providers are also responsible for the management of the entire database including backup, administration, restoration, reorganization, and migration. Cloud-based database systems such as Google BigTable, Amazon Simple DB, and Apache HBase allow users to submit queries to databases with generic schemas. Google Cloud SQL allows users to create, configure, and use relational databases within Google App Engine applications. Data privacy and security remain the key concerns with DBaaS (Lehner, 2010).

3.1.4 Backend as a Service (BaaS)

Backend as a Service (BaaS), a type of IaaS, provides web and mobile app developers a way to connect their applications to backend cloud storage with added services such as user management, push notifications, social network services integration using custom software development kits and application programming interfaces. BaaS users save time and effort in having a consistent way to manage backend data and services ("Backend as a Service", n.d.).

3.1.5 Desktop as a Service (DTaaS)

Another widely-used instance of an infrastructural service is Desktop as a Service (DTaaS) or Desktop Virtualization. We refer the reader to a brief description that appears in Section 2.5 on Virtualization.

3.2 Platform as a Service (PaaS)

Platform as a Service (PaaS), a system level service, provides users with a computing platform for the development, testing, deployment, and management of applications (Stallings and Case, 2013). Users build their own applications using programming languages and tools supported by PaaS providers. These applications then run on a provider's infrastructure and/or are delivered to end-users via the Internet from the provider's servers. PaaS providers (e.g., Amazon Elastic Beanstalk, Windows Azure Compute, and Google App Engine) bring together middleware such as databases, operating systems, and tools to support software development and delivery on a pay-per-use basis. PaaS users gain efficiency and productivity with a standardized application development process without the cost and complexity of allocating computer and storage resources to match demand for development and testing activities (Hurwitz, 2012).

3.3 Software as a Service (SaaS)

Software as a Service (SaaS), an application level service, allows users to access a provider's applications from various devices through a thin client interface such as a web browser (Stallings and Case, 2013). SaaS providers (the best-known example is salesforce.com) use a multi-tenant architecture to deliver a single application to thousands of users on a subscription basis. SaaS users gain access to needed applications without the hassles associated with software licensing, installation, maintenance, upgrades, and applying patches. SaaS is especially appealing to small businesses that cannot afford to own and manage high-end enterprise software such as accounting, invoicing, human resource management, customer relationship management, and enterprise resources planning. In addition, SaaS desktop applications (e.g., Google Apps, Office 365, Zoho Office)

provide collaborative possibilities that allow users from remote locations to work together on the same application document in real-time via the Web (Hurwitz, 2012).

3.3.1 Testing as a Service (TaaS)

Testing as a Service (TaaS), provides users with software testing capabilities such as generation of test data, generation of test cases, execution of test cases, and test result evaluation on a pay-per-use basis (Yu et al., 2010). Software testing requires costly and extensive computing resources such as servers, storage, and network devices but for a limited time. Consequently it makes sense to outsource testing tasks to TaaS providers. For example, UTest offers functional, security, load, localization, and usability testing services ("Software Testing", n.d.).

3.3.2 API as a Service (APIaaS)

API as a Service (APIaaS) is closely related to SaaS, but instead of delivering full-blown applications as in SaaS, APIaaS provides Application Programming Interfaces (API) for users to exploit functionality of such Web services as Google Maps, payroll processing (e.g., by ADP Inc.), and credit card processing services (e.g., through Merchant Express). APIaaS offered by PaaS providers such as Google App Engine (Google, Inc., 2012) allows developers to build feature-rich applications to perform various functionalities including: application log keeping and accessing, large data set generation and processing (MapReduce), Secure Socket Layer encrypted applications, website performance analyses and optimization (PageSpeed), location aware queries, user authentication, instant messaging, instant update browser channel establishment, application tasks scheduling and execution, web content retrieval, and language translation.

3.3.3 Email as a Service (EaaS)

Email as a Service (EaaS), an instance of SaaS, provides users with an integrated system of emailing, office automation, records management, migration, and integration services with archiving, spam blocking, malware protection, and compliance features. Emailing services include calendaring, contacts and instant messaging, mobile device integration, and search capabilities. Office automation services include web conferencing, document sharing, and browser-based office productivity suites. Records management services include integrating document management with email, and providing APIs for records searching and management. Migration services include migrating email systems and data, end user training, and migrating mobile users. Integration services include development and technical maintenance for integration of applications and project management. EaaS users reap the benefits of saving on licensing and maintaining the hardware and software of a company's email system ("Email as a Service (EaaS)", n.d.).

3.4 Data as a Service (DaaS)

Data as a Service (DaaS) provides data on demand to a diverse set of users, systems, or applications. Leading DaaS providers such as DataDirect offer software to connect business applications to data whereby data connectivity for distributed systems is simplified and streamlined. Data encryption and operating system authentication are commonly provided for added security. DaaS users have access to high-quality data in a centralized place and pay by volume or data type, as needed. However, because the data is owned by the providers, users can only perform read operations on the data. Nonetheless with the global data volume reaching 1.8 zettabytes (a zettabyte is about a trillion gigabytes) in 2011 and growing by a factor of nine in five years (Gantz, 2011), attention has been shifted to Big DaaS such as Google's Public Data

service that aggregates, manages, and provides access to data on public institutions and government agencies (EMC Solutions Group, 2012). Google DaaS users can use Google Public Data Explorer to mash up and visualize data dynamically.

3.5 Security as a Service (SECaaS)

Security as a Service (SECaaS) is a new approach to security in which cloud security is moved into the cloud itself whereby cloud service users will be protected from *within* the cloud using a unified approach to threats. Four mechanisms of cloud security are currently provided: email filtering, web content filtering, vulnerability management, and identity management (Getov, 2012). Email services are protected where they reside against malware, spam, and phishing threats through email filtering. Web content filtering includes URL filtering, HTTP header screening, page content and embedded links analyses, and outgoing web traffic monitoring to block sensitive information such as IDs, credit card information, and intellectual property from being compromised. Vulnerability management protects clients from a shared environment using application firewalls between virtual machines, virtual intrusion detection systems, cloud antiviruses, and virtual private networks linking virtual machines. Identity management centralizes identification requests to ensure standards compliance, single sign-on interoperability, and provisions of identification, authentication, authorization, and accountability functionalities.

4. CLOUD COMPUTING AND WEB 2.0/WEB 3.0 INITIATIVES

We have just described the different Cloud Computing services available to customers. As previously noted, the NIST (Mell and Grance, 2011) defines Cloud Computing as, " ... a model for enabling ubiquitous, convenient, on-demand network access to a shared pool of configurable computing resources (e.g., networks, servers, storage, applications, and services) that can be rapidly provisioned and released with minimal management effort or service provider interaction." This view of Cloud Computing has given rise to some confusion with another term that is currently very popular in computing circles, namely, Web 2.0. Here, we define Web 2.0 and attempt to draw distinctions and relationships between Cloud Computing and Web 2.0.

The term Web 2.0 was first introduced by Dinucci (1999) in the article, "Fragmented Future." Dinucci observed then that we were glimpsing the beginning of a new way of using the web that she termed Web 2.0 in contrast to its predecessor, Web 1.0. Web 1.0 (Getting, 2007) is the original World Wide Web as conceived in 1989 by Tim Berners-Lee while a researcher at CERN. Web 1.0 is a "read only" web in the sense that content providers and consumers are considered distinct groups and all that consumers could do was to search for and consume web content provided by others. There was very little user interaction with the web and with other users and very little content provision by the typical consumer. Online advertising, e-catalogs, e-brochures, and online shopping carts are all part of the Web 1.0 experience.

We are presently at a different stage of using the web which is termed as the "read-write" web by Berners-Lee. Today, we have services like those listed below where many of us are both content providers and consumers:

- **Blogs:** The maintenance of "web logs;" e.g., the Nudge blog.
- **Twitter:** A "micro-blogging" service with a restriction of 140 characters per "tweet"; e.g., Jet Blue's use of tweets to answer consumer queries about flights and service ("JetBlue Airways (JetBlue) on Twitter", n.d.).
- **Mashups:** Websites created by users by drawing on content from other websites

such as raidsonline.com (a mapping mash-up) and bizrate.com (a shopping mashup).
- **Facebook:** for social networking; e.g., Skittles' Facebook Fan Page.
- **MySpace:** for social networking but with an emphasis on music.
- **LinkedIn:** for professional networking.
- **YouTube:** for video sharing.
- **Podcasting:** distributing audio or video content to gadgets like cell phones, MP3 players, laptops, and desktops from internet servers.

This "interactive" web is what Dinucci termed as Web 2.0 as far back as 1999 when such use was emerging. According to Dinucci, Web 2.0 would also eventually be distinguished by its ability to allow users to interact with it using gadgets such as televisions (e.g., YouTube and Netflix access via AppleTV), Car Dashboard equipment (for navigation, yellow pages), cell phones (for weather, navigation, flight status updates, news), gaming consoles (for linking players with one-another over the net using, e.g., Sony 's PlayStation or Microsoft's XBox), personal digital assistants (palmtop computers or PDAs such as the iPod Touch), etc., collectively labeled "portable, web-ready" devices. The hardware, interface, and performance characteristics of each device are quite different from the others. Yet, Web 2.0 would be accessible from these different platforms apart from desktop machines running web browsers like Firefox, Explorer, Safari, and Chrome.

O'Reilly (2008) notes that virtually all Web 2.0 applications are cloud applications. From this perspective, Cloud Computing applications encompass Web 2.0 applications and Cloud Computing offers a myriad of tools that enable the facile construction and delivery of Web 2.0 applications. Further, Web 2.0 proponents note that the term denotes not just a set technical specifications for a "new/improved" Web, but represents a set of economic, social and technology trends that collectively form the basis for the next generation

Internet. As such, the ongoing Cloud Computing trend, which clearly is a socio-technological trend driven largely by economic considerations, may be regarded as an enabler of Web 2.0. Lastly, efforts are underway for a move toward what Berners-Lee terms the "read-write-execute" web or Web 3.0. Web 3.0 seeks to:

1. Transform the entire web into a distributed, global data base system housing not only structured content as present day data-driven web sites require but also less structured content such as emails, documents, audio, images, and video;
2. Rely heavily on artificial intelligence (intelligent agents, in particular) and natural language processing in assisting users with search in a context-sensitive and personalized manner (the iPhone Siri Intelligent Personal Assistant is an example),;
3. Transform the web into a Semantic Web whereby ontological meta data to aid intelligent agents is embedded in the web along with associated web content data, and
4. Rely heavily on real-time, 3-D content presentation using the ISO X3D file format and XML (Extensible Markup Language) to offer rich, visual communication of web content where applicable.

In our view, many of the ongoing developments in Cloud Computing may also be regarded as enablers of the Web 3.0 vision.

5. PURPORTED BENEFITS OF CLOUD COMPUTING

The current high levels of interest in, and the positive press enjoyed by, Cloud Computing are fueled in part by its perceived benefits. Perry (2008) notes that the ideal Cloud Computing infrastructure would possess the following desirable characteristics:

- **Self-Healing:** In case of failure, there will be a hot backup instance of the application ready to take over without disruption. When a backup becomes the primary, the system launches a new backup.
- **SLA-Driven:** The system is dynamically managed by service-level agreements that define policies such as how quickly responses to requests need to be delivered.
- **Multi-Tenancy:** The system is built in a way that allows several customers to share infrastructure with mutual opacity and without compromising privacy and security.
- **Service-Oriented:** The system allows composing applications out of discrete, reusable, loosely-coupled services. Changes to, or failure of, a service will not disrupt other services.
- **Virtualized:** Applications are decoupled from the underlying hardware. An application may rely on Grid Computing and multiple applications could run on a single computer.
- **Linearly Scalable:** The system will scale predictably and efficiently (linearly) with growing demand.
- **Data, Data, Data:** The key to many of the above desirable characteristics is management of data: its distribution, partitioning, security and synchronization using technologies like Amazon's SimpleDB (large-scale relational databases) and in-memory data grids.

According to premier Cloud Computing vendor, Salesforce.com, given a properly-implemented Cloud Computing solution, a client should experience some or all of the following benefits:

- **Proven Web-Services Integration:** Cloud Computing technology is much easier and quicker to integrate with other enterprise applications.

- **World-Class Service Delivery:** Cloud Computing infrastructures offer much greater scalability, complete disaster recovery, and impressive uptime numbers.

- **No Hardware or Software to Install:** Cloud Computing requires significantly lesser capital expenditures to get up and running.

- **Faster and Lower-Risk Deployment:** No more waiting months or years and spending millions of dollars before anyone gets to log into your new solution. Cloud Computing technology applications are alive in a matter of weeks or months, even with extensive customization or integration.

- **Support for Deep Customizations:** The Cloud Computing infrastructure not only allows deep customization and application configuration, it preserves all those customizations even during upgrades and with evolving needs, thus freeing up organizational IT resources.

- **Empowered Business Users:** Cloud computing technology allows on-the-fly, point-and-click customization and report generation for business users, so IT doesn't spend significant time on such tasks.

- **Pre-Built, Pre-Integrated Apps:** Hundreds of pre-built applications and application exchange capabilities are either pre-integrated into larger, off-the-shelf applications or available for quick integration to form new applications.

6. CHALLENGES FACING CLOUD COMPUTING

6.1 Challenges from a Provider Perspective

Like any technology before it, Cloud Computing, must submit to the NFLT (No Free Lunch Theo-

rem!), its positives notwithstanding. According to a 2012 survey of senior executives at 179 Cloud service providers by KPMG Int'l (Krigsman, 2012), there are several challenges that providers perceive in fostering widespread adoption/deployment of Cloud Computing as Figure 2 depicts.

Observe that the top three perceived challenges relate to establishing a value proposition. The survey also identifies perceived confusion on the part of Cloud Services customers (Krigsman, 2012):

Less than half of the providers in the survey feel their customers are informed or well-informed about Cloud Computing at the executive level. Only 43 percent believe users are aware of cloud costs vis-à-vis their existing IT services, and a similar proportion feel they do not fully understand cloud security, pricing models, integration with existing infrastructure and service level agreements (SLAs).

6.2 Challenges from a Customer Perspective

It appears that even as organizations appear enthusiastic about Cloud Computing in general, and many indicate that launching cloud applications is a major priority, several seem to harbor insecurities about getting their feet wet. IDC estimates that global spending on Cloud Computing will be $148 billion by 2014 and K. Bailey (CMO, Verizon Enterprise Solutions), places the figure closer to $600-$750 billion (Knorr, 2012). While this represents only about 20% of estimated spending on all of IT in 2014, the projections for the future are even more bullish.

The InfoWorld Cloud Computing Special Report, 2012, identifies nine challenges faced by customers new to Cloud-based IT application deployment (i.e., continued Cloud Computing evolution):

Figure 2. Cloud provisioning challenges (adapted from: Krigsman 2012)

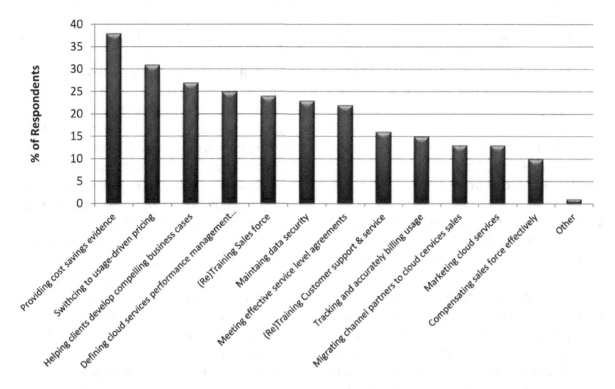

- Developers might find that legacy configurations used in production are hard to port over to a cloud environment, without significant modifications, for running tests against a newly-developed, equivalent, Cloud-based application. (To ease the process, though, vendors like iTKO have emerged with offerings like Lisa that assist in moving legacy applications to the cloud).

- High-end applications that have extreme data security or regulatory restrictions, or rely on legacy (e.g., Cobol-based) coding projects, aren't suited for cloud development.

- Cloud Computing could be a disruptive technology. In house developers often dislike disruption to set ways and prefer working with familiar toolsets. Top management encouragement, training, and, if necessary, staff changes, are options to explore in fostering acceptance.

- There is a dearth of documentation to help developers understand Cloud-based tools and their use. This could change with increasing adoption or organizations will have to hire outside consultants for help.

- Unless an organization is careful, its developers could easily forget to turn off Cloud-based services when not needed and unnecessarily run up rental charges.

- Organizations must be clear about licensing agreements with cloud vendors or be unpleasantly surprised with what they can or cannot accomplish with cloud-based resources.

- Cloud developers usually do not have open access to the provider's infrastructure, applications, and integration platforms. This could pose challenges in integrating in-house applications with cloud-based applications and even in integrating multiple cloud-based applications. Reliance on providers who make available appropriate

Application Program Interfaces (APIs) is important.

- Cloud Computing is in an evolutionary state and the pace of change is rapid. Organizations must work with vendors to keep abreast of best practices as they rapidly evolve.

6.3 A Note on Security, Interoperability, and Portability Concerns

Concerns relating to security, interoperability, and portability in cloud-based service deployments pervade both service providers and consumers and the NIST notes that these concerns are the top three barriers to broader cloud services adoption. From the consumer side, relinquishing data and applications control to a third party, having to share IT resources with other consumers, and the lock-in relationship with a cloud provider are major considerations that they must weigh when balancing the risk and benefits of adopting Cloud Computing.

To meet general IT security requirements, organizations need to have security control provisions to protect and preserve the integrity, availability, and confidentiality of IT resources from unauthorized access, disruption of service, theft, misuse, malicious attacks, and such (NIST, 1995). Cloud Computing presents unique security challenges that go beyond these general security requirements. These added challenges stem primarily from two sources: the use of Virtualization and a multi-tenant environment inherent to Public, Community, and Hybrid cloud environments (see Section 5 for descriptions).

Virtualization helps with cloud scalability. However, Virtualization creates added data integrity and confidentiality issues due to vulnerabilities in hypervisors (Robinson, 2010). A compromised hypervisor could potentially damage all systems that it hosts (Scarfone, 2011). Another virtualization related security challenge is to separate the

data, locations, virtual machines, API calls, transactions, etc., of each tenant in a multi-tenant setting from those of other tenants for confidentiality and integrity assurance. An intruder can gain access to not only one client's data/applications on the cloud but every other client's data/applications as well by simply exploiting flaws in the cloud's multi-tenancy design or insecure APIs. Indeed, data breaches are considered the most serious of security threats with Cloud Computing (Cloud Security Alliance, 2013). A provider must prevent a single security breach from impacting the entire cloud environment. The scale and complexity of the network architecture underlying Cloud Computing further complicates attempts to understand security vulnerabilities in order to properly address and reduce risks to acceptable levels.

Cloud Computing, with its many interconnected components of hardware, software, data, and telecommunications, has to be fully interoperable in order to deliver a seamless flow of information and services. To be fully interoperable users need to have the ability to integrate and consolidate their data, applications, and systems across cloud infrastructures and among cloud providers. The idea for an "Intercloud," where Cloud Computing services including data, storage, computing, etc., are ubiquitous and interoperable in a Web-based network of clouds across different domains, platforms and geographies, is currently being investigated under a joint research project between IBM and the European Union called "Reservoir" or Resources and Services Virtualization Without Barriers (Sacharen and Hunter, 2008). New Virtualization and Grid technologies will be needed to enable the level of interoperability envisioned in Intercloud. Other technological challenges that must be addressed include the ability to manage and distribute large-scale workloads to optimize economic and quality of service requirements, negotiate and specify service level agreements, as well as design and manage a network of over 100,000 data centers spanning large geographic distances.

Portability is the flexibility to move data and applications from one cloud provider to another or between Private and Public cloud environments (www.webopedia.com). This amounts to relaxing the lock-in requirement with a specific cloud service provider so that users have complete control of their data and/or applications. The ability to import/export large volumes of data, the ownership management and access control of shared or collaborative data, as well as the security and authentication mechanisms involved to support this level of portability remain a technological challenge of Cloud Computing (Fitzpatrick, 2010).

7. CONCLUSION

In this chapter, we first traced the history of Cloud Computing from its early roots in Time Sharing with mainframe computer systems, through Peer-to-Peer and Client-Server computing, Grid Computing, Utility Computing, Virtualization, and Service-oriented Architecture. We then introduced Cloud Computing as a distinct step in this evolution where the emphasis is on ease of provision of various services to users. Following this discussion, we explored four models of Cloud Computing deployments, namely, Private, Public, Hybrid, and Community clouds. We then turned our attention to the many different kinds of services provided by cloud service providers and summarized key aspects of the different services available today. Given our understanding of cloud-based services, we explained the role that Cloud Computing plays as an enabler of today's Web 2.0 and the future Web 3.0. We round out our examination of Cloud Computing by articulating the benefits accruable and the challenges one faces with Cloud Computing.

Despite its lengthy evolutionary history, the field of present-day Cloud Computing is as yet in its nascent stages and is going through its share of teething troubles. At the time of this writing, two major cloud service outages were making headlines. Netflix, the online video service provider experienced service outage in the US East Region, through a backend-failure Christmas eve through Christmas day, 2012 (Chernicoff, 2012). Netflix was hosted on Amazon's Backend-as-a-Service (Baas) cloud. To complicate matters, Netflix has been let down at least thrice, to date, by its cloud services provider, Amazon (Dines, 2012). Previously, a July 2012 Amazon outage impacted Netflix, Pinterest, and Instagram. The following week, on Dec 28, 2012, Microsoft's Azure cloud-based storage service for the South-Central US experienced partial outage. The STaaS outage, initially expected to be resolved in a few hours, continued in excess of 50 hours. Soluto, a company that runs a PC diagnostics tool for Windows customers worldwide, had migrated to Azure in 2010 following inability of its private storage infrastructure to handle sudden load spikes. These are a few recent examples. Many of us have experienced cloud-based email service (EaaS) outages with providers like Hotmail, Yahoo, and Gmail over the years.

While the outlook for migration to cloud services looks bullish according to the cloud pundits, incidents such as these should cause prospective clients to pause, re-consider, and proceed with caution. At the very least, mission-critical applications may not be ready for the cloud without extensive and expensive failsafe measures in place. Moreover, clients must be willing to accept possible cloud-services failures as an integral part of running business on the cloud, much as they must be willing to accept inevitable services outages for their non-cloud-deployed services.

REFERENCES

Altnam, D. (2012). *Three reasons private clouds are winning over the business world*. Retrieved December 2012 from http://www.business-2community.com/tech-gadgets/three-reasons-private-clouds-are-winning-over-the-business-world-0362241

Backend as a Service. (n.d.). Retrieved December 2012 from http://en.wikipedia.org/wiki/Backend_as_a_service

Batch Processing. (n.d.). Retrieved December 2012 from http://en.wikipedia.org/wiki/Batch_processing

Beal, V. (2012). *The difference between server and desktop virtualization?* Retrieved March 2013 from http://www.webopedia.com/DidYouKnow/Computer_Science/difference_between_server_and_desktop_virtualization.html

Biddick, M. (2011). *Cloud storage: Changing dynamics beyond services*. Retrieved December 2012 from http://reports.informationweek.com/abstract/24/7534/Storage-Server/research-cloud-storage.html

Biswas, S. (2011). *Quotes about cloud computing (and some background information on them)*. Retrieved December 2012 from http://www.cloudtweaks.com/2011/03/quotes-about-cloud-computing-and-some-background-information-on-them/

Bort, J. (2012). *Larry Ellison just took on Amazon with a new cloud service*. Retrieved December 2012 from http://www.businessinsider.com/larry-ellison-just-took-on-amazon-with-a-new-cloud-service-2012-9

Butler, B. (2012). *Are community cloud services the next hot thing?* Retrieved December 2012 from http://www.networkworld.com/news/2012/030112-are-community-cloud-services-the-256869.html

Chernicoff, D. (2012). *A less than merry Christmas for Netflix*. Retrieved December 2012 from http://www.zdnet.com/a-less-than-merry-christmas-for-netflix-7000009187/

Chunawala, Q. S. (n.d.). *Early batch-oriented operating systems, in what on earth is a mainframe-the sum and substance of a mainframe*. Retrieved April 2013 from http://www.mainframe360.com

Cloud Computing. (n.d.). Retrieved December 2012 from http://en.wikipedia.org/wiki/Cloud_computing

Cloud Security Alliance. (2013). *The notorious nine: Cloud computing top threats in 2013*. Retrieved March 2013 from http://www.cloudsecurityalliance.org/topthreats

Conroy, S. P. (2011). *History of virtualization*. Retrieved March 2013 from http://www.everythingvm.com/content/history-virtualization

Dines, R. (2012). *How Amazon ruined my Christmas*. Retrieved December 2012 from http://www.zdnet.com/how-amazon-ruined-my-christmas-7000009215/?s_cid=rSINGLE

Dinucci, D. (1999, April). Fragmented future. *Print Magazine*, 220-222.

Email as a Service (EaaS). (n.d.). Retrieved December 2012 from http://www.gsa.gov/portal/content/112223?utm_source=FAS&utm_medium=print-radio&utm_term=eaas&utm_campaign=shortcuts

EMC Solutions Group. (2012). *Big data-as-a-service: A marketing and technology perspective*. Retrieved December 2012 from http://www.emc.com/collateral/software/white-papers/h10839-big-data-as-a-service-perspt.pdf

Farber, D. (2008). *Oracle's Ellison nails cloud computing*. Retrieved December 2012 from http://news.cnet.com/8301-13953_3-10052188-80.html

Fitzpatrick, B. W., & Lueck, J. J. (2010). The case against data lock-in. *Communications of the ACM*, *53*(11), 42–46. doi:10.1145/1839676.1839691

Gantz, J. (2011). *Extracting value from chaos*. Retrieved December 2012 from http://www.emc.com/digital_universe

Getov, V. (2012). Security as a service in smart clouds – Opportunities and concerns. In *Proceedings of the IEEE 36th Annual Computer Software and Applications Conference* (COMPSAC), (pp. 373-379). IEEE.

Getting, B. (2007). *Basic definitions: Web 1.0, web 2.0, web 3.0*. Retrieved March 2013 from http://www.practicalecommerce.com/articles/464-Basic-Definitions-Web-1-0-Web-2-0-Web-3-0

Google Chrome Team. (2010). *20 things I learned about browsers and the web*. Retrieved December 2012 from http://www.20thingsilearned.com/en-US

Google, Inc. (2012). *Google app. engine – The platform for your next great idea*. Retrieved December 2012 from https://cloud.google.com/files/GoogleAppEngine.pdf

Grid Computing Info Center. (n.d.). Retrieved December 2012 from http://gridcomputing.com

Grid Computing. (n.d.). Retrieved December 2012 from http://en.wikipedia.org/wiki/Grid_computing

Grush, M. (2011). *A community cloud strategy for the education enterprise*. Retrieved December 2012 from http://campustechnology.com/articles/2011/09/08/a-community-cloud-strategy-for-the-education-enterprise.aspx

Hurwitz, J., Bloor, R., Kaufman, M., & Halper, F. (2012). *Cloud services for dummies*. Retrieved December 2012 from http://www.businesscloudsummit.com/sites/all/themes/bcsummit/downloads/Cloud%20Services%20for%20Dummies.pdf

Hurwitz, J., Bloor, R., Kaufman, M., & Halper, F. (2013). *Service-oriented architecture for dummies*. Retrieved March 2013 from http://www.dummies.com/Section/id-612246.html

InfoWorld. (n.d.). *Cloud computing deep dive: The journey to the private cloud*. Retrieved December 2012 from http://computerworld.com.edgesuite.net/insider/infoworld_private_cloud_insider.pdf

Interactive Computing. (n.d.). Retrieved December 2012 from http://pdp-1.computerhistory.org/pdp-1/index.php?f=theme&s=2&ss=1

JetBlue Airways (JetBlue) on Twitter. (n.d.). Retrieved March 2013 from https://twitter.com/jetblue

Knorr, E. (2012, February). Shaking up the data center: 2011-a year of surging private cloud and public cloud build-outs, cloud computing deep dive. *InfoWorld Special Report*.

Kodali, R. R. (2005). *What is service-oriented architecture? An introduction to SOA*. Retrieved March 2013 from http://www.javaworld.com/javaworld/jw-06-2005/jw-0613-soa.html

Krigsman, M. (2012). *Cloud research: Cost matters most and confusion remains*. Retrieved December 2012 from http://www.zdnet.com/cloud-research-cost-matters-most-and-confusion-remains-7000009136/

Lehner, W., & Sattler, K. (2010). Database as a service (DBaaS). In *Proceedings of the International Conference on Data Engineering* (ICDE), (pp. 1216-1217). Long Beach, CA: ICDE.

Marko, K. (2012). *State of storage 2012*. Retrieved December 2012 from http://reports.informationweek.com/abstract/24/8697/Storage-Server/Research:-State-of-Storage-2012.html

McKendrick, J. (2010). *NASA's nebula: A stellar example of private clouds in government.* Retrieved December 2012 from http://www.zdnet.com/blog/service-oriented/nasas-nebula-a-stellar-example-of-private-clouds-in-government/5267

Mell, P., & Grance, T. (2011). *The NIST definition of cloud computing.* Retrieved December 2012 from http://csrc.nist.gov/publications/nistpubs/800-145/SP800-145.pdf

Minar, N., & Hedlund, M. (2001). A network of peers: Peer-to-peer models through the history of the internet. In *Peer-to-peer: Harnessing the power of disruptive technologies.* Retrieved December 2012 from http://oreilly.com/catalog/peertopeer/chapter/ch01.html

Network as a Service. (n.d.). Retrieved December 2012 from http://en.wikipedia.org/wiki/Network_as_a_service

NIST. (1995). *An introduction to computer security: The NIST handbook (Special Publication 800-12).* Gaithersburg, MD: National Institute of Technology.

O'Dell, J. (2012). *Adobe acquires behance to bring more community into creative cloud.* Retrieved December 2012 from http://venturebeat.com/2012/12/20/adobe-acquires-behance/

O'Reilly, T. (2008). *Web 2.0 and cloud computing.* Retrieved March 2013 from http://radar.oreilly.com/2008/10/web-20-and-cloud-computing.html

Perry, G. (2008). *How cloud and utility computing are different.* Retrieved December 2012 from http://gigaom.com/2008/02/28/how-cloud-utility-computing-are-different/

Public Cloud Examples and Case Studies. (n.d.). Retrieved December 2012 from http://www.cloudpro.co.uk/cloud-essentials/public-cloud/case-studies

Raman, T. V. (2009). Toward 2w, beyond web 2.0. *Communications of the ACM, 52*(2), 52–59. doi:10.1145/1461928.1461945

Robinson, N., Valeri, L., Cave, J., Starkey, T., Grauz, H., Creese, S., & Hopkins, P. (2010). *The cloud: Understanding the security, privacy and trust challenges.* Brussels: Directorate-General Information Society and Media, European Commission. doi:10.1017/CBO9780511564765.012

Rouse, M. (2009a). *Private cloud.* Retrieved December 2012 from http://searchcloudcomputing.techtarget.com/definition/private-cloud

Rouse, M. (2009b). *Public cloud.* Retrieved December 2012 from http://searchcloudcomputing.techtarget.com/definition/public-cloud

Rouse, M. (2010). *Hybrid cloud.* Retrieved December 2012 from http://searchcloudcomputing.techtarget.com/definition/hybrid-cloud

Rouse, M. (2012). *Community cloud.* Retrieved December 2012 from http://searchcloudstorage.techtarget.com/definition/community-cloud

Sacharen, C., & Hunter, J. (2008, February 5). IBM and European Union launch joint research initiative for cloud computing. *IBM News Room.* Retrieved March 2013 from http://www-03.ibm.com/press/us/en/pressrelease/23448.wss

Scardino, S. (2005). *Spreadsheet/personal computing kills off time sharing.* Retrieved December 2012 from http://corphist.computerhistory.org/corphist/view.php?s=stories&id=46

Scarfone, K., Souppaya, M., & Hoffman, P. (2011). *Guide to security for full virtualization technologies* (Special Publication 800-125). National Institute of Standards and Technology. Retrieved March 2013 from http://csrc.nist.gov/publications/nistpubs/800-125/SP800-125-final.pdf

Software Testing. (n.d.). Retrieved December 2012 from http://www.utest.com

Stallings, W., & Case, T. (2013). *Business data communications: Infrastructure, networking and security* (7th ed.). Upper Saddle River, NJ: Prentice Hall.

Strickland, J. (2008). *How utility computing works.* Retrieved December 2012 from http://computer.howstuffworks.com/utility-computing.htm

Subramanian, K. (2011a). *Hybrid clouds.* Retrieved December 2012 from http://www.trendmicro.com/cloud-content/us/pdfs/business/white-papers/wp_hybrid-clouds-analyst-ksubramanian.pdf

Subramanian, K. (2011b). *Public clouds.* Retrieved December 2012 from http://www.trendmicro.com/cloud-content/us/pdfs/business/white-papers/wp_public-clouds-analyst-ksubramanian.pdf

Utility Computing. (n.d.). Retrieved December 2012 from http://en.wikipedia.org/wiki/Utility_computing

Worldwide LHC Computing Grid. (n.d.). Retrieved December 2012 from http://wlcg.web.cern.ch/

Yu, L., Tasi, W., Chen, X., Liu, L., Zhao, Y., Tang, L., & Zhao, W. (2010). Testing as a service over cloud. In *Proceedings of the 5th International Symposium on Service Oriented System Engineering* (SOSE), (pp. 181-188). SOSE.

Zhou, M., Zhang, R., Zeng, D., & Qian, W. (2010). Services in the cloud computing era: A survey. In *Proceedings of the 4th International Universal Communication Symposium,* (pp. 40-46). Beijing, China: Academic Press.

Chapter 2
Rationale for Use of Cloud Computing:
A QoS-Based Framework for Service Provider Selection

Amir Zeid
American University of Kuwait, Kuwait

Ahmed Shawish
Ain Shams University, Egypt

Maria Salama
British University in Egypt, Egypt

ABSTRACT

Cloud Computing is the most promising computing paradigm that provides flexible resource allocation on demand with the promise of realizing elastic, Internet-accessible, computing on a pay-as-you-go basis. With the growth and expansion of the Cloud services and participation of various services providers, the description of quality parameters and measurement units start to diversify and sometime contradict. Such ambiguity does not only result in the rise of various Quality of Service (QoS) interoperability problems but also in the distraction of the services consumers who find themselves unable to match quality requirements with the providers' offerings. Yet, employing the available QoS models that cover certain quality aspects while neglecting others drive consumers to perform their service selection based only on cost-benefit analysis and performance evaluation, without being able to perform subjective selection based on a comprehensive set of well-defined quality aspects. This chapter presents a novel QoS ontology that combines and defines all of the existing quality aspects in a unified way to efficiently overcome all existing diversities. Using such an ontology, a comprehensive broad QoS model combining all quality-related parameters of both service providers and consumers for different Cloud platforms is presented. The chapter also provides a mathematical model that formulates the Cloud Computing service provider selection optimization problem based on QoS guarantees. The validation of the provided model is addressed in the chapter through extensive simulation studies conducted on benchmark data of Content Delivery Network providers. The studies report the efficient matching of the model with the market-oriented different platform characteristics.

DOI: 10.4018/978-1-4666-5788-5.ch002

1. INTRODUCTION

The promise of cloud computing is its potential to shift paradigms away from fixed IT assets to more flexible resource allocation on demand with the promise of realizing elastic, Internet-accessible, computing on a pay-as-you-go basis. Standing at different level of hardware and software stack levels - Infrastructure as a Service (IaaS), Platform as a Service (PaaS) and Software as a Services (SaaS), this form of service provides several benefits to consumers; no cost for purchasing, free of maintenance, accessibility through Internet, and high availability. Computing services are offered on-demand according to an auto-scaling paradigm following the pay-as-you-go financial model. Such flexible key tenets will lead Cloud Computing to become the next wave of technological revolution that will be able to provide IT-services required by business.

Although Cloud Computing is growing rapidly, its Quality of Service (QoS) still poses significant challenges, especially in the context of service provider selection and quality assurance. Various QoS models have been adopted by different service providers and consumers for describing QoS information. This diversity leads to the use of different QoS descriptions as well as different concepts, scales and measurements of, sometimes, the same QoS factor. Such ambiguity not only results in an increase of various QoS interoperability problems, but also in the confusion of consumers, who find themselves unable to match their quality requirements with provider' offerings. While Cloud service providers are increasingly offering novel services, it becomes a challenging task for Cloud consumers to select the appropriate service provider based on predefined QoS requirements.

Most of the current QoS models focus only on one quality factor such as transparency or security (Pauley, 2010), (Catteddu, 2010), and neglect others. Even those models that cover multiple QoS factors are tailored only for certain service platforms, such as SaaS, or certain applications

domain, such as Customer-Relationship Management (CRM) applications (La & Kim, 2009) (Heart, Tsur, & Pliskin, 2010) (Armstrong & Djemame, 2009). Under such limited QoS models, the consumers often find themselves unable to perform independent subjective service selection based on a comprehensive set of well-defined quality aspects. Hence they perform it based on either cost-benefit analysis (Kondo, Javadi, Malecot, Cappello, & Anderson, May 2009), (Klems, Nimis, & Tai, 2009) or performance evaluation (Xiong & Perros, 2009), (Pathan, Broberg, & Buyya, 2009) measured only by response time and throughput. Meanwhile, existing selection approaches developed in the service computing community (i.e. grids and web services) cannot be directly migrated to the Cloud environment due to the difference in their service model structure. Yet optimal service provider selection based on QoS requirements for the purpose of maximizing the consumer's utility is still uncovered for Cloud Computing as it should be. By that, the necessity of developing a general framework, that gathers all of the QoS factors with a unified description, scale and measurement unit, becomes crucial. Such a framework should overcome QoS interoperability problems and all its consequent ones.

This chapter presents a novel QoS ontology that combines and defines all of the existing quality aspects in a unified way to efficiently overcome all existing diversities in expressing QoS aspects. Using such ontology, a comprehensive broad QoS model combining all quality related parameters of both service providers and consumers for different Cloud platforms – (IaaS, PaaS, SaaS). The model sustains the extension of QoS attributes according to specific situation, to support QoS-guaranteed Cloud service selection. The chapter also provides a mathematical model that formulates the Cloud Computing service provider selection optimization problem based on a multi-dimensional QoS approach, to satisfy the consumer quality requirements. The mathematical model assists decision makers in selecting the optimal Cloud service provider, incorporating a comprehensive set of well-defined quality aspects. The validation of the provided model is addressed in the chapter through extensive simulation studies conducted on benchmark data of Content Delivery Network providers (Cloud Harmony: benchmarking the Cloud, 2001). The overall validation is representing a typical selection problem scenario.

The chapter is organized as follows. Section 3 introduces the background and related work on the available QoS and service selection models. In section 4, the QoS framework including the QoS ontology and the QoS model is presented. In section 5, the service provider selection problem is addressed in addition to the formulation of QoS parameters and the mathematical model. Section 6 covers the conduct simulation studies that validate the efficiency of the provided model. Finally, the chapter conclusion and future work are in section 7.

2. BACKGROUND

This section discusses the related research work of the available QoS models that has been developed for Cloud Computing services. Some models focused on certain service platforms only; like IaaS, or PaaS, or SaaS (La & Kim, 2009) (Heart, Tsur, & Pliskin, 2010) (Armstrong & Djemame, 2009); while others focused on a single quality aspect such as performance, availability or transparency only (Pauley, 2010), (Catteddu, 2010) (Catteddu & Hogben, Cloud Computing Risk Assessment, 2009) (Stantchev & Schröpfer, 2009) (Cao & Li, 2009).

Also discussed is the background of service selection models. The available techniques developed in the Cloud Computing context have been only developed based on performance evaluation (Xiong & Perros, 2009), (Pathan, Broberg, & Buyya, 2009) and cost-benefit analysis (Kondo, Javadi, Malecot, Cappello, & Anderson, May 2009), (Klems, Nimis, & Tai, 2009). Also, existing

service selection approaches developed in service computing community (Zeng, Benatallah, Ngu, Dumas, & Kalag, 2004) (Yu, Zhang, & Lin, 2007) (Yu, Zhang, & Lin, 2007) (Vanderster, Dimopoulos, R., & Sobie, 2009) (Chunlin & Layuan, 2006); i.e. grids and web services; are discussed.

It is worth noting that the utility function is incorporated in the proposed model as a mathematical tool.

2.1 QoS Models

Models developed for Cloud Computing services traditionally focused on certain service platforms only; while others focused on a single quality aspect such as performance, availability or transparency.

QoS models have been developed for Software-as-a-Service (SaaS), while others focused on Infrastructure-as-a-Service (IaaS) and Platform-as-a-Service (PaaS) by considering only computing resources performance. In (La & Kim, 2009), authors were concerned with developing high quality SaaS Cloud services and focused only on reusability, availability and scalability properties. Authors in (Heart, Tsur, & Pliskin, 2010) carried out evaluation criteria for SaaS vendors for selecting the suitable offer, considering the technology-specific evaluation criteria beside the financial feasibility. Regarding IaaS and PaaS, (Armstrong & Djemame, 2009) was concerned with the management and resources performance like processors, memory, storage and networking issues. It should be noted that QoS as defined is not just limited to performance and availability but extends to a wide range of other quality aspects that should be covered. In addition, developing QoS models for a particular platform focuses on certain quality attributes while neglecting others, and this is the case in the available QoS models.

Other Cloud-based QoS models have been developed focusing on a single quality aspect. For example, an empirical evaluation of Cloud provider transparency has been conducted in

(Pauley, 2010). The developed methodology segmented the evaluation into four key domains: security, privacy, audit and service level agreement. Authors in (Catteddu & Hogben, Cloud Computing Risk Assessment, 2009) allowed an informed assessment of the security of using Cloud computing, providing security guidance for potential and existing users of Cloud computing. While in (Catteddu, 2010), the authors outlined both security benefits and risks resulting from using Cloud computing, covering the technical and legal implications. Authors in (Stantchev & Schröpfer, 2009) described the formalization of QoS levels as a main precondition for the negotiation of SLAs. It dealt also with the performance and the availability as non-functional properties while addressing their enforcement in the Cloud computing environments. Nevertheless, QoS cannot be defined through a single quality parameter, as it should be defined through a range of parameters that describe the services requested by the consumers. Other researchers (Cao & Li, 2009) emphasize on the common quality attributes between provider and consumer. However, they reported a limited number common attributes like response time, cost, and availability.

The available QoS ontologies for Internet services were specially designed for web services and tailored according to its nature. It is noted that the Web service technology targets to build and run only distributed processes and applications accessible via the Internet; while Clouds offer multiple service models (i.e., IaaS, PaaS and SaaS) with the purpose of enabling dynamic resources allocation for running web services. Also, web services encapsulate application functionality and information resources only; while each Cloud service model encapsulates certain computing resources. For instance, IaaS offers virtualized hardware and computational resources; such as memory, CPU, storage and operating systems; on top of which customers can build their own infrastructure. SaaS provides customers with various kinds of applications that are accessible

anytime and anywhere; including web services. These issues reflect that the Cloud is a computing platform that offers services from a wider scope and range. Thus due to the difference in nature between the two technologies, applying the available web services ontologies in the Cloud will lead to incorrect definition of the QoS parameters. Therefore, proposing a new ontology tailored based on the Cloud's nature is crucial.

Moreover, the previously defined QoS ontologies were not comprehensive; i.e. not combining all the attributes required for defining properly the QoS parameters. The famous available ontologies such as "OWL-Q" and "onQoS" prove this claim. For instance, the "OWL-Q" ontology has weak support for QoS priority, quality level, and QoS mandatory. It does not also include concrete definitions of common QoS properties. The "onQoS" ontology does not mention many other characteristics of QoS properties, such as unit, impact direction, dynamism, QoS relationships, etc.

Hence, defining cloud's quality parameters using the available QoS ontologies that were designed for web services will lead to an incorrect definition. This is due to the difference in nature between the two technologies. Moreover, the previously defined QoS ontologies were not comprehensive; i.e. not combining all the attributes required for defining properly the quality parameters.

The available QoS ontologies for Internet services were specially designed for web services and tailored according to its nature. It is noted that the Web service technology targets to build and run only distributed processes and applications accessible via the Internet; while Clouds offer multiple service models (i.e., IaaS, PaaS and SaaS) with the purpose of enabling dynamic resources allocation for running web services. Also, web services encapsulate application functionality and information resources only; while each Cloud service model encapsulates certain computing resources. For instance, IaaS offers virtualized

Table 1. Cloud computing services classification

Category	Characteristics	Product Type	Vendors & Products
SaaS	Customers are provided with applications that are accessible anytime and from anywhere.	Web applications and services (Web 2.0)	SalesForce.com (CRM) Clarizen.com (Project Management) Google Documents, Google Mail (Automation)
PaaS	Customers are provided with a platform for developing applications hosted in the Cloud.	Programming APIs and frameworks; Deployment system.	Google AppEngine Microsoft Azure Manjrasoft Aneka
IaaS/HaaS	Customers are provided with virtualized hardware and storage on top of which they can build their infrastructure.	Virtual machines management infrastructure, Storage management	Amazon EC2 and S3; GoGrid; Nirvanix

hardware and computational resources; such as memory, CPU, storage and operating systems; on top of which customers can build their own infrastructure. SaaS provides customers with various kinds of applications that are accessible anytime and anywhere; including web services. These issues reflect that the Cloud is a computing platform that offers services from a wider scope and range. Thus, due to the difference in nature between the two technologies, applying the available web services ontologies in the Cloud will lead to incorrect definition of the QoS parameters. Therefore, proposing a new ontology tailored based on the Cloud's nature is crucial.

Moreover, the previously defined QoS ontologies were not comprehensive; i.e. not combining all the attributes required for defining properly the QoS parameters. The famous available ontologies such as "OWL-Q" and "onQoS" prove this claim. For instance, the "OWL-Q" ontology has weak support for QoS priority, quality level, and QoS mandatory. It does not also include concrete definitions of common QoS properties. The "onQoS" ontology does not mention many other characteristics of QoS properties, such as unit, impact direction, dynamism, QoS relationships, etc.

Because many service providers and consumers use different QoS descriptions, concepts, scales and measurements for QoS, it is necessary to find

a unified QoS description. This is because any comparison cannot be performed without such unification. This diversity goes also across providers' advertisements, consumers' requirements and the agreed SLA. Besides, different platforms and domains require different QoS properties. Therefore a more comprehensive, efficient and flexible method to express QoS is crucial. Table 1 summarizes the nature of these categories and lists some major players in the field.

2.2 Service Selection Models

The available techniques developed in the Cloud Computing context have been only developed for performance evaluation and cost-benefit analysis.

With respect to performance evaluation, only response time and throughput has been considered. In (Xiong & Perros, 2009) (Jacob & Davie, 2005), the authors focus on the response time from the perspective of the customer who is more inclined to request a statistical upper bound on its response time rather than an average response time. This chapter introduces the concept of the response time percentile. That is, the time to execute a service request is less than a pre-defined value with a certain percentage of time. The throughput is also considered as an important performance factor in a wide range of applications. For example, in Content Delivery Networks (Buyya, Yeo,

Venugopal, Broberg, & Brandic, 2009) (Pathan, Broberg, & Buyya, 2009), the service deployment is optimized based on average throughput; as well as its utility that was measured as the fraction of processed requests (throughput) or the total evaluation (weighted throughput).

On the other hand, cost-benefit analysis has also been conducted on the Cloud Computing services. In (Kondo, Javadi, Malecot, Cappello, & Anderson, May 2009), a comparison between Clouds and grids was done in terms of performance and resource requirement in the context of cost-benefits. The results were that cost efficiency varies depending on the platform size, where a minimum number of nodes is sufficient for a grid to become cost effective for a short period of time, while Clouds of the same size are more efficient to support a long term scientific project. Calculating cost metric and estimating the value of the Cloud in terms of opportunity costs have been proposed in (Klems, Nimis, & Tai, 2009). Such framework helps decision makers to estimate and compare Cloud Computing costs for conventional IT solutions. In general, despite of the effort done to analyze the cost-benefit, consumer utility is not considered.

It is worth noting that there have been some efforts done to address the QoS evaluation topic as standalone metrics like transparency, availability, reliability, and reputation. The author in (Pauley, 2010) focused on how a business assesses Cloud providers' transparency. An instrument has been developed for evaluating a Cloud provider's transparency from security, privacy, and service level competencies aspects.

Due to the absence of a unified QoS ontology for Cloud Computing, the available selection approaches are based either on a single quality parameter or on performance evaluation. Hence, the provider evaluation will not take into consideration the consumer quality concerns and requirements. On the other hand, the available service selection approaches that were developed for other service computing communities like grids and web services, address different other purposes such as service composition and resources allocation.

In the web services context, utility functions have been used for service composition and optimization. In (Zeng, Benatallah, Ngu, Dumas, & Kalag, 2004), authors addressed the issue of selecting web services, in a way that maximizes user satisfaction, which is expressed as utility functions over QoS attributes. The main objective of the formulated utility function was service composition, i.e. selecting web services to compose a final one. Authors in (Yu, Zhang, & Lin, 2007) presented algorithms to select service components according to application-dependent performance requirements. In fact, the maximization of utility function under end-to-end QoS constraints has not taken into consideration multi-dimensional QoS constraints and attributes. Meanwhile, tackling the service optimization problem was addressed in (Lee, Lehoczky, Rajkumar, & Siewiorek, 1999) using utility values. Optimization was performed by allocating a single finite resource to satisfy QoS requirements of multiple applications along multiple QoS dimensions.

Considering non-QoS based approaches, authors in (Menascé, Casalicchio, & Vinod, 2010) have addressed the problem of finding the set of service providers that minimizes the total execution time of the business process. This technique is limited only to two selection parameters that are the cost and execution time. An end-to-end framework to manage user-centric services was presented in (Zhao, Lage, & Crespi, 2011). The management is performed by firstly learning end-user's intent through daily events, recommending relevant functionalities, and then selecting the services that offer the required functionalities based on the user's selection rules. Since the service provider selection problem differs from both service composition and service optimization problems, the previously mentioned available models will not fit the addressed selection problem, even with some modifications. Thus, utility functions formulated for various purposes cannot fit with the provider selection problem for a user whose target is selecting a Cloud provider.

In the grid context, utility has been mainly used for re-source allocation. In (Vanderster, Dimopoulos, R., & Sobie, 2009), authors have introduced a utility model for resource allocation of computational grids. While in (Chunlin & Layuan, 2006), authors have considered multiple QoS-based grid resource scheduling. Although Cloud and grid computing paradigms have many points in common, QoS-based models are already developed for different purposes. Thus, these models cannot be adopted in the Cloud Computing context, especially when addressing the service provider selection problem.

To sum up, approaches developed for web services and grids cannot be directly migrated to the Cloud environment. Similarities between both could be considered in terms of resousces allocation and scheduling. Meanwhile, previous work from Grid Computing cannot be applied, as different applications are being addressed. While Grid Computing primarily assists scientists with computationally expensive problems, Cloud Computing addresses businesses' applications that are of varying scale and complexity over the Web. Although back-end technologies may be similar, the target groups and typical use cases for Grids and Clouds are very different.

2.3 Utility Functions

Developing a model for optimal provider offering selection shows the necessity of incorporating mathematical tools that deal with maximizing the utility of the cloud consumer. Therefore, in the following part, "the utility function" will be discussed as one of those tools. The utility function has been previously introduced by (Pauley, 2010) for mapping system's state to a common scale, representing response time and number of QoS goals met. In (Catteddu, 2010), the authors formulated

utility-maximization problem with quantitative expressions, with the aim at improving content-serving utility of Content Delivery Clouds. From their perspective, utility-maximization can be achieved from perceived utility measured by processed requests (throughput). A utility metric has been formulated for this purpose.

3. QoS FRAMEWORK

This section describe the design of a comprehensive QoS model that incorporate all quality parameters currently known and defined in the clouds context, such that it can cover all quality aspects of both service providers and consumers of different cloud platforms like IaaS, PaaS and SaaS . This is because it incorporates all quality parameters currently known and defined in the Cloud's context.

The model also sustains the extension of QoS attributes according to specific situation; by that it can be implemented by a domain-specific level of QoS properties. For example, the quality parameters of an IaaS platform are found in the model; among them response time, throughput and scalability. To support PaaS model, dependability, integrity and manageability are added to the model. Interoperability, robustness and accessibility quality factors are found to support SaaS. Other common factors between all platforms, such as economics, are also presented. Using QoS properties, performance, reliability, availability and economics are referred as non-functional properties of Cloud services. Moreover, the model sustains the extension of QoS attributes according to specific situation, to support QoS-based Cloud service provider selection, provision and Service Level Agreement (SLA) monitoring.

A general overview of the QoS framework is depicted in Figure 1. In the following, the components with the framework are described in details (Salama, Shawish, & Kouta, 2011).

Figure 1. Hierarchy of the QoS Framework

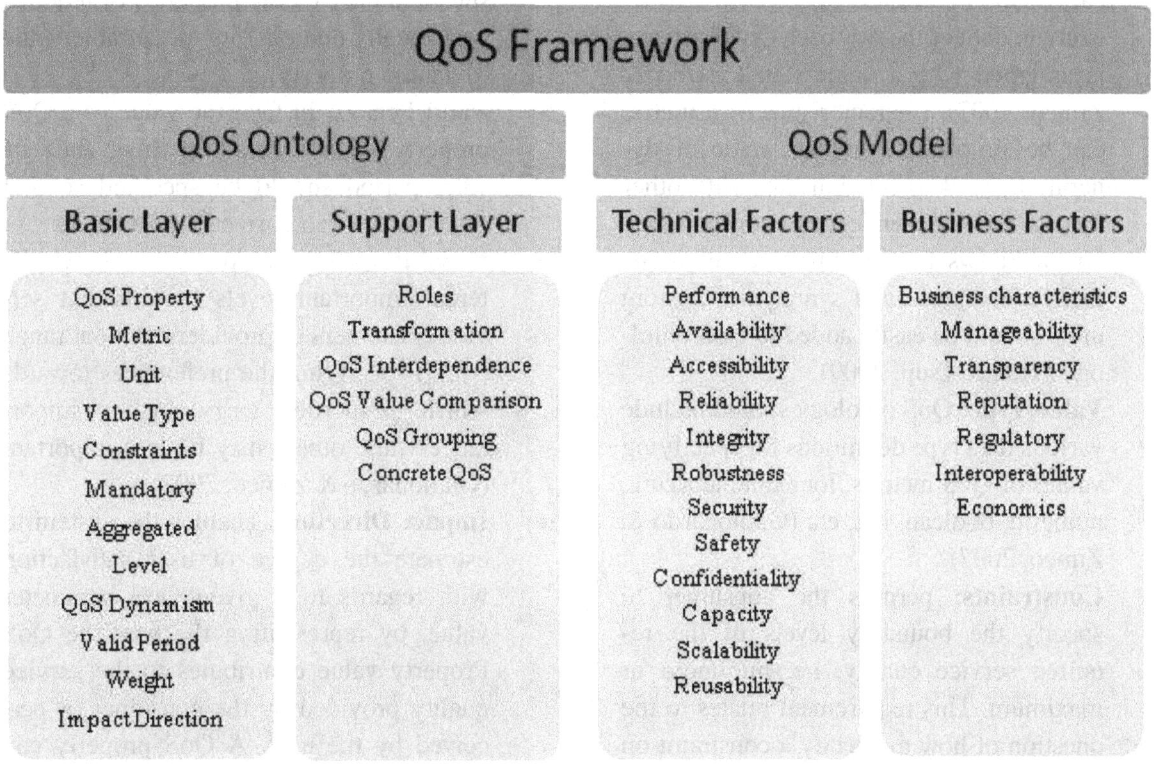

QoS Framework

QoS Ontology		QoS Model	
Basic Layer	**Support Layer**	**Technical Factors**	**Business Factors**
QoS Property	Roles	Performance	Business characteristics
Metric	Transformation	Availability	Manageability
Unit	QoS Interdependence	Accessibility	Transparency
Value Type	QoS Value Comparison	Reliability	Reputation
Constraints	QoS Grouping	Integrity	Regulatory
Mandatory	Concrete QoS	Robustness	Interoperability
Aggregated		Security	Economics
Level		Safety	
QoS Dynamism		Confidentiality	
Valid Period		Capacity	
Weight		Scalability	
Impact Direction		Reusability	

3.1 QoS Ontology

The development of a comprehensive QoS model requires clear and unified definitions for different QoS concepts such as QoS properties, metrics, and units that are employed in QoS advertisements, QoS requirements or SLAs (Tran & Tsuji, 2009). This is why an ontology is needed in order to solve the interoperability of QoS. The addressed QoS ontology offers a unified QoS description for both providers and consumers. Moreover, it solves semantic descriptions and ambiguity issues. The QoS ontology specifies how the information of service quality will be described; i.e. specifies the basic attributes that will be used to describe QoS factors in a unified and consistent manner.

In the following subsections, the QoS ontology is presented in two layers. First, the Basic Layer encloses the definitions of the basic attributes

(e.g., QoS properties, metrics, and units) that will be utilized in the QoS model. Second, the Support Layer presents some auxiliary means (e.g., transformation, values comparison, and others) to support the modeling of the QoS properties.

3.1.1 QoS Ontology Basic Layer

QoS Ontology Basic Layer encloses definitions of the basic attributes that will be employed to define all QoS factors. Such attributes depict how to define, describe, and measure any QoS factor. They are listed as follows:

- **QoS Property:** represents a measurable non-functional requirement of a service within a given domain. A QoS Property is a set of attributes of cloud service quality characteristics and may be refined into multiple levels of sub-characteristics; also called QoS Parameter.

- **Metric:** defines the way each QoS Property is assigned with a value (Giallonardo & Zimeo, 2007). Characteristics of a metric can be simple or complex, static or dynamic as well as relationships with other metrics like independence or correlation.
- **Unit:** Allows for various types of units, their equivalence and synonyms. Custom units should be easily added to QoS ontology (Tran & Tsuji, 2009).
- **Value Type:** QoS ontology should include various data type definitions for specifying values of QoS metrics, for example string, numeric, boolean, list, etc (Giallonardo & Zimeo, 2007).
- **Constraints:** permits the consumer to specify the boundary levels of the required service quality; i.e. minimum or maximum. This requirement relates to the question of how to specify a constraint on a QoS property. Almost all existing approaches assume simple operators like >, <, =, >=, =< for expressing QoS constraints. However other operators related to value types of string, list, etc. are supported (Tran & Tsuji, 2009).
- **Mandatory:** This requirement allows specifying which QoS properties are required while others may be optional (Yin, Yang, P., & Chen, 2010).
- **Aggregated:** A quality property is said to be an aggregated one if it is composed from other qualities. For instance, the price performance ratio aggregates price and performance (Yin, Yang, P., & Chen, 2010).
- **Level:** specify different quality levels of a service so that the most appropriate quality levels for the user demands can be chosen. This way of organization helps in creating different usage modes (Giallonardo & Zimeo, 2007).

- **QoS Dynamism:** A QoS property can be specified once (static property) or requires periodically updating its measurable value (dynamic property).
- **Valid Period:** In fact, the value of a QoS property is not fixed all the time. Thus, its valid period should be specified so that other parties can correctly evaluate it.
- **Weight:** QoS properties often have different important levels by different service consumers or providers. A float range ([0,1]) specifying the preferences towards which properties carry higher importance while others may be less important (Giallonardo & Zimeo, 2007).
- **Impact Direction:** enables the system to estimate the degree of user satisfaction with regards to a given QoS parameter value, by representing the way the QoS Property value contributes to the service quality provided by the consumer or perceived by the user. A QoS property can have one of five impact directions: negative, positive, close, exact, and none (Tran & Tsuji, 2009).

QoS Ontology is illustrated in Figure 2.

3.1.2 QoS Ontology Support Layer

Modeling QoS properties using the previously cited attributes entailed a concrete support, due to the current diversity in metrics and units for the same QoS property, the interdependence between the provider and consumer, as well as the fact of correlation between QoS properties. Such support emerges in grouping factors of similar characteristics, transformation of values and metric units and others. Support Layer defines auxiliary means to sustain modeling QoS using the basic attributes previously defined in the Basic Layer as follows:

Figure 2. QoS Ontology Basic Layer

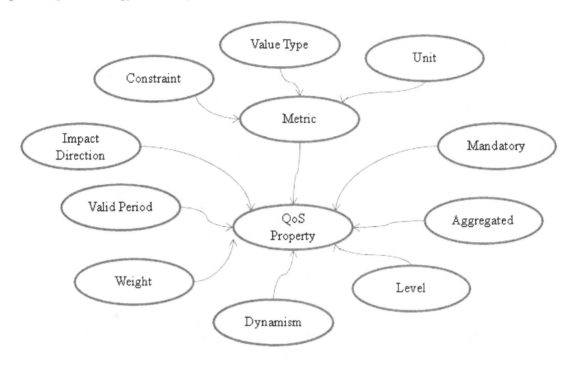

- **Roles:** Besides providers and consumers service quality evaluation, other third-party participants like certificate authorities and security providers should also be supported in a process of measurement and evaluation of QoS information.
- **Transformation:** Providers and consumers may be familiar, use or understand different metrics for the same QoS properties. Therefore, QoS ontology supports for converting and transforming QoS metrics as well as values and units of related metrics.
- **QoS Interdependence:** Not just a service consumer requires QoS from a service provider but a service provider can also specify its QoS demands that a requester must guarantee in order to get expected QoS from executing provider service (Tondello & Siqueira, 2008).
- **QoS Value Comparison:** Not all QoS properties have same mechanism for comparing their values. For example, numeric

based QoS properties are compared differently from string based ones.
- **QoS Grouping:** Allow for grouping QoS properties that share similar characteristics or impact in order to facilitate the evaluation and computing of the whole QoS value.
- **Concrete QoS:** A minimum set of common and domain-independent QoS properties should be defined, as the model presented in the following section.

3.2 QoS Model

The QoS model describes the concrete level of quality requirements. It defines the QoS properties, which are the non-functional attributes of the service. This definition is completed using the vocabulary of the QoS ontology previously defined. The model aims to support several QoS-based processes; such as service selection, and Service Level Agreement (SLA) monitoring.

Figure 3. Sample of the QoS Framework – A QoS Property (Performance) modeled using QoS Ontology

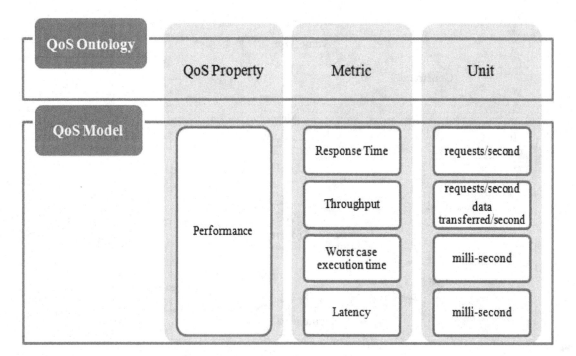

The defined QoS properties are a set of domain-independent quality concepts and can be widely used by various Cloud Computing applications. The model also supports the extension of QoS attributes according to specific situation; by that it can be completed by a domain-specific level of QoS properties; like scientific applications or CRM applications domain. Each quality factor is described in light of the ontology, where each one is defined as a QoS property with a specific metric providing the necessary information of how to measure, compare and assess its value. Figure 3 illustrates sample of QoS factors defined based on the QoS ontology.

In the QoS model, QoS properties are classified into two main categories: technical factors and business factors. Technical factors include performance, availability, reliability and others; while business factors are mainly concerned with manageability, transparency, economics and others. Figure 4 illustrates the QoS properties combined in QoS model.

3.2.1 Technical QoS factors

In this section, we present QoS factor for Cloud Computing, along with their measuring parameters and the assessments methods. These include performance, availability, accessibility, reliability, integrity, robustness, security, safety, confidence, stability, capacity, scalability, and reusability.

- **Performance:** means the total effectiveness of the service and can be measured in terms of response time, throughput (transaction rate), worst-case execution time and latency.
  - *Response time* is the time a service takes to respond to various types of requests. Response time is a function of load intensity, which can be measured in terms of arrival rates (such as requests/second) or number of concurrent requests. For IaaS, it may represent the interval from the

Figure 4. QoS properties of the QoS Model

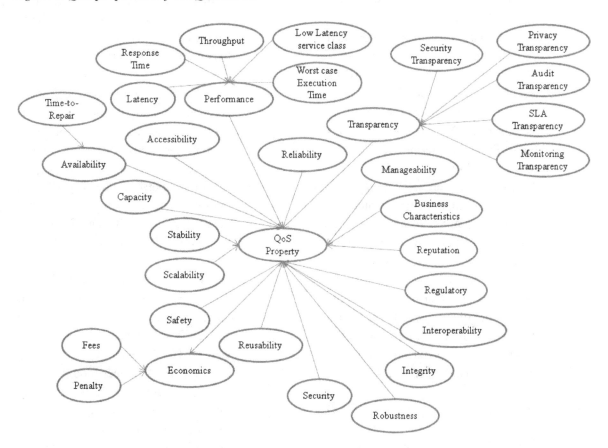

requirement sending of cloud service consumers to cloud service implements competition, which is calculated as follows:

$$CloudServiceQoSresponse_{time}(S) = Time_{transfers}(S) + Time_{run}(S) \qquad (1)$$

Among this, $Time_{transfers}(S)$ on behalf of the transmission time from requirement sending to results return and it can be gained by cloud service monitor; $Time_{run}(S)$ represent cloud service implements time and it also can be obtained by cloud service monitor [83]. As for providers' concern, it may be defined as the time it takes to an entity to respond a request and send

a response to the requester (Cao & Li, A Service-Oriented Qos-Assured and Multi-Agent Cloud Computing Architecture, 2009).

There is also the concept of *perceived response time*, which is the time a user senses as the beginning of input and the end of the response (Blanquer, Hernández, Segrelles, & Torres, 2008). From another customer's perspective, a customer may be more inclined to request a statistical bound on its response time than an average response time. For instance, a customer can request that 95% of the time its response time should be less than a given value. Therefore, a *percentile of response time* that characterizes the statistical response time should be considered as a performance metric. That is, the time to execute a service request is less than a pre-defined value with a certain percentage of time. The metric has been used by IBM's researchers as well as it has also been called a percentile delay by scientists at Cisco and MIT Communications Future Program (Inter-provider Quality of Service, 2006).

○ *Throughput* is the rate at which a service can process requests and represents the number of equivalent requests completed within a time frame. A general and broadly accepted definition of performance is to observe the system output $\omega(\delta)$ that represents the number of successfully served requests (or transactions) from a total of input $\iota(\delta)$ requests during a period of time, that is calculated as follows:

$$\omega(\delta) = f(\iota(\delta)) \tag{2}$$

This definition of performance corresponds to *transaction rate* – the system guarantees to process n requests during time period t (Stantchev & Schröpfer, 2009). QoS measures can also include the maximum throughput (number of service requests served at a given time period) or a function that describes how throughput varies with load intensity. It depends on the request nature, and should be measured by dedicated testers and fixed tests. In data transmission, throughput is the amount of data moved successfully from one place to another in a given time period. (Blanquer, Hernández, Segrelles, & Torres, 2008).

○ Worst-case execution time of a computational task is the maximum length of time a task could take to execute on a specific hardware plat-

form. Knowing worst-case execution times is of prime importance for IaaS.

○ *Latency* is the round-trip time between sending a request and receiving the response.

○ *Low Latency service class* is a measurement for synthetic traffic designed to model the performance of aggregate customer traffic and is characterized by three network performance metrics: one-way latency, one-way packet loss, and one-way delay variation (Xiong & Perros, Service Performance and Analysis in Cloud Computing, 2009). All metrics should be defined for packets that are representative of the traffic that will use that class. Thus they should use IP/UDP/RTP packets with a payload size of 160 bytes (representative of common VOIP codecs today).

The *single instance of the one-way delay* measurement is defined as the time the test packet traverses the network segment(s) between two reference points. The Metric is defined as a time from the time first bit of the packet is put on the wire at the source reference point to the time the last bit of the packet is received at the receiver reference point.

Packet loss ratio is defined as a metric measured for packets traversing the network segment between the source reference point and the destination reference point. The metric is reported as the number of lost packets at the destination reference point divided by the number of packets sent at the sender reference point to that destination.

A definition of the *IP Packet Delay Variation* can be given for packets inside a stream of packets. The singleton measure of packet delay variation for a pair of packets within a stream of packets is defined for a selected pair of packets in the stream going between two measurement points.

- **Availability:** is the quality aspect of whether the service is present or ready for immediate use.
  - It can be presented by the probability of services can be accessed successfully or the percentage of time that a service is operating. Larger values represent that the service is always ready to use while smaller values indicate unpredictability of whether the service will be available at a particular time.
  - Associated with availability is *time-to-repair* (TTR) that represents the time it takes to repair a service that has failed. Ideally smaller values of TTR are desirable. It has been defined traditionally as a binary metric that describes whether a system is "up" or "down" at a single point of time.
  - Also, a common extension of this definition is to compute the average percentage of time that a system is available during a certain period – this is a typical availability measure that describes a system as having 99.999% availability, for example (Stantchev & Schröpfer, 2009). It can be measured by [number of requests completed/requests submitted] and total time that an entity is available (Blanquer, Hernández, Segrelles, & Torres, 2008) as well as using the following equation:

$$CloudServiceQoS_{availability}(S) = A/N \qquad (3)$$

where *N* express the request times that consumer want to use cloud service *S* during a certain period of time; *A* express the accessible times of cloud service *S* (Cao & Li, A Service-Oriented Qos-Assured and Multi-Agent Cloud Computing Architecture, 2009).

- **Accessibility:** is the quality aspect of a service that represents the degree it is capable of serving a request, despite the fact that there could be situations when a service is available but not accessible. It may be expressed as a probability measure denoting the success rate of a successful service instantiation at a point in time.

- **Reliability:** is the quality aspect of a service that represents the degree of being capable of maintaining the service and service quality, by indicating the ability to correctly carry out the requested functionalities. It is a comprehensive evaluation of the quality of service [ISO 9126], denoting the continuity of service provision (Stantchev & Schröpfer, 2009). Cloud service reliability is mainly concerned with how probable that the cloud can successfully provide the service requested by users (Yang, Tan, Dai, & Guo, 2009). The number of failures per month or year represents a measure of reliability of a service. Reliability also shows the capacity that cloud service accurately implements its function and the times of validation and invalidation can be acquired by cloud service monitor, which is calculated as follows:

$$CloudServiceQoS_{reliability}(S) = R/M \qquad (4)$$

where, *R* express the times of called and successful implements of the cloud service *S*; *M* on behalf of the total called times of the cloud service *S*.

- **Integrity:** is the quality aspect of how the service maintains the correctness of the interaction in respect to the source. It denotes that there are no improper changes of the system (Stantchev & Schröpfer, 2009).

Proper execution of transactions will provide the correctness of interaction. A transaction refers to a sequence of activities to be treated as a single unit of work. All the activities have to be completed to make the transaction successful. When a transaction does not complete, all the changes made are rolled back. From a security background, integrity is considered as a measure of the service's ability to prevent unauthorized access and preserve its data integrity.

- **Robustness:** is the fault tolerance when you input non-normal data and invoke service incorrectly. Fault tolerance is generally implemented by error detection and subsequent system recovery (Laprie, 1995). Test cases for expected faults should be run and report the percentage of faults covered.

- **Security:** is the quality aspect of providing confidentiality and non-repudiation by authenticating the parties involved, encrypting messages, and providing access control. Security has added importance because service invocation occurs over the public Internet. The service provider can have different approaches and levels of providing security depending on the service consumer. Security properties include the existence and type of authentication mechanisms the service offers, confidentiality and data integrity of messages exchanged, non-repudiation of requests or messages, and resilience to denial-of-service attacks [ISO 9126]. Security levels should be agreed between the consumer and provider and propagated in the agreed SLA. It could be measured in two quality scales; either true/false, or high/medium/low (Blanquer, Hernández, Segrelles, & Torres, 2008).

- **Safety:** is an attribute that assures there are no catastrophic consequences on the user and the environment (Stantchev & Schröpfer, 2009).

- **Confidentiality:** denotes the absence of unauthorized disclosure of information (Laprie, 1995).

- **Stability:** is the change rate of service's attributes, such as its service interface and method signatures [ISO 9126] for SaaS. It could be measured by the number of changes over a certain period of time.

- **Capacity:** is the number of concurrent requests a service allows. When the service goes beyond its service capacity to work, its reliability and availability will be adversely affected.

- **Scalability:** defines whether the service capacity can increase as the consumer's requirement. Services with low scalability would suffer at the time of peak requests and so lose their reputations by consumers (La & Kim, 2009). This aspect can be checked with the following questions:
  ○ Can the platform accommodate more users and increasingly intensive calculations?
  ○ Are there no storage limits?
  ○ Can scale up to more space be done easily?

- **Reusability:** is a key criterion for cloud services, and commonality is the main contributor to reusability; that is cloud services with high commonality will yield higher reusability. Commonality in general denotes the amount of potential applications which need a specified feature such as a component or a service. Hence, a commonality of a feature can be computed as the followings;

$$Commonality(S) = A(S)/T \qquad (5)$$

where, $A(S)$ expresses the number of applications needing the service S and T denotes the total number of target applications.

If every application in the domain needs the given feature, the value of Commonality will be 1. It would be desirable to include features with high Commonality into the target SaaS. The range of the metric is between 0 and 1 (La & Kim, 2009).

3.2.2 Business QoS factors

In this section, we present business related QoS factor for Cloud Computing, along with their measuring parameters and the assessments methods. These include business characteristics, manageability, transparency, reputation, regulatory, interoperability, and economics.

- **Business characteristics:** must be considered in a service provider evaluation. The following characteristics should be considered for the provider (Pauley, 2010):
  - Length in business (in years).
  - Published security breaches.
  - Published privacy breaches.
  - Published outages.
  - Published data loss.
  - Having similar customers, applications, scale and customer base.
- **Manageability:** Questions reflecting aspects related to the manageability of the service should be addressed. Manageability covers the following points:
  - Administration; what (user and programmatic) interfaces do the consumer has to manage the application, and how can on-premises administrators mash up your client-facing management tools with their own.
  - Backwards compatibility of changes; which "dimensions of change" (i.e. functional changes, platform changes, environment changes) will impact any on-premises processes, or systems that we have depending on the newly introduced application.
  - User interface customization; what are the options for customizing the user interface, whether this requires code or configuration and by whom.
  - Developer toolkit; what is the developer experience for our team when interfacing with the cloud platform and services, and whether there are SDKs, libraries and code samples.
  - Exploiting on-premises capabilities; whether this application makes use of any existing on-premises infrastructure capabilities such as email, identity, web conferencing, analytics, telephony, etc.
- **Transparency:** Transparency evaluation is segmented into four key domains: security, privacy, external audits/certifications, and service-level agreements (Pauley, 2010); as follows:
  - Security Transparency; checks whether there is a portal area for Security Information, the Security Policy and white papers on Security Standards are published, whether an email address or online chat is provided to field additional questions, security professional services (such as security assessments of customer environments) are offered, Security Certified (COBIT, ISO 27000, NIST SP800-53), Members of ENISA or CSA, usage of the ENISA or CSA recommendations for governance, and staff security education and certifications, employees CISSP, CISM, or other Security Certified.
  - Privacy Transparency; checks whether there is a portal area for Privacy Information, the Privacy Policy and white papers on Privacy Standards are published, whether an email address or online chat is provided to field additional questions, privacy professional services (such as privacy assessments of customer environments)

are offered, Privacy Policy managed over the time, and staff privacy education and certifications, employees CIPP, or other Privacy Certified.

○ Audit Transparency; is the service provider comply with Statements on Auditing Standards (SAS) No. 70 type II13, Payment Card Industry Data Security Standard (PCI – DSS), Health Insurance Portability, Accountability Act (HIPAA), and Sarbanes-Oxley (SOX) as control groups that the provider use for auditing.

○ Service Level Agreements; checks whether SLA is offered, that service levels apply to all the services provided, use of a service level management process such as Information Technology Infrastructure Library (ITIL) and are employees ITIL Certified.

○ Monitoring; are performance monitoring tools (such as utilization, response time and availability), monitor tools for resource utilization and demand patterns provided and is remote availability and quality testing of networked resources performed.

- **Reputation:** expresses the creditability of the service provider and mainly depends on users' experiences. Reputation can be seen as the sum of subjective customer's rating and objective QoS advertising messages credibility, taking into consideration to reduce the impact of malicious rating (Cao & Li, A Service-Oriented Qos-Assured and Multi-Agent Cloud Computing Architecture, 2009).

- **Regulatory:** is the quality aspect of the service in conformance with the rules, the law, compliance with standards, and the established SLA.

- **Interoperability:** defines such a service that is compatible with the standards [ISO 9126]. Checking if the service provider is a member of Cloud Standards groups (ENISA, CSA, CloudAudit, OCCI) is a useful check.

- **Economics:** From an enterprise perspective, costs are important but so too are customer relationships, public image, flexibility, business continuity and compliance. Users need to consider the benefits, risks and the effects of cloud computing on their organizations and usage-practices in order to make decisions about its adoption and use: the potential for reduced costs could be just one of the persuasively significant benefits of cloud computing offerings (Khajeh-Hosseini, Sommerville, & Sriram, 2010).

○ It is represented by the fees paid when a consumer use a service provided by cloud service provider, that is, pay-per-use, and it can be realized by cloud service meterage (Cao & Li, A Service-Oriented Qos-Assured and Multi-Agent Cloud Computing Architecture, 2009).

○ One more metric to consider is the penalty that the provider will be charged of, in case the service was not delivered. This penalty is considered compensation for the loss that will be encountered by the consumer.

3.3 Discussion

In this section, a general and flexible QoS ontology to express QoS information in a unified way was designed and a comprehensive QoS model was demonstrated, to cover all quality aspects of both service providers and consumers of different cloud platforms. The model sustains the extension of QoS attributes according to specific situation, to support QoS-assured cloud service selection, provision and Service Level Agreement (SLA) monitoring. Diverse QoS factors, defined in the QoS model, will be integrated in the service selection process.

4. QoS-BASED UTILITY MODEL FOR PROVIDER SERVICE SELECTION

This section emphasizes on the QoS utility-based model for optimal Cloud service provider selection in market-oriented Cloud Computing platforms. Matching the characteristics of various kinds of Cloud Computing services, the addressed model can be applied on the selection of providers of all kinds of services. Such kinds of Cloud services include IaaS, PaaS and SaaS. Also, various applications are hosted within each kind of platforms; i.e. in SaaS, applications such as Customer Relationship Management (CRM) and Content Delivery Network (CDN) are hosted.

In contrast with previous approaches of selection problem, the integrated utility approach allows various QoS metrics, including economic ones, to be objectively de-fined and implemented in the selection process. Various QoS factors integration enables the consumers with a mean for expressing their QoS condition, so the selection process can proceed on a QoS basis.

This section is organized into sub-sections as follows; the first sub-section we discuss how the process of selecting the Cloud provider will be conducted by the consumer. The second sub-section presents how diverse QoS factors are formulated, represented in our model and integrated within the two phases of the selection process previously described in part A. Finally, the problem is mathematically formulated in the third sub-section.

4.1 Selection Methodology

The addressed selection methodology includes three main sequential phases; primary selection, dominance selection and utility selection. Figure 5 illustrates the selection process.

Primary selection should take place first, where evaluating the service offerings and yielding a set of services matching the consumer's minimum requirements is the main target. Pre-assessment process defines the QoS minimum requirements, in terms of QoS attributes, that will determine whether the service offering can fit into the consumer's organization as evaluation criteria.

Next, Dominance selection is performed on the set of service offerings meeting the minimum requirements. Dominance selection is simply done to check whether there exists any service offering that dominates another one in terms of all QoS attributes previously defined in the primary selection phase. The main objective of this stage is to eliminate the number of offerings that will pass to the next phase.

Utility selection is then performed only on the set of service providers that passed the dominance selection. The utility function will be used in our model to objectively evaluate the consumer's benefits (utility) of each possible Cloud service offering. Selection is, then, performed based on utility-maximization between such alternatives. Using the utility function, the selection problem can be naturally formulated as a utility-maximization problem; the utility-maximization problem finds the optimal service offering among the set of selection alternatives which maximizes the global utility sum.

Accordingly, a successful service offering has two main objectives: to provide the needed functionality and to provide the needed Quality of Service (QoS).

This approach uses utility functions in the context of the addressed QoS framework with the goals to meet the minimum requirements and maximize the total utility for the consumer. Fig-

Figure 5. The selection process

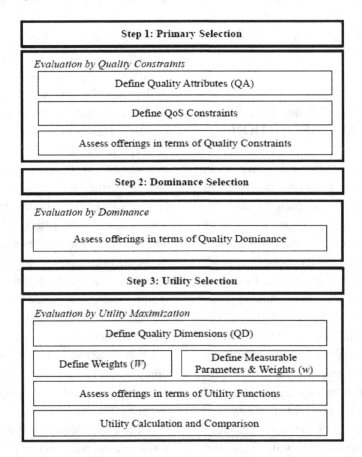

ure 6 provides a schematic representation of the problem and the addressed methodology (Salama, Shawish, Zeid, & Kouta, 2012).

The differentiation between the available providers is performed based on the QoS commitment listed in each provider's Service-Level-Agreement (SLA) contract. Such differentiation may be also based on the performance metric gathered from the user trials. Generally, the values listed in the provider's SLA are the actual metrics recording the level of service in terms of several attributes; otherwise in case of violating such SLA the provider will be incurred penalties that are also listed in the same SLA.

The efficiency of this approach lies in terms of minimum requirements fulfillment and overall utility maximization including monetary cost minimization. It also addresses the lack of tools the Cloud service consumers pose when evaluating service providers' offerings. This is done by integrating a wide range of QoS constraints and dimensions and allowing various QoS parameters including economic metrics to be objectively defined and considered in the selection process.

4.2 Formulating Quality Parameters

The previously presented selection process raises the need to model the QoS factors in a tailored way. Fitting the selection model, two major concepts are implemented. First, a simple set of QoS attributes (QA) is defined for the primary selection process. For each QoS attribute a constraint

Figure 6. Selection Methodology

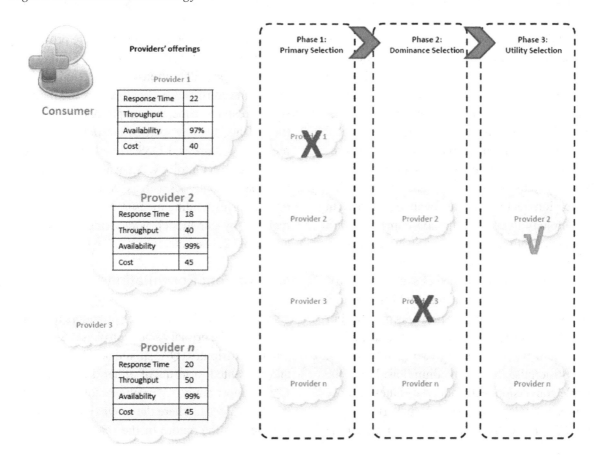

value - minimum or maximum - is specified expressing the consumer's requirement regarding the corresponding quality attribute. QAs will be also used for dominance selection. Second, a bigger set of QoS dimensions (QD) is defined for the utility-based selection process. For each QD, a set of measurable parameters is then defined.

The flexibility supported by the model to include various QoS attributes and dimensions make it suitable for different Cloud Computing services: SaaS, PaaS or IaaS. For instance, factors such as reusability, availability and scalability of the software will be applied in case of SaaS, while in case of IaaS factors like performance and availability of resources such as processors memory, storage and networks will be considered. As a matter of fact, characterization of the services

facilitates the determination of the appropriate QoS attributes and dimensions for the selection process. It is also worth noting that Quality Attributes and Dimensions can be extended by addition or removal according to the user QoS requirements. In addition, quality parameters may also be extended within one Quality Dimension. Moreover, those dimensions and their parameters are weighted upon consumer preferences. Therefore, the selection will be performed based, not only on the consumer minimum requirements, but also on the highest quality possible.

QoS Attributes & QoS Dimensions are selected from the provided QoS Model, either from technical or business factors. They may refer to the same factor, but they are implemented by two different expressions; Attributes and Dimensions. QAs are meant to be simpler than QDs in order to fit the first two phases of the selection methodology, while QDs were needed to implement different metrics in order to reflect the consumer utility.

Taking into consideration the non-scalar QoS parameters like security, privacy, and business factors; a simple conversion technique has been developed to convert the values of the non-numerical parameters into numeric ones. Such new features make it possible for the addressed selection model to incorporate non-scalar parameters. A simple conversion technique has been developed in the ontology to convert the non-numerical QoS parameters into numeric ones. Such new feature makes it possible for the service selection model to incorporate QoS parameters such as security, privacy, and business factors, which was not possible in the available or previous models. For instance, security level, as a non-scalar parameter, could be measured in two quality scales; either true/false, or high/medium/low. Using the simple conversion technique, the values of those non-numerical parameters are converted to 1/0 and 3/2/1 respectively. By that, such numerical

values could be easily incorporated in the utility function calculation.

To assess the QoS among multiple providers in a meaningful way, it is essential to specify QoS properties that will be used in the selection process and define consistently the attributes and metrics such as response time, throughput, and availability time. Thus, QoS properties are defined by the previously addressed QoS Model and modeled using the QoS Ontology. An example for modeling QoS attributes, as well as QoS dimensions an d their corresponding measurable parameters, as required by our model, is described in Table 1 and Table 2, respectively.

4.3 Problem Formulation

Assume that n cloud services providers are considered for the primary selection phase. A set of m Quality Attributes (QA) should be firstly selected and presented in terms of either a lower bound C_j^{min} or upper bound C_j^{max} value as follows: { C_1^{min} C_2^{min} $,..., C_m^{max}$ }, where the usage of C_j^{min} or C_j^{max} is based on the nature of the selected attribute.

Table 1. QoS attributes

QoS Attribute	Description
Response Time	the time experienced by the consumer to get serviced
Throughput	the number of requests completed within a time frame
Availability Time	total time that the service is available
Service Value	denotes the economic dimension for a unit of service (1 GB storage, 1 CPU hour)

Table 2. QoS Dimensions and corresponding measurable parameters

QoS Dimension	Description	Measurable QoS Parameters
Performance	describe how fast and successfully the cloud can provide the requested service	response time, worst-case execution time, throughput
Dependability	concerned with how probable the cloud can successfully provide the requested service	availability time, reliability level (high/medium/low) [Note: these levels are assigned based on the percentage of availability]
Reputation	expresses the creditability of the service provider	Consumers' rating, advertising messages credibility
Service Value	denotes the economic dimension	service fees to be paid

Attributes like response time will be presented in terms of upper bound C_j^{max} while attribute like throughput will be presented in terms of lower bound C_j^{min}. Here, it should be noted that the value of either C_j^{min} or C_j^{max} is actually assigned by the consumer to illustrate the required level of QoS. Each of the n providers is then investigated based on the selected QAs. Each provider i, where $i \in \{1,\ldots,n\}$, is presented in terms of $\{r_{i1}, r_{i2}, \ldots, r_{im}\}$ where the value r_{ij} describes the performance of the provider i in terms of the quality attribute j. The input values are either mentioned in the Service-Level-Agreement (SLA) contracts guaranteed by the provider or gathered from the user trials. The input values are either mentioned in the Service-Level-Agreement (SLA) contracts guaranteed by the provider or gathered from the user trials. Obtaining valid and reliable QoS values is not addressed in this work, where, it is assumed that the published QoS values are trusted and reliable.

The primary selection will take place as follows:

Each provider i, presented by $\{r_{i1}, r_{i2}, \ldots r_{im}\}$ is compared term by term correspondingly with the pre-determined QAs upper or lower bounds $\{C_1^{min}, C_2^{min}, \ldots, C_m^{max}\}$.

The provider i is rejected if for any term r_{ij}, where $j \in \{1,\ldots,m\}$, $(r_{ij} < C_j^{min})$ for those QAs with lower bound (subject to maximization), or $(r_{ij} > C_j^{max})$ for those QAs with upper bound (subject to minimization).

By the end of the primary selection phase, only k_1 providers, where $k_1 \leq n$, will be promoted to the next phase of the selection processes. Those providers are the ones that fulfill the consumer's primary threshold.

Next, the dominance selection will be performed as follows. For each provider i, where $i \in \{1,\ldots,k_1\}$, its QAs will be checked against QAs of all other providers. The provider i is rejected if all terms were dominated by another provider i', where $i' \in \{1,\ldots,k_1\}$. For any term r_{ij}, where $j \in \{1,\ldots,m\}$, $(r_{ij} < r_{i'j})$ for those QAs with lower bound (subject to maximization), or $(r_{ij} > r_{i'j})$ for those QAs with upper bound (subject to minimization).

After the dominance selection phase, providers with QAs dominated by another provider; i.e. providers with all QAs poorer than another provider; will be eliminated. Thus, only k_2 providers, where $k_2 \leq k_1$, will be promoted to the next phase of selection.

Next, the utility selection will take place as follows. For each provider i, where $i \in \{1,\ldots,k_2\}$, the consumer utility value will be calculated to illustrate the expected gain that the consumer may obtain if the provider i is selected. A linear utility function $f(U_i)$ is defined to specify such utility value. Firstly, the consumer should select a group of m QoS Dimensions (QD) as a base-reference for differentiation between the k candidate providers. By giving the user the freedom to select the QDs, he will be indirectly formulating the utility function itself. The QDs selection is not a complicated task for the user, as he will be selecting his main concerns compared to mathematically formulating a utility function. Choosing QDs will be performed based on the requirements of the user. For instance, financial applications require high throughput rather than fast response time, while CRM application in a call center requires faster response time. Guidelines on how to choose QDs are out of the scope of this paper. Thus the selected QoS dimensions should illustrate the main concerns of the consumer such as performance, dependability, reputation, and service value and represented by the calculated value u_{ij}, where $j \in \{1,\ldots,m\}$. The consumer will also assign a weight W_j for each of these QDs. The value of $W_j \in [0,1]$, and

$$\sum_{j=1}^{m} W_j = 1.$$ The weight specified for each QD is not absolute, but relative and directly reflects the importance of that QoS Dimension for the user. Weights of all dimensions sum up to 1, by that, weights are normalized; i.e. the weight of each

dimension is relative to the weights of other dimensions. It is important to note that the assigned value of each weight also reflects the relative importance of the QD with respect to the others based on the consumer's concerns.

The weights are mathematically represented as previously described. Although when the consumer has the task of assigning those mathematical values, a problem will arise. From the consumer side, weights will be settled using a simple algorithm as follows. After choosing the set of QDs, the consumer will be asked to arrange those QDs in an ascending order from the least important to the highest important. And, the first QD will be automatically assigned an importance degree of 1. Then, the consumer will be asked to assign an importance degree for the second QD, relative to the first QD, and so on each QD will get an importance degree relative to its previous one. For instance, the consumer will assign an importance degree of 2 in case this QD is twice important than the first one, or 1 if it is with the same importance. By that, the consumer will freely assign importance degree values without being constrained by the mathematical rule that equates all weights to 1. All importance degree values assigned by the consumer are then scaled to sum up to 1.

For instance, each provider i will be denoted by a group of utility values $\{u_{i1}, u_{i2},...,u_{im}\}$ that describe the performance of such provider with respect to the m selected QDs. Thus, the global utility function $f(U_i)$ associated with provider i is computed as follows:

$$f\left(U_i\right) = \sum_{j=1}^{m} u_{ij} * W_j \qquad (6)$$

The calculation of the utility value u_{ij} is addressed as follows. Any quality dimension j, where $j \in \{1,..,m\}$, is defined by a group of measurable parameters P_{jl}, where $l \in \{1,..,q_j\}$, and q_j is the size of this group. For example; a quality dimen-

sion like the performance is defined in terms of measurable parameters like response time, worst-case execution time, and throughput. Each of these parameter P_{jl} is further associated with a weight w_{jl}, where for $w_{jl} \in [0,1]$, and $\sum_{l=1}^{q_j} w_{jl} = 1$. Varying P_{jl}, different parameters can be considered for one QoS dimension. For instance, the performance dimension, if $P_{ijl} = 1/T_i$, then this factor will be considered for minimization (assuming that T_i denotes the response time). As well as throughput (number of requests processed within a certain time frame) can be considered for maximization. Notably, the assigned value of w_{jl} should reflect the relative importance of such parameter with respect to the other parameters inside the quality dimension.

Based on the above description, one can compute the utility value u_{ij} for a single QD j associated with provider i as follows:

$$u_{ij} = \sum_{l=1}^{q_j} P_{ijl} * w_{jl} \qquad (7)$$

Accordingly, by applying the same methodology for the rest QDs, the overall utility function will be formulated as follows:

$$f\left(U_i\right) = \sum_{j=1}^{m} \left(\sum_{l=1}^{q_j} P_{ijl} * w_{jl} \right) * W_j \qquad (8)$$

Finally, by computing the utility value associated to each provider, the optimal provider will be the one with the highest utility value.

4.4 Discussion

In this section, the QoS utility-based model for optimal cloud service selection is presented. The model can be applied on the selection of all kinds of Cloud Computing service, by allowing various QoS metrics to be objectively defined and implemented in the selection process. Diverse QoS factors, that have been defined in a unified way by the QoS ontology and defined in the QoS model, were integrated in the selection process. Various QoS factors integration, including economic ones, enables the consumers with a mean for expressing their QoS condition, so the selection process can proceed on a QoS basis.

5 VALIDATION AND VERIFICATION

This section focuses on demonstrating the efficiency of the model developed. The developed tool is presented in detail and simulation conducted along with experimental studies are addressed. The main purpose of the empirical work was to run a typical selection problem that a cloud consumer may face when having multiple offerings from multiple providers. Two empirical pieces of work were held, one as a simulation and another one using benchmark data. The setup of the empirical work is introduced in sub-section 1. Finally, the empirical work results are presented in sub-section 2.

The main objectives of the simulation and experimental studies were to:

- Investigate the complications of a basic classical selection.
- Study the effect of QoS factors on the selection problem.
- Evaluate the efficiency of the QoS-guarantees utility model and measure the consumer utility.

5.1 Empirical Work Setup

The empirical work processes a typical selection problem that a cloud consumer may face when having multiple offerings from multiple providers.

Two experiments were held for this purpose. The first one was held using simulation data (presented in sub-section 1) and the second one was performed using benchmark data (presented in sub-section 2).

5.1.1 Simulation Setup

Simulation data used in the experimental study has been published in (Limam & Boutaba, 2010). This simulation setting has been established for evaluation under a more realistic environment. Consider a set of 20 software services $P_i, i = 1..20$, say, for instance, 20 storage service providers, with 20 different quality attributes, as illustrated in Table 3.

As commonly new providers are constantly introduced into the market, this feature is produced by assigning to different providers a randomly generated parameter *Arrival Time to Market* (ATTM) that refers to the time at which the service starts being available. Considering the dependability quality dimension, uptime parameter has been randomly generated ranging from 97.99 to 99.99 percent, as well as for the service value dimension, different costs ranging from 70 to 90. Since the acquired service is storage, failures that may occur from time to time and time taken for recover presents important quality attributes to be considered for the performance dimension. Two more randomly generated simulation parameters are defined for each service provider: *Time Between Failures* (TBFs), which refers to the shortest time that separates two consecutive failures, and *Time to Recovery* (TTR), which refers to the longest time the service will take to recover from any failure. At each failure, the recovery time is randomly generated with TTR as an upper bound (the upper bound for all TTRs being set to 50), and the next failure will take place after a randomly generated time, not shorter than TBF (the lower bound for TBFs being set to 50 and the upper bound to 400).

For the primary selection phase, Table 4 shows the list of the considered quality attributes, and their upper or lower bounds. These values are assigned by the consumer based on his own interest,

Table 3. Simulation parameters: Service offerings data

Provider	Fees	Uptime	TBF	TTR	ATTM
0	74.0	97.99	165	14	0
1	98.0	97.99	184	25	86
2	81.0	99.99	133	43	44
3	71.0	98.99	151	47	83
4	98.0	97.99	105	11	71
5	75.0	99.99	177	26	43
6	76.0	97.99	182	42	28
7	100.0	99.99	156	44	92
8	77.0	99.99	116	16	46
9	81.0	99.99	188	32	82
10	74.0	99.99	123	26	89
11	75.0	98.99	111	48	71
12	98.0	97.99	186	17	63
13	81.0	97.99	142	34	66
14	81.0	99.99	180	42	65
15	73.0	98.99	120	44	73
16	80.0	99.99	149	29	10
17	81.0	99.99	176	20	6
18	88.0	97.99	102	30	6
19	92.0	97.99	185	14	41

Table 4. Simulation parameters: Quality attributes, weights and boundaries values

QoS Attribute	Range	Constraint
Time to Recovery (TTR)	15 – 50	Max. 45
Uptime	97.00 – 99.99	Min. 98%
Service fees	71.0 – 100.0	Max. 85

Table 5. Simulation parameters: Quality dimensions, parameters and weight values

QoS Dimension	Weight (W_j)	QoS Parameters	weight (w_j)
1. Dependability	0.40	1.1 Uptime	0.60
		1.2 Time to Recovery (TTR)	0.40
2. Performance	0.25	2.1 Time Between Failures (TBF)	1.0
3. Reputation	0.10	3.1 Arrival Time To Market (ATTM)	1.0
4. Service Value	0.25	4.1 service fees to be paid	1.0

within a range of values, previously specified, in order to make it easier for the consumer.

With respect to the utility value calculation, Table 5 holds the set of QoS dimensions and their assigned weights, along with the measurable parameters for each dimension.

5.1.2 Experiment Setup

In the SaaS category, there is delivery of use-specific services over the Internet (such as Customer Relationship Management software, Content Delivery Networks and email). The benefit of SaaS clouds is that clients can only focus on the use of the software and do not have to worry about the cost and effort to keep software licenses nor handling up-to-date. While vendors have concentrated their effort on the improvement of performance, resource consumption and scalability, other cloud characteristics have been neglected. Clients face difficult problems of resource discovery and automatic services selection; dynamic sharing toward efficient management of resources; QoS and reputation of providers and clients; fault tolerance; cloud security and ease of use have been neglected.

An experiment was performed to present the selection problem, based on a specific sector of applications that use cloud computing, Content Delivery Network (CDN). Benchmark data published in (Cloud Harmony: benchmarking the Cloud, 2001), listing all available providers for CDN, has been used for performing the experiment. A set of 14 providers has been considered in our experiment. The benchmark has published four kinds of quality tests that have been performed on the available providers; including large files download, small files download, network latency and availability. For the first three tests, the following parameters have been measured: Time (seconds), Min. Mb/second, Max. Mb/ second, Median Mb/ second and Average Mb/second. As for the availability, *Availability Report for Last 365 Days* has been published. To illustrate the

flexibility of our model to incorporate different types of QoS parameters; even the non-scalar ones, the "Security" parameter has been added to the experiment data and emerged into our selection process. The security level is assessed here based on three levels; low, medium and high, where each provider is randomly assigned one of these levels. CDN Providers benchmark data is summed up in Table 6.

Considering the selection criteria, first for the primary selection phase, Table 7 shows the list of the considered quality attributes, and their upper or lower bounds. These values are assigned by the consumer, within a specified range of values.

With respect to the utility value calculation, Table 8 holds the set of QoS dimensions and their assigned weights, along with the measurable parameters for each dimension.

5.2 Results and Discussion

5.2.1 Simulation Results

Using the addressed model, primary selection is firstly performed. By checking the first provider P_0, the offering will be rejected, as not all its quality attributes satisfy the imposed constraints; the uptime (97.99%) is lower than the minimum allowed (98%). Same for P_1, the uptime (97.99%) is lower than the constraint and the fees (98) surpass the maximum allowed value (85). While checking, P_2 indicates the approval of such provider. It can easily note that all of the quality attributes of P_2 satisfy the imposed constraints, as TTR (43) is not higher than the maximum constraint (45), uptime (99.99%) is greater than the minimum constraint (98%) and fees (81) are less than the maximum value allowed (85). Thus, the providers P_2, P_5, P_8, P_9, P_{10}, P_{14}, P_{15}, P_{16} and P_{17} will pass to the next phase of selection. Applying dominance selection, none of those providers will be rejected as none of them dominates one another in all QAs. The utility calculation is then performed.

Table 6. Experiment Parameters: Providers data

	Service Provider	Security Level	Availability	Large File Download Tests					Small File Download Tests					Network Latency Tests				
				Time (secs)	Min Mb/s	Max Mb/s	Median Mb/s	Avg Mb/s	Time (secs)	Min Mb/s	Max Mb/s	Median Mb/s	Avg Mb/s	Time (secs)	Min ms	Max ms	Median ms	Avg ms
P$_1$	Akamai CDN	L	100.00%	14.7	0.26	0.26	0.26	0.26	22.24	0.06	0.57	0.1	0.19	0.9	136	162	139	145
P$_2$	Amazon CloudFront	M	100.00%	14.41	0.27	0.27	0.27	0.27	10.3	0.09	0.31	0.19	0.17	1.77	129	137	131	132.11
P$_3$	CacheFly CDN	M	100.00%	16.91	0.23	0.23	0.23	0.23	12.12	0.13	0.33	0.22	0.23	2.02	128	136	130	130.7
P$_4$	CDNetworks CDN	H	100.00%	14.32	0.27	0.27	0.27	0.27	15.24	0.11	0.3	0.23	0.21	2.07	126	134	131	130.4
P$_5$	CloudFlare	L	99.94%	16.4	0.23	0.23	0.23	0.23	18.32	0.1	0.19	0.17	0.15	2.75	301	311	307	306.33
P$_6$	Edgecast CDN	L	99.99%	19.86	0.19	0.19	0.19	0.19	17.05	0.2	0.24	0.22	0.22	2.01	127	136	131	131.2
P$_7$	Highwinds CDN	M	99.91%	34.34	0.21	0.23	0.23	0.22	6.17	0.17	0.36	0.23	0.25	1.97	131	138	135	134.78
P$_8$	Internap CDN	M	100.00%	15.56	0.25	0.25	0.25	0.25	12.27	0.15	0.31	0.25	0.23	2.36	133	163	138	145.11
P$_9$	Level 3 CDN	H	100.00%	15.1	0.25	0.25	0.25	0.25	12.61	0.07	0.21	0.14	0.13	2.71	246	2464	2464	1355
P$_{10}$	Limelight CDN	L	100.00%	16.44	0.23	0.23	0.23	0.23	12.09	0.11	0.21	0.18	0.18	2.22	138	144	141	140.78
P$_{11}$	MaxCDN	M	100.00%	14.8	0.26	0.26	0.26	0.26	10.17	0.17	0.31	0.24	0.24	3.39	128	208	163	159.6
P$_{12}$	Rackspace Cloud Files CDN	M	99.99%	14.45	0.26	0.26	0.26	0.26	12.72	0.11	0.26	0.18	0.18	1.83	126	131	129	128.89
P$_{13}$	VoxCAST CDN	L	99.99%	15.81	0.24	0.24	0.24	0.24	16.14	0.17	0.28	0.21	0.21	1.04	128	130	129	128.83
P$_{14}$	Azure CDN	H	99.98%	21.02	0.18	0.18	0.18	0.18	18.65	0.1	1.28	0.27	0.44	1.88	141	165	146	147.63

Table 7. Experiment parameters: Quality attributes, weights and boundaries values

QoS Attribute	Range	Constraint
Availability	98% - 100%	Min. 99.95%
Large File Download - Max Mb/s	0.15 - 0.30	Min. 0.20
Small File Download - Time (secs)	5.00 - 25.00	Max. 14.00

Table 8. Experiment parameters: Quality dimensions, parameters and weight values

QoS Dimension	Weight (W_j)	QoS Parameters	weight (w_j)
1. Large File Download	0.35	1.1 Max Mb/s	0.60
		1.2 Avg Mb/s	0.40
2. Small File Download	0.25	2.1 Time (secs)	0.70
		2.2 Median Mb/s	0.30
3. Network Latency	0.40	3.1 Time (secs)	0.35
		3.2 Avg ms	0.65
4. Secuirty Level	0.10	4.1 Level (L/M/H)	1

The utility values for each QD is firstly calculated using Equation 7, introduced in the previous chapter. For example, the first QoS dimension utility value that present the dependability is calculated by summing its parameters (Uptime and TTR) times their weights respectively (0.60, 0.40); noting that TTR was inverted as it is subject to minimization and TBF was not. A utility function is then calculated out of the utility values of all quality dimensions times their corresponding weights using Equation 8, also introduced in the previous chapter. The detailed calculations related to provider P_2 are shown in Table 9. The calculated utility values for providers that passed to the second phase are illustrated in Figure 7. Hence, the optimal provider is P_9 since it yields maximum utility value (79.21).

5.2.2 Experiment Results

Following the addressed model, primary selection is firstly performed. By checking the first provider Akamai CDN (P_1), the offering will be rejected, as not all its quality attributes satisfy the imposed

constraints; the time for small files download is (22.24) is greater than the maximum allowed (14.00). While checking, Amazon CloudFront (P_2) indicates the approval of such provider. It can easily note that all of the quality parameters of P_2 satisfy the imposed constraints, as availability (100.00%) is not less than the minimum constraint (99.95%), max. Mb/s for large files download (0.27) is greater than the minimum constraint (0.20) and time for small files download (10.3) are less than the maximum value allowed (14.00). Continuing with the same approach, the providers P_2, P_3, P_4, P_8, P_9, P_{10}, P_{11}, and P_{12} will pass to the next phase of selection and the utility calculation is then performed.

The utility values for each QD is firstly calculated. For example, the first QD utility value that present Large Files Download is calculated by summing its chosen parameters (Max Mb/s and Avg Mb/s) times their weights respectively (0.60, 0.40). For the utility values calculation, it is important to note that quality parameters subject to minimization (for example, time for small files download) are inverted. A utility function is then

Figure 7. Simulation results (Utility functions)

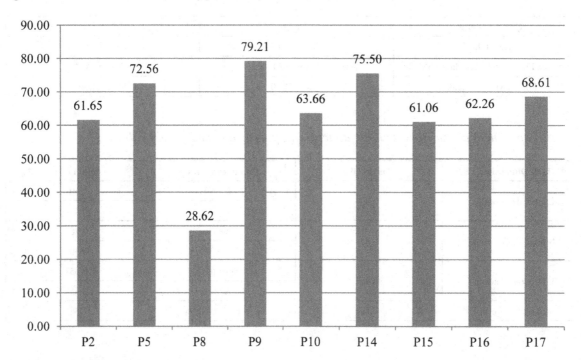

Table 9. Utility calculations for provider P2

QoS Dimension	QoS Parameters	P₂	u₂ⱼ	U₂ⱼ	U₂ * Wⱼ
1. Dependability	1.1 Uptime	99.99	59.99	60.00	24.00
	1.2 Time to Recovery (TTR)	43.00	0.01		
2. Performance	2.1 Time Between Failures (TBF)	133.00	133.00	133.00	33.25
3. Reputation	3.1 Arrival Time To Market (ATTM)	44.00	44.00	44.00	4.40
4. Service Value	4.1 service fees to be paid	81.00	0.01	0.01	0.003
					$f(U_2) = 61.65$

Table 10. Utility calculations for provider Amazon CloudFront (P2)

QoS Dimension	QoS Parameters	P₂	u₂ⱼ	U₂ⱼ	U₂ * Wⱼ
1. Large File Download	1.1 Max Mb/s	0.27	0.16	0.270	0.095
	1.2 Avg Mb/s	0.27	0.11		
2. Small File Download	2.1 Time (secs)	10.30	0.03	0.162	0.065
	2.2 Median Mb/s	0.19	0.13		
3. Network Latency	3.1 Time (secs)	0.56	1.15	1.153	0.288
	3.2 Avg ms	132.11	0.00		
					$f(U_2) = 0.448$

Figure 8. Experiment results (Utility functions)

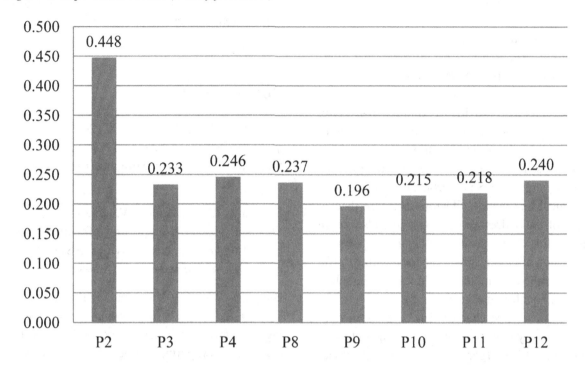

calculated out of the utility values of all quality dimensions times their corresponding weights. The detailed calculations related to provider P_2 are shown in Table 10. The calculated utility values for providers that passed to the second phase are illustrated in Figure 8. Hence, the optimal provider is P_2 since it yields maximum utility value (0.448).

5.2.3 Discussion

The simulation example scenario demonstrated the simple implementation of the proposed model. Meanwhile, using straight forward comparison based on single quality parameters will restrain implications in the selection process and will not lead to the optimal selection. For instance, although P_0 retains better TTR, and fees than P_9 and same uptime, P_0 didn't succeed to yield a higher utility value.

The performed experiment presented a real selection problem that a consumer may face. It was performed on Content Delivery Network (CDN) applications which recently turned to use cloud computing. While there are several CDN providers, it becomes hard to differentiate between them in terms of performance and the problem becomes more complicated when it is for optimal service selection. Optimal service selection cannot be performed by comparing a single quality attribute. For instance, although P_2 (Amazon CloudFront) showed the highest utility value, it was difficult to obtain this result by directly comparing quality attributes as it did not show the highest values for all quality attributes.

Throughout the empirical study, it is worth noting that the consumer preferences towards the quality metrics, presented in the specified weights, affected the calculations and hence the obtained results. Also, utility functions have mathematically reflected the needs of the consumer and converted it to the optimum selection.

6 CONCLUSION

This chapter introduced a general and flexible QoS ontology for expressing QoS information in a unified way. QoS ontology encloses basic attributes and auxiliary means for modeling QoS properties. The chapter also provided a comprehensive QoS framework covering all quality needs of both providers and consumers of various services' platforms. The provided framework incorporates a wide range of QoS properties, varying between technical and business factors and described in light of the addressed ontology. It is also worth noting that the proposed framework supports the extension of QoS attributes according to specific application domain, to be used for service selection and quality monitoring.

Moreover, the chapter also covered an integrated utility QoS-based model for the optimum selection of Cloud service providers. This model incorporate a wide range of QoS attributes and dimensions for the purpose of selecting the optimum provider reporting the best performance based on the consumer's interest. Hence, it can be reasonably described as a 3-dimensional model, covering the selection problem for different Cloud platforms and applications.

Evidently, all of the consumer quality requirements are fully taken into consideration to select the optimal provider. Furthermore, the economical factor was embedded in the selection process, so the consumer establishes an economical selection along with quality attributes. It is also worth noting that the structure of the model is flexible enough to accommodate any new quality attributes and dimensions. In addition, the model also shows the ability to be easily adjusted to meet any level of the QoS requirements through the adjustment of the internal attributes and dimensions weights.

Cloud Computing: a market-oriented distributed computing paradigm consisting of a collection of inter-connected and virtualized computers that are dynamically provisioned and presented as one or more unified computing resources based on service-level agreements established through negotiation between the service provider and consumers.

REFERENCES

Armstrong, D., & Djemame, K. (2009). *Towards quality of service in the cloud.* Paper presented at the 25th UK Performance Engineering Workshop. Leeds, UK.

Blanquer, I., Hernández, V., Segrelles, D., & Torres, E. (2008). A supporting infrastructure for evaluating QoS-specific activities in SOA-based grids. *Distributed and Parallel Systems*, 167–178.

Buyya, R., Yeo, C., Venugopal, S., Broberg, J., & Brandic, I. (2009). Cloud computing and emerging IT platforms: Vision, hype, and reality for delivering computing as the 5th utility. *Future Generation Computer Systems*, 25(6), 599–616. doi:10.1016/j.future.2008.12.001

Cao, B., & Li, B. (2009). A service-oriented QoS-assured and multi-agent cloud computing architecture. *Cloud Computing*, 5531, 644–649. doi:10.1007/978-3-642-10665-1_66

Catteddu, D. (2010). Cloud computing: Benefits, risks and recommendations for information security. *Web Application Security*, 72, 17. doi:10.1007/978-3-642-16120-9_9

Catteddu, D., & Hogben, G. (2009). *Cloud computing risk assessment.* Greece: European Network and Information Security Agency.

Chunlin, L., & Layuan, L. (2006). QoS based resource scheduling by computational economy in computational grid. *Information Processing Letters*, 98(3). doi:10.1016/j.ipl.2006.01.002

Cloud Harmony: Benchmarking the Cloud. (2001). Retrieved June 27, 2011, from http://cloudharmony.com

Giallonardo, E., & Zimeo, E. (2007). More semantics in QoS matching. In *Proceedings of IEEE Inter. Conf. Service-Oriented Computing and Applications* (pp. 163–171). Newport Beach, CA: IEEE.

Heart, T., Tsur, N., & Pliskin, N. (2010). Software-as-a-service vendors: Are they ready to successfully deliver? *Global Sourcing of Information Technology and Business Processes*, *55*, 151–184. doi:10.1007/978-3-642-15417-1_9

Jacob, P., & Davie, B. (2005). Technical challenges in the delivery of interprovider QoS. *IEEE Communications Magazine*, *43*(6), 112. doi:10.1109/MCOM.2005.1452839

Khajeh-Hosseini, A., Sommerville, I., & Sriram, I. (2010). Research challenges for enterprise cloud computing. *CoRR, abs/1001.3257.*

Klems, M., Nimis, J., & Tai, S. (2009). Do clouds compute? A framework for estimating the value of cloud computing. *Designing E-Business Systems: Markets, Services, &. Networks*, *22*, 110–123.

Kondo, D., Javadi, B., Malecot, P., Cappello, F., & Anderson, D. (2009). Cost-benefit analysis of cloud computing versus desktop grids. In *Proceedings of IEEE Int. Symp. on Parallel & Distributed Processing*. Washington, DC: IEEE Computer Society.

La, H., & Kim, S. (2009). A systematic process for developing high quality SaaS cloud services. In *Proceedings of 1st Int. Conf. on Cloud Computing* (pp. 278–289). Beijing, China: IEEE.

Laprie, J.-C. (1995). Dependable computing and fault tolerance: Concepts and terminology. In *Proceedings of 25th International Symp. Fault-Tolerant Computing* (pp. 27–30). Pasadena, CA: IEEE.

Lee, C., Lehoczky, J., Rajkumar, R., & Siewiorek, D. (1999). On quality of service optimization with discrete QoS options. In *Proceedings of 5th IEEE Real-Time Technology and Applications Symp.* (pp. 276-286). Washington, DC: IEEE Computer Society.

Limam, N., & Boutaba, R. (2010). Assessing software service quality and trustworthiness at selection time. *IEEE Transactions on Software Engineering*, *36*(4), 559–574. doi:10.1109/TSE.2010.2

Menascé, D., & Casalicchio, E., & Vinod. (2010). On optimal service selection in service oriented architectures. *Journal of Performance Evaluation*, *67*(8). doi:10.1016/j.peva.2009.07.001

MIT. (2006). Inter-provider quality of service. Cambridge, MA: MIT Communications Futures Program (CFP) Quality of Service Working Group.

Pathan, M., Broberg, J., & Buyya, R. (2009). Maximizing utility for content delivery clouds. In *Proceedings of 10th Int. Conf. on Web Information Systems Engineering* (pp. 13-28). Berlin: Springer-Verlag.

Pauley, W. (2010). Cloud provider transparency: An empirical evaluation. *IEEE Security and Privacy*, *8*(6), 32–39. doi:10.1109/MSP.2010.140

Salama, M., Shawish, A., & Kouta, M. (2011). *Generic ontology-based QoS model for cloud computing*. Paper presented at the International Conference on Computer and Information Technology (ICCIT 2011). Amsterdam, The Netherlands.

Salama, M., Shawish, A., Zeid, A., & Kouta, M. (2012). Integrated QoS utility-based model for cloud computing service provider selection. In *Proceedings of 36th Annual IEEE Computer Software and Applications Conference* (COMPSAC 2012). IEEE.

Stantchev, V., & Schröpfer, C. (2009). Negotiating and enforcing QoS and SLAs in grid and cloud computing. *Advances in Grid and Pervasive Computing*, *5529*, 25–35. doi:10.1007/978-3-642-01671-4_3

Tondello, G., & Siqueira, F. (2008). The QoS-MO ontology for semantic QoS modeling. In *Proceedings of ACM Symp. Applied computing* (pp. 2336–2340). ACM.

Tran, V., & Tsuji, H. (2009). A survey and analysis on semantics in QoS for web services. In *Proceedings of Inter. Conf. on Advanced Information Networking and Applications* (pp. 379–385). IEEE.

Vanderster, D., Dimopoulos, N. R. P.-H., & Sobie, R. (2009). Resource allocation on computational grids using a utility model and the knapsack problem. *Future Generation Computer Systems*, *25*(1). doi:10.1016/j.future.2008.07.006 PMID:21308003

Xiong, K., & Perros, H. (2009). Service performance and analysis in cloud computing. In *Proceedings of 2009 Congress on Services – I (SERVICES 09)* (pp. 693-700). Washington, DC: IEEE Computer Society.

Yang, B., Tan, F., Dai, Y., & Guo, S. (2009). Performance evaluation of cloud service considering fault recovery. In *Proceedings of 1st International Conference on Cloud Computing* (CloudCom 09) (pp. 571–576). Beijing, China: IEEE.

Yin, B., & Yang, H., P., F., & Chen, X. (2010). A semantic web services discovery algorithm based on QoS ontology. *Active Media Technology*, *6335*, 166–173. doi:10.1007/978-3-642-15470-6_18

Yu, T., Zhang, Y., & Lin, K. (2007). Efficient algorithms for web services selection with end-to-end QoS constraints. *ACM Trans. on the Web*, *1*(1).

Zeng, L., Benatallah, B., Ngu, A., Dumas, M., & Kalag, J. (2004). QoS-aware middleware for web services composition. *IEEE Transactions on Software Engineering*, *30*(5), 311–327. doi:10.1109/TSE.2004.11

Zhao, Z., Lage, N., & Crespi, N. (2011). User-centric service selection, integration and management through daily events. In *Proceedings of 2011 IEEE Inter. Conf. Pervasive Computing and Communications* (pp. 94-99). IEEE.

KEY TERMS AND DEFINITIONS

Cloud: A large pool of easily usable and accessible virtualized resources (such as hardware, development platforms and/or services). These resources can be dynamically reconfigured to optimum resource utilization. This pool of resources is typically exploited by a pay-per-user model in which guarantees are offered by the Infrastructure Provider by means of customized SLA's.

Infrastructure-as-a-Service (IaaS): A provision model in which an organization outsources the equipment used to support operations, including storage, hardware, servers and networking components, where the service provider owns the equipment and is responsible for housing, running and maintaining it and the client typically pays on a per-use basis.

Platform-as-a-Service (PaaS): A Cloud service model which offers an environment on which developers create and deploy applications and do not necessarily need to know how many processors or how much memory that applications will be using.

Software-as-a-Service (SaaS): A software distribution model in which applications are hosted by a vendor or service provider and made available to customers over a network, typically the Internet.

Chapter 3
Is the Cloud the Future of Computing?

Joseph M. Kizza
University of Tennessee – Chattanooga, USA

Li Yang
University of Tennessee – Chattanooga, USA

ABSTRACT

Cloud computing as a technology is difficult to define because it is evolving without a clear start point and no clear prediction of its future course. Even though this is the case, one can say that it is a continuous evolution of a computer network technology. It extends client-server technology that offers scalability, better utilization of hardware, on-demand applications and storage, and lower costs over the long run. It is done through the creation of virtual servers cloned from existing instances. The cloud technology seems to be in flux; hence, it may be one of the foundations of the next generation of computing. A grid of a few cloud infrastructures may provide computing for millions of users. Cloud computing technology consists of and rests on a number of sound, fundamental, and proven technologies. This includes virtualization, service-oriented architectures, distributed computing, and grid computing. Based on these fundamental and sound computing principles, one wonders whether cloud computing is the next trajectory of computing. This chapter discusses this in depth and also looks at the security issues involved.

1. INTRODUCTION

Cloud computing as a technology, in its present form, is difficult to define because it is evolving without a clear start point and no clear prediction of its future course is known yet. However, one can say that cloud computing has gone beyond the client-server paradigm in networking environment which offers scalability, increased utilization of hardware, on-demand software applications and storage. Cloud computing lowers cost of operation over the long run through employing virtual servers which lead to instantaneous increased performance and fast response to any emerging hardware, software or service demands. With the current trends in cloud technology, it may be that in the next few years, a grid of a few cloud

DOI: 10.4018/978-1-4666-5788-5.ch003

infrastructures may provide computing for millions of users.

Cloud computing technology consists of and rests on a number of sound, fundamental and proven fundamental technologies including virtualization, service oriented architectures, distributed computing, grid computing, broadband networks, software as a service, browser as a platform, free and open source software, autonomic systems, web application frameworks and service level agreements (Mell, 2011). We will discuss cloud computing based on these technologies.

First let us start by giving a broader but specific view of the technology, what it is composed of and how it works. According to NIST (Mell, 2011), cloud computing is a model for enabling ubiquitous, convenient, on-demand network access to a shared pool of configurable computing resources like networks, servers, storage, applications and services that can be rapidly provisioned and released with minimal management effort or service provider interaction. So for the remainder of this chapter, we are going to focus on this model of computing and discuss its benefits and security concerns.

2. HISTORICAL DEVELOPMENT OF THE CLOUD INFRASTRUCTURE

Traditionally data center computing models were mainly based on a client-server model architecture and design relying firmly on a three-tier architecture design that included access, distribution and core switches connecting relatively few clients and meeting limited client needs compared to today's cloud services models. Each server was dedicated to either a single or limited applications and had IP addresses and media access control addresses. This static nature of the application environment worked well and lent itself to manual processes for server deployment or redeployment. According to both Jim Metzler and Steve

Taylor of Network World (Metzler, 2011), they primarily used a spanning tree protocol to avoid loops. Recent dramatic advances in virtualization technology, distributed computing, rapid improvements and access to high-speed Internet have all had dramatic influences on the current models of computing and data center. From services on demand to unprecedented elasticity in resource acquisition, users now have an array of choices at hand on demand and in quantities of choice. The services are fully managed by the provider, with the user as a consumer. Let us briefly look at those characteristics that have come to define cloud computing as a technology (Mell, 2011).

- **Ubiquitous Network Access:** The recent ubiquitous access to computer networks and services attribute to advances and use of high speed Internet and virtualization technology. Advances and development in these technologies have increased the repertoire of computing services a customer can select from. With more options came the high specialization and quality of services that a customer can expect.

- **Measured Service:** The increase in the repertoire of services available to users has been enhanced by cloud services' elasticity, flexibility, on demand capabilities thus allowing for these services to be metered. The concept of metered services allows customers to get what they want in the required amounts at the time they want the service. One of the most popular characteristics of cloud computing technology is measured or metered service for most, if not all, of the cloud services including storage, processing, bandwidth and active user accounts. This *pick-what-you-can-afford-to-pay-for* principle based on metering results in an automatic control and optimization of cloud technology resource use based on the type of service and these statistics can be reported as needed thus providing transparency for both the provider and consumer.

- **On-Demand Self-Service:** Traditionally, acquisition of computing services demanded perpetual ownership of software or computing hardware and sustainable technical support to help with computing services. Those models are phasing out when we have cloud computing as a flexible model where consumers of computing services are no longer restricted to rigid traditional models of ownership or boxed services. Now, a consumer is able to not only automatically provision any computing services and capabilities as needed but also to determine the time and how long to use the provisioned services.

- **Rapid Elasticity:** The ability to resize and dynamically scale the virtualized computing resources at hand such as servers, processors, operating systems and others to meet the customer's on-demand needs is referred to as computing service elasticity. To meet elasticity demands on computing resources, the provider must make sure that there are abundant resources at hand that to ensure that end-users' requests are continually and promptly met. Amazon's EC2 is a good example of a web service interface that allows the customer to obtain and configure capacity with minimal effort.

- **Resource Pooling:** As noted in the NIST report, the provider's computing resources are pooled to serve multiple consumers using a multi-tenant model, with different physical and virtual resources dynamically assigned and reassigned according to consumer demand. These fluctuating and unpredictable customer demands are a result of new cloud computing flexibility, access and ease of use.

There are other characteristics common to cloud computing beyond the five we have discussed above. Among these are (Mell, 2011):

- **Massive Scale:** That the cloud offers the resources at a massive scale on demand.

- **Virtualization:** In fact, this is the linchpin of the cloud technology. The cloud is possible because of virtualization of the fundamental functionalities of the physical machine.

- **Free (or Near Free) Software:** Software as needed from the cloud.

- **Autonomic Computing:** In a sense that you scale computing resources at a time you want them on the fly.

- **Multi-Tenancy:** Because of cloud's massive scale and easy access of those resources, cloud computing can accommodate a large number of users at a time.

3. CLOUD COMPUTING SERVICE MODELS

Infrastructure as a Service (IaaS)

Cloud computing offers flexibility and autonomy that allow customers to manage and control system resources via a web-based virtual server instance API. Customers are able to start, stop, access, and configure operating systems, applications, storage and other fundamental computing resources without interacting with the underlying physical cloud infrastructure.

Platform as a Service (PaaS)

This is a set of software and product development tools hosted on the provider's infrastructure and accessible to the customer via a web-based virtual server instance API. Through this instance, the customer can create applications on the provider's platform over the Internet. Accessing the platform via the web-based virtual instance API protects the resources because the customer cannot manage or control the underlying physical cloud infrastructure including network, servers, operating systems, or storage.

Software as a Service (SaaS)

Ever since the beginning of computing software, over the years, the key issue that has driven software development has been the issue of the cost of software. Trying to control the cost of software has resulted into software going through several models. The first model was the home developed software where software users developed their own software based on their needs and they owned everything and were responsible for updates and management of it. The second model, the traditional software model was based on packaged software where the customer acquired more general purpose software from the provider with a license held by the provider and the provider being responsible for the updates while the customer is responsible for its management. However, sometimes, software producers provide additional support services, the so called premium support, usually for additional fees. Model three was the Open Source model led by a free software movement starting around the late 80s. By the late 1980, free software turned into open source with the creation of the Open Source Initiative (OSI). Under the name of "open source" philosophy, some for-profit "free software" started to change the model from purely free software to some form of payment in order to support updates of the software. The open source software model transformed the cost of software remarkably. Model Four consisted of Software Outsourcing.

The outsourcing model was in response to the escalating cost of software associated with soft-ware management. The component of software management in the overall cost of software was slowly surpassing all the costs of other components of software including licensing and updates. In model four, the software producer takes on the responsibility of the management of that software because software is still licensed from the software company on a perpetual basis.

Software model five is Software as a Service (SaaS). Under this model, there is a different way of purchasing. Under SaaS, there is the elimination of the upfront license fee. All software applications are retained by the provider and the customer has access to all applications of choice from the provider via various client devices through either a thin client interface, such as a web browser, a web portal or a virtual server instance API. The cloud user's responsibilities and actual activities in the use of and operations of the requested cloud services is limited to user-specific application configuration settings, leaving the management and control of the underlying cloud infrastructure including network, servers, operating systems, storage, or even individual application capabilities to the cloud provider.

4. CLOUD COMPUTING DEPLOYMENT MODELS

There are four cloud deployment models: public, private, hybrid, and community (Mell, 2011).

Public Clouds

The public clouds provides access to computing resources for the general public over the Internet allowing customers to self-provision resources typically via a web service interface on a pay-as-you-go basis. One of the benefits of public clouds is to offer large pools of scalable resources on a temporary basis without the need for capital investment in infrastructure by the user.

Private Clouds

Unlike public clouds, private clouds give users immediate access to computing resources hosted within an organization's infrastructure and premises. Users, who are usually in some form of a relationship with the cloud owner, choose and scale collections of resources drawn from the private cloud, typically via web service interface, just as with a public cloud. Also the private cloud is deployed within and uses the organization's existing resources and is always behind the organization's firewall subject to the organization's physical, electronic, and procedural security measures. Security concerns are addressed through secure-access virtual private network (VPN) or by the physical location within the client's firewall system. In this case, therefore, private clouds offer a higher degree of security.

Hybrid Clouds

A hybrid cloud combines the computing resources of both the public and private clouds, which helps businesses to take advantage of secured applications and data hosting on a private cloud, while still enjoying cost benefits by keeping shared data and applications on the public cloud. This model is also used for handling cloud bursting, which refers to a scenario where the existing private cloud infrastructure is not able to handle load spikes and requires a fallback option to support the load. Hence, the cloud migrates workloads between public and private hosting without any inconvenience to the users. Many PaaS deployments expose their APIs, which can be further integrated with internal applications or applications hosted on a private cloud, while still maintaining the security aspects. Microsoft Azure and Force.com are two examples of this model.

Community Clouds

A community cloud is shared by several organizations with the same policy and compliance considerations. This helps to further reduce costs as compared to a private cloud, as it is shared by larger group. Some state-level government departments requiring access to the same data relating to the local population or information related to infrastructure, such as hospitals, roads, electrical stations, etc., can utilize a community cloud to manage applications and data.

5. BENEFITS OF CLOUD COMPUTING

Cloud computing as a model of computing is very exciting and has tremendous benefits for those who dare to use it. It is not only exciting when you come to learn it, but it also has an array of benefits including but not limited to leveraging on a massive scale, homogeneity, virtualization, low cost software, service orientation, and advanced security technologies (Mell, 2011).

- **Reduced Cost:** The biggest benefit from all cloud computing benefits to a company perhaps lies in cost savings. Whether it is a small, medium or large scale manufacturing business there are essential cost benefits in using a cloud model for most of the company's computing needs. The biggest issue here is the fact that cloud computing is operated remotely off company premises except a few devices needed for accessing the cloud resources via a web portal. This means that company personnel can do the same amount of work on fewer computers by having higher utilization, save on not housing data centers on premises, save on personnel for running the data center, save on expenses that would normally be essential for running a data center on the premises. There are documentary evidences to support these views from industry experts. In the words of Greg Papadopoulos, the CTO from Sun Microsystems (Farber, 2008), hosting providers bring 'brutal efficiency' for utilization, power, security, service levels, and idea-to-deploy time. And there are savings on power consumption since there are few computers on premises. Currently, servers are used at only 15% of their capacity in many companies and 80% of enterprise software expenditure is on installation and maintenance of software.

- **Automatic Updates:** Our economy is now an online economy because most of, if not all businesses, are now online and depend on software applications for day to day services. Software is continuously changing and as business functionalities change, software need to be changed or updated. The cost of software updates and management has always been on the rise, usually surpassing the cost of new software. For companies to stay competitive and in many cases afloat, they must be consistently updating and changing software. The business of software updates and software management and licensing is a big drain on company resources. So having automatic updates and management from the cloud provider can be a great relief to any company. But updates are not limited to only software. Also not worrying about hardware updates is cost effective for companies.

- **Green Benefits of Cloud Computing:** Although cloud computing energy consumption has seen a vigorous debate and this debate is continuing, pitting those claiming that cloud computing is gobbling up resources as large cloud and social networking sites need daily megawatts of power to feed insatiable computing needs and those who claim that the computing model is indeed saving power from mil-

lions of servers left idling daily and consuming more power. We will discuss this more in the coming sections. For now, we think that there are indeed savings in power consumption by cloud computing.

- **Remote Access:** With a web portal access to the cloud, company employees may be able to work while they are on the road, home or in the office. This is of great benefit to the company so that there is no down time because somebody is not in the office.

- **Disaster Relief:** Many companies live in constant fear disasters occurring when they have company vital data stored on premises. No one likes to be a victim of large-scale catastrophes such as devastating hurricanes, earthquakes, and fires and of course terrorist attacks. Such misfortunes can create havoc to the companies' vital data and disrupt operations even if there were limited physical damage. Additionally, there are smaller disasters like computer crashes and power outages that can also wreak havoc on a company's vital data. While this is possible, there are many companies, especially small ones that may not even have any disaster recovery plan and some who have it may not be able to execute it effectively. This fear can be overcome with investments in cloud technology. Company's vital back up data can be safely stored on secure data centers on the cloud instead of in the company's server room.

- **Self-Service Provisioning:** Cloud computing allows users to deploy their own virtual sets of computing resources like servers, network, storage, and others, as needed without the delays, competency and complications typically involved in physical resource acquisition, installation and management. The cloud owners, irrespective of their physical location, not only can they provide all the computing resources your organization needs but also have the necessary capacity needed to monitor, manage and respond to the organization's daily and hour by hour infrastructure, software and platform requirements.

- **Scalability:** Because of the minute by minute monitoring capability of cloud computing of an organization's computing needs and the ability to increase or reduce the required resources as the demand increases or decreases, cloud computing offer the best infrastructure, platform and software scalability that cannot be matched in any owned computing facility.

- **Reliability and Fault-Tolerance:** Because the cloud provider, with qualified professionals and experience, monitors the computing requirements of a client company and can easily scale to demand, cloud computing offers a high degree of reliability and fault-tolerance.

- **Ease of Use:** To attract more customers, cloud provider has and must make the user interface friendly so that customers can scale into the cloud with the least effort.

- **Skills and Proficiency:** Some of the most sought after assets from a cloud provider are professionalism and a vast skill set provided to the customers. Companies, especially small ones, would pay a high price to get an employee with the skills set, efficiency, proficiency and experience found with cloud center staff.

- **Response Time:** Depending on the bandwidth at the company web portal, cloud computing services normally have speed because the computing resources provided are modern and powerful to be able to accommodate large number of users.

- **Mobility:** Because of web portal interface to the Cloud, cloud computing essentially is a mobile computing platform, allowing the users to access their applications.

- **Increased Storage:** Storage is a main function from cloud computing. Because of this, it is cheap and readily scalable to need.

- **Other Benefits:** Other benefits beyond those we descussed above include, providing a high quality of service (QoS), providing a high quality, well-defined and stable industry standard API and on demand availability of computing resources based on "at hand" financial contraints.

- **Security:** We are going to discuss this more in the coming section, but cloud computing, because of its individual virtual machines created per use, security provision has already been built in. In addition to these built in provisions due to virtualization, the Cloud model also offers a strong authentication regime at the browser interface gateway, a security mechanism that is individually and quickly set up and torn down as needed and a strong validation and verification scheme that is expensive to deploy at an individual client-server model.

6. SECURITY, RELIABILITY, AVAILABILITY AND COMPLIANCE ISSUES OF CLOUD COMPUTING

The cloud computing model as we know it today did not start overnight. The process has taken years moving through seven software models beginning with in-house software, licensed software normally referred as the traditional model, open source, outsourcing, hybrid, software as a service and finally the Internet model, the last two being part of the cloud computing model. When one carefully examines the cloud servicing model, one does not fail to notice the backward compatibilities or the carryovers of many of the attributes that characterized software through all the models. While this brings the benefits of each one of those software models, but also many, if not all of the software complexity and security issues in those models were carried over into the cloud computing model. Because of this, our first thought was to discuss the security issues in the cloud computing model through the prism of these models. It is tempting but we are going to follow a different path while keeping the reader rooted into the different software models. Security is and continues to be a top issue in the cloud computing model. The other three related issues are performance, compliance and availability. We will discuss all four in this section but since security is the number one issue, we will address it first.

We want to start the discussion of cloud computing security by paraphrasing Greg Papadopoulos, CTO of Sun Microsystems who said that cloud users normally "trust" cloud service providers with their data like they trust banks with their money. This means that they expect the three issues of security, availability and performance to be of little concern to them as they are with their banks (Farber, 2008). To give a fair discussion of the security of anything, one has to focus on two things that are the actors and their roles in the process you are interested in securing and the application or data in play. The application or data is thought of in relation to the temporal state it is in. For example the states of data are either in motion between the remote hosts and the service provider's hypervisors and servers or in the static state when it is stored at remote hosts, usually on the customer's premises or in the service provider's servers. The kind of security needed in either one of these two states is different.

6.1. Delegated Security Responsibilities in the Cloud

In the cloud computing model, the main players are the cloud provider, the customer who is the data owner and who seeks cloud services from the cloud provider and the user who may or may not be the owner of the data stored in the cloud. The security responsibilities and expectations of each one of these players are different. The first

two players have delegated responsibilities to all who work on their behalf. To fully understand these delegated responsibilities assigned to each one of these, we need to look at first the marginal security concerns resulting from the peripheral system access control that always result in easiest breach of security for any system, usually through compromising user accounts via weak passwords. This problem is broad affecting both local and outsourced cloud solutions. Addressing this and all other administrative and use security concern requires companies offering and using cloud solutions to design an access control regime that covers and requires every user, local or remote, to abide by these access policies including the peripheral ones like the generation and storage of user passwords. Additionally, employees need to be informed of the danger of picking easy passwords and to understand the danger of writing a password down or divulging a password to anyone. Access control administration is so important that cloud providers spend large amounts of resources to design a strong assess control regimes.

6.2. Security of Data and Applications in the Cloud

Security is arguably the most relevant concern preventing players' entry in the cloud. Threats posing to data, applications and users in the cloud are determined by a large number of technologies it comprises. The most relevant threats for the cloud have recently been shown in (Archer, 2010).

- **Threat 1: Abuse and Nefarious Use of Cloud Computing.** IaaS providers bring the illusion of unlimited compute, network, and storage capacity. However, IaaS offerings have hosted the botnets, Trojan horses, and software exploits.
- **Threat 2: Insecure Interfaces and APIs.** Cloud Computing providers expose a set of software interfaces or APIs that customers use to manage and interact with cloud ser-

vices. Provisioning, management, orchestration, and monitoring are all performed using these interfaces. The security and availability of general cloud services is dependent upon the security of these basic APIs.

- **Threat 3: Malicious Insiders.** This is amplified in the cloud by "the convergence of IT services and customers under a single management domain, combined with a general lack of transparency into provider process and procedure".

- **Threat 4: Shared Technology Issues.** IaaS vendors deliver their services in a scalable way by sharing infrastructure. Monitor environment for unauthorized changes/activity.

- **Threat 5: Data Loss or Leakage.** This threat increases in the cloud, due to the architectural or operational characteristics of the cloud environment (e.g. insecure APIs, shared environment, etc.).

- **Threat 6: Account or Service Hijacking.** Phishing, fraud, and exploitation are well-known issues in IT. The cloud adds a new dimension to this threat: "if an attacker gains access to your credentials, they can eavesdrop on your activities and transactions, manipulate data, return falsified information, and redirect your clients to illegitimate sites. Your account or service instances may become a new base for the attacker".

- **Threat 7: Unknown Security Profile.** The reduction of cost of ownership induced by the cloud also resulted in more complex analysis of a company's security posture. More tenants imply increased complexity in detecting who and how the cloud infrastructure is used.

We will then discuss the security of data and applications in the cloud. To do this we need to focus first on the security and role of the hypervisor

and then the servers on which user services are based. A hypervisor is also called virtual machine manager (VMM), which is one of many hardware virtualization techniques allowing multiple operating systems to run concurrently on a host computer. The hypervisor is piggybacked on a kernel program, itself running on the core physical machine running as the physical server. The hypervisor presents to the guest operating systems a virtual operating platform and manages the execution of the guest operating systems. Multiple instances of a variety of operating systems may share the virtualized hardware resources. Hypervisors are very commonly installed on server hardware, with the function of running guest operating systems, that themselves act as servers. The security of the hypervisor therefore involves the security of the underlying kernel program and the underlying physical machine, the physical server and the individual virtual operating systems and their anchoring virtual machines.

6.2.1. Hypervisor Security

The key feature of the cloud computing model is the concept of virtualization. It is virtualization that gives the cloud the near instant scalability and versatility that makes cloud computing so desirable a computing solution by companies and individuals. The core of virtualization in cloud computing is the easy process of minting of virtual machines on demand by the hypervisor. The hypervisor allocates resources to each virtual machine it creates and it also handles the deletion of virtual machines. Since each virtual machine is initiated by an instance, the hypervisor is a bi-directional conduit into and out of every virtual machine. The compromise of either, therefore, creates a danger to the other. However, most hypervisors are constructed in such a way that there is a separation between the environments of the sandboxes (the virtual machines) and the hypervisor. There is just one hypervisor, which services all virtual sandboxes, each running a guest operating system. The hypervisor runs as part of the native monolithic operating system, side-by-side with the device drivers, file system and network stack, completely in kernel space. So, one of the biggest security concerns with a hypervisor is the establishment of covert channels by an intruder. According to the Trusted Computer Security Evaluation Criteria, TCSEC, a covert channel is created by a sender process that modulates some condition (such as free space, availability of some service, wait time to execute) that can be detected by a receiving process. If an intruder succeeds in establishing a covert channel, either by modifying file contents or through timing, it is possible for information to leak from one virtual machine instance to another (Violino, 2010).

Also since the hypervisor is the controller of all virtual machines, it, therefore, becomes the single point of failure in any cloud computing architecture. That is, if an intruder compromises a hypervisor then the intruder has control of all the virtual machines the hypervisor has allocated. This means that the intruder can even create or destroy virtual machines at will. For example, the intruder can perform a denial of service attack, by bringing down the hypervisor which then brings down all virtual machines running on top of the hypervisor.

The processes of securing virtual hosts differ greatly from processes used to secure their physical counterparts. Securing virtual entities like a hypervisor, virtual operating systems and corresponding virtual machines is more complex. To understand hypervisor security, let us first discuss the environment in which the hypervisor works. Recall that a hypervisor is part of a Virtual Computer System (VCS). In his 1973 thesis in the Division of Engineering and Applied Physics, Harvard University, Robert P. Goldberg defines a virtual computer system as a hardware-software duplicate of a real existing computer system in which a statistically dominant subset of the virtual processor's instructions execute directly on the host processor in native mode. He also gives

two parts to this definition, the environment and implementation (Goldberg, 1973).

- **Environment:** That the virtual computer system must simulate a real existing computer system. Programs and operating systems which run on the real system must run on the virtual system with identical effect. Since the simulated machine may run at a different speed from the real one, timing dependent processor and I/O code may not perform exactly as intended.

- **Implementation:** Most instructions being executed must be processed directly by the host CPU without recourse to instruction by instruction interpretation. This guarantees that the virtual machine will run on the host with relative efficiency. It also compels the virtual machine to be similar or identical to the host, and forbids tampering with the control store to add an entirely new order code.

In the environment of virtual machines, a hypervisor is needed to control all the sandboxes (virtual machines). Generally in practice, the underlying architecture of the hypervisor determines if there is a desired true separation between the sandboxes. Robert P. Goldberg classifies two types of hypervisor (Goldberg, 1973):

- **Type-1 (or native, bare metal) hypervisors** run directly on the host's hardware to control the hardware and to manage guest operating systems. See Figure 1. All guest operating systems then run on a level above the hypervisor. This model represents the classic implementation of virtual machine architectures. Modern hypervisors based on this model include Citrix XenServer, VMware ESX/ESXi, and Microsoft Hyper-V. The most common commercial hypervisors are based on a monolithic architecture below. The underlying hypervisor services all virtual sandboxes, each running a guest operating system. The hypervisor runs as part of the native monolithic operating system, side-by-side with the device drivers, file system and network stack, completely in kernel space.

- **Type-2 (or hosted) hypervisors** run just above a host operating system kernel such as Linux, Windows and others as in Figure 2. With the hypervisor layer as a distinct second software level, guest operating systems run at the third level above the hardware. The host operating system has direct access to the server's hardware like host CPU, memory and I/O devices and is responsible for managing basic OS services. The Hypervisor creates virtual machine environments and coordinates calls to CPU, memory, disk, network, and other resources through the host OS. Modern hypervisors based on this model include KVM and VirtualBox.

The discussion so far highlights the central role of the hypervisor in the operations of virtual machine systems and it points to its central role in securing all virtual machine systems. Before we look at what can be done to secure it, let us ask ourselves what security breaches can happen to the hypervisor. Some malicious software such as rootkit masquerade themselves as hypervisors in self-installation phases.

Neil MacDonald, Vice President and a Gartner Fellow (MacDonald, 2011) reported his observation about hypervisor and the vulnerabilities associated with it in his blog titled as "Yes, Hypervisors Are Vulnerable". His observation is summarized below:

- The virtualization platform (hypervisor/VMM) is software written by human beings and will contain vulnerabilities. Microsoft, VMware, Citrix, and other, all of them will and have had vulnerabilities.

Figure 1. Type-1 Hypervisor

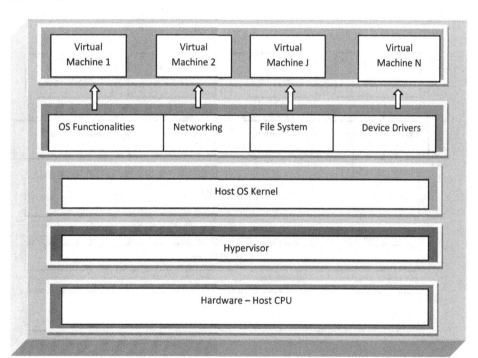

- Some of these vulnerabilities will result in a breakdown in isolation that the virtualization platform was supposed to enforce.
- Bad guys will target this layer with attacks. The benefits of a compromise of this layer are simply too great.
- While there have been a few disclosed attacks, it is just a matter of time before a widespread publicly disclosed enterprise breach is tied back to a hypervisor vulnerability.

There have been a growing number of virtualization vulnerabilities. Published papers have so far shown that the security of hypervisors can be undermined. As far back as 2006, Samuel T. King, Peter M. Chen, Yi-Min Wang, Chad Verbowski, Helen J. Wang and Jacob R. Lorch demonstrate in their paper "SubVirt: Implementing malware with virtual machines", the use of type of malware, which called a virtual-machine based rootkit (VMBR), installing a virtual-machine monitor underneath an existing operating system and hoists the original operating system into a virtual machine.

In their study, the authors demonstrated a malware program that started to act as its own hypervisor under Windows. We know that the hypervisor layer of virtualization, playing the core role in the virtualization process is very vulnerable to hacking because this is the weakest link in the data centre. Therefore attacks on hypervisor are on the rise. Data from the IBM X-Force *2010 Mid-Year Trend and Risk Report* show that every year since 2005, vulnerabilities in virtualization server products, the hypervisors, have overshadowed those in workstation products, an indication of the hackers interest in the hypervisors. The report further shows that 35% of the server virtualization vulnerabilities are vulnerabilities that allow an attacker to "escape" from a guest virtual machine to affect other virtual machines, or the hypervisor itself. Note that the hypervisor in *type-1* environment is granted CPU privilege to access all system I/O resources and memory. This makes it a security threat to the whole cloud

Figure 2. Type-2 Hypervisor

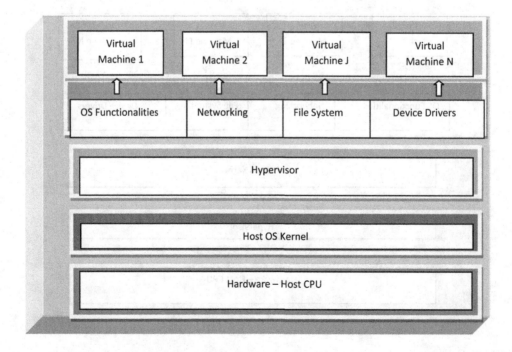

infrastructure. Just a single vulnerability in the hypervisor itself could result in a hacker gaining access to the entire system, including all the guest operating systems. Because malware run below the entire operating system, there is a growing threat of hackers using malware and rootkits to install themselves as a hypervisor below the operating system thus making them more difficult to detect. In *type-2* hypervisor configuration, Figure 2, the microkernel architecture is designed specifically to guarantee a robust separation of application partitions. This architecture puts the complex virtualisation program in user space, thus every guest operating system uses its own instantiation of the virtualization program. In this case, therefore, there is complete separation between the sandboxes (virtual boxes), thus reducing the risks exhibited in type-1 hypervisors.

An attack, therefore, on *type-2* hypervisors can bring down one virtual box, not more and cannot bring down the cloud infrastructure as is the case in *type-1* hypervisors.

According to Samuel T. King et al, overall, virtual-machine based rootkits are hard to detect and remove because their state cannot be accessed by software running in the target system. Further, VMBRs support general-purpose malicious services by allowing such services to run in a separate operating system that is protected from the target system (King, 2006).

6.2.2 Securing Load Balancers

For every hypervisor, there is a load balancer, used to route traffic to different virtual machines to help spread traffic evenly across available machines. A Loadbalancer in a hypervisor plays a vital role of ensuring a fair distribution of available load to all virtual machines especially during high traffic and ensuring the full utilization of the cloud infrastructure. Elastic load balancers play a central in the cloud infrastructure along the following lines:

- It listens to all traffic destined for the internal network and distributes incoming traffic across the cloud infrastructure.
- Automatically scales its request handling capacity in response to incoming application traffic.
- It creates and manages security groups associated with each instance and provides additional networking and security options if and when needed.
- It can detect the health of the virtual machines and if it detects unhealthy load-balanced virtual machine, it stops routing traffic to it and spreads the load across the remaining healthy virtual machines.
- It supports the ability to stick user sessions to specific virtual machines.
- It supports SSL termination at the Load Balancer, including offloading SSL decryption from application virtual machines, centralized management of SSL certificates, and encryption to backend virtual machines with optional public key authentication.
- It supports use of both the Internet Protocol version 4 and 6 (IPv4 and IPv6).

Due to the load balancer's ability to listen and process all traffic that is destined to the internal network of the cloud, it is a prime target for attackers. If a load balancer was compromised an attacker could listen to traffic and may compromise secure traffic destined to outside the network. Additionally, if the load balancer is compromised along with a virtual machine - traffic could be directed to an unsecure internal server where further attacks are launched (Hotaling, 2003). Because the load balancer is a single point in the cloud infrastructure, it very vulnerable to denial-of-service (DoS) attacks which lead to disruption of cloud activity.

What is the best way to secure the load balancer from attacks? A load balancer is normally secured through proper configuration and monitoring of the balancer's logs. This is achieved through restriction of access to administration of the balancer itself by configuring the load balancer to only accept administrative access over a specific administrative network. This administrative network should be connected to the administrative only network. Limiting access over the administrator network greatly limits the number of users with access to the load balancer (Kizza, 2013).

6.2.3 Virtual Operating Systems Security

Besides the hypervisor, the virtualization system also hosts virtual servers each running either a guest operating system or another hypervisor. And on the peripheral of the virtual machine system are the consoles and hosts. Through each one of these resources, the virtual machine system can be susceptible to security vulnerabilities. Let us briefly look at these below:

Host Security

Through hosts like workstations, user gain access to the virtual machine system, hence to the cloud. Two problems are encountered here:

- **Escape-to-Hypervisor Vulnerabilities:** that allow intruders to penetrate the virtual machine from the host.
- **Escape-to-Host Vulnerabilities:** that allow vulnerabilities in the virtual machine to move to the hosts.

Guest Machines

Guest machines running guest operating system can also pose a security problem to the cloud. However, as we saw in the previous chapter, vulnerabilities in the guest virtual machines are confined to that machine and they rarely affect other machines in the system.

6.3 Security of Data in Transition: Cloud Security Best Practices

With the vulnerabilities in the cloud we have discussed above, what is the best way to protect the user of the cloud? For a cloud customer, the key areas of concerns are virtualization technology security vulnerabilities that may be encountered during the use of the cloud that may affect the customer, unauthorized access to customer data and other resources stored or implemented in the cloud, whether the cloud provider uses strong enough encryption to safeguard customer data, secure access and use of cloud applications and secure cloud management. Let us next discuss the best practices that try to address some of these concerns.

6.4 Service Level Agreements (SLAs)

A service-level agreement (SLA) is a service contract between the provider of a service and the client defining the level of expected service in terms of security, availability and performance. The Cloud service-level agreements (SLAs) are a series of service contracts between cloud providers and clients to define the level(s) of service based on the types of services sought by the client because the effectiveness of these contracts depend on how well maximized and tailored these services are to the particular needs of each client. For example, the security of services sought by a client may depend on the tier of cloud offering the client is using. To see how involved and intricate these documents can be, take an example of security concerns. For IaaS, the security responsibilities are shared with the provider responsible for physical, environmental, and virtualization security, while the client takes care of the security in applications, operating system, and others. Now if we change the service model to SaaS, the provider is responsible for almost every aspect of security.

6.5 Data Encryption

The moment data leaves your end-point web-cloud access point in your location, it travels via a public network and stored in shared environment – the cloud. In a public or in a shared environment, data can be intercepted and infiltrated by intruders from within and outside the cloud and during transmission from man-in-the-middle crypto-analysis. To prevent these kinds of breaches strong encryption and authentication regimes are needed. Encryption to safeguard any kind of data breaches require a strong access control and authentication to all web-based cloud resource interfaces, encryption of all administrative access to the cloud hypervisor, all access to applications and data.

6.6 Interface and API Security

Most cloud access instances are web-based. A set of APIs to manage and interact with cloud services are typically exposed (provisioning, monitoring, etc.). Most security breaches to stored data originated from Web applications or APIs. Cloud security therefore depends on strong security controls of these basic cloud APIs.

7. FUTURE CHALLENGES

Many of the cloud security issues just reflect traditional web application, networking, and data-hosting problems although we have been relating them with cloud specific element throughout the chapter. Issues, including phishing, downtime, data loss, password weakness, and compromised hosts running botnets, will remain to be challenges in cloud computing environments. *Scalability* is a paramount problem for securing current clouds at the level of physical infrastructure. Denial of service (DoS) attacks is easier in an environment with a high number of cloud users if not appropriately managed. *VM image management* is an issue since VM images

need to be moved from in-house trusted facilities to a cloud provider through unsecured networks. VM encryption techniques are weakened by the fact that VMs are usually large files. *Virtual networks* are also subject to some security concerns such as how to securely and dynamically establish data paths for communicating distant VMs. The cloud leads to a drop in security as the traditional controls such as virtual local-area networks (VLANs) and firewalls prove less effective during the transition to a virtualized environment. Trust management and auditability remain challenging cloud security. The establish zones of trust in the cloud, the virtual machines must be self-defending, effectively moving the perimeter to the virtual machine itself. Enterprise perimeter security only controls the data that resides and transits behind the perimeter. In the cloud computing world, the cloud computing provider is in charge of customer data security and privacy. The assumption of full trust in IaaS providers might not be true. The complex chain of trust introduced by different cloud stakeholders can be further complicated by the federation of an application's component across different cloud providers (Rodero-Merino, 2012). Some cloud-specific approaches (Santos, 2009) introduced a third external trusted authority to guarantee that the cloud provider could not gain access in the deployed VMs. Enterprises are often required to prove that their security procedure conforms to regulations, standards, and auditing practices regardless of the location of the system at which the data resides. Achieving auditability without sacrificing performance is yet to be accomplished. Auditors should be independent third parties, which are different from current practice in which cloud providers record and maintain their own audit logs. To change this, several efforts are under way, for example, the CloudAudit (www.cloudait.org) is developing an API which supports "audit, assertion, assessment, and assurance for cloud providers".

REFERENCES

Archer, J., Boheme, A., Cullinarie, D., Puhlmann, N., Kurtz, P., & Reavis, J. (2010). Top threats to cloud computing. *Cloud Security Alliance*. Retrieved from http://www.cloudsecurityalliance. org/topthreats

Farber, D. (2008). Cloud computing on the horizon. *CNET News*. Retrieved from http://news. cnet.com/8301-13953_3-9977517-80.html

Goldberg, R. P. (1973). *Architectural principles for virtual computer systems*. National Technical Information Service (NIST), U.S. Department of Commerce. Retrieved from http://www.dtic.mil/ cgi-bin/GetTRDoc?AD=AD772809&Location= U2&doc=GetTRDoc.pdf

Hotaling, M. (2003). IDS load balancer security audit: An administrator's perspective. *SANS Institute*. Retrieved from http://it-audit.sans.org/ community/papers/ids-load-balancer-security-audit-administratorsperspective_119

King, S. T., Chen, P. M., Wang, Y., Verbowski, C., Wang, H., & Lorch, R. (2006). SubVirt: Implementing malware with virtual machines. In *Proceedings of the 2006 IEEE Symposium on Security and Privacy*, (pp. 314–327). IEEE. Retrieved from http://web.eecs.umich.edu/~pmchen/ papers/king06.pdf

Kizza, J. M. (2013). *Guide to computer network security* (2nd ed.). Berlin: Springer. doi:10.1007/978-1-4471-4543-1

MacDonald, N. (2011). Yes, hypervisors are vulnerable. *Gartner Blog Network*. Retrieved from http://blogs.gartner.com/neil_macdonald/2011/01/26/yes-hypervisors-are-vulnerable/

Mell, P., & Grance, T. (2011). *The NIST definition of cloud computing* (NIST Special Publication 800-145). NIST. Retrieved from http://csrc.nist. gov/publications/nistpubs/800-145/SP800-145. pdf

Metzler, J., & Taylor, S. (2011). The data center network transition: Wide area networking alert. *Network World*. Retrieved from http://www.network-world.com/newsletters/frame/2011/080811wan1. html?source=nww_rss

Rodero-Merino, L., Vaquero, L. M., Gil, V., Galán, F., Fontán, J., Montero, R.S., & Llorente, I. M. (2010). From infrastructure delivery to service management in clouds. *Future Generation Computer System, 26*(8), 1226-1240. DOI=10.1016/j. future.2010.02.013

Santos, N., Gummadi, K. P., & Rodrigues, R. (2009). Towards trusted cloud computing. In *Proceedings of HotCloud*. San Diego, CA: USE-NIX. Retrieved from http://www.usenix.org/event/ hotcloud09/tech/full_papers/santos.pdf

Violino, B. (2010). Five cloud security trends experts see for 2011. *CSO: Security and Risk*. Retrieved from http://www.csoonline.com/ar-ticle/647128/five-cloud-security-trends-experts-see-for-2011

Chapter 4
Different Perspectives of Cloud Security

M. Sundaresan
Bharathiar University, India

D. Boopathy
Bharathiar University, India

ABSTRACT

Cloud storage systems can be considered to be a network of distributed datacenters that typically use cloud computing technology like virtualization and offer some kind of interface for storing data. To increase the availability of the data, it may be redundantly stored at different locations. Basic cloud storage is generally not designed to be accessed directly by users but rather incorporated into custom software using API. Cloud computing involves other processes besides storage. In this chapter, the authors discuss different viewpoints for cloud computing from the user, legal, security, and service provider perspectives. From the user viewpoint, the stored data creates a mirror of currently available local data. The backup feature allows users to recover any version of a previously stored data. Synchronization is the process of establishing consistency among the stored data. From the legal viewpoint, provisions regulating the user processing and storage of the data must have to be constant from when the data is stored in the cloud. The security viewpoint requires interaction with the Web application, data storage, and transmission. The service provider viewpoint requires the maximum level of cloud storage service at the minimum cost.

CLOUD SECURITY

New computing models are always facing the problems like security, controllability, accessibility, portability, operability. Cloud computing model is not an exceptional from this list. The security problem is vital issue in cloud computing. The Cloud Service Providers (CSP), Cloud Service Vendors (CSV) and Cloud Service Users (CSU) are facing real time problems and still they are trying to come out from the issues. The security issues differ and vary based on the following perspectives and they are:

DOI: 10.4018/978-1-4666-5788-5.ch004

1. Service Provider perspective
2. User Perspective
3. Security Perspective
4. Legal Perspective

1. Service Provider Perspective

The Cloud Service Providers are classified into three types, based on the kind of service they provide. Here the consumer plays a major role.

- Software as a Service Provider (SaaS) The consumer is provided the capability to use the provider's applications running on a cloud infrastructure. The applications are accessible from various client devices through a thin client interface such as a web browser (for example, web-based email). The consumer does not manage or control the underlying cloud infrastructure that includes network, servers, operating systems, storage, or even individual application capabilities, with the possible exception of limited user-specific application configuration settings.

- Platform as a service Provider (PaaS) The consumer is provided the capability to deploy onto the cloud infrastructure consumer-created or acquired applications created using programming languages and tools supported by the provider. The consumer does not manage or control the underlying cloud infrastructure that includes network, servers, operating systems, or storage, but has control over the deployed applications and possibly application hosting environment configuration.

- Infrastructure as a service Provider (IaaS) The consumer is provided the capability to provision processing, storage, networks, and other fundamental computing resources where the consumer is able to deploy and run arbitrary software, which can include operating systems and applications. The consumer does not manage or control the underlying cloud infrastructure but has control over operating systems; storage, deployed applications, and possibly limited control of some of the networking components (for example, host firewalls).

The cloud computing is an umbrella term. The cloud service providers are interlinked between them with the certain limitations and conditions. According to that some important and mandatory things are discussed below.

1.1 Connectivity

The Connectivity between the service providers is the most important aspect. So to avoid the confusion and misleading, some important things are framed and followed by them. This may help them to provide the secured services to their clients.

1.1.1 SSL

The Secure Socket Layer is used to provide a secure communication channel. When the application is independent, it is optimized for Hyper Text Transfer Protocol (HTTP) and usually used for secure communication with a web server. SSL (Secure Sockets Layer) is the standard security technology for establishing an encrypted link between a web server and a browser. This link ensures that all data passed between the web server and browsers remain private and integral. The complexities of the SSL protocol remain invisible to your customers.

1.1.2 Virtual Private Networks

A VPN securely transports IP packets across the Internet backbone by establishing tunnel endpoints that negotiate a common encryption and authentication scheme prior to transport. Virtual private network enables a computer to send and receive data across shared or group or public networks as if it were directly connected to the private network, while benefitting from the functionality, security and management policies of the private network. A VPN connection across the Internet is similar to a wide area network (WAN) link between the sites

1.1.3 Firewalls

Firewalls are standards for every Cloud Service Provider (CSP). A usual setup is having an outer firewall, a Demilitarized Zone (DMZ) with web servers and an inner firewall (may be from a different vendor) that protects the applications, databases etc. Of course an Application Service Provider (ASP) could have a much more complicated firewall setup, for example compartmentalize applications or customers. If each customer has a different port assigned the firewall can be configured to only allow connections from specific IP addresses to go through the firewall. The correct setup is very important and has to be done by trained personnel. Maintenance is important: it shouldn't happen that each firewall administrator creates her/his own set of rules on top of the old ones. A firewall can never be the only defense against outside intruders.

1.2 Authentication and Authorization

Authentication can happen through a lot of different means. Certificates are considered as one of the more secure forms of authentication. Others are fixed and dynamic passwords. Once authenticated, authorization provides role based access.

1.2.1 Certificates

Digital Certificates / Certificates are a vital component of network security. By establishing the identity of people and electronic assets using a wired or wireless network, Digital Certificates / Certificates authenticate that their holders — people, web sites, and network resources such as routers — are who or what they claim to be.

One of the most difficult questions when dealing with certificates is how to deal with CRLs (Certificate Revocation Lists). Another question is who is to be accepted as the issuer or whether to accept self signed certificates.

1.2.2 Passwords

If the ASP relies on fixed passwords as the only way to authenticate users, a strict password policy is absolutely necessary. Dynamic passwords are much more secure and usually use a hardware or software token. An example is RSA's SecureID. If an ASP decides to use dynamic passwords it has to distribute the token to the customer. The combination of certificates and fixed passwords for authentication is considered very secure, while allowing for easier implementation than dynamic passwords (Newton, 2011).

1.2.3 Authorization

Once authenticated, the access level of the customer can be determined. This enables the ASP to offer some kind of self service for the customer, e.g. a customer can add users, change the password of existing users etc. to restrict the access to hosts and files.

1.3 Administration

The administration has the major responsibility to handle the service requiring customers, the service providers should satisfy the customer security in service providing and its related area. The security aspects are presented in the way of:

1.3.1 Security Policy

One of the most important things an ASP has to have is a Security Policy. All ASP operations are governed by its security policy. It deals with questions like which personnel is authorized to access a customer's application and data and under what conditions, it answers questions about qualified security staff and potential screening procedures.

Other areas covered by the Security Policy are procedures and processes for events like Denial of Service (DoS) attacks, unavailability for other reasons, breach of data integrity, incident response strategy etc. A big ASP customer might want to have a customized Security Policy.

1.3.2 Ongoing Assessments

Cloud Service Providers (CSP) could use vulnerability scanners on a regular basis to find weaknesses in its network. Another possibility is to hire an outside company for a security assessment.

1.3.3 Physical Access Control

Most of the time an ASP actually uses a collocation provider like Exodus or Above Net for the services it is hosting. These companies have strict access controls to the cage where the ASP's machines reside and only authorized personnel can get there. If this is not the case the ASP has to have strict physical access controls in place.

2. The User Perspective

The user perspective section introduces the typical and salient innovations of cloud storage services. A particular service must offer at least one of these innovations and may offer multiple or combination of innovations at the same time or required time.

2.1 Features

In the following section, an explanation of the innovations like copy, backup, synchronization and sharing are described.

2.1.1 Copy

The copy innovation creates a mirror of current local data in the cloud storage. The typical user wants to assure that the data is available in position even if local hard disk crashes or drops out. Further, the user wants to access the data from any place, even if the user's own hardware is not available. Therefore, an access via web browser is quite usual, for a service providing a copy innovation.

In contrast to the backup innovation where data is stored at certain times the copy innovation usually stores data continuously or according to the condition given by the user. A storage service may provide a short retention period; e.g. 50 days, to recover deleted data but this time is too short to satisfy the definition of a backup innovation as given by the service provider.

Typically, there are different ways to store the data in the cloud. The user may manually store files or folders in online storage using the internet browser, or the user may use client software provided by the cloud service vendor. Such client software has to be locally installed by the user and may be used for the automatic upload of all files from a given folder belonging to the user to the cloud storage provider space.

2.1.2 Backup

The backup innovation allows recovering any version of a previously stored file or directory over a long period of time. The typical user wants to sustain his intellectual property and to fulfill compliance requirements.

Creating backups using cloud services is an automated process of periodically making copies of data, transmitting these copies to and storing them in the cloud storage so that they may be used to restore the original after a data loss event has taken place.

Cloud backup service providers usually offer software to be installed in local hardware, enabling the customer to select the data to be backed up to the cloud storage, to configure the retention period as well as a schedule for the backup. The client software either runs continuously in the background so that newly created or changed files are backed up immediately or the software is configured to perform the backup on a regular basis. The task of the client software is to check which data needs to be backed up, that is to recognize files added or changed since the previous backup files.

Additionally, the client software could enable the customer to monitor the backup process of their files, i.e. the customer is able to view the backup files and restore files history. This might be implemented as a continuously written log file where all actions are recorded in a single place.

Copy and backup is actually the same process, during copy the user have to select the object and copy it and paste it to destination place (different place) and this has to be done annually, but in case of backup the files are copied automatically by using backup softwares. Backup softwares are of different types based on the type of the files and they are name accordingly as: Copy backups, Crashed Consistency backup, daily backups, differential backups, incremental and normal backups. In simple terms, while in copy the user cannot restore that file which was affected, but using the back up method, user can restore the file using the restore point while the file is crashed or corrupted. In copy the file was updated continuously or periodically. But in backup the file was backed up with date wise i.e. if the user file corrupted or crashed, the restore point was used to restore that file with the data which was stored before the last saved work.

2.1.3 Synchronization

Synchronization is the process of establishing consistency among data from different cloud storage sources. The typical user has a set of devices, e.g. a laptop, a tab and a smartphone, and the user wants to have all data available on all of his devices and that all data can be changed according to the device.

The client software must be able to detect conflicts that occur if a file has been changed on two devices in different ways. The software should offer a number of choices to the user: merge the files, overwrite one version, or keep both versions by applying a renaming scheme.

2.1.4 Sharing

Data sharing is the process of sharing data with other subscribers of the same service, with a closed group of people from the outside, or with everybody. The typical user wants to collaborate with colleagues and project partners or to share data with his friends or to publish data.

Depending on the service, the shared data has a set of fixed or configurable access rights like read, write, upload or delete. If the write access is enabled for more than one user, synchronization problems arise which is described previously.

2.2 Interfaces

This section explains the different interfaces that can be used to access the data at the cloud storage provider.

2.2.1 Browser Interface

A web browser interface is a method to access data from any place even on a device which has no client installed and is owned by somebody who is not identical to the user who has submitted the data to the cloud. A browser interface is sometimes preferred by companies that do not want to spend too much time to manage software for their employees. Further, it is wanted by private users who appreciate a way to share their data, e.g. photos from the last holidays, wherever they are, even on foreign devices.

2.2.2 Application Programming Interface

Most cloud storage providers grant their users, access to an Application Programming Interfaces (API). This API can be used by developers to directly integrate access to the cloud storage service into applications, e.g., to provide games for a mobile device across multiple devices and platforms. If the API supports advanced features such as deduplication or access to revisions of files previously saved within the cloud storage, these can be integrated to enhance the capabilities of in-house applications.

In order to provide an API for customers, cloud storage providers need to expose a web service or web application which can be accessed using a standardized communication protocol. The majority of cloud storage providers offering an API either expose standard web services leveraging the Simple Object Access Protocol (SOAP) (Hadley, 2003) or use the Representational State Transfer (Fielding, 2000) in the form of RESTful web services. In order to facilitate cloud storage API usage, developers are generally provided with Software Development Kits (SDK).

2.3 Optimization

This section explains the optimization techniques deduplication, delta encoding and compression, which are provided by some services in order to save bandwidth.

2.3.1 Deduplication

The term Deduplication (also Data Deduplication) describes a popular technique that allows cloud storage providers to significantly decrease the amount of needed storage space. The principle of deduplication is as follows: only a single copy of each piece of data is stored. If a user wants to store data that the cloud storage provider already has stored in the past, the storage provider simply creates a link to that data instead of storing another copy. There are some variations of how deduplication may be realized:

1. File level deduplication vs. block level deduplication: File level deduplication means that only a single copy of each file will be stored. Block level deduplication means that each file will be split up into blocks and only a single copy of each block will be stored. Identical files or blocks are detected by comparing the hash value with a list of known files or blocks.

2. Server-side deduplication vs. client-side deduplication: In the case of server-side deduplication, each file a user wants to store is transmitted to the cloud storage provider. For every file, the provider checks if he has to store the file or only needs to create a link to an already stored file. The user cannot detect if the cloud storage provider uses data deduplication. In the case of deduplication by the client, the client software transmits the hash value of the file to the cloud storage provider. Only if the provider is not already in possession of the file it will be transmitted. This variation of data deduplication has the effect of not only saving storage space, but also bandwidth. It is easy to detect if a cloud storage provider uses this kind of data deduplication by inspecting the log files or observing the amount of data that is transferred.

3. Single user deduplication vs. cross user deduplication: Single user deduplication means that data deduplication is carried out separately for each user: If user A wants to store a file he has already stored in the past or in a different folder, the cloud storage provider only creates a link to that file. In the case of cross user deduplication, data deduplication is carried out across all users: If user A wants to store a file that another user B has already stored, the cloud storage provider only creates a link to that file instead of storing an additional copy.

In general, data deduplication is carried out completely in the background which means that the user usually cannot choose whether data deduplication should be used or not. Deduplication may cause security problems.

2.3.2 Delta Encoding

A popular technique for minimizing data transfer and thus saving bandwidth is to only upload the differences to a previously uploaded file instead of transferring the whole file. Suppose that a user wants to store a file that only slightly differs from a previously stored file. In this case, it is not necessary to upload the entire file. Instead, it is sufficient to only upload those parts of the file differing from the previous version along with additional information needed to reconstruct the file on the server. A common method to implement this kind of optimization is the algorithm used by the rsync tool (Rsync, 2013). The principle is to split a file into chunks of fixed size. For each chunk, it is checked whether the cloud storage provider has already stored in this chunk or not (e.g. by sending a hash value of the chunk). Only those chunks that do not match any chunk already stored by the cloud storage provider will be uploaded.

Delta encoding does not make sense if the service cannot decrypt data because two cryptograms of slightly modified inputs may differ completely.

2.3.3 Compression

A simple way to save bandwidth is to compress data on client-side. The drawback is that compression consumes computing power, which may cause trouble to users of storage services where transmission of data to the cloud is a continuous process. Compression can be combined with delta encoding and works fine with encrypted data, if applied before encryption. And also one has to be very careful in choosing the right compression methodology lossless or lossy.

3. The Security Perspective

This section defines a minimal set of security requirements and appropriate measures to reach them that cloud storage services have to be considered sufficiently secure for usage. These requirements will be applied to the cloud storage

services and compared to the results obtained in the upcoming analysis.

The security requirements include the interaction with the web application via browser, the actual data storage and transmission as well as basic features of the cloud storage client applications and special features such as file sharing and publication. Last but not least, some requirements have been defined concerning the minimization of collected data by various processes revolving around interaction with cloud storage services.

In general, there are some more security requirements that will not be addressed here, e.g. logging by the cloud storage service provider or security clearance of the employees.

3.1 Registration and Login

Before customers are able to use a cloud storage provider to synchronize or back up personal data, they have to complete a registration process. Cloud storage providers usually require the creation of a user account before any services can be used. On the one hand, it is the interest of the service provider to establish a single point of contact through which all subsequent configurations, logging and - above all - accounting will take place. On the other hand, a customer who wishes to entrust personal data to the service provider wants to be certain that he communicates with the intended service and - above all - establishes a relationship of trust and contracts the service provider to perform its duties as pledged. During the registration process, the service provider and the new customer agree upon credentials which must later be used to log in for accessing the service. If at any time an attacker is able to eavesdrop on the communication, he might obtain the credentials, compromise the account and gain access to uploaded data. Beyond that, if an attacker is able to manipulate the messages exchanged between customer and service provider, he might act as a proxy and defraud both of them. In order to prevent these attacks, all communication between service provider and customer must be secured in terms of authenticity, confidentiality and integrity. The de-facto standard to achieve these goals on the web is to use the Transport Layer Security (TLS) protocol (Dierks, 2008). Since service providers need to authenticate themselves against the client machine by presenting a certificate, customers can examine it and use it to verify that they are really communicating with the intended service provider. That way, they have a means to detect impending phishing attacks, where attackers host a website which looks very similar to the intended service and try to get users to enter their credentials.

In case of a security breach, the easiest way to minimize potential data theft is to limit data collection to the bare minimum needed to operate the service - this approach is also called "data minimization". The absence of valuable personal data might even make the service less attractive to financially-orientated attackers.

When customers register to access services which are free of charge, apart from the email address only a unique key like a user name is needed to tie the customer to an account (Hushmail, 2013). However, storage services that need to be paid for necessitate the collection of the customer's accounting data.

Even if an attacker is not able to directly glean (Collect gradually and bit by bit) any credentials, he can still attempt to guess them. The login systems of service providers are publicly accessible and can therefore be used to attempt a brute-force attack or dictionary attacks on the credentials. In order to prevent these kinds of attacks, service providers should enforce sufficiently complex passwords - ideally 12 characters long and containing letters, numbers and special characters. But even then, guessing attacks may prove successful given enough time. To this end, service providers should implement measures to make these attacks infeasible such as time penalties or a temporary account lock down after a certain amount of incorrect login attempts within a given time frame (BlueKrypt, 2013).

Under ideal circumstances, a service provider would provide an authentication method which not only relies on the knowledge of credentials but rather demands possession of a token such as a smartcard. Alternatively, an access code could be sent to another physical device such as a mobile phone which has to be entered in addition to the credentials in order to login. Such authentication schemes - usually called two-factor authentication - combine something that is known to the user, like username and password with something he owns, like a mobile phone or smartcard. Overall, these schemes can significantly increase the security level of the login process.

Assuming that an authentication mechanism with a sufficiently high security level has been established by the service provider, additional measures should be implemented to protect standard processes during account management.

The email used by the customer should be verified during registration by sending an activation link used to complete the process. This prevents a possible incrimination where an attacker registers using an email address which does not belong to him.

Frequently, customers forget the credentials used to log into the service and need a way to create or receive new ones. If the system was implemented in such a way that new credentials were directly created as soon as the customer requested them, an attacker could abuse the password-reset process to effectively bar a customer's access to the service - this is also called a denial-of-service attack. To prevent this possibility, a link leading to a password-reset form or temporary credentials which have to be changed directly after logging in could be sent via email to the customer. Service providers should refrain from using questions about the user's social background like "name of the user's pet" or "user's first car" as a means to allow login to the system. Such questions facilitate social engineering attacks on user accounts if an attacker has some knowledge about the user's social background.

But sometimes it is not even necessary for an attacker to break into a system in order to glean information about a service provider's customers. Feedback from the web application such as careless error messages can be exploited for information gathering.

3.2 Transport Security

Cloud storage providers usually provide client software which assists users in setting up their synchronization or backup schemes on the local devices. The actual transmission of all data with the remote storage servers is also handled by the client software. Attackers may be able to steal credentials, learn the contents of private data or even manipulate it if the communication between the client and the remote server is not sufficiently secured. Therefore, the server must authenticate itself to the client and all communication should be encrypted and its integrity ensured.

It is important to use appropriate cryptographic functions. All primitives, like symmetric and asymmetric encryption functions and hash functions should be up to date. This includes the algorithms as well as their parameters, like key lengths. If keys are generated this should be done by a secure high-entropic key generator. The Algorithms and protocols should always be public, as stated by Kerckhoff's principle. Keeping these things secret is always a risk that does not increase security but decreases it dramatically.

Developing a cryptographic protocol is a very difficult task. In the past, even protocols designed by well-respected experts have failed. So it is in most cases a bad idea to invent a new algorithm for a well known problem, especially if a widely accepted solution is available.

The standard protocol Transport Layer Security (TLS) offers an established solution for transport security (Dierks, 2008). There should be overwhelming reasons for replacing it by something else for the same task.

3.3 Encryption

The main reason to use a cloud storage provider - for both individuals and companies - is to always have a backup of valuable data. Arguably a reason for this is that personal data or sensitive company data is highly valuable in either sentimental or financial terms. Before cloud storage became popular, individuals and companies had personal backup strategies to protect against data loss, but these almost always relied on additional physical devices usually at the same location as the original data. Since the stored data was under the control of its owner, protection of the data itself was not always regarded as imperative. Nowadays, data is often entrusted to cloud storage providers on servers visible on the public Internet. Frequent discoveries of security vulnerabilities facilitate successful external attacks with ensuing data thefts. Additionally, there can be internal attacks from within the cloud storage provider itself. Therefore, the data itself should be protected in such a way that even in the event of a successful attack, the contents of the stored data remain confidential. To this end, all data needs to be stored on the remote servers in encrypted form. There are several cryptographically secure encryption schemes available which can be used freely. Cloud storage providers often offer a general encryption of all data stored on their servers using a company key which is known only to them.

Therefore, all data should be encrypted on the client system before the data is transmitted into the cloud using a key unknown to the service provider. Standalone software may be used to encrypt all data on the client system, but this has drawbacks: The software has to be installed, administrated and operated on all client systems in addition to the client software of the cloud storage provider. The key used to encrypt the data needs to be distributed to all devices which are used to access the stored data. In the event that this key is lost, the data can never be decrypted again. As a precautionary measure, all keys used to encrypt data could be integrated into some kind of key escrow system to guard against data loss.

All keys that are used for encryption should be generated at random respectively pseudo random. This requirement ensures that two cryptograms of the same clear text are different. Some products use a password to derive a cryptographic key. This has the disadvantage that just a small part of the key space can be reached by passwords. To produce a good key more entropy is required. A good example for this principle is the TrueCrypt disk encryption system, where key derivation is based on a password and on keyfiles. A keyfile can be any kind of file, for example the user's favorite song as MP3. The keyfile is cryptographically mixed with the password to get a high entropic input for the key derivation function. A signing of data by the user enhances security because it enables the user to verify his data.

3.4 File Sharing

Sharing files appears in three different flavors:

1. Sharing files with other subscribers of the same service.
2. Sharing files with a closed group of non-subscribers.
3. Sharing files with everybody.

In any case the service should describe clearly which flavor of sharing is used. This is not a technical point but it is important because the difference between file publication and file sharing with a closed user group is very unclear for users. Hence, data that is dedicated to a closed group may be revealed to the public.

Sharing files with selected people, as in the first two cases, creates a closed user group and the sharing user has the role of an administrator within this group. General security requirements for these cases are:

1. The files that are being shared should only be accessible to the closed user group that was decided by the sharing user.
2. It should also be possible to revert sharing for each individual file.
3. A list of files currently being shared by the user could be accessed in the web interface or in the client application.
4. It should be possible to deal with different access rights and at any time the sharing user should be able to grant, edit or remove individual access rights.
5. If client-side encryption is used, sharing files should not weaken the security level. In particular, the cloud storage service provider should not be able to read shared files.
6. If client-side encryption is used, a disinvited user should be excluded by cryptographic means from the closed user group. In particular, this means that an encryption key that is known by the disinvited user can no longer be used for the encryption of new files.

Sharing files with selected non-subscribers is usually accomplished by providing a URL which is distributed to the intended group. Knowing this URL means having the right to access the file and the security requirements are:

1. The URL should be obfuscated (unintelligible):
   a. The URL should not contain any information about the user, the file or the folder structure. Otherwise it might be possible for an attacker to guess filenames or to gain information about registered users.
   b. If no credentials are used, the URL should contain a randomly generated unique identifier. Taking the average number of shared documents into account, there should be enough different possible values so that it is infeasible for

an attacker to successfully guess valid links. If the identifier size is too small or the identifier is simply incremented for each published document, an attacker may iterate over all possible links and thereby access all currently published files.

2. If the shared file is hosted on a web server, the cloud storage service provider should take care to exclude the file from being indexed by search engines.

3. Ideally, a cloud storage provider would provide an option to secure shared files with credentials chosen by the user. This would not only disable access to anyone outside of the intended user group, but also prevent the indexing of any published files.

3.5 Deduplication

Data deduplication is employed by many storage providers since it enables them to save large amounts of storage space, thereby reducing costs.

There are also some privacy issues that should be kept in mind as demonstrated by (Harnik, 2010). However, these privacy issues can only occur if the cloud storage provider uses both client-side and cross user deduplication. If this is the case, the following attacks may occur:

1. An attacker who has an account at the cloud storage provider can use the deduplication feature to learn which files are already stored at the cloud storage provider: He transmits a file and observes what happens. If his client software does not upload the file, the attacker knows that this file already exists at the cloud storage provider. That is, he knows that at least one other user has the same file, but he does not know which one.

2. The previously described attack may also be used to find out information about a specific customer of the cloud storage provider: Assuming the attacker knows that a specific

user A stores his medical examination results at the cloud storage provider, and these medical examinations are inscribed in a standard form with simple yes/no questions. The attacker could then create different versions of such results of medical examinations by using the standard form. In each version he inserts the user's name and he answers the questions with either 'yes' or 'no'. After that, he consecutively uploads these files to the cloud storage provider and observes what happens. If one of these files is not uploaded, the attacker knows that user A already stored this file, and thus the attacker knows the results of user A's medical examination.

One solution to reduce the privacy risks concerning data deduplication is presented in (Harnik, 2010). It is based on the introduction of a random threshold which will be assigned to every stored file and which is kept secret by the storage provider. Deduplication will only be done if the number of uploads of a file exceeds this file's specific threshold. An attacker, who wants to learn if a specific file has already been uploaded by another user, has to repeatedly upload this file until deduplication is performed. But if the storage provider performs deduplication, the attacker cannot tell if deduplication has been carried out because another user already uploaded the file before or because the attacker himself was the first who uploaded the file and now exceeded the threshold. This solution provides the advantages of data deduplication (although incurring additional expenses) to both the provider and the user while not exposing the user to any potential privacy threats.

One of the attacks described in (Mulazzani, 2011) is using the deduplication feature and in principle enables an attacker to download files of other users. However, the attacker would need to know the hash values of the files he wants to download. Using a well-known hashing algorithm with a sufficiently large hash size, the probability that an attacker can guess valid hashes for (random or specific) files is negligible.

Ideally, the provider would only use client-side deduplication within a single account or, when using cross-account deduplication, would always upload any files added by the user even if they are already on the server, thereby disabling any useful feedback to the potential attacker. There are currently no known privacy issues when only server-side deduplication is being used.

3.6 Multiple Devices

In the time of ubiquitous computing devices, a typical user has multiple devices to access his data depending on his current location. This might include the computer he has at home, his computer at work and his smartphone. Still, he wants to be able to access all his data in its most recent version from the device that is currently being used. Therefore, multiple different machines will have to be associated with a single account.

The way a new location is added to a cloud storage account is of paramount importance when considering the security of said account. Multiple devices appear in the context of the synchronization feature, but also in the context of backup or storage where multiple, independent devices can be managed within one account without sharing data.

During the installation on a new device, the user will have to provide the credentials he created during the registration process to associate the new device with his account. After the initial login, the credentials are usually stored locally. This trade-off between usability and security allows the user to directly use cloud storage applications without having to enter his credentials every time. In the case of the Dropbox "config. db" attack, it was sufficient to copy a single file from the computer of the user in order to gain access to his account. The attack was hard to detect since there was no notification shown to the user when the new device was added by the attacker.

To prevent this kind of attack, any devices that are added to a cloud storage account, including the first, should have to be activated by the user. This could be done by sending an activation email to the address that was used to register the account.

Even if the credentials are kept secure and are never compromised, there might be other ways for third parties to gain access to the user's data. For example, when a smartphone is lost that was used to access files stored at a cloud provider, the person who finds the phone will be able to access these files using the cloud storage application on the phone. Therefore, the user should be able to remove specific devices from his account. This should be done by showing a list of devices currently associated with the account, either in the client application itself, in the web interface of the cloud provider, or, ideally, on both. To make the management of attached devices easier, the user should be able to choose a name for the new device he wants to add to his account.

3.7 Update Functionality

Running outdated software poses security risks since vulnerabilities that have already been fixed in newer versions will still be present in the old version and could be exploited by an attacker. Therefore, the client software could regularly check for updates. If a new version is found a notification should be shown to the user who then can decide whether he wants to update the program directly or at a later time. Alternatively the client software could automatically download and apply updates without any user interaction.

3.8 Server Location

The cloud storage provider should indicate where its servers are located, i.e., in which country the user's data will be ultimately stored. Ideally, the storage provider would offer different storage locations from which the user can choose.

In the preceding sections, several security requirements concerning cloud storage providers have been described. Security requirements are to be fulfilled. So that users can be relatively sure that measures against the most common threats taken are mandatory. The additional requirements are not absolutely necessary, but they potentially increase the security level of the storage service and are as such desirable.

4. Legal Perspective

Laws and legal provisions regulating the use, processing and storage of data have to be adhered to when storing data in the cloud storage. This applies to all parties involved: the cloud user who stores data in the cloud, the cloud service provider who offers cloud storage services and potential subcontractors who provide resources or infrastructures for the cloud service provider. In this context, a cloud user may be an individual or a business company. Each of the aforementioned parties is subject to legal regulations and provisions of the country in which the respective party is based. These legal regulations and provisions may concern personal rights, data security or access rights for fiscal or law enforcement authorities and may differ from country to country. In general, the cloud user is primarily responsible for his data and its processing.

4.1 Legal Regulations in Germany

In Germany, several legal provisions and laws regulate the use, processing and archiving of data. Those legal requirements must be adhered to by cloud users when storing data in the cloud storage.

Data which concerns the personal rights of others, so-called personal data, has to be protected according to the German Federal Data Protection Act. The cloud user (an individual or a business company) is responsible to ensure data protection when storing personal data in the cloud. There is no legal regulation for individuals storing data which only concerns themselves. Companies are, in addition, subject to further legal regulations regardless whether they are using cloud storage or not (Europa, n.d.). The following sections analyze which legal regulations must be adhered to by cloud users.

4.1.1 Data Protection

In Germany, the Federal Data Protection Act regulates the handling of personal data in order to protect individuals against infringement of their right to privacy. It applies to the collection, processing and use of personal data, which includes, according to FDP Act 3(1).

... any information concerning the personal or material circumstances of an identified or identifiable natural person (data subject).

Personal data may be any information concerning a company's employees, business partners, suppliers or customers or any other information which can be (directly or indirectly) attributed to a natural person.

In practice, the data protection law will apply to almost every business application, unless the collected data is completely anonymized. Pseudonymization, in FDP Act 3(7) named as `aliasing', may be a method to achieve a level of privacy sufficient to permit data processing as well.

The FDP Act also applies to personal data gathered, processed or used in the cloud. The responsible entity to guarantee the protection of the personal data is defined in FDP Act 3(7) as the controller:

Controller shall mean any person or body which collects, processes or uses personal data on his, his or its own behalf, or which commissions others to do the same.

In cloud computing the controller is the cloud user, i.e., the companies or individuals which store data in the cloud.

One possibility to achieve the protection of the personal data is to use a private cloud, where all devices are under complete control and legal responsibility of the controller (cloud user). In this case the cloud user himself has to take all necessary measures to ensure data security and data privacy according to FDP Act. The disadvantage of using a private cloud is that the cloud user has to buy, build and manage the hardware and software themselves and thus may not benefit as much from the advantages cloud computing offers as when using a public cloud.

If the cloud user chooses a public cloud service, he commissions someone else (the cloud provider) to store his data, with the result that the cloud user loses control to some extent over his data and its safety. According to FDP Act 3(7) cloud computing can legally be seen as Contract Data Processing, which is regulated by FDP Act 11. A company delegating the processing of personal data to a third party - the cloud provider - is required to ensure that the third party complies with the FDP Act.

This includes the following topics:

- Careful selection of the provider, including a written contract that includes all items from FDP Act 11(2), which comprises, for example, the following articles:
  ○ The duration of contract work.
  ○ Data security measures to be taken according to FDP Act 9. The provider's (monitoring) obligations.
  ○ Any right to issue subcontracts.
  ○ The cloud users monitoring rights.
  ○ The return of data storage media and the deletion of data recorded by the provider after the work have been carried out.

- Making sure that personal data is not transferred outside the European Economic Area (EEA) according to FDP Act 4b.
- Making sure that the data processor provides an adequate level of protection, i.e. the cloud user shall verify compliance with the technical and organizational measures taken by the cloud provider before data storing begins and regularly thereafter FDP Act 11.

According to FDP Act 11(2) no.6 the above mentioned items apply not only to the cloud provider as the prime contractor but also to potential basic cloud storage providers, which may act as subcontractors.

Exception: Cloud computing outside the EEA is legally not regarded as 'contractual data processing' as mentioned above. If the personal data (in the cloud) is not processed in Germany, in another European Union Member State, or another state party to the Agreement on the EEA 3(8), cloud computing is legally seen as a data transfer FDP Act 4b.

4.1.2 Further Legal Provisions

Besides the data protection requirements, further legal provisions concerning retention of data or fiscal requirements have to be met by a company when using cloud computing. The following list contains some examples of regulations with which a German company has to comply:

In general, the cloud user has to make a contract with the cloud provider which contains all necessary provisions e.g. governing the liability of the cloud provider and potential cloud subcontractors towards the cloud user.

When choosing a cloud provider for the storage of tax-relevant data, a company must take into account the location (country) where a cloud provider and potential subcontractors store the data.

The use of cloud storage in the financial, insurance, telecommunication, or health care sectors may have further (legal) implications as these sectors have their own specific rules and provisions. In general, the legal implications and problems when processing (personal) data in the cloud are not yet sufficiently addressed and solved. It is recommended that:

With international regulations in place; it would doubtless be possible to make cloud-based data processing independent of location, and to mandate that cloud-based data processing be governed exclusively by the law that applies to the user or to the cloud provider in direct contractual relationship with the user. So far, however, there is no evidence of efforts in this direction. Given the inconsistency and in some cases the inadequacy or total absence of national laws on data processing in general and data privacy in particular, it is unrealistic to expect international standards for the moment. As a result, we have no alternative but to implement a clear system of legal protections that begins with the data controller, i.e., the cloud user.

4.1.3 Certification and Guidelines

Besides the problem of closing a written contract in a dynamic cloud environment, cloud users, especially small and medium sized companies, often lack the resources and the experience to make the right decisions when choosing a cloud provider, to understand all legal implications when using cloud services, and to be able to assess cloud providers. A solution for these problems may be the use of certified cloud services and the study of already existing guidelines concerning cloud computing. However, users often cannot evaluate the relevance of such certifications.

The following list provides some certification entities and guidelines:

Statement on Auditing Standard No. 70 (SAS 70) is an audit guide, whose latest version has been issued by the American Institute of Certi-

fied Public Accountants (AICPA) in May 2009. An analogous German standard "IDWPS 951" based on SAS 70 has been issued by the German "Institut der deutschen wirtschaftsprufer". SAS 70 is a guideline for service auditors that assess internal controls of service organizations or service providers, e.g. cloud providers. The audit can only be performed by an independent Certified Public Accountant (CPA). SAS 70 is not a pre-determined set of standards that a service provider must meet to "pass", i.e. the evaluation criteria can be customized. The control may refer to application development, maintenance, security and access, data processing or business continuity (GDPdU, 2002).

At the end of a SAS 70 audit, the service auditor issues a report including his opinion on whether the controls were suitably designed, placed in operation, and operating effectively.

There are two types of Service Auditor's Reports:

- Type I report contains the service organization's description of controls at a specific point in time (e.g. June 30, 2011).
- Type II report includes a Type I report and additionally a description of detailed testing of the (cloud) service provider's controls over a minimum six month period (e.g. January 1, 2011 to June 30, 2011) and the results of those tests.

A SAS 70 report has no validity period. However, most service providers will have the SAS 70 audit conducted annually.

The standard specifies requirements for the management of IT security in companies. It provides:

a model of establishing, implementing, operating, monitoring, reviewing, maintaining and improving a documented Information Security Management System (ISMS) within the context of the organization's overall business risks. It specifies requirements for the implementation of security controls customized to the needs of individual organizations. The ISMS is designed to ensure the selection of adequate and proportionate security controls that protect information assets. (30)

Organizations with such ISMS can be audited and certified compliant with the standard ISO 27001.

The EuroCloud SaaS Quality Seal has just been introduced. Therefore, only little experience has been made regarding the relevance of this certification.

4.2 Legal Regulations in the EU

4.2.1 The Data Protection Directive

In 1995, the EU established Directive 95/46/EC (Data Protection Directive), which had to be integrated into the laws of each nation belonging to the European Economic Area (EEA) by the end of 1998. The directive aims to protect the rights and freedoms of persons and sets strict limits on the collection and use of personal data (OECD, 2013). It relates to:

- The quality of the data
- The legitimacy of data processing
- Information to be given to the subject
- The right to object to the collection

In these Guidelines24, they defined a set of seven basic principles for national application which include the following:

- The Use Limitation Principle mandates that personal data should not be disclosed, made available or otherwise be used except by the authority of law or with the consent of the data subject.
- The Collection Limitation Principle mandates that there should be limits to the collection of personal data.

- The Purpose Specification Principle mandates that data collection be carried out according to a certain purpose which has to be defined in advance to the actual collection.
- The Disclosure Principle mandates that data subjects should be informed as to who is collecting their data.

4.2.2 The Safe Harbor Framework

The Safe Harbor framework was created in cooperation between the US department of commerce and the EU to ensure the safe passage of data from Europe to the US and was approved by the EU in 2000. Companies that want to be a part of the Safe Harbor agreement have to comply with the rules defined by the agreement. These rules include, among others

- The notification of individuals about the purposes of data collection
- The access for individuals to personal information about them
- The obligation of the company to protect personal information from loss, misuse and unauthorized access

There is no external validation required to join the Agreement, the joining company has to self-certify to the Department of Commerce that it adheres to the Safe Harbor Framework. This has been one of the points criticized ever since the creation of the agreement in 2000. Although the Federal Trade Commission is authorized to enforce the Safe Harbor Framework, there have only been seven cases in the last ten years where the FTC has filed complaints against companies that violated Safe Harbor Principles.

A German association of regulatory authorities for the enforcement of data protection in the private sector has published a resolution on the Safe Harbor Agreement .In this resolution, they declare that a European company which wants to transfer personal data to an American company has to verify that the American company correctly implements the Safe Harbor Principles (Ramasastry, 2009).

4.2.3 Recommendations

European laws significantly restrict the transfer of personal data outside of the EEA. The European Data Protection initiative requires the processing and storage of personal data within the EEA (Europa, n.d.). Their thinking is summarized by the following statement:

There is no privacy in the European cloud, or any public cloud outside of the United States where a US-based or wholly owned subsidiary company is involved.

4.3 Legal Regulations in the USA

4.3.1 The Patriot Act

The USA PATRIOT Act was signed into law in 2001 in response to the terror attacks of September 11, 2001 (USA PATRIOT Act, 2001). The case study "How the USA PATRIOT act can be used to access EU data" shows how the PATRIOT Act could be used in the context of cloud computing. It affects not only data that is stored in the US in accordance with the Safe Harbor Agreement but also data that is physically stored in Europe. The latter case is also relevant when the data is being stored by a European company that is a subsidiary of an American company (EuroCloud, 2011). Confirmation of this point came directly from Microsoft. A company representative was asked at the launch of their new cloud service whether Microsoft can

... guarantee that EU-stored-data, held in EU based data centers, will not leave the European Economic Area under any circumstances ǀ even under a request from the Patriot Act.

The reply was:

"Microsoft cannot provide these guarantees. Neither can any other company." This would apply, for example, to all files stored in the Azure platform and Office365.

Summary

This chapter has elaborately discussed about the cloud security in different perspectives as such as service provider, user, security and legal. Various aspects related to security on the cloud have been covered. Connectivity, authentication, authorization, certificates, passwords have been dealt with. From the legal point of view, the legal procedures followed in different countries like Germany, EU and USA have been covered. In other countries, procedures are yet to be developed in the legal perspective.

REFERENCES

BlueKrypt. (2013). Retrieved from http://www.keylength.com/en/

Dierks, T., & Rescorla, E. (2008). *RFC 5246 - The transport layer security (TLS) protocol version 1.2.* RFC.

EuroCloud. (2011). Retrieved from http://www.eurocloud.org

Europa. (n.d.). *Summaries of EU legislation.* Retrieved from http://europa.eu/legislation_summaries/information_society/data_protection/l14012_en.htm

Fielding, R. (2000). *Architectural styles and the design of network-based software architectures.* (PhD thesis). University of California, Irvine, CA.

GDPdU. (2002). *Principles of data access and auditing of digital documents*. Retrieved from http://www.avendata.de/downloads/e-GDPdU.pdf

Hadley, M., Nielsen, H., Mendelsohn, N., Gudgin, M., & Moreau, J. (2003). *SOAP version 1.2 part 1: Messaging framework*. Retrieved from http://www.w3.org/TR/2003/REC-soap12-part1-20030624/

Harnik, D., Pinkas, B., & Shulman-Peleg, A. (2010). Side channels in cloud services: Deduplication in cloud storage. *IEEE Security & Privacy, 8*(6), 40–47. doi:10.1109/MSP.2010.187

Hushmail. (2013). Retrieved from http://www.hushmail.com/

Mulazzani, M., Schrittwieser, S., Leithner, M., Huber, M., & Weippl, E. (2011). *Dark clouds on the horizon: Using cloud storage as attack vector and online slack space*. USENIX Security.

Newton, D. (2011). *Dropbox authentication: Insecure by design*. Retrieved from http://dereknewton.com/2011/04/dropbox-authentication-static-host-ids/

OECD. (2013). *OECD guidelines on the protection of privacy and transborder flows of personal data*. Retrieved from http://www.oecd.org/document/18/0,2340,en_2649_34255_1815186_1_1_1_1,00.html

Ramasastry, A. (2009). *The EU-US safe harbor does not protect US companies with unsafe privacy practices*. Retrieved from http://writ.news.findlaw.com/ramasastry/20091117.html

Rsync. (2013). Retrieved from http://rsync.samba.org/

USA Patriot Act. (2001). Retrieved from http://www.fincen.gov/statutes_regs/patriot/index.html

Chapter 5
A Framework for Compliance and Security Coverage Estimation for Cloud Services:
A Cloud Insurance Model

Dipankar Dasgupta
University of Memphis, USA

Durdana Naseem
University of Memphis, USA

ABSTRACT

Many organizations are adopting cloud services to reduce their computing cost and increase the flexibility of their IT infrastructure. As cloud services are moving to the mainstream to meet major computing needs, the issues of ownership and chain of custody of customer data are becoming primary responsibilities of providers. Therefore, security requirements are essential for all service models (while the degree of defensive measures may vary) along with satisfying industry standard compliances. The authors develop an insurance framework called MEGHNAD for estimating the security coverage based on the type of cloud service and the level of security assurance required. This security coverage estimator may be useful to cloud providers (offering Security as a Service), cloud adopters, and cloud insurers who want to incorporate or market cloud security insurance. This framework allows the user/operator to choose a cloud service (such as Saas, Paas, IaaS) and other pertinent information in order to determine the appropriate level of security insurance coverage. This chapter describes an extension to the MEGHNAD (version 2.0) framework by incorporating security-related compliances. The compliance for each sector requires specific protection for online data such as transparency, respect for context, security, focused collection, accountability, access, and accuracy. The MEGHNAD tool can also generate a SLA document that can be used for monitoring by a certified Third-Party Assessment Organization (3PAO).

DOI: 10.4018/978-1-4666-5788-5.ch005

1. INTRODUCTION

With rapidly changing computing and Information Technologies, it is becoming more expensive for companies and organizations to regularly update/purchase hardware and software licenses and keep big IT departments with highly technical professionals. Cloud computing has evolved the concept of how we deploy, maintain, and access software, platforms, and infrastructure utilizing the high-speed Internet connectivity. Analysts forecasting a long-running trend where all types of business services will be virtualized, enabling massive interoperability, which will potentially lead to huge cost savings. So the cloud computing is becoming more attractive because of the possibilities in significant cost reduction in IT operations.

While some small and medium size companies are moving to cloud services for their IT need, they are very concerned about data privacy, security and compliance requirements (such as PCI DSS, HIPAA, GLBA, SOX, etc.). For example, HIPAA (Health Insurance Portability and Accountability Act) requires insurance portability, administrative simplification and fraud enforcement like privacy and security. Another example, PCI-DSS compliance, was set up to improve the Information Security of financial transactions related to credit and debit cards. GLBA (Gramm-Leach-Bliley Act) compliance requires analyzing the risks before moving customer information into emerging technology models. While security requirements are essential for all service models, as these three segments have differences and similarities, they vary in the degree of defensive measures and should be considered by organizations when selecting a cloud service. In any cloud service, satisfying compliance requirements will ensure the following:

- Best and improved protection of companies' critical data and its availability.
- Reduce the liability due to security breach.

- Timely audition to ensure full compliancy and reporting.
- Cost efficient service that meets the customer needs.

To guarantee the above-mentioned benefits, the cloud provider needs to be carefully assessed by each customer or 3PAO to assure that the key requirements of security and compliances are met (Dokras, 2009). Moving application and data to the cloud has many advantages but when it comes to sensitive data it is yet very risky. It is important to understand the cloud architecture, access control and network security and "know where your data is and know where your data is going." (Pennell, 2011).

2. CLOUD SERVICE MODELS AND COMPLIANCES

Cloud computing facilitates delivering services over the Internet are also known as cloud services. In this section we will describe different cloud service models, compliances and the necessity of SLA document with proper information on security coverage.

2.1. Cloud Service Models

Cloud computing has three main different service models which provide services at different levels (DoD, 2011), (Rackspace Hosting, 2011) as illustrated in Figure 1.

2.1.1 Software as a Service (SaaS)

In SaaS, the vendor uses the cloud service to host software applications for the customers. The vendor controls and maintains the physical computer hardware, servers, network, operating systems, and software applications. The customers have very limited control on settings specific to the user. Some SaaS vendors includes CRM,

Figure 1. Different service models and their hierarchy

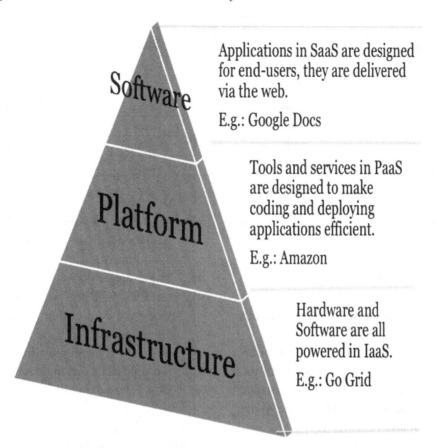

Microsoft Office 365, Groupon, Google services such as Gmail, Google Docs (Strickland, 2008), etc. For example, services offered by SaaS for Google Docs:

- The applications are not tied to the specific computer; therefore the users need not store any information as the information will be stored in the cloud system.
- User can access the file form anywhere in the world via web access.
- By using the SaaS, Google can manage the Google software from a central location and deliver to users based on "one to many" model.

- Users are not required to download any upgrades or patches; they are handled by Google at the SaaS level.

2.1.2 Platform as a Service (PaaS)

In PaaS, the vendor uses the cloud services to provide infrastructure for the customers. It enables customers to use web servers and deploy web applications and other software developed by customers. The vendor controls and maintains the physical computer hardware, servers, network, operating systems and server applications. The customer controls and maintains software applications. It protects data and storage as a service. Example PaaS vendor services includes Amazon Web Services (Amazon web services, 2013),

Table 1. Different service models with who controls what?

Service Models			
Components	**SaaS**	**PaaS**	**IaaS**
Network	Vendor	Vendor	Vendor
Servers	Vendor	Vendor	Vendor
Operating Systems	Vendor	Vendor	Consumer
Storage	Vendor	Vendor	Consumer
Application	Vendor	Consumer	Consumer
Configurations	Consumer	Consumer	Consumer

Google App Engine etc. For example, Amazon uses Services PaaS such as:

- Infrastructure and application services which allow the user to run everything in the cloud from data to the mobile applications.
- It provides different services like develop, test, host and maintain applications to fulfill the application development process.
- It builds scalability of deployment of software, which also provides support for load balancing and fail overs.
- Common standards are provided for services like web services, databases, team collaboration, billing, etc.

2.1.3 Infrastructure as a Service (IaaS)

In IaaS, the vendor provides computer hardware plus the memory, storage, network connectivity, CPU processing. The vendor controls and maintains the physical computer hardware. The customer controls and maintains the operating systems, software applications. Example IaaS vendor services include Amazon Elastic Compute Cloud (EC2), Go Grid and Rackspace Cloud. For example, Go Grid (GoGrid Cloud Hosting, 2010), as an IaaS provides:

- The user to create virtualized IT configurations by giving the control over the environment,
- The users can create their own infrastructure that will provide those features, services and control that is better than other cloud services.
- It allows dynamic scaling by supporting multiple users on single hardware.
- Cost is based on utility based model

Recently, SearchCloudComputing.com team examines 13 big and small cloud service providers who are trying to compete with cloud leader Amazon Web Service (AWS), they are making headway in IaaS and PaaS offerings in significant ways (Cloud Computing Digest 2013).

Based on the general terms that sits over a variety of services among IaaS, PaaS, SaaS, it is important to understand the different aspects of cloud computing and assess who controls what in the different service models. Table 1 gives an overview of which components are controlled by the vendor and which are controlled by customers in different service models.

2.2 Compliance Standards

The term compliance defines a set of rules and regulations, which creates the ability to act according to the order and creates a standard to maintain. The need for security and data privacy are critical with the increase in technology outsourcing and remote data storage. Security and compliances policies and regulations can provide an organization a baseline for protection. Proper infrastructure with network security, system certifications, timely auditing and user involvement are the major parameters for compliance. Without addressing security issues for compliance can lead to huge financial losses via damage recovery, service interruption, notification costs, fines etc. Some of the key industry base compliance include PCI-DSS, HIPAA, GLBA, SOX, SAS 70 and FISMA.

- **PCI-DSS** stands for the Payment Card Industry (PCI) Data Security Standard (DSS). It was setup to encourage and enhance cardholder data security by the major card companies that use credit or the debit cards for the financial transaction. The PCI Security Standard Council (PCI Security Standards Council, 2010) has comprised a minimum set of 12 requirements for protecting cardholder data.

- **HIPAA** stands for Health Insurance Portability and Accountability Act (HIPAA) requires insurance portability, administrative simplification and fraud enforcement like privacy and security. Congress introduced it in 1996 that aims to protect the privacy of patient information in healthcare industry (SearchSecurity, 2009). The HIPAA standards are classified into 6 major categories of requirements to ensure that health information of patients remain secure (CASHRUN, 2010; Lawson, 2003).

- **GLBA** is Gramm-Leach-Bliley Act of 1999 (Fortinet, 2006)). It requires financial institutions to develop, implement, and maintain a program that protects the privacy and integrity of customer records. Also requires analyzing the risks before moving

the customer information into emerging technology models.

- **SOX** is the Sarbanes-Oxley Act of 2002 Legislation that came in to existence in response to the high profile Enron and WorldCom financial scandals to protect shareholders and the general public from accounting errors and fraudulent practices in the enterprise. SOX is not a set of business practices and does not specify how a business should store records; rather, it defines which records are to be stored and for how long (Spurzem, 2007).

- **SAS 70** represents Statement on Auditing Standards. It consists of Type I and Type II complaints. American Institute of specified Public Accounts (AISPA) used for report on controls placed in operation and tests of operating effectiveness in 1992 (NDB Accounts and Consults, 2008). Service organization provides services to some other companies such as Payroll companies, medical centers, data centers and SAAS. This standard is not only technology or security audit its both wrapped together.

- **FISMA:** The Federal Information Act of 2002 was established to address the importance of information security related to both the economic and national security interests of the United States. It maintains minimum-security requirements and controls to be abided by all federal agencies (NetWrix, 2013).

- **ISO 27001** is the formal set of specifications against which organization may seek independent specification of their Information Security Management Systems; it specifies requirement for the establishment, implementation, monitoring and review, maintenance and improvement of management system (ISO/IEC Certification standards, 2013).

Figure 2. Various aspects of deciding cloud services

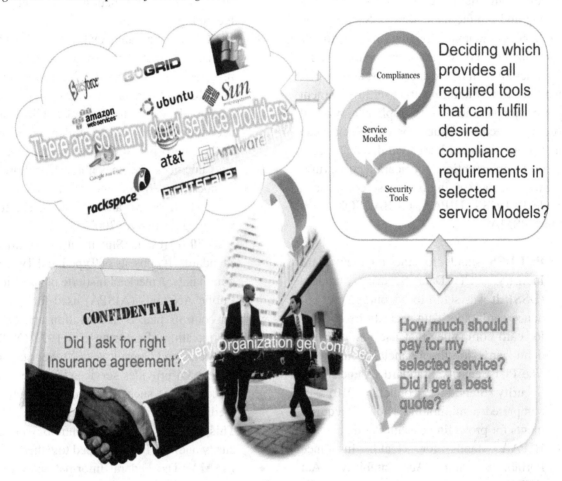

The Increase demand in security compliances and cloud computing services, every company states to best provide all checklists required for different compliance. When requested by organizations, vendors provide assurances by hiring third-party vulnerability assessments, also encrypting inbound and outbound data, arranging scheduled monitoring, and sometimes facing liability in the event of a breach or service degradation, etc. (Hasan, 2007). This requires vendors to implement what the organizations may not be able to do for them without incurring significant expense.

Consider a payment industry where the 12 requirements of PCI DSS must be satisfied by the Vendor Organizations to provide security certification, but it increases the cost. Hence,

when an organization wants to use only Platform as a Service, then they may not need the vendor to fulfill all the requirements compared to the organization that request for Software as a Service from the cloud.

The main problem is when relying on cloud computing partners many organizations tend to overlook the importance of finding the right compliance vendor and the responsibilities they bear for ensuring ongoing compliance with appropriate sector. Figure 2 illustrates various factors to consider before moving to cloud services and selecting a provider.

All the current existing tools provide a framework that fulfill all the requirements for the particular sector compliance but do not filter the requirements that are necessary based on individual service model. In this paper we address this problem by developing the relational model for compliance with the service model. The developed tool will also provide coverage estimations against each tool with compliance requirement mapping. This will help to analyze the estimate and compare with the quotes offered by the service provider.

Once the organization mapping is done the tool generates a SLA document in the PDF format for the customers, which they can use to find the right vendor and use as a service agreement between them. This framework will also provide the companies a tool to test risk and compliances against cloud service providers.

2.3 Service Level Agreement (SLA)

The Service Level Agreement (SLA) is similar to having a warranty before buying a car. SLA serves as an agreement between the Cloud Service Provider and the Customer. The objectives of this agreement is to make sure that the proper security measures are in place with clear description of service to be provided and supported to the customer by the service provider. In cloud there are many services like networks, geographic locations, data storage, availability, authentication, access, availability etc. SLA sets expectations for both the service provider and customers and serves as a roadmap for services used, expected or unexpected changes (Diaz, 2011).

The customer should be engaged during the establishment of SLAs and contractual obligations to ensure that security requirements are contractually enforceable.

• Metrics and standards for measuring performance and effectiveness of information security management should be established prior to moving into the cloud. At a minimum, organizations should understand and document their current metrics

and how they will change when operations are moved into the cloud and where a provider may use different (potentially incompatible) metrics.

• Due to the lack of physical control over infrastructure by customers, in many cloud computing deployments, SLA's, contract requirements, and provider documentation play a larger role in risk management than with traditional, enterprise owned infrastructure.

• Due to the on-demand provisioning and multi-tenant aspects of cloud computing, traditional forms of audit and assessment may not be available or may be modified. For example, some providers restrict vulnerability assessments and penetration testing, while others limit availability of audit logs and activity monitoring. If these are required per your internal policies, you may need to seek alternative assessment options, specific contractual exceptions, or an alternative provider better aligned with your risk management requirements. An SLA should address the following:

  ○ What type of data classification system does the provider use?
  ○ What are the service legal agreement issues?
  ○ What is the long term viability of the provider?
  ○ What happens if there is a security breach?
  ○ What is the disaster recovery/business continuity plan?

2.4 Cloud Security and Compliance Tools

While base level security is essential for all types of cloud services, more specialized security tools are also needed for different cloud services. For example, in SaaS focus should be web applications--providing email service requires spam filter, white/black listing of websites. Platform as a Service (PaaS) cloud requires deploying and running customer-created applications, needing secure communication (VPN), multi-client process isolation and availability of on-demand access. Infrastructure as a Service (IaaS) usually rents processing, storage, network capacity, and other computing resources, and require load balancers and multiple firewalls. For different types of cloud services, the cloud provider and customers/subscribers retain and/or relinquish controls over application, middleware, OS, hardware to some extent and play different roles. In SaaS, the cloud subscriber has only user level access and limited administrative level control over the application configuration whereas the provider retains full admin control over the applications, middleware, operating system and hardware. In IaaS, the subscriber has some control over applications, middleware and guest OS whereas the provider holds control on the hardware and the hypervisor. Similarly, PaaS requirements lie between these two extremes. Hence, service type is an important aspect of cloud security coverage. It's evident that, in case of SaaS, the subscriber shouldn't be concerned about IDS, Firewalls etc. Hence, emphasis on Firewalls/IDS should be very low while estimating the coverage. In case of PaaS, the subscriber has more control and the provider can offer additional security coverage or overlapping protection with multiple tools. Following security tools is essential security for organizations to satisfy the compliances:

- *WatchGuard* (WatchGuard, 2009) is an easy-to-manage network security tool that provides small and enterprise offices compliance solutions. They also provide solutions that deliver security, performance and rock-solid reliability for different industries like Hospitality, Education, Energy, Healthcare and Finance. WatchGuard uses XTM multi-functional firewalls, Next generation Firewall etc. This tool provides all

the required software and act as a vendor for the organizations that are looking for cloud computing compliances services. It is a very comprehensive tool that is useful to all kind of service sectors with high-end technology.

- *Trust Wave* (TrustWave, n.d.) is the leading provider of on-demand data security and payment card industry compliance management solutions to businesses and organizations throughout the world. They also provide solutions that deliver security, performance and rock-solid reliability for different industries like Hospitality, Education, Energy, Healthcare, Government agencies, POS Providers, Retailers, Utilities, Hosting Providers, Higher Education and Finance Services. It provides services from small business to large companies with different cloud components. It was awarded as 2011 finalist for best security company.

- *FedRAMP Program,* Federal Risk and Authorization Management Program (FedRAMP, 2012) is a government-wide program that provides a standardized approach to security assessment, authorization and continuous monitoring for cloud-based services. FedRAMP uses a "do once, use many times" framework that intends to saves costs, time, and staff to conduct redundant agency security assessments and process monitoring reports. FedRAMP uses a security risk model that can be used by different agencies based on a consistent security baseline. The FedRAMP PMO can create a framework for agencies to utilize the security authorization. This framework requires Federal agencies to use FedRAMP when assessing, authorizing, and continuously monitoring cloud services. Four distinct areas of FedRAMP security authorization process are: Security Assessment, Leverage the Authority to Operate (ATO), Continuous Monitoring and 3PAO

(Third party assessment organization) Accreditation. Third Party Assessment Organizations (3PAO) perform initial and periodic assessment of CSP systems as per the FedRAMP requirements, provide evidence of compliance and play an ongoing role in ensuring CSPs meet requirements. FedRAMP provisional authorization must include an assessment by an accredited 3PAO to ensure a consistent assessment process [FedRAMP, 2012].

- *CISCO* (CISCO Systems, n.d.) organizes a key to business in building and maintaining the trust of customers in reducing risk and improving security. Cisco helps in collecting data by monitoring controls and enforcement, security and industrial participation and leadership. It also helps in storing data, transferring/sharing data, and retaining /deleting data with security.

- *McAfee* helps to optimize for continuous PCI compliance through a layered security model that mitigates vulnerabilities and reduces the likelihood of data loss and theft. It also provides services for cost-effective scanning and assessment. Delivering more than just security technology, McAfee has specific solutions for point-of-sale systems, ATMs, databases, and other components in the scope of your PCI infrastructure. McAfee PCI Compliance solutions utilize the best of McAfee technology, including Global Threat Intelligence, as well as industry-leading system-level change prevention to ensure the continuous integrity of your PCI systems (McAfee, 2013).

2.5 Cyber Security Insurance

Cyber insurance is in existence for last 25 years (Phil Ins, 2011; Cyber-InsuranceMetrics, n.d.). It is used to protect businesses from Internet-based risks, and damages. For example, Chubb's Cybersecurity insurance package (CHUBB, 2011)

claims to be designed by cyber risk experts to address the full breadth of risks associated with doing online businesses.

- The CIS (CIS, 2010) defined seven security functions to make cost-effective business decisions: Incident Management, Vulnerability Management, Patch Management, Application Security Configuration Management, Change Management and financial metrics.

- The Index of Cyber Security (CyberSecIndex, 2011) is a sentiment-based measure of the risk for a spectrum of cybersecurity threats to assess cybersecurity insurance policy. This index features 15 sub-indices to measure malware threats, intrusion pressures, insider threat, industrial espionage, information sharing and media and public perception, etc.

- CyberFactors (Moore, 2010), is a company that evaluates cloud providers for risk, creates warranties to help customers and cloud policies for insurers.

Cloud security insurance is a way towards enterprise risk management where there is a security of financial compensation in case a failure occurs at the cloud service provider (Ghatak, 2012). With increase cloud technology platform usage there is a rising demand for an insurance policy to cover for potential losses in the event of a failure or data breach. A cloud service enabled with insurance will be a better business model and the insurance companies see cloud services or cloud technologies as business enabling technologies. Different service level parameters play a critical role in choosing suitable cloud computing insurance such as performance of a service, security of a service, availability and reliability of a service, scalability of service, disaster recovery and business continuity, auditing and logging, service integration and interdependency. For example, CloudInsure is a Cloud Insurance platform designed to address

Figure 3. An illustration of Cloud insurance which is analogous to health insurance

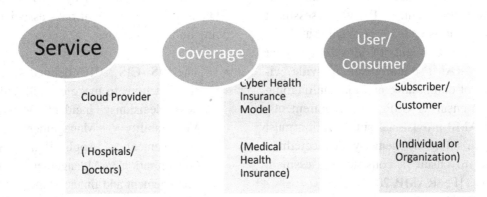

emerging liabilities within the cloud environment. Figure 3 gives an analogy of cloud insurance to health insurance.

3. A CLOUD INSURANCE MODEL: MEGHNAD

The MEGHNAD (Dasgupta, 2011a; Dasgupta, 2011b) is a framework to estimate security coverage (based on the preferred insurance level), focusing on the features of security techniques, tools and Compliance requirements for different cloud models under various operating conditions. It is a Java-based framework to estimate security coverage for different type of service offerings while addressing different compliance requirements. This uses a knowledgebase of cloud-related security tools (reviewing their features, effectiveness and consumer reports in mitigating risks) and applies an intelligent search and optimization technique (a multi-objective genetic algorithm) which works as a specialized *Cloud Doctor* in prescribing security toolsets based on the cloud services and the level of security assurance required. The optimization method used in the MEGHNAD is scalable to accommodate tool specific configuration settings, and customer-required standards and compliances to make a fine-grained coverage estimate. It also provides

a visualization interface to analyze results and detailed reports on recommended security tools, their costs and estimated/quantifiable coverage. This framework is tested with various cloud service security requirements; it has 100 security tools from six defense levels.

3.1 MEGHNAD Architecture

In assuring security coverage of a cloud service, it is important to consider service requirement, security need for that service and best practices necessary for employees and their processes. The MEGHNAD framework consists of three input modules, one processing unit and an output GUI as shown in Figure 4. A knowledge base is created with existing cyber security tools and techniques which are applicable to different cloud environment. Characteristics of each tool are considered including features, cost, performance index, constraints, known vulnerabilities, risk factors, etc. The expert input, organizational information, service type, and cyber hygiene practices are provided as 'Customer Info.' The input module in 'Parameter Setting,' feeds user preferences and the operator input to run the search engine that utilizes Genetic Algorithms (Deb, 2002). It determines an optimal set of security tools for a certain level of coverage while providing the requested cloud service. The output module

Figure 4. Cloud Security Coverage Architecture with various sub modules [Dasgupta and Rahman 2011]

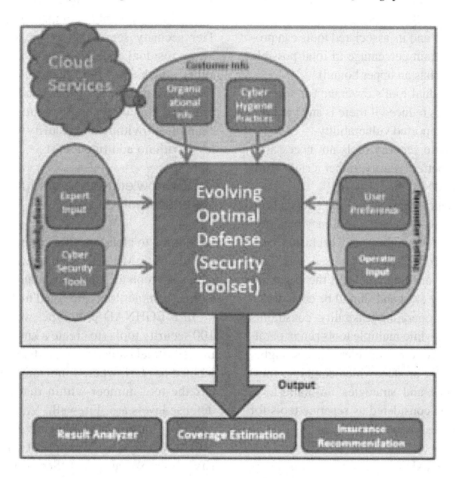

includes user console, result analyzer to help the user to review the characteristics of the security toolset. Recommendations are provided showing security tools to be used, their operating costs and security coverage and compliances in the form of a detailed report.

3.1.1 Assumptions and Constraints

The notion of security coverage is very different from the traditional insurance aspects of coverage. For instance, an insurance company checks which practices the client has implemented (Phil Ins., 2011), while insuring a client for the coverage from cyber attacks and the insurance premium depends accordingly. In this case, the insurer is not

offering any security tools to harden the client's defense albeit indirectly encouraging the client to increase their self-defense capability. With the cloud a different type of coverage will emerge which will be offered by the cloud providers to their subscribers as security assurance/insurance. The cloud providers have to use various security products from multiple vendors and need to integrate them seamlessly so that the desired security coverage can be achieved.

The underlying assumptions are considered in developing the MAGHNAD framework:

- A single tool/technique cannot provide 100% security coverage and has limited capacity in terms of overall security

- A multi-level defense strategy provides better in-depth security coverage
- Each level and its associated tools can provide a certain percentage of total possible coverage (has an upper bound)
- An Individual tool's coverage (or security index) gets reduced if there is any yet to be resolved reported vulnerability
- Using more security tools not necessarily provide better security, rather a right combination does
- Dependency constraint (Tool 2 depends on Tool 1 i.e. one security tool may be a prerequisite for another) and exclusion constraints (Tool 2 cannot be used with Tool 1 or using one tool precludes the use of another) may exist and should be considered
- Different operating/feasibility constraints may exist while multiple tools run in parallel and need to be considered accordingly
- Any vendor product which combines multiple tools and strategies for multi-level defense is considered as separate tools for coverage estimation

The MEGHNAD framework can estimate the security coverage for a desired assurance level i.e. selecting an insurance tier is equivalent to having an expectation of a certain level of security coverage. This developed estimator is primarily for cloud providers or 3PAOs to offer a feasible combination of security products in order to meet customers' security expectation while satisfying all their service requirements.

3.1.2 Security Services (Assurance Levels)

We considered five assurance tiers (as shown in Table 2), where Tier I assures highest level of security coverage. Depending on the Tier selection for a security service, the MEGHNAD provides solutions satisfying the coverage range

and cost range of the chosen tier, accordingly, if the cloud subscriber company seeks a higher Tier security service, they presumably have lower residual risk of service failure due to cyber attacks. On the other hand, Basic Tier security coverage is a must and needs to be provided for all types of cloud services; for example, providing one security tool from each level with no additional cost.

3.1.3 Knowledgebase of Multilayer Defense Tools

In addition to cloud specific security tools mentioned earlier, MEGHNAD framework used a list of security tools for supporting multi-level defense (some examples tools are listed in Table 3).

In MEGHNAD prototype, we listed about 100 security tools (to create a knowledge base) in six critical categories or defense levels, and labeled as *(l, t)*, where *l* indicates its level and *t* is the tool number within that level. These defense levels are 'Firewall,' 'Authentication,' 'Access Control,' 'Monitoring & Response,' 'Offline Analysis' and 'Application/Web Security' tools. We assigned 'Security Index (*SI*)' for individual product/tool and calculate average by their respective level weights. It returns a set of solutions and their weighted coverage. Some of the tools (except level 3, Access Control which also provide 20% coverage) that we are using in our implementations are listed in Table 3.

Enterprise-wide access control schemes usually adopt based on their access policy, procedure, standard guidelines; accordingly, we will consider 5 types of access control schemes as Level 3 defense strategies (MAC, DAC, RBAC HRBAC and ABAC) in our initial framework. We will also assume that tools at each level can offer limited maximum coverage, which is a certain percentage of the overall security coverage.

Table 2. Security services tiers and corresponding coverage

Security Service	Expected Security Coverage (%)
Tier I	90-99
Tier II	80-90
Tier III	70-80
Basic	50-70

Table 3. Shows a partial list of tools that we use to create the knowledgebase; a detailed list of security-related tools is available elsewhere. We assumed that tools at each level can offer limited maximum coverage, which is a certain percentage of coverage

Category / Level	Security tool	Vendor	Tool Features
Firewalls (Level 1) Max. possible Coverage 20%	Secure PIX Firewall	Cisco Systems Inc.	Network layer firewall performing stateful inspection, its function as VPN endpoint appliance too.
	Gauntlet 5.0	PGP Security	It is a proxy based firewall. Use application and adaptive proxies and PKI server.
	Microsoft Forefront UAG 2010	Microsoft	Provides endpoint security management. Web application firewall. And perform ontent inspection.
Authentication (Level 2) Max. possible Coverage 20%	Identity Enforcement Platform (IEP)	SecureAuth	It integrates tokenless 2-factor authentication, SSO, access, and user management services to simplify and secure access for cloud and web applications, VPN resources, and mobile devices.
	Kaspersky Password Manager 4	Kaspersky Lab	It captures login credentials automatically. It can also handle multipage and proprietary login. It has on demand password generator and it offers convenient password management by means of grouping and automatic form filling.
	LastPass 1.72	LastPass	Stores encrypted passwords online for accessing from anyplace. Performs Two factor authentication. Uses One-time passwords. Allow Flexible automatic password capture and playback.
Monitoring & Response (Level 4) Max. possible Coverage 20%	Cisco Adaptive Security Appliances (ASA) 5500 Series	Cisco Systems Inc.	Control network and application activity by using context-aware security parameters. Advanced intrusion prevention system (IPS) with Global Correlation.
	Dragon IPS	Enterasys Secure Networks	Can integrate with switches, firewalls, and routers can be used as an HIDS or an NIDS
	Snort	Sourcefire, Inc.	Network—based intrusion detection system (NIDS). Able to perform real time traffic analysis and packet logging. Protocol analysis, content searching, content matching etc.
AV Tools/ Offline Analysis (Level 5) Max. possible Coverage 10%	Norton Antivirus	Symantec Corporation	Checks files from Web, e-mail, IM etc. Effective intrusion prevention system. It has interactive threat map.
	McAfee AntiVirus Plus 2010	McAfee (Intel)	Enhanced cloud based active protection.
Others (Level 6) Max. possible Coverage 10%	Spyware Terminator 2.0	Crawler, LLC	Web Security Guard warns about phishing Web sites and other dangerous sites.
	Web of Trust (WOT)	WOT Services	Based on websites' reputation, it can be used as add-ons with popular web browsers.

3.1.4 Determining Optimal Security Toolset

The problem of estimating cloud security coverage (of a collection of security tools) is formulated as a multi-objective (Coverage, Cost and Performance) search and optimization problem. An optimal toolset is then determined using genetic search which can find solutions on the pareto-front of the search space. Genetic Algorithms (GAs) represent a class of general-purpose adaptive search methods that mimic the metaphor of natural biological evolution. Genetic algorithms operate on a population of candidate solutions applying the principle of survival of the fittest to produce better and better approximations to a solution.

Security Index and Security Coverage

Effectiveness of a security tool, we called *Security Index* is measured using two opposite factors: *Customer Rating (CR)* is determined using customers, reviewers and security experts ratings (between *0.0* and *5.0*) based on features, testing and evaluation; and tool's maximum vulnerability (*MV*) as maximum *CVSS* score [40, 41] which is between *0* and *10*. If a tool has any vulnerability, corresponding *SI* decreases since vulnerabilities provide an attacker with exploitation opportunities. For a tool with one or more vulnerabilities, the *SI* is reduced using the following formula,

$$SI_{(l,t)} = \frac{SI_{max} \times CR_{(l,t)}}{CR_{max}} \times \frac{1 + \frac{(CVSS_{max} - MV_{(l,t)})}{CVSS_{max}}}{K}$$

where $MV_{(k,t)}$ = Maximum CVSS Severity among all the vulnerabilities reported for the tool. If a tool has no vulnerability then we consider $MV=0$. We assumed $CVSS_{max} = 10.0$, $CR_{max}=5.0$, $SI_{max}=10.0$ and K (=2 here) is a constant.

Table 4 gives a list of currently available security products and their *Security Indexes*. These values will be updated on a regular basis to keep the information current and to accurately estimate security coverage in cloud. Illustration of calculating a tool's *Security Index* is given with three examples:

1. Gauntlet Firewall 5.0 has two vulnerabilities registered in the National Vulnerability Database (NVD) [40] with CVSS severity of 7.5 for both vulnerabilities. So, the value of *MV* for this tool is 7.5. If the *CR*, assigned by security expert is 4.5 then

$$SI = \frac{10.0 \times 4.5}{5.0} \times \frac{1 + (10.0 - 7.5) \times \frac{1}{10.0}}{2.0} = 5.62$$

2. Microsoft Forefront UAG 2010 Gold firewall has four vulnerabilities as mentioned in NVD with CVSS severity values 4.3, 4.3, 4.3 and 5.8. If the expert assigned *CR* for this tool is 4.0, our framework assigns, *SI = 5.68*.

3. Cisco Adaptive Security Appliances (ASA) 5500 Series" has several vulnerabilities registered in the NVD with *MV*=7.8, In this case *SI* can be calculated in a similar way.

We next calculated maximum possible coverage assumed Table 3 (Column 1), and is denoted as $w_{(l)}$ for each level, $l = 1..L$. We represent a solution S by a vector of vectors, $[S_{(1)} ... S_{(6)}]$ where $S_{(l)}$ is a vector of integers representing tools from level l used in the solution S and $S_{(l, i)}$ is used to refer to the ith integer of this vector. Solution, S, may contain zero or more tools from a level, l, whose *SI* values are used to calculate the effective coverage of multiple tools at each level, called *Level Security Index*, $LSI_{(S, l)}$, using the following algorithm:

Table 4. A list of some currently available security products; their Security Indexes (SI) are calculated based on various review reports and customer ratings. Here MV is set to 0 in all cases as we have not yet checked their CVSS scores

Security Product Type and Name	Tool Review Rating			CR	MV	SI
	PC Magazine	CNET	Expert			
Firewalls						
Panda Global Protection 2012	2.5	3.0	4.5	3.33	0	6.67
Norton 360 Version 5.0	4.5	5.0	3.5	4.33	0	7.16
iBoss Home Parental Control Router/Firewall	4.0	3.0	5.0	4.0	0	7.0
ZoneAlarm Firewall 9.2	4.5	5.0	4.5	4.67	0	7.34
Authentication						
LastPass Password Manager 1.72	5.0	5.0	4.5	4.83	0	7.42
Kaspersky Password Manager 4	4.0	N/A	4.0	4.0	0	7.0
Antivirus						
ZoneAlarm Extreme Security 2012	4.0	2.5	3.5	3.33	0	6.67
Avast! Internet Security 6.0	3.5	4.5	4.0	4.0	0	7.0
Microsoft Security Essentials 2.0	3.0	4.0	5.0	4.0	0	7.0
AVG Internet Security 2011	2.5	4.5	2.0	3.0	0	6.5
McAfee Antivirus Plus 2010	4.0	4.5	3.5	4.0	0	7.0

i. $ASI_{(S, 1)} = 0.0$

ii. for i = 0 to size($S_{(l)}$)-1 do

    a. $ASI_{(S,l)} += \dfrac{(SI_{max} - LSI_{(S, l)}) \times SI_{(k, S_{(l,i)})}}{SI_{max}}$

iii. End

iv. $LSI_{(S,l)} = w_{(l)} \times \exp\{-\dfrac{(ASI_{(S,l)} - SI_{max})^2}{2\sigma^2}\}$

Value of μ is set to 10.0 (same as SI_{max}) and *ASI* is the aggregated *SI*. Security experts can set σ^2 (=8.0 here). In the above algorithm, $w_{(l)}$ is the maximum possible coverage from each level (as given in Table 2, Column 1). The overall security coverage for all levels is calculated as,

$$Overall\ Security\ Coverage_{(S)} = \{\sum_{l=1}^{L} LSI_{(S,l)}\}\%$$

Here, *L* is the total number of levels.

It is to be noted that selected toolset need to be properly configured to achieve maximum performance. Benchmark and evaluation of cyber-security tools also provide guidelines in assigning *CR* for each tool. For example, the report on Cisco Firewall Version 2.2.0 mentioned several scorable benchmark configurations.

Estimated Cost

In this framework, the cost is related to the purchasing/licensing and operating cost of security products as determined by the cloud service provider. For higher tier insurance more rigorous/multiple tools will be recommended. If the cost for the tool, *t* at level *l* is $C_{(l, t)}$, then the total cost is calculated as $\sum_{l=1}^{L} \sum_{i=0}^{size(S_{(k)})-1} C_{(l, S_{(l,i)})}$ for each candidate solution, *S*.

In addition, we also have taken into consideration other factors such as cyber hygiene practices, organization size in terms of employees, systems etc.

Performance

Initially, we considered the performance index (between 0.0-100.0) is considered according to the efficiency of security tools such as CPU usage, memory usage, response time etc. where the performance score to be represented by $P_{(l, t)}$ of a tool, *t* at level *l*.

In our approach, a set of security tools is selected through a guided stochastic search process based on their security index, cost and performance index as objectives in order to deploy in cloud for security as a service.

3.2 Determining an Optimal Set of Security Tools Optimization

We used a variant of multi-objective genetic algorithm (MOGA), called NSGA-II (Durillo, 2006)]) as search and optimization. We have extended

the *JMetal* [Saxena et. al, (2002, April)] library to perform search in multi-objective space. i.e. search for an optimal security toolset. Genetic algorithms operate on a population of candidate solutions applying the principle of survival of the fittest to produce better and better approximations to a solution. In general, in order to successfully employ GA to solve a problem, one needs to identify the following four components:

- **Syntax of the chromosome:** Represent the problem space.
- **Interpretation of the chromosome:** Decoding and checking the feasibility.
- **Fitness Measure of the chromosome:** Determine the quality of solutions.
- **Genetic Operators:** Crossover and mutation operators are used to manipulate candidate solutions.

Genetic algorithm works with a population of candidate solutions (chromosomes). The fitness of each member of the population (point in search space) is computed by an evaluation function that measures how well an individual performs with respect to the problem domain. We extended the *JMetal* [GA Library] library to perform search in multi-objective space. In order to minimize cost and maximize coverage and performance for a chosen security service tier, we used the following formula as minimization of fitness measure,

In order to minimize cost and maximize coverage & performance for a chosen security service tier, we formulated the search as a minimization problem for fitness measure:

1. Residual Risk: 100% − *Overall Security Coverage* $_{(S)}$
2. Cost Index:

$$\frac{\sum_{k=1}^{L} \sum_{i=0}^{size(S_{(k)})-1} C(k, S_{(k,i)})}{\text{Upper range of cost for the chosen insurance service}}$$

Figure 5. Representation of the security coverage problem

Chromosomal Representation

Figure 5. Representation of the security coverage problem

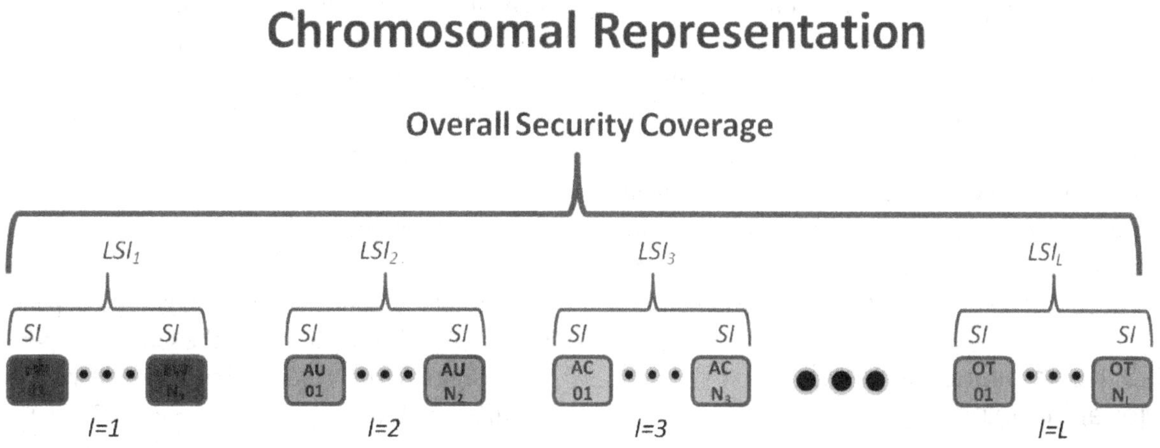

3. Performance Index:

$$100.0 - \frac{\sum_{k=1}^{L} \sum_{i=0}^{size(S_{(k)})-1} P(k, S_{(k,i)})}{\sum_{k=1}^{L} size(S_{(k)})}$$

We have encoded the problem instance (candidate solution) using six array variables representing six levels (e.g. firewall, authentication, monitoring, etc.) as shown in Figure 5.

In our initial design, we make level 1 (Firewall), Level 2 (Authentication) and Level 4 (Monitoring & Response) systems mandatory meaning all solution must contain tools/implementations for such categories of services. We configured level 3 (Access Control), Level 5 (Offline Analysis) and Level 6 (Others) optional tools. As mentioned earlier, each level contributes their coverage (LSI) in order to calculate overall security coverage.

It is to be noted that a solution may or may not contain security tools from all levels. The GA parameters will be set using the 'Operator Input Panel.' The better-performing members will be rewarded and individuals showing poor performance will be punished or discarded i.e. candidate solutions violating constraints will be penalized by reducing their fitness values in each objective. A pool of feasible solutions will be discovered when the genetic search terminates. These solutions will be ranked based on an overall weighted fitness score and also based on individual objective.

3.3. An Extended Version: MEGHNAD V 2.0

MEGHNAD V 2.0 is an enhancement to the Java based framework MEGHNAD (Dasgupta, 2011a; Dasgupta, 2011 b). With addition to the security continuously this enhancement introduced the compliance aspect in the tool. MEGHNAD have inbuilt multi-level defense strategy that can provide in-depth security coverage and with the vast knowledgebase of 100 security tools in six different categories as defense levels. The processing used JMetal Genetic algorithms that improve the estimator performance and liability on coverage estimation. We extended the original framework by adding six different industry standards compliance requirements to the knowledgebase for PCI DSS, HIPAA, GLBA, SOX, SAS 70 and FISMA. These compliance requirements are mapped to the security model and compliance requirement into different categories based on the "who controls what matrix?"

In this Version 2.0, we take the user input of organization type and if any required security compliance with the cloud model and suggest the compliance requirements needed by the organization and also to generate the mapped checklist of compliance requirements. Finally, the framework generates a Service level agreement document for the customer to use as a guide to select the appropriate vendor and also use as an agreement between the vendors to satisfy the compliance.

3.3.1 Compliance to Service Model Mapping Process

The security model and compliance requirement are mapped into different categories based on the "who controls what matrix?" described in section 2.2 Table 1.

The work involved understanding the concepts of Cloud Computing, security Model and Compliances. This involved extensive research on the subject. As a first step all security tools and techniques available for multilevel protection of different cloud services, then secondly, find compliance for different sectors, gathered requirements for the compliances (PCI DSS [LogRhythm, (April, 2011)], HIPAA, FISMA, etc), mapped those requirement in a matrix based on "Who controls what in cloud". Table 5 and Table 6 provide the

mapping for two compliance standards and other standards are similarly mapped. This mapping was developed manually, which produced the steps to develop an algorithm to provide as base to the new version of MEGHNAD framework (as shown in Figure 6).

3.3.2 Expert Input Panel

The prototype implemented an expert input panel as discussed in earlier, where the security experts can assign *CR* to any tool, assign coverage weights to different levels and set variance ($\sigma2$) of the Gaussian function used to estimate coverage. CVSS Severity is added as a tool quality from this panel. This panel also provides the interface to manipulate constraints information to create the Knowledgebase. This panel corresponds to the input module 'Knowledgebase.'

3.3.3 Operator Input Panel

This panel is used to input information regarding organizational facts and cyber hygiene practices. Critical organizational information comprises of the number of users, hardware/software assets and web/application servers etc. This panel has the interface for parameter setting of the Genetic Algorithm such as the population size, maximum

Table 5. HIPAA requirement mapping matrix

R No	Requirement	Service Models		
		SAAS	PAAS	IAAS
1	Security Management Process: Review permission settings and correct access right.	Yes	No	No
2	Assigned Security Responsibility: Identify the security official who is responsible for the development and implementation of the policies and procedures required by this subpart for the entity	Yes	No	No
3	Workforce Security: Ensure that only authorized workforce members have access to Electronic Protected Health Information	Yes	Yes	No
4	Information Access Management: Implement policies and procedures for accessing Electronic Protected Health Information	Yes	Yes	No
5	Access Control: Allow access only to the authorized workforce	Yes	Yes	Yes
6	Audit Control: Record and examine activities for Electronic Protected Health Information	Yes	Yes	Yes

Table 6. PCI DSS requirement mapping matrix

R No	Requirement	Service Models		
		SAAS	PAAS	IAAS
1	Install and maintain a firewall configuration to protect cardholder data	Yes	Yes	Yes
2	Do not use vendor-supplied defaults for system passwords and other security parameters	Yes	Yes	No
3	Protect stored cardholder data	Yes	Yes	No
4	Encrypt transmission of cardholder data across open, public networks	Yes	Yes	No
5	Use and regularly update anti-virus software	Yes	Yes	No
6	Develop and maintain secure systems and applications	Yes	No	No
7	Restrict access to cardholder data by business need-to-know	Yes	Yes	Yes
8	Assign a unique ID to each person with computer access	Yes	Yes	No
9	Restrict physical access to cardholder data	Yes	Yes	No
10	Track and monitor all access to network resources and cardholder data	Yes	Yes	Yes
11	Regularly test security systems and processes	Yes	Yes	Yes
12	Maintain a policy that addresses information security	Yes	No	No

Figure 6. MEGHNAD V 2.0 architecture

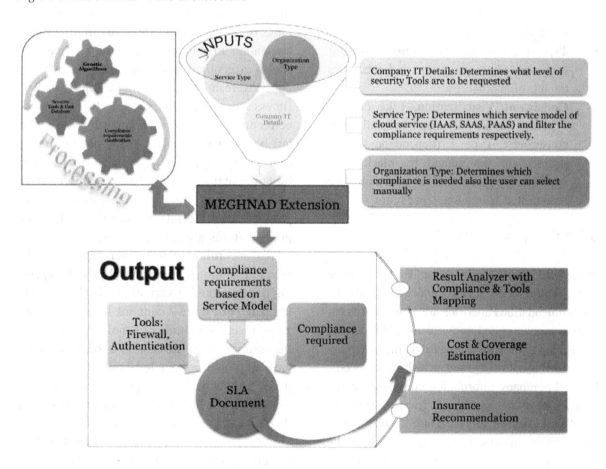

number of evolutions, selection strategy, mutation probability, crossover probability, crossover/mutation type, etc.

When the GA terminates, post-processing is performed to eliminate infeasible solutions, and calculate the overall weighted fitness score. The prototype offers an interface to change weights for Coverage, Cost and Performance objectives and rearrange solutions based on the objective preference. The user is also able to rank the solutions based on any of these three objectives.

3.3.4 Handling Constraints

The developed tool supports two types of constraints, which are

- **Type I: Dependency constraints.** This constraint type helps us to model real world scenarios where one security tool may be a prerequisite for another.
- **Type II: Exclusion constraints.** This is for scenarios where using one tool precludes the use of another.
- **Constraint Visualization.** Like defense systems, we use polylines to visualize the constraints. Type I (dependency) constraints are represented by black lines whereas Type II (exclusion) constraints are represented by red lines (in Figure 7).

3.3.5 Compliance Panel

In the MEGHNAD V 2.0, we added compliance & its requirements panels, which maps to the Recommendation Panel for equivalent security essentials in color-coded representation. This panel is used to input information regarding the Company information, data usage and its technology needs. Critical company information comprises of the number of users, hardware/software assets and web/application servers etc. Once the user inputs the Company information, the user is taken to the next Panel which recommends the Compliance information and input information of the Service model desired by the Company is captured. In this Panel the user can also select any other desired Compliance and the type of security service (i.e. Tier I, II, III or basic tier) which helps the tool to generate requirements according to the preferred selection.

Based on the Compliance Panel Input, the tool to recommends the user what type of compliance is needed for the company. This information along with the other compliance the user selected including the Security Service Tier is used as Input to filter the requirements needed to be requested from cloud computing provider or the vendor for the company to be compliant.

3.3.6 User Console, Visualization and Result Analyzer

In Figure 7, the output module 'Result Analyzer' ranks the solutions and show summary, recommendation in multiple visual representations. It also offers the filtering of solutions by user-defined thresholds in one or more objectives. The fitness scores are scaled between 0% - 100% for better understanding and comparing results. On left bottom panel, polylines are used to represent the solutions where levels are represented by horizontal lines. The lines contain discrete points representing individual security tool/product classified into the level/category. The products/tools are arranged from left to right, sorted according to the coverage index. The selected solution is represented by the lines passing through tools at various levels. The bottom left panel of Figure 7 contains several red lines going through a number of tools. According to the assumption of the design, a solution cannot have all tools from one level only. On the other hand, if the solution line goes through a point located on the left margin at a particular level then no tool is selected from that level.

As the user ranks the solutions based on their overall or any other individual objective and selects

Figure 7. Main panel of security coverage estimator (MEGHNAD 2.0) showing results of a typical run

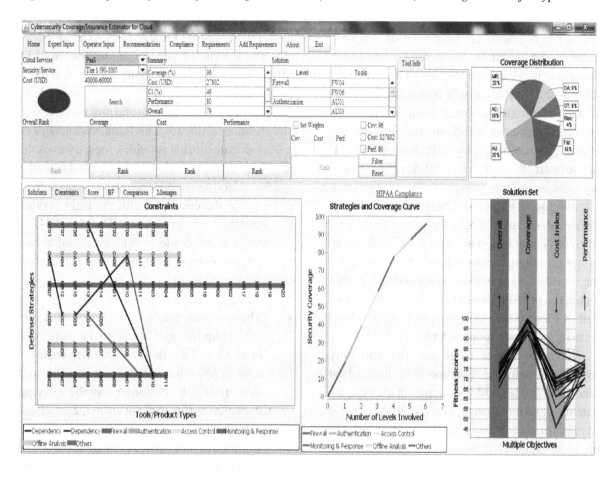

one of those ranked solutions, corresponding lines are painted in red; other lines (unselected solutions) are painted in black. The central panel at the bottom row shows the estimated coverage for the selected solution. It also shows which types of tools/products are available in this solution. The panel at the bottom right area shows the ranked solutions according to fitness scores. The red lines show the fitness scores of the selected solution.

The 'Coverage Distribution' panel lies above 'Objective Fitness' panel at the top right corner. It includes a pie chart showing the contribution of various tools in the estimated coverage. The white portion of the pie chart shows the residual

risk. Users can filter the solutions' list using the control available on the left of the pie chart. The other two tables beside the tools information table are used to show detail about the solution selected by the user. For convenience to the user, the prototype implementation comes with filtering mechanism based on fitness score thresholds for individual objectives.

In our configuration, we make Level 1 (Firewall), Level 2 (Authentication) and Level 4 (Monitoring & Response) systems mandatory, meaning all solutions must contain tools/implementations for such categories of services. We configured Level 3 (Access Control), Level 5 (Offline Analysis) and Level 6 (Others) optional.

CONCLUSION

Cloud environments are becoming increasingly more attractive both in commercial sector and in mission-critical operations; also Government's "cloud-first" initiative will make the transition faster. For mission-oriented resilient cloud environment, assurance and survivability are key enabling factors for deployment. Best effort security support (as a Service Level Agreement) will not work as military using cloud services cannot afford frequent data losses, breaches and unavailability of services. From the cloud providers' point of view, it is also not a good business model of not providing a certain level of assurance for the services. So to mitigate risks and attacks in a cloud, the providers need to include security as a part of their service offerings, making the cloud security insurance more acceptable.

However, Proper cloud security can only happen through a combination of vigilance, best practices, and technology, including encryption, patching, and monitoring. The shift to the cloud is an opportunity to rethink security from the ground up, to re-architect networks and data centers in a way that closes existing gaps. The feds are helping agencies do this with a growing body of guidance such as NIST's 68-page document on cloud security and controls required as part of the forthcoming FedRAMP security authorization program (Hoover, 2011). This chapter discussed a framework for cloud insurance model (called MEGHNAD) with embedding most critical security requirements of industry ccompliances. Cloud Computing provides services as per usage and service models, the more customer delegate the IT infrastructure to cloud it becomes increasingly important to continuously monitor Quality of Service (QOS) as the data security and compliance is a continues ongoing responsibility. Therefore, finding the right service provider with required terms in SLA Document is the backbone of any service. This new version of framework categorizes the compliance requirements that need to be

requested from the vendor based on the service model for different industry standards such as PCI DSS, HIPAA, SOX, GLBA, SAS 70 and FISMA etc. The optimized genetic algorithms used in MEGHNAD are applied to the compliance mapping with the security tools, which is scalable to customer-required standards and provide coverage and insurance estimates. This framework generates a SLA document that provides security compliance requirements terms to be requested from the vendor. Also the vendors can use this document to persuade the customer with the right service they need in a cost effective way. The MEGHNAD framework can provide companies a tool to test risk and compliances for cloud services based on the industry standard.

- The customer gets a clear idea of what services requirements need to be requested in order to be compliant in their business sector. Also the vendors can use the tool to convince the customer thereby offering the right service they need in a cost effective way.
- Combining the operational benefits of the cloud with enterprise security needs can provide necessary control over their users and their access to cloud and on-premise applications.

REFERENCES

Amazon. (2013). *Amazon web services*. Retrieved from http://aws.amazon.com/

CASHRUN. (2010). *The importance of PCI DSS compliance*. Retrieved from http://www.cashrun.com/1038/the-importance-of-pci-dss-compliance

CHUBB Group of Insurance Companies. (2011). *ForeFront portfolio 3.0 cyber security insurance*. Author.

CIS. (2010). *The CIS (center for internet security) security metrics v1.1.0*. Author.

CISCO. (n.d.). *Privacy and security compliance journey-cisco systems*. Retrieved from http://www.cisco.com/web/about/doing_business/legal/privacy_compliance/index.html

Cloud Computing Digest. (2013). *Thirteen cloud service providers to watch in 2013*. Author.

Cyber-InsuranceMetrics. (n.d.). *Cyber-insurance metrics and impact on cyber-security*. Retrieved from http://www.whitehouse.gov/files/documents/cyber/ISA%20-%20Cyber-Insurance%20Metrics%20and%20Impact%20on%20Cyber-Security.pdf

CyberSecIndex. (2011). *New index measures cyberspace safety, the index of cyber security*. Retrieved from http://www.cybersecurityindex.org/

Dasgupta, D., & Rahman, M. (2011a). A framework for estimating security coverage for cloud service insurance. In *Proceedings of ACM Proceeding of the Seventh Annual Workshop on Cyber Security and Information Intelligence Research (CSIIRW)*. ACM.

Dasgupta, D., & Rahman, M. (2011b). Estimating security coverage for cloud services. In *Proceedings of IEEE International Conference on Privacy, Security, Risk, and Trust*. IEEE.

Deb, K., Pratap, A., Agarwal, S., & Meyarivan, T. (2002). A fast and elitist multiobjective genetic algorithm: NSGA-II. *IEEE Transactions on Evolutionary Computation*, 6(2). doi:10.1109/4235.996017

Diaz, A. (2011). *Service level agreements in the cloud: Who cares?* Wired Cloudline. Retrieved from http://www.wired.com/cloudline/2011/12/service-level-agreements-in-the-cloud-who-cares/

DoD. (2011). *Cyber security operations centre initial guidance*. Retrieved from http://etherealmind.com/wp-content/uploads/2011/04/Cloud_Computing_Security_Considerations-1.pdf

Dokras, S. et al. (2009). *The role of security in trustworthy cloud computing*. RSA Security Inc.

Durillo, J. J., & Nebro, A. J. (2006). jMetal: A Java framework for multi-objective optimization. Academic Press.

FedRAMP. (2012). *Concept of operations (CONOPS)*. Retrieved from http://www.gsa.gov/graphics/staffoffices/FedRAMP_CONOPS.pdf

Fortinet. (2006). *Simplified GLBA compliance for community banks using fortinet hardware, software and partner services* (Whitepaper WPR127-0806-R1). Retrieved from http://www.fortinet.com/doc/whitepaper/GLBA-Compliance.pdf

Ghatak, A. (2012). *Cloud insurance for ramping up cloud adoption*. TechRepublic Blog. Retrieved from http://www.techrepublic.com/blog/datacenter/cloud-insurance-for-ramping-up-cloud-adoption/5606

GoGrid Cloud Hosting. (2010). *The cloud pyramid: Cloud infrastructure*. Retrieved from http://pyramid.gogrid.com/cloud-infrastructure/

Hasan, R., Winslett, M., & Sion, R. (2007). *Requirements of secure storage systems for healthcare*. Stony Brook, NY: Network Security and Applied Cryptography Lab. doi:10.1007/978-3-540-75248-6_12

Hoover, N. (2011). *Cloud security: Better than we think?* Retrieved from http://www.informationweek.com/government/cloud-saas/cloud-security-better-than-we-think/231902850

ISO/IEC Certification Standards. (2013). Retrieved from http://www.iso27001security.com/html/27001.html

Lawson, N., Orr, J., & Klar, D. (2003). The HIPAA privacy rule: An overview of compliance initiatives and requirements. *Defense Counsel Journal, 70*, 127–149.

LogRhythm. (2011). *PCI and PA DSS compliance with LogRhythm.* Author.

McAfee. (2013). *PCI DSS compliance/McAfee compliances solution.* Retrieved from http://www.mcafee.com/us/solutions/compliance/pci-compliance.aspx

Moore, T. (2010). The economics of cybersecurity: Principles and policy options. *International Journal of Critical Infrastructure Protection, 3*(3-4), 103–117. doi:10.1016/j.ijcip.2010.10.002

NDB Accounts and Consults. (2008). *Introduction to SAS 70 audits.* Retrieved from http://www.sas70.us.com/SAS70TrainingvideoI.php

NetWrix. (2012). *FISMA compliance.* Retrieved from http://www.netwrix.com/FISMA_Compliance.html

NIST SP-800-66. (2008). *An introductory resource guide for implementing the health insurance portability and accountability act (HIPAA) security rule.* National Institute of Standards and Technology. Retrieved from http://csrc.nist.gov/publications/nistpubs/800-66-Rev1/SP-800-66-Revision1.pdf

PCI Security Standards Council. (2010). *Requirements and security assessment procedures.* Retrieved from https://www.pcisecuritystandards.org/documents/pci_dss_v2.pdf

Pennell, J. (2011). *Defining best practices in cloud computing.* IOActive, Inc. Retrieved from http://www.ioactive.com/cloud-computing.html

Phil Ins. (2011). *Network security & privacy liability coverage supplement.* Philadelphia Insurance Companies. Retrieved from www.phly.com/products/forms/MiscForms/NetworkSecurityCoverageSupplement.pdf

RackSpace. (2011). *Understanding the cloud computing stack SaaS, PaaS, IaaS.* Retrieved from http://broadcast.rackspace.com/hosting_knowledge/whitepapers/Understanding-the-Cloud-Computing-Stack.pdf

SearchSecurity Inc. (2009). *HIPAA compliance manual: Training, audit and requirement checklist.* Retrieved from http://searchsecurity.techtarget.com/tutorial/HIPAA-compliance-manual-Training-audit-and-requirement-checklist

Spurzem, R. (2007). *SOX definition.* SearchCIO. Retrieved from http://searchcio.techtarget.com/definition/Sarbanes-Oxley-Act

Strickland, J. (2008). *How GoogleDocs works.* Retrieved from http://computer.howstuffworks.com/internet/basics/google-docs.htm

Trust Wave. (n.d.). Risk management and compliance solutions. *Trust Wave Inc.*

U.S. Department of Health and Human Services. (n.d.). *Privacy rule summary by United States department of health & human services HIPAA compliance tools.* Retrieved from http://www.hhs.gov/ocr/privacy/hipaa/understanding/

WatchGuard. (2009). *How to meet PCI DSS requirements.* Retrieved from http://www.watchguard.com/docs/whitepaper/wg_pci-summary_wp.pdf

Chapter 6

Securing Business IT on the Cloud

Bina Ramamurthy
University at Buffalo, USA

ABSTRACT

In this chapter, the author examines the various approaches taken by the popular cloud providers Amazon Web Services (AWS), Google App Engine (GAE), and Windows Azure (Azure) to secure the cloud. AWS offers Infrastructure as a Service model, GAE is representative of the Software as a Service, and Azure represents the Platform as a Service model. Irrespective of the model, a cloud provider offers a variety of services from a simple large-scale storage service to a complete infrastructure for supporting the operations of a modern business. The author discusses some of the security aspects that a cloud customer must be aware of in selecting a cloud service provider for their needs. This discussion includes the major threats posed by multi-tenancy in the cloud. Another important aspect to consider in the security context is machine virtualization. Securing these services involves a whole range of measures from access-point protection at the client end to securing virtual co-tenants on the same physical machine hosted by a cloud. In this chapter, the author highlights the major offerings of the three cloud service providers mentioned above. She discusses the details of some important security challenges and solutions and illustrates them using screen shots of representative security configurations.

1. INTRODUCTION

Security is of utmost concern to the users of cloud computing, understandably so; businesses are typically handing over data, information, computational models, computations, and in many instances the whole IT operation of their organization to a cloud services provider. On the other end, securing the cloud and its resources is all the more critical for the cloud providers, for the survival of their own business. While there are lot of skepticism about the security and trustworthiness of the "cloud" (Chen, 2010), one must understand that the cloud is indeed a

DOI: 10.4018/978-1-4666-5788-5.ch006

composition (combination) of many existing technologies (Reese, 2009). These technologies have successfully used a variety of security measures from basic user authentication to sophisticated PKI based digital certificates (Bishop, 2005). In fact, contrary to common belief, the cloud may offer an effective model for enforcing the security measures uniformly across all applications, data and services hosted by it. It is with this assumption that we approach the discussion in this chapter, where we elaborate on the security challenges and solutions in the existing cloud models. We will examine the approaches to securing the cloud end-to-end, from the perimeter to a processor inner core. Specifically we look at the security models implemented by three of the prominent cloud providers: Amazon Web Services (AWS), Google Cloud Platform (Google) and Windows Azure (Azure). The purpose of the discussion here is to assure the readers that the cloud providers indeed have taken extraordinary measures to secure the cloud and are constantly working on making it even more secure. In this chapter we will focus mainly on AWS security features in detail, along with a few important security features of Google cloud and Windows Azure.

2. BACKGROUND/OVERVIEW

The Internet innovation changed the way computing and information technology being done. When the Internet protocol Version 4 IPV4 was defined by IETF RFC 791 in 1981, nobody anticipated the extent of the growth of the internet (*Limitations, 2013*). It is hard to believe security specifications were not part of this initial RFC. In fact, security was retrofitted by an optional IPSec protocol to secure network communication packets. Security has come a long way since these early days of the Internet. As the major businesses, such as healthcare and education are increasingly getting digital, security plays a critical role in protecting the information privacy and also for assuring the

continuity of the businesses. Business consortiums have come up with standards and regulations for security and privacy in their respective domains and cloud providers have been quite eager to comply with these rules and regulations. For instance, all three cloud providers discussed here have been certified by the ISO 27001-standard (*ISO, 2013*) that covers an extensive list of best practices for security management.

3. SECURING THE BUSINESS OPERATIONS ON THE CLOUD

A high level view of the cloud-based system architecture is shown in Figure 1. The client side shown on the left depicts the exponential growth in mobile devices, social networks, and the diversity of application domains. Data generated by these technological advances has been characterized by variety, veracity, high volume and high velocity (the four V's) (Zikopoulis, 2012). Data generated offers a gold mine of intelligence and most businesses desire to take advantage of this. This warrants large and efficient storage and secure access to the data and algorithms. Businesses have been increasingly relying on the cloud to address these newer demands as shown below in Figure 1.

Figure 1 shows an organization with the entire IT operations deployed on the cloud; *IT on the cloud* is a popular model among the recent start-ups, with Instagram, Netflix and Pinterest hosting the majority of their operations on the cloud (*Case studies, 2013*). Popular attraction of cloud infrastructure is in the on-demand, quick to install and uninstall, pay-as-you-go provisioning of the common services to support a business. While cloud services may be indispensable for start-ups, it has been an equally popular choice for maintaining legacy services (e.g. 32-bit applications), and for addressing variability in demands at large organizations. Thus the cloud serves a wide range of needs of the modern business organization. A full-fledged commercial cloud provider such as

Figure 1. Architecture of a cloud-based system

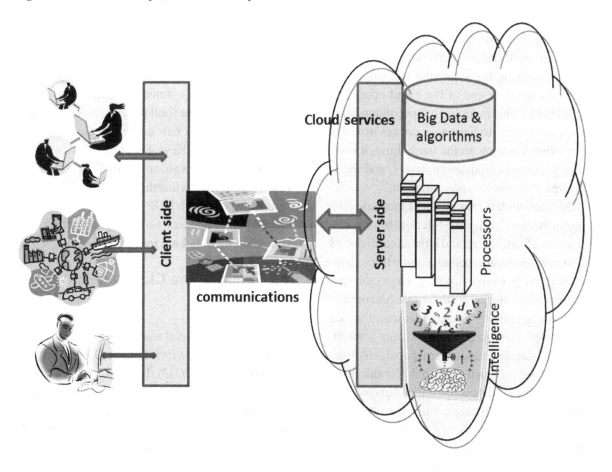

Amazon or Google supports a much richer collection of services than a traditional internal IT department does to the typical average business organization. These extra services demand extra security. Moreover such features as virtualization (Hess, 2010) and co-tenancy of multiple clients on the same network or processors cause an additional level of security issues. We will identify these issues and discuss how these are addressed by the popular cloud providers.

4. AMAZON WEB SERVICES

Amazon (AWS) offers a comprehensive suite of IT resources on the cloud that are exposed to the clients as web services (WS) and accessed

using REST (Fielding, 2000) or SOAP APIs. Once the instances and infrastructure have been established on the cloud using web services, client can communicate with them using traditional TCP/IP protocols. AWS has implemented quite an elaborate security stack with its operations and infrastructure, leveraging its deep expertise in online business. The cloud services are after all the byproduct of its innovative online store business. The Amazon online business has experienced its share of security issues with outages and DDoS (Distributed Denial of Service) (Bishop, 2005). Experience in addressing these has helped in framing the security for its cloud offering. The AWS cloud has issued a manifesto (*AWS Security, 2013*) that elaborates the security processes in place for its cloud services. In this document, it advocates a shared responsibility model with the cloud client and the cloud server both providing a reasonable baseline security environment. This shared responsibility of security is emphasized by clearly specifying the steps that a client should take to secure their end of the cloud operations (Varia, 2011). This is similar to how online banks require the clients to have a secure environment for communicating with the bank through using strong passwords, updated browsers, and recent operating systems versions and so on.

The data centers and physical machines that make up the cloud components have to be protected and secured from natural and intentional disasters. AWS provides environmental security through fire detection and suppression, power, temperature and climate control, and proper disposal of decommissioned storage devices and regular maintenance. AWS compliance program also covers a variety of security standards and several popular industry specific standards such as HIPPA (Health Insurance Portability and Accountability Act) and CSA (Cloud Security Alliance). Business continuity management is accomplished through high availability, quick incidence response and transparent communication through such features as service health dashboard and security and compliance center interfaces. In the next sections we discuss specific issues related to information technology.

4.1 Secure Access to Resources and Infrastructure

The network supporting the cloud has security features such as gateways, proxies and firewall settings for controlling access to cloud services.

For example Figure 2 shows the security group setting for a hypothetical business Acme Inc. The business establishes secure access to its cloud infrastructure by defining the rules for access. For example, as shown in Figure 2 on the bottom right, only accesses granted for external parties is through RDP (port 3389), SSH (port 22), some custom ports (49000-50000) and HTTPS (443).

The rules are collectively identified as AcmeInc security group. Such security groups can help in transparently applying a business' security policies of across the board for all its applications.

Once the network infrastructure is established on the AWS cloud, connection to the network can be through a secure shell protocol using the public key/private key pair authentication as shown in Figure 3 (AcmeKey). Secure-shell accesses to the Linux instances are authenticated through the key pair generated while the access to the Windows instances is through RDP (Remote Desktop Protocol) authentication using digital certificates generated by the cloud instance.

4.2 Securing the Cloud against Attacks

AWS provides several methods to thwart attacks from outside. Since its infamous DDoS attack of 2000 (*Bosworth, 2002*) that also affected Yahoo and Ebay, Amazon has taken extraordinary measures to address well-known attacks. Amazon has applied the experience gained as the world's largest online retailer in protecting its business and cloud services. It spreads the resources at diverse locations and also uses proprietary techniques to mitigate DDoS attack. The man in the Middle (MITM) (*Bishop, 2005*) attacks are prevented by server authentication and by encouraging use of SSL for interaction with services. IP spoofing is prevented by a firewall-infrastructure that can be customized to allow access at specific ports. This is illustrated in Figure 2, where the only allowed accesses to the server are through RDP, SSH and HTTPS and a range of ports for general use (49000-50000). All the other ports are shut down for access. Port scanning by any customer is a violation of the Amazon agreement. A customer needs to get prior approval even for their WAN port scan for vulnerability audits.

Many worry about usage of virtual machines (VM) on the cloud, especially about multiple VMs residing on the same physical machine (co-

Figure 2. Screen shot of security group in AWS

Figure 3. Private/public key pair creation for authenticating access

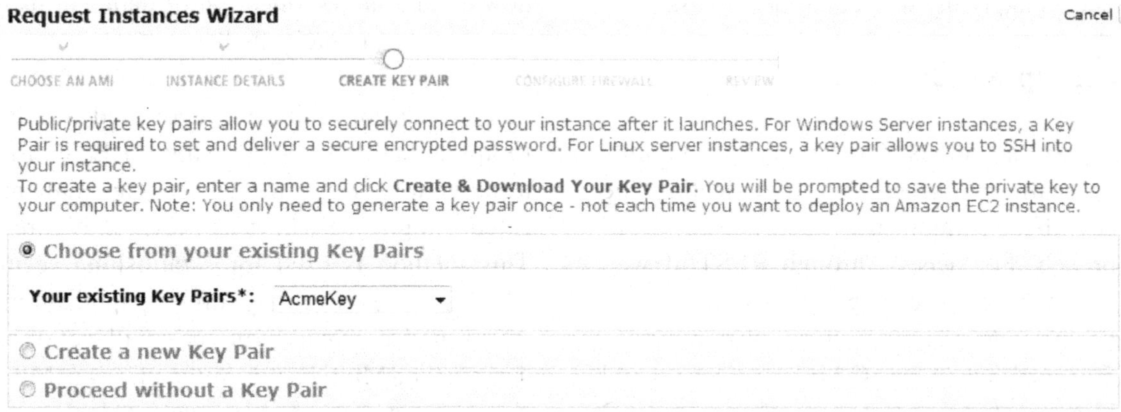

Figure 4. Security credential and access key pairs

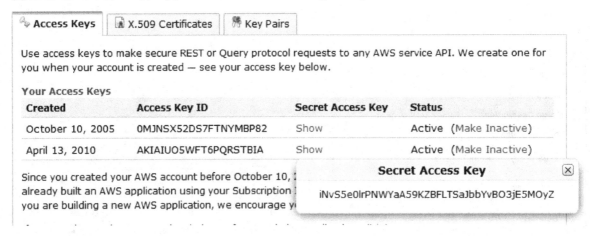

tenancy), sniffing ports of others and snooping on the cache. These are clearly identified as problems and AWS does provide ample protection against these. However customers are also advised to protect sensitive data with encryption. All the software installed and infrastructures configured adhere to well established reviews and audits, and the configuration management servers are well protected internally with controlled access.

4.3 Endpoint Defense

The first line defense for the server end points from malicious access is authenticating the user with the common user name and password approach. For access through RESTful web services based user-applications and tools, AWS provide access keys. It also provides X.509 certificates for SOAP-based access and public-private key-pair to securely access EC2 instances, clusters and in general, any AMIs (Amazon Machine Images). Figure 4 shows the security credentials for RESTful access to Amazon services from client programs. The access key pair defined by the Access Key ID

and Secret Access Key generated by the AWS are shown. (Of course these pairs have been deleted after this screen shot was taken.)

S3 (Simple Storage Service) is a global storage space that can be accessed by logging into Amazon web services using the username and password credentials. However S3 interface does not provide a convenient way to upload or download a large collection of data automatically or programmatically. There are open source tools available such as S3Fox (*S3Fox, 2013*) that provide convenient and dedicated interface to upload and download using a RESTful interface. Accesses from such tools are authenticated using Access keys as shown in Figure 5. This method is used for establishing secure RESTful access from any software applications. Amazon also provides an optional level of security called Multi Factor Authentication (MFA) using codes generated by special devices. In this case a new one-time password is generated by a MFA device, and then is entered along with the regular username and password credentials.

Figure 5. S3Fox account manager authentication

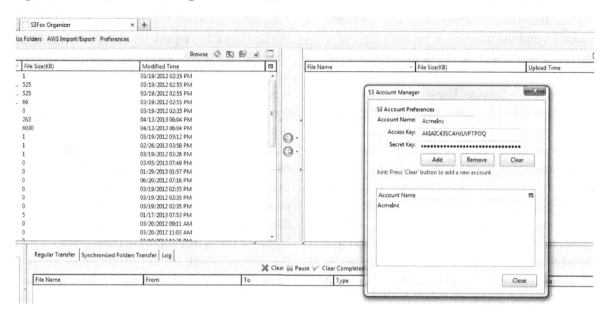

4.4 Securing the AWS Services

Amazon offers a variety of cloud services each with its own security features. We discussed secure access to S3 in section 4.3. In general, many of the security measures are applicable generally to all the services. In this section we will discuss few of the services including EC2 (Elastic Compute Cloud) and Virtual Private Cloud (VPC).

4.4.1 Elastic Compute Cloud (EC2)

The centerpiece of the Amazon cloud offering is the EC2 service and it is also the most commonly used service. It allows users to launch an instance of various versions of Linux and Windows, clusters of machines, pre-loaded machine images and workflows. The instances are realized using Xen hypervisor with multiple levels of security rom 0-3, 3 being the least. In the virtualized mode the host operating system is at level 0 and the guest or user operating system at level 1 and the applications at level 0, thus providing security through separation of the operating levels.

4.4.2 Virtual Private Cloud (VPC)

At the outset VPC offers security through anonymity. Typically non-VPC services are launched at public IP addresses in Amazon's domain. VPC offers private IP addresses of user's choice as specified by the RFC 1918 and the ability to define a subnet within this VPC. All the security features discussed above such as firewall, security group can be applied. Besides the typical security features users can configure access control lists (ACLs) that contain rules to grant and deny access to the VPC at fine granular levels of IP address, port number etc. AWS also provides a virtual private gateway and allows for configuration of the virtual subnet behind a NAT (Network Address Translator); Amazon also provides NAT machine images (AMI) that can be readily configured and used.

5. GOOGLE CLOUD PLATFORM

Google cloud platform is also an offshoot of a very successful business where security is given highest priority. Unlike AWS where the infrastructure is directly exposed to the client at the TCP/IP level; the typical offering of the Google cloud resources and the interaction between the client and cloud server is at the application (app) level. Thus we have the classification of Google cloud as Software as a Service. The security strategy for the Google cloud is drawn from its experiences with its search and related businesses. Its cloud security strategy is clearly defined in 10 different components (*Google's Approach, 2013*) beginning with corporate security policies, to disaster recovery and business continuity. Google cloud model consists of popular applications such as Gmail, Google App Engine, Google Drive, Google Cloud Storage etc. Thus most of the accesses is at the application level and is controlled through user name and password authentication. These application level accesses implicitly provide the first line of defense against attacks from outside. Unlike AWS, native system attributes such as ports and operating systems are hidden behind the application. Internal interactions between the front-end and the back-end production systems are controlled by short-lived personal certificates issued by Google's internal certificate authority.

5.1 Google App Engine

We have chosen to discuss the security features of Google App Engine (among the many cloud services offered by Google) that allows for application deployment on the cloud. Besides the usual user authentication for the deployment of the application, it provides an elaborate monitoring dashboard as shown in Figure 6. This dashboard provides elaborate but an intuitive interface to the application monitoring for the business that deployed the application. For example Figure 6 shows the load curve, incoming and outgoing bandwidth and the number of requests etc. This allows a business to monitor any anomalous access patterns. The green band for the outgoing bandwidth in Figure 6 is indeed indicating that outgoing bandwidth has exceeded a predetermined

limit indicated by a black vertical line. This may indicate an anomaly that needs to be addressed. While Figure 6 is a peek into the operating of an application, Figure 7 shows the status of the cloud infrastructure element memcache. This figure is representative of the monitoring done by Google for possible anomalies in the normal behavior of the system. In this case, at the point A in the load curve, memcache becomes partially unavailable and the yellow exclamation point indicates that Google is investigating the reasons for this anomalous behavior. Thus a combination of authentication of the application user, monitoring by the business that deployed the application and the internal watch by Google provides a strong multi-level security for the applications deployed on the Google cloud.

5.2 Data Storage

AWS provides clear separation among the data from various sources. Google on other hand does not segregate among customers' data and Google's own data in the sense they are all stored in homogeneous machines in large data-centers managed by Google at various geographic locations. Thus the same security measures used for Google's own data secure customers' data and storage on the cloud. Unlike AWS users' access to the data and cloud storage is through applications that can ensure a further level of front-end security through isolation. Also the operating systems run on Google's servers is based on proprietary design and is a version of Linux customized for running Google applications with strict control over unauthorized modifications.

6. WINDOWS AZURE

Windows Azure model is really an extension of the Microsoft Windows environment to provide the cloud services. Windows Azure SDK for Visual Studio extends the basic Visual Studio and

Figure 6. Google App engine dashboard

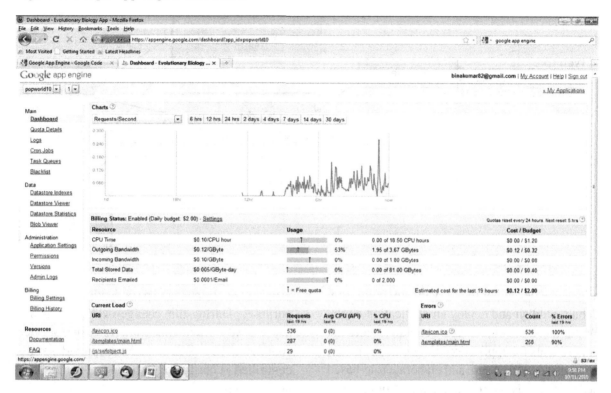

Figure 7.Memcache status and investigation

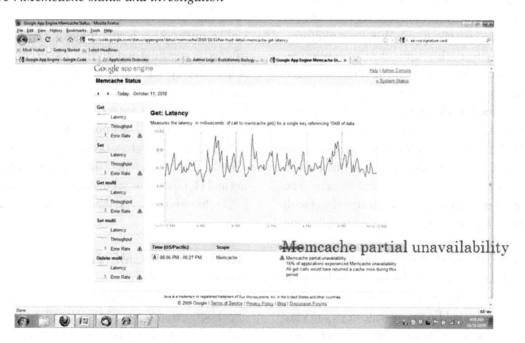

Figure 8. Components of Windows Azure cloud platform

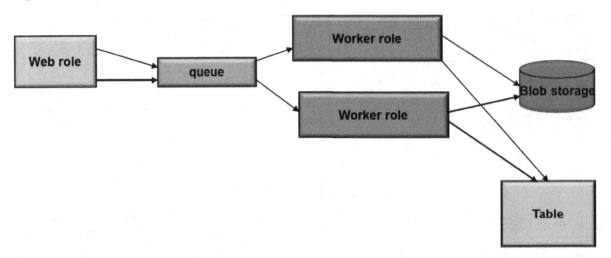

allows the developer to easily create, build, run, debug, publish and deploy an application on the Windows Azure cloud. Azure cloud provides the components for application development such as AppFabric, SQL Azure and elaborate role-based access methods. Various application components are defined by the platform: blobs, tables, queues and drives; various logical roles are provided for mapping the clients to the servers: web role and worker role. All these components make Azure cloud highly specific to the Windows platform. Windows Azure defines a platform for developing cloud applications for the existing Windows users, resulting in a Platform as a Service (PaaS). Of the three cloud models discussed in this chapter, Windows Azure is the most proprietary.

The first level of defense for accessing an application is the Windows Live ID as part of the federated identity management system. The developers use self-signed certificates along with Live ID. The cloud services are exposed using RESTful Web services.

As seen in Figure 8, the web role and the worker role provides the security by isolating the cloud resources from the applications. In accessing the cloud resources public key-private keys pairs are used. Two keys are generated one primary key and a secondary key. Primary key is the one used for normal access. However it is recommended that primary keys be changed periodically for security purposes. During this change-over a secondary key is used for authentication, to ensure service continuity. Thus Windows Azure provides well-controlled security for its cloud resources and applications.

7. SUMMARY

Unlike many other technologies for remote distributed computing and storage, cloud computing is here to stay, since it is founded on strong fundamentals. Cloud is democratizing computing by making computing accessible to masses just like any utility service. The impact of the cloud on the global society and global commerce is immense. Cloud is poised to change the way we do computing and IT. Given this scenario, securing the cloud is a technological as well as a social imperative.

ACKNOWLEDGMENT

This work is partially supported by the National Science Foundation grants NSF-DUE-CCLI-0920335 and NSF-OCI-CITEAM-1041280, and an educational grant from amazon.com.

REFERENCES

Amazon Web Services, Cloud Computing: Compute, Storage, Database. (n.d.). Retrieved April 2013 from http://aws.amazon.com/

App. Engine & Google Developers. (n.d.). Retrieved April 2013 from https://developers.google.com/appengine/

AWS Security and Compliance Center. (n.d.). Retrieved April 2013 from http://aws.amazon.com/security/

Berners-Lee, T. (2009). *Program integration across application and organizational boundaries*. Retrieved April 2013 from http://www.w3.org/DesignIssues/WebServices.html

Bishop, M. (2005). *Introduction to computer security*. Reading, MA: Addison-Wesley Professional.

Bosworth, S., Kabay, M., & Whyne, E. (2009). *Computer security handbook*. Hoboken, NJ: Wiley.

Case Studies. (n.d.). Retrieved April 2013 from https://aws.amazon.com/solutions/case-studies/

Chen, Y., Paxson, V., & Katz, R. (2010). *What's new about cloud computing security?* (Master's thesis). UC Berkeley, Berkeley, CA. Retrieved from www.eecs.berkeley.edu/Pubs/TechRpts/2010/EECS-2010-5.pdf

Fielding, R. (2000). *Architectural styles and the design of network-based software architectures*. (doctoral Dissertation).

Google Cloud Platform. (n.d.). Retrieved April 2013 from https://cloud.google.com/

Google's Approach to IT Security. (n.d.). Retrieved April 2013 from https://cloud.google.com/files/Google-CommonSecurity-WhitePaper-v1.4.pdf

Hess, K., & Newman, A. (2010). *Practical virtualization solutions: Virtualization from the trenches*. Upper Saddle River, NJ: Prentice Hall/Pearson Education.

ISO 27001: An Introduction to ISO 27001 (ISO27001). (n.d.). Retrieved April 2013 from http://www.27000.org/iso-27001.htm

Jennings, R. (2011). *Cloud computing with the Windows Azure platform*. Indianapolis, IN: Wiley.

Limitations of IPV4. (n.d.). Retrieved April 2013 from http://www.omnisecu.com/tcpip/ipv6/limitations-of-ipv4.htm

Reese, G. (2009). *Cloud application architectures: Building applications and infrastructure in the cloud*. Sebastopol, CA: O'Reilly.

Rhoton, J., & Haukioja, R. (2011). *Cloud computing architected*. New York: Recursive Press.

S3Fox Organizer. (n.d.). Retrieved April 2013 from http://www.s3fox.net/

Varia, J. (2011). *Architecting for the cloud: Best practices*. Retrieved from media.amazonwebservices.com/Whitepaper_Security_Best_Practices_2010.pdf

Zikopoulos, P., Eaton, C., Deutsch, T., Deroos, D., & Lapis, G. (2012). *Understanding big data: Analytics for enterprise class Hadoop and streaming data*. New York: McGraw-Hill.

Section 2
Regulatory and Industry Compliance

Chapter 7
Meeting Compliance Requirements while using Cloud Services

S. Srinivasan
Texas Southern University, USA

ABSTRACT

Compliance with government and industry regulations is an essential part of conducting business in several sectors. Many of the requirements revolve around financial, privacy, or security aspects. Most of the requirements are due to federal regulations in USA while some are industry requirements that are applicable globally. Even some of the federal regulations in USA apply to service providers abroad when they are providing service to entities in USA. In that sense, all of the compliance requirements discussed here apply to a global audience. In this chapter, the authors discuss in detail the scope of the Health Insurance Portability and Accountability Act, Sarbanes-Oxley Act, Federal Information Security Management Act, Gramm-Leach-Bliley Act, Payment Card Industry Requirements, and the Statement on Auditing Standards 70. These compliance requirements concern protecting the customer data stored in the cloud with respect to confidentiality and integrity. Several of these requirements have significant enforcement powers associated with them, and businesses need to take these requirements seriously and comply. The compliance aspect involves gathering and reporting appropriate information on a regular basis. The authors present details on all these aspects in this chapter.

1. INTRODUCTION

Many businesses are required to meet certain compliance requirements either by the government or by the industry in which they operate. For many years businesses were able to gather

the necessary data for compliance because they owned their IT system. With the popularity of cloud computing many businesses, both large and small which use cloud services, have to gather the necessary data in order to meet the compliance requirements. In this chapter we will identify the necessary compliance requirements and how businesses could meet those requirements with

DOI: 10.4018/978-1-4666-5788-5.ch007

respect to some of the major laws and industry requirements. These are: Health Insurance and Portability Act (HIPAA), Sarbanes-Oxley Act (SOX), Gramm-Leach-Bliley Act (GLBA), Federal Information Security Management Act (FISMA), Payment Card Industry (PCI), and Statement on Auditing Standards 70 (SAS 70). These requirements are put in place to provide adequate security and privacy for the data related to financial transactions, health care records, and credit cards. Some of these laws were enacted to address the abuse of trust placed in businesses. All the requirements specified in this chapter relate to laws and requirements in USA. Because of the worldwide reach of many multinational corporations in USA many of these laws and requirements extend beyond USA and are applicable in other countries as well when they relate to businesses in USA. Thus the implications of the use of the cloud services globally have implications when it is related to an American business.

Use of cloud services by its very design leaves the control of the computing infrastructure outside the control of the business using the cloud service. Many surveys have confirmed that this lack of control is a major concern for businesses when it comes to data security. Some technologies are better suited to protecting confidential information than others. Antonopoulos and Gillam discuss many of the fundamental issues associated with cloud computing in their book (Antonopoulos, 2010). Their book provides further amplification on many of the topics discussed in this book. Information Technology is a necessary conduit to facilitate business transactions of all kinds. Today businesses gather vast amounts of data effortlessly from every type of action an individual performs with a business. Some of these data may contain confidential information related to a person's health or financial standing. The various laws and industry requirements that we will discuss in this chapter address aspects related to privacy and security of such data. In many cases the requirements involve processes and data flow aspects

that businesses follow. For the cloud computing industry there is an international organization called Cloud Security Alliance (CSA) that offers guidelines and forums (Cloud Security Alliance, 2013). CSA is the leading industry supported group that provides guidelines to service providers and customers worldwide. Major corporations and government agencies that participate in CSA activities are: Amazon Web Services, Google, Microsoft, HP, Cisco, RSA, Rackspace, Oracle, US Department of Defense, and Salesforce.

Before analyzing the compliance aspects that we set out to discuss in this chapter, we discuss some of the important literature on this topic first. The growth of cloud computing is discussed in detail by Armbrust, et al in their View of Cloud Computing (Armbrust, 2010). One of the main contributions of this work is that cloud computing takes advantage of economies of scale in locating their data centers. Furthermore, many cloud providers depend on open source software since licensing models for commercial software are often a handicap for growth of cloud computing. In the influential paper "Hey, You, Get Off of My Cloud" the authors Ristenpart, Tromer, Schacham and Savage argue that the major risk in cloud computing is data co-location for multiple users. These authors recommend two ways to mitigate this risk by blocking network-based co-residence checks or a customer using all the virtual machines on a physical server irrespective of how much computing resource they need on a single server (Ristenpart, 2009). Since the growth of cloud computing is rapid, Sengupta, Kalgud and Sharma examine the security aspects in the cloud and the future research directions. Their analysis discusses the major concerns in cloud computing such as the physical security of the cloud providers' system, the way the cloud provider handles data in their servers and in backup systems, access control for the various cloud resources for the customer, and how the providers support compliance aspects (Sengupta, 2011). We conclude this brief review of current literature with the work of Yang and

Tate in which they categorize the contributions of nearly 150 research articles (Yang, 2012).

Our goal in this chapter is to present details on compliance required by federal laws and industry standards. We will discuss how a business must design its business processes in order to gather the necessary data for compliance requirements. In some cases the cloud service user must enter into a specific agreement with the cloud service provider in order to gather the necessary data. We will give examples of processes and technological approaches that will support meeting these compliance requirements. In the next several sections we will describe the major laws and industry requirements first and then follow it up in the last section about how to meet many of the compliance requirements when using a cloud based solution.

2. HIPAA

Health Insurance Portability and Accountability Act (HIPAA) was enacted in 1996 to address the health care challenges people face when they switch or lose jobs (HIPAA, 2013). In many instances the insurers were excluding people for a set period of time from coverage under the pre-existing clause for any type of medical condition. HIPAA was enacted to address this problem whereby the insurers were required to continue medical coverage for people for a set period of time under the same terms they were in when they switched or lost jobs. Thus, HIPAA facilitated mobility of people from one job to another as well as movement from one place to another without fear of job lock. Simultaneously, HIPAA added data security and privacy aspects when it came to dealing with a person's health data. First, HIPAA clearly delineated that the individual about whom the health data has been gathered must consent when the data is shared with others. Second, the organizations such as hospitals that gather health data of individuals must have verifiable processes to protect the data from being exposed to unau-

thorized people. Third, anyone collecting health care data about an individual must have a clear purpose for such collection. Any individual or organization violating these principles is subject to severe penalties. Even though HIPAA mandated that patients must consent to sharing their health data for any purpose, the USA PATRIOT Act that was enacted in the aftermath of the September 11, 2001 terrorist attacks exempted law enforcement from notifying or seeking permission of the patient when their health data was required for any investigative purposes. This Act, commonly referred to as the Patriot Act, stands for Uniting and Strengthening America by Providing Appropriate Tools Required to Intercept and Obstruct Terrorism. It was reauthorized in 2005 with some minor changes.

As discussed above, the principal scope of HIPAA is to protect and secure patient data. For this reason HIPAA violations are seriously prosecuted. Consequently, people dealing with HIPAA are adequately trained in handling sensitive data. One of the HIPAA requirements is that organizations that collect health care data about individuals must have a process to protect the data, its storage must be encrypted and any transmission of data to other parties must follow strict security protocols. Today many health care providers such as hospitals, pharmacies, laboratories and insurers are required to comply with HIPAA requirements and prove to their licensing bodies that they are compliant. In order to meet the compliance requirements organizations must gather data. When health care data is prepared for creating policies and procedures the data must de-identify the individual. When data is owned by the organization they will be in a better position to comply with these requirements. However when the data is stored in the cloud and transmitted over the internet, then meeting the compliance requirements are more challenging.

A major modification to the HIPAA rules were announced on January 25, 2013 in light of the introduction of electronic medical records and use of cloud services in health care. The changes proposed to the HIPAA rules under this revision are intended to enhance the Health Information Technology and is known as the HITECH Act. This stands for Health Information Technology for Economic and Clinical Health and was enacted in 2009 to take advantage of the technological capabilities to ensure sharing of health records as well as protecting the security and privacy of such data. These new rules clarify the responsible party for any HIPAA violation. A health care organization such as a hospital, pharmacy, laboratory or a health insurance company is known as the 'covered entity' under this rule. Organizations such as IT vendors who provide services to facilitate transmission and storage of electronic health data are known as 'business associates.' Under the 1996 HIPAA requirements only the covered entities were responsible for data security, privacy and protection unless they had an explicit arrangement with a vendor for these purposes. An analysis of the data breaches related to health data reveals that many of them happened with the loss of mobile devices such as laptops, flash drives and PDAs that were used by the business associates. Since the use of these types of devices is only growing more, the responsibility for data protection had to be identified clearly. With the advent of cloud computing, the modified rules hold the business associates responsible for protection of health data because they deal with much of the data processing. As mentioned before there is a severe penalty for any violation. For example, a business associate will be fined $1.5 million per violation under the modified rule as part of the HITECH Act. Moreover, the HITECH Act removes the exemption provided under the original HIPAA rules which allowed for revocation of penalties if the violations were corrected within a 30 day period. Given the severity of the penalties that many businesses would face, they have to take adequate protective measures to guard against any violation.

HIPAA rules require each covered entity to have written plans for:

1. disaster recovery
2. data backup
3. emergency mode operation

Besides these requirements, each covered entity should also take prudent steps to encrypt all protected health information both in transit and at rest, have access controls in place and an audit process to verify that these requirements are met. The audit results will be used in providing evidence for compliance requirements. These are considered prudent measures and assume that the covered entity has control over the information system infrastructure and storage. Given today's widespread use of cloud services organizations that use cloud services must have adequate measures to verify the compliance aspects related to these three expectations. We will address this aspect in greater detail later in this chapter in section 8.

The Electronic Medical Record (EMR) provision of HIPAA was intended to facilitate sharing of medical information among the various entities involved in providing health care to individuals (Federal Register, 2013). Often health records of individuals were held by the providers for their exclusive use. This practice prevented providing quality health care whereby certain parties in the health care loop needed additional information about the patients but were unable to obtain them in a timely manner. The availability of EMR facilitates storing the data related to a patient in a shareable database that other providers could access under proper access control. Cloud Computing is a natural conduit for this purpose. By using the cloud all providers will be able to load their data for a patient in a shareable database without having to have the necessary computing infrastructure to manage the complex computing system. In Europe such a centralized system exists for many years because each individual has a health identification card that has basic information about the individual and the use of this card enables health care providers around Europe to transfer health data for the patient to the central storage which then becomes available for other providers to use. In Europe's model the individual's health identification card serves the authentication purpose for accessing the confidential health data. In Europe such a model works well because of nationalized health care. For USA, the suitable method to share necessary health data is facilitated by the cloud services but the authentication part is still the responsibility of the customer who provides access to selected individuals.

When multiple providers start loading EMR data for individuals the volume of data stored in the database grows very rapidly. In order to process such volumes of data rapidly Google developed the MapReduce process. An open source implementation of MapReduce is Hadoop by Apache software. Many of the cloud solution providers in the medical field implement the Hadoop technology to handle large volumes of data. One of the major EMR providers is GE Health Care's Centricity program. MedCloud, in partnership with GE Health Care, provides a cloud based solution to physicians to implement EMR in their practices. The major benefits of this cloud based approach is the ability to get a robust service implemented quickly at a lower cost and not have the need to have an IT specialist on staff to manage the system. This Software as a Service (SaaS) solution provides the physicians with the necessary HIPAA certified system that is scalable. Other comparable high-end cloud based solutions for EMR are AdvancedMD, AthenaHealth and MedPlus.

3. SARBANES-OXLEY ACT (SOX)

Sarbanes-Oxley Act (SOX) was enacted in 2002 as a direct result of the financial abuses of companies like Enron, WorldCom, Tyco, and Xerox as well as external auditors like the Arthur Anderson

Company. All these companies, other than Xerox, went out of business because of direct financial fraud or abetting such action. SOX mandated strict compliance requirements for internal controls and accountability for all publicly traded companies. These compliance requirements have created a new set of businesses that specialize in helping organizations comply with SOX requirements. Businesses find the SOX compliance an expensive proposition. SOX compliance requires extensive record keeping and performing periodic audits. The general expectation for data retention for SOX compliance is five years. Because of the stringent requirements for compliance, financial frauds in publicly traded companies are going down. It is attributed that SOX compliance has cost businesses, especially small and medium sized business, significant sums of money without adequate return.

One of the requirements of SOX was the creation of Public Company Accounting Oversight Board responsible for developing audit report standards and rules and overseeing the audit of public companies. This was incorporated in the Act as a watchdog for potential false reporting by external auditors of publicly traded companies (SOX, 2002). In order to comply with SOX, companies had to gather data periodically to include in their reports. Gathering such data based on inventory, attempted breach of computing resources, possible loss of data, etc requires automated processes. For example, a Radio Frequency Identification (RFID) based inventory management system will be able to provide the necessary data quickly. Aspects related to attempted data breaches are gathered from log information. Since the SOX compliance requirements are multi-faceted there is need for plenty of different forms of data. So, a business should have the necessary processes to gather such data periodically. Collecting such data becomes somewhat easier if the organization controls the computing infrastructure. Since all aspects of SOX reporting are tied to extensive computerized record keeping, computer logs play an important role. When a business with a SOX compliance requirement uses a cloud based service for their computing services then they have to work with their service provider to obtain the necessary data for reporting purposes. We will address this aspect in detail in section 8 of this chapter.

Gathering the necessary data for SOX compliance is expensive for many businesses. Many new businesses that specialize in helping organizations with SOX compliance have developed systems and processes to gather the required data. This level of diversity in data gathering is a cause for concern as many businesses do not have the necessary financial resources to invest in the integration of multiple tools available. Thus the proposed solution to fix financial fraud in the form of SOX Act has the unintended consequence of affecting business growth as businesses are consumed by the compliance requirements. For this reason the Act was amended multiple times since its enactment to exempt certain types of businesses from the compliance requirements.

SOX Act applies to businesses in USA. Many of the businesses in USA also have subsidiaries or partners in other countries. Since the compliance requirements apply to all businesses in USA they are obligated to collect the necessary financial and other data from their overseas subsidiaries and partners. In this sense the scope of SOX Act extends beyond USA even though the enforcement powers and penalties are limited to USA. Like HIPAA discussed earlier, enforcement of SOX compliance requirements are very strict in order to maintain the public's trust in publicly traded companies. The significance of the Act lies in the fact that many other countries have also adopted compliance requirements similar to SOX to overcome the financial problems faced by many European countries.

4. GRAMM-LEACH-BLILEY ACT (GLBA)

Gramm-Leach-Bliley Act (GLBA) was enacted in 1999 as a result of large banks, financial services companies and insurance companies lobbying to repeal the prohibition of Glass-Steagall Act from mergers among these three entities. With the passage of GLBA banks and financial services companies were allowed to merge and develop new financial products. It is also known as the Financial Services Modernization Act. This Act was aimed at financial services companies that provided consumer loans, insurance products, or financial/investment advice to consumers to inform their customers of their data sharing practices, safeguarding of sensitive data and privacy protection policies. The three main sections of the Act are the Financial Privacy Rule, the Safeguards Rule and the Pretexting provisions (GLBA, 2006). All three of these sections are governed by compliance requirements. The Financial Privacy Rule places restrictions on what types of financial information an organization can collect and disseminate. The Safeguards Rule requires the financial institutions to have policies and procedures to protect the financial information of individuals that they collect. The Pretexting Rule prohibits an organization to collect information under false pretenses. Most organizations are required to provide compliance reports with regard to the Safeguards Rule.

The more visible implementation of Gramm-Leach-Bliley Act is the requirement that every organization disclose their privacy policies with regard to protection of any sensitive information that they collect and how they share it with other organizations. The scope of this bill was deregulatory in nature and so large financial houses were able to develop risky and creative financial products in the mid-2000s which resulted in the global financial meltdown in late 2008.

As a result, the Dodd-Frank Act was passed in 2010 to regulate the financial industry and set up oversight councils. Another important aspect of GLBA is section 501(b) which requires all financial institutions to adequately protect and secure all non-public personal information of their customers. Today, organizations find it easy to collect lot of non-public personal information about their customers based on their electronic footprint. Some of this information is gathered from Voice-over-IP (VoIP) transactions. This results in volumes of data being gathered about each customer. Both VoIP and Cloud Computing are two rapidly evolving fields that businesses see beneficial to them from a cost perspective. As part of GLBA compliance requirements businesses should carefully evaluate the risks posed by these new technologies since the laws often lag behind technological capabilities. As an example, consider the customer expectation to deposit a physical check with an electronic image of the check sent over the internet to the financial institution. This process is known as Remote Deposit Capture (RDC) and it deals with sensitive information in the form of images which contain confidential data such as customer bank account number. As part of the GLBA compliance the bank would be expected to show the types of internal controls it has in place to protect the RDC transaction. The type of controls developed for this process would come from the risk assessment that the bank conducts noting the ways in which the images are transferred to the banking center. This risk assessment is different from the organizational risk assessment of its data center which would be required as part of SOX compliance discussed earlier. Thus the main thrust of GLBA compliance would be to know that organizations should focus on information protection for each of its processes rather than counting on the capabilities of the technology.

5. FEDERAL INFORMATION SECURITY MANAGEMENT ACT (FISMA)

The Federal Information Security Management Act (FISMA) was enacted in 2002 with the aim of protecting all federal information systems. This Act applies only to federal systems. Since the federal government is a major player as a regulator in various areas such as transportation, banking and finance, utilities, commerce, etc the scope of this Act extends far and wide. This Act recognizes the significance of information security to economic and national security matters (FISMA, 2010). In order to strengthen the federal information security requirements, the National Institute of Standards and Technology (NIST) has been given the responsibility to develop the necessary procedures and policies to reduce the risks. NIST has developed extensive guidelines for federal information security, which would also apply to the private sector for information protection. We will discuss next the NIST information security guidelines.

NIST SP800-18 is a significant set of guidelines (NIST, 2006) for protecting federal information systems. As the first step, NIST requires all federal agencies to have an inventory of their information systems. Maintaining this inventory will enable the agency to identify the level of security and access restrictions each system must have in order to protect the overall security. As part of meeting the FISMA compliance requirements the Department of Homeland Security and the Department of Justice have developed the tool called CyberScope. This tool helps gather data in manual and automated manner related to IT Asset Inventory, System Configuration and Vulnerability Management. These are all essential to protecting all federal information systems. As a result of FISMA, in 2011 all Cabinet Departments provided automatic feed to CyberScope. It is worth noting that the US Congress is monitoring FISMA compliance as shown in the chart below

Figure 1. FISMA compliance by all cabinet departments in 2011
Note: *Developed from Office of Management and Budget, FISMA Compliance Report 2011*

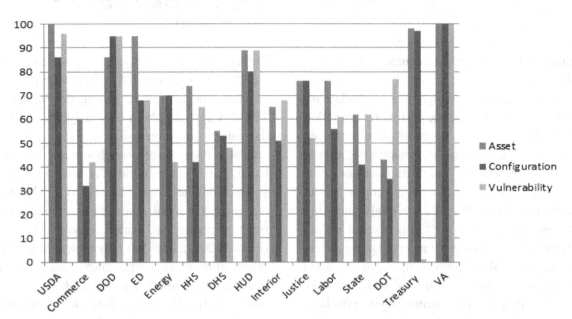

(Figure 1) (OMB, 2012). This chart shows the level to which each Cabinet Department is able to provide data feed to CyberScope in each of the three areas identified.

This analysis shows that because of FISMA the Treasury Department is able to note that their system is not able to generate the necessary data to verify compliance. So they need to devote the necessary resources and people to comply.

6. PAYMENT CARD INDUSTRY (PCI)

Payment Card Industry (PCI) standards are developed for the benefit of protecting consumer credit card data generated by thousands of businesses globally. This industry-led effort is managed by the PCI Security Standards Council, a global consortium of the five major credit card brands – Master Card, Visa, American Express, Discover, JCB (Japan Credit Bureau) International. The primary goal is to set compliance standards that must be followed by all merchants participating in

the credit card network. PCI compliance requirements apply to all members who accept credit cards either online or offline. The Data Security Standard (DSS) is the chief guideline from PCI to protect customer data (PCI, 2013). The type of compliance varies by size of business and the compliance requirements and penalties are administered by the individual payment brand such as MasterCard and Visa. The three main components of PCI DSS are Assess, Remediate and Report. The Assessment part involves knowing the systems used in processing credit card data. This assessment includes knowing the vulnerabilities of the system. The Remediate aspect requires the business to fix the vulnerabilities and at the same time take steps to collect only the required data. The Report feature is the compliance part and it involves submission of the periodic reports to the associated banks and card brands.

The main goal of PCI DSS is to prevent, detect and react to security incidents involving credit card processing. Most of the highly publicized violations such as the one involving the Heartland Payment Credit Card system occurred due to technical and process failures. In the case of Heartland Systems, which deals with over 175,000 merchants and 100 million credit card transactions per month, the breach occurred in 2008. This is not an isolated case. According to PrivacyRights.Org more than 510 million records have been breached since 2005. That is why PCI-DSS implementation is critical to businesses and monitoring compliance of the PCI requirements is essential. In order to address the vulnerabilities the merchants should take steps to secure the point-of-sale system, store data securely and allow only encrypted communications from their hotspots. The last one may pose a problem to customers but they should be required to have the suitable API in order to use the hotspot. For example, if the hotspot is from Starbucks then the hotspot user should have the necessary API with encryption enabled. At present the hotspot recommendation above is not mandated by PCI and as such is a potential vulnerability in the payment processing system.

PCI security involves building a firewall that restricts all traffic from untrusted nodes and networks. Another requirement is the prohibition of direct access from the Internet and any system that holds card holder data. In spite of the recommendation from PCI to store only the necessary data, a survey by Forrester Consulting shows that businesses hold a variety of data as follows:

Credit card numbers 81%
Credit card expiration dates 73%

Card verification codes 71%
Customer data 57%

Businesses store such data to facilitate customer ease of use of their system. Unfortunately this practice opens up the possibility for hackers to steal sensitive information about credit cards. Businesses that follow any of these practices should be required to encrypt all stored data. Given the periodic breach of credit card data, the enforcement of PCI DSS standards compliance appears to be inadequate.

PCI DSS contains 12 requirements. Even though each of these requirements is significant in offering the necessary protection to the credit card transaction, Requirement 9 especially requires the business to restrict access to customer data that they store. This is a very basic requirement in any asset that is being protected. When the business loses control over the storage of that asset because of choice of technology such as cloud computing, then the business should have adequate measures to validate that such data is being protected by the cloud service provider. There is not enough case law to know where the liability would rest. Just as we emphasized in the GLBA section, the business should assess the risks in each of their processes when it comes to capturing and storing sensitive data. Another expectation from PCI DSS is that each business must change the default password provided by the equipment vendor in order to access the internal system or to communicate data to the transaction authorization system.

Table 1. PCI data storage guideline

Type of Data	Data Storage Permitted	Encryption Required
Credit card number	Yes	Yes
Cardholder Name	Yes	No
Expiration Date	Yes	No
Card Verification Value	No	n/a
Full magstripe data	No	n/a
PIN	No	n/a

Every business using a PCI system must have a data retention policy that is consistent with legal requirements and purge unwanted data periodically. Table 1 shows which data could be stored and which data should be encrypted when stored.

We discussed above some of the data storage restrictions associated with PCI DSS compliance. In addition to the above requirements, PCI compliance requires the business to restrict physical access to data storage devices, logical access to data content and have an audit trail to track data access. Further, the business organization must have policies for secure data backup, data breach notification and incident response plan.

7. STATEMENT ON AUDITING STANDARDS 70 (SAS 70)

Statement on Auditing Standards 70 (SAS 70) was developed by the American Institute of Certified Public Accountants (AICPA) in 1993. It is a comprehensive audit of the procedures and controls used by an organization and this audit is widely recognized. There are two types of SAS 70 audits – Type I and Type II. Type I Audit is performed for a specific point in time and is usually a precursor to a Type II audit which is more exhaustive (SAS, 2013). Type II audit closely follows many of the Internal Control requirements mentioned in the Sarbanes-Oxley Act. This audit also meets the compliance requirements associated with Health Insurance Portability and Accountability Act and Gramm-Leach-Bliley Act. The SAS 70 Audit does not follow a checklist for audit; instead it relies on the AICPA's standards for field work, quality control and reporting requirements. The audit report is the considered opinion of the auditor on processes as well as financial controls in place in the organization. Because of this type of freedom that the auditor has the SAS 70 Audit reports have wide variance in their reporting. The mere fact that a service provider underwent a SAS 70 Type II Audit does not mean anything in particular

with respect to the sufficiency or reliability of the controls the organization has. The onus is on the business planning to use the services of the provider by examining the audit report for conclusions and recommendations of the auditor.

Type I Audit is limited in scope and less expensive for the organization. However, its results are not sufficient to meet the compliance requirements of SOX, HIPAA and GLBA. An organization that has not had an external audit about their internal financial controls will benefit from a Type I Audit. Type II Audit is more exhaustive and expensive for an organization. The Auditor would benefit from a Type I Audit report as it would have helped the organization prepare all the necessary internal compliance reports that would form part of the Type II Audit report. In Type II Audit the Auditor tests and reports on the operating effectiveness based on tests done over a six month period. This exhaustive report is widely accepted and its findings support the organization's claims on meeting the necessary compliance requirements.

When some service providers, be it on the cloud or VoIP or something similar, follow the path of SAS 70 Type II Audit for compliance, it only means that the provider meets many of the auditing standards for compliance which are widely recognized. This vendor compliance would not absolve any client of their responsibility in meeting the specific compliance requirements that are expected for their line of business. We will discuss this in greater detail relative to cloud computing in the next section.

8. SUPPORT FOR COMPLIANCE REQUIREMENTS IN CLOUD SERVICES

Cloud services are becoming popular because of the flexibility it offers. It is especially attractive for small and medium sized businesses because of the cost savings it offers and the high level of computing service that they would be able to afford. Simultaneously businesses are expected to meet certain compliance requirements depending on their line of business. As we discussed in the previous sections there are federal laws that mandate certain levels of compliance with regard to protecting customer information, affording customer privacy for the data that they collect and meeting certain industry standards. In this section we will explore in detail the benefits and drawbacks relative to meeting the necessary compliance requirements.

In this section we highlight the compliance provisions supported by the major cloud service providers. Amazon Web Services (AWS) is the largest cloud service provider globally and they support the computing requirements for small, medium and large businesses (Amazon Web Services, 2013). They offer all three types of cloud services – SaaS, PaaS and IaaS. For compliance purposes our focus would be on AWS' ability to provide the cloud customers the necessary means to gather the required compliance data in an automated manner for their public cloud offerings. As a first step, AWS is SAS 70 Type II compliant. This helps organizations in meeting their HIPAA and SOX compliance. Other major providers such as Google, Microsoft and Salesforce are also SAS 70 Type II audit compliant. All these providers enable the customers to gather the necessary compliance data in an automated manner, which is key to meeting the compliance requirements. Moreover, this frees up the cloud service providers from devoting their time and effort to gather the necessary compliance data for their customers.

HIPAA compliance requirements apply to all organizations that provide health related services. Both HIPAA and HITECH Acts support electronic storage, access and retrieval of patients' health data. Because of the sensitive nature of the information being handled all users that come in contact with health data are expected to be HIPAA certified so that they understand the requirements of the law and the penalties that apply when the law is violated. The law's requirements, when

enacted, assumed that the organization had the ability to control the resources in order to comply with the requirements. Over the past decade newer technologies have evolved that are changing the way people access their personal data and where organizations keep the data. In this context cloud computing and mobile devices have added many layers of complexity in meeting the HIPAA requirements. We will now explore the benefits and constraints that cloud computing presents in meeting the HIPAA compliance requirements.

Hospitals, health clinics, laboratories, pharmacies, insurance companies, and physicians are all expected to comply with HIPAA requirements as part of their business license. All these entities note the benefits that a cloud service provider offers, especially with regard to system availability, remote accessibility, demand elasticity and usage based cost. Depending on the size of the business entity the cloud service chosen varies. The simplest of these services is Software as a Service (SaaS) where the cloud service provider provides all infrastructure and software applications. In this type of service the client simply focuses on their core strengths and benefits from the service provided by the cloud service provider. The total control on hardware, storage of data, backup and security of software applications rests with the service provider. The customer is responsible for providing the necessary access credentials to their users and the service provider is responsible only to validate the access credentials for authentication. The service provider will have no knowledge of the sensitivity of the data being stored and so will not be able to provide any differentiated data protection. So the service provider would not feel responsible for any compliance requirements with regard to the data generated, stored and transmitted through their systems. Given this type of different expectations from the customer and service provider with regard to security, it is important to spell out appropriate responsibilities in the contract for service. In cloud contracts, customer is the "data controller" and the service provider is the "data processor." So, the obligations of the data processor are less compared to the data controller. This understanding is reflected in the Ponemon Institute study. The 2013 Ponemon Institute Study reported that majority of cloud service providers felt that it is not their responsibility to protect customer data (Ponemon, 2013).

We discussed above the SaaS service where the customer would lack control on many of the infrastructure aspects with regard to compliance. There are two other types of services – Platform as a Service (PaaS) and Infrastructure as a Service (IaaS). In PaaS the customer has slightly more control over the system they choose for cloud service and in IaaS the customer has lot more control over the system. In order for meeting the compliance requirements the customer must have plenty of visibility on the controls that the cloud service provider has in place. The importance of compliance for the customer is reinforced by a Cloud Security Alliance survey about the leading constraints on cloud adoption. In this survey, based on a scale of 1 to 5, customers ranked the significance of their ability to meet regulatory compliance at 4.01, which had the ranking of 4 out of 11(Cloud Security Alliance, 2013). Also, the customer must have trust in the ability of the service provider to offer privacy and security. It takes time to build this trust. Cloud customers must evaluate the risks to their clients before deciding to use cloud services. One way to protect client data would be to encrypt all transactions and store the keys locally while storing the encrypted data on the cloud for the flexibility it offers. This bifurcated approach requires additional processing capabilities before accessing the stored data. Often customers are attracted to the cloud by the benefits and flexibility it offers. Customers should also evaluate the security aspects prior to making a commitment to use cloud services. This can be accomplished by evaluating third party reports such as SAS 70 Type II Audit report and ISO 27001 certification achieved by the cloud provider.

One of the large companies that has been very successful in providing cloud service is Salesforce. It specializes in Customer Relations Management (CRM) over the cloud. Since its introduction nearly 15 years ago it has grown into a very mature organization that provides its customers several ways to meet their compliance requirements. To start with, Salesforce is SAS 70 Type II certified. The privacy protection provisions for customer data that Salesforce offers supports compliance requirements of GLBA and HIPAA. Many businesses try to leverage their social media presence and it adds another layer of requirement for compliance especially with respect to data protection. Salesforce has a service similar to LinkedIn called Chatter that is integrated with its main CRM product offering in the cloud (Salesforce, 2013). The significance of Chatter is that it enables the users to capture and archive all customer communications automatically in order to meet their compliance requirements. Salesforce partners with other third party providers so that their encryption service is available to their customers in order to meet the compliance requirements of FISMA, PCI, GLBA and HITECH.

Compliance with laws and industry standards strengthens a company's information processing capabilities and offers protection under liability claims. In this regard the compliance requirements extend beyond the country or region for which the compliance requirements apply. We have already identified the impact of SOX beyond USA. In a similar manner, the US-EU Safe Harbor agreements and the International Safe Harbor Privacy Principles extend the scope of the compliance requirements beyond these regions. It is worth noting that many of these compliance aspects are discussed in detail by Chaput and Ringwood in their article on Cloud Compliance (Chaput, 2010).

Often compliance expectations assume that the organization that owns the data is responsible for protecting the data. In the traditional computing models organizations controlled the location where they stored the data. In cloud computing, be it SaaS, PaaS, or IaaS, the cloud service provider may not be able to provide the physical location of the data since they have their data centers distributed around the world, with backup systems equally spread out. For this reason it will be very difficult for the cloud customer needing data location information for compliance purposes to certify about physical security of data storage and backup systems. So, the cloud customer must obtain this information prior to finalizing a cloud service provider for their needs. During this phase of the evaluation the customer should try to obtain peer assessments of the service provider's ability to provider compliance data. This might also require the service provider to identify potential references. Even though this might be helpful, lack of an external reference should not be considered as negative as many businesses may not be willing to take time to answer questions from other businesses. What is more important for a customer to know is what happens to their data at the end of the contract and what type of Service Level Agreement (SLA) that they could expect from the service provider regarding data availability. The customer should be told when their data would be purged from the provider's storage at the end of their contract and how the provider will facilitate transfer of all data to another service provider chosen by the customer. This transfer aspect should spell out any costs associated with the data transfer and the bandwidth that the service provider would be able to dedicate. Many businesses fail to work out the details at the beginning of their contract on these aspects as the customers accumulate large volumes of data, often in peta bytes, over a period of time. The following hypothetical scenario is worth noting as an example in this respect. Company AllForAll contracts with a major cloud service provider for SaaS service and stores all data generated over one year with the provider. During the period of the one year contract AllForAll's data storage has reached one peta byte. At the end of the contract AllForAll plans to move to a different service

provider and asks the service provider to transfer all their data. Service provider offers a rate plan with three different tiered pricing as follows:

Based on this hypothetical data transfer rate availability and cost by the service provider, the time and money it will take AllForAll to move their data to a new service provider would be as follows:

The analysis shown in Tables 2 and 3 are intended to show that there is a significant cost and time involved when a customer decides to move from one provider to another. Providers do not make it easy for customers to move by using proprietary storage solutions for storage. This aspect is known as *stickiness* in spite of touting the fact that the cloud service is pay-as-you-go model and there is no requirement for any long term contract for the service or the level of service. The primary reason for stickiness being a potential problem is the lack of universal standards for data storage in the cloud.

In our analysis of cloud services relative to compliance requirements we have identified some key issues that a cloud customer must be aware of prior to switching to cloud service. In this regard another important question to be answered by the service provider is the access to customer data in case the service provider goes out of business. This is achieved by having access to data backup systems for the customer. Cloud computing is evolving rapidly and there is no standard yet that customers could rely on for meeting their compliance requirements. Since cloud computing uses distributed resources there is even more uncertainty and lack of control for cloud customers regarding the physical security of the system. From the service provider perspective any time that they have to perform a manual operation to gather the necessary data for the customer, it is expensive.

Cloud service providers would benefit from having a lot of automation in their systems so that they can provide log data in an automated manner to the customer. The internal control processes

Table 2. Hypothetical data transfer rate and cost

Tier Level	Data Transfer Rate	Transfer Cost
1	10 GB/s	$0.15 / GB
2	100 GB/s	$3 / 100GB
3	500 GB/s	$25 / 500GB

Table 3. AllForAll Company estimated time and cost for 1 petabyte data transfer

Tier Level	Time Required to Transfer all Data	Cost of Data Transfer
1	≈ 1 day + 4 hrs.	$15,000
2	≈ 2 hrs. + 50 mts.	$30,000
3	≈ 34 mts.	$50,000

that the service provider has initiated should be transparent to the customers. Cloud service providers have built-in automated processes for acquiring and releasing additional computing or storage resource on demand. They have to leverage the expertise gained from this process to provide enough transparency in systems processing so that the customers can meet their varying compliance requirements. In this context it is worth noting the dilemma faced by service providers with regard to knowing the value of any data stored by the customers. Given the level of automation expected by the customers, it will be impossible for the service provider to know which data needs higher level of protection. This is one reason why many service providers think that they are not responsible for security and privacy of customer data.

Small and medium sized organizations may use cloud services in a big way but their resource requirements are much less when compared to enterprise level organizations. In many large organizations, given the nature of budgeting, internal controls and approval processes, many units within the organization find it easy to subscribe to cloud services for specialized needs. Since cloud computing is still an evolving technology, enterprises do not have a centralized approval process for subscribing to cloud services by in-

dividual units within the organization. At present the practice in many organizations is such there is a mushrooming of subscriptions to cloud services because it is easy to subscribe to specialized SaaS applications that the business unit needs. This practice has resulted in disparate data that does not integrate well between applications. This problem has been identified as the result of Cloud Identity Management (CIM). CIM has become a focus in many large enterprises because the security offered by the enterprise firewall is no longer available when people in the enterprise use cloud services as needed without getting clearance from a central group in the enterprise. Many large organizations have noticed this problem and are instituting centralized approval processes for all cloud services. As a result of this effort large organizations have noticed that many of the specialized requests for cloud services could be met internally. A related effort in this regard is discussed later as a standardization process initiated by the Internet Engineering Task Force.

Another important cloud service is data backup. Cloud backup requires an automated process. Furthermore, the customer should have automated validation that the backup succeeded. Users also have the ability to require on-demand backup of sensitive data. Companies providing the backup service to customers should provide the end user to have access to log data that is compiled at the end of the backup process. Federal regulations require record maintenance for a certain period of time based on the type of data being stored. Cloud service provides the ability to maintain a large amount of such information as needed. One of the compliance requirements involves proof of data archival which the customer should be able to obtain from the cloud provider as part of their general archival process. Backup is only a part of the backup and recovery system that is required under HIPAA. As mentioned earlier the backup process is automated. The recovery process on the other hand is on-demand and it does not require any manual handling by the cloud service provider. The end user should be able to select the file or folder for recovery and they will be decrypted and restored to the location of choice.

Some of the compliance requirements involve the type of documentation that the cloud service provider would be able to provide. This involves the cloud service provider providing a successful completion of SAS 70 Type II Audit for their system. Another type of audit information that would be useful for the customer is the OCR (Office of Civil Rights) Audit result that the service provider could provide their customers in order to show evidence of privacy protection. The customer could then use this information in their compliance reporting requirement.

Next, we look at some of the major applications that many organizations, both large and small, use. One such is Google Apps. It is a SaaS application that many businesses use. As we pointed out earlier SaaS, in general, lacks support for many compliance requirements. Noting the importance to customers of the ability to capture the relevant data for compliance, the CloudLock feature in Google Apps provides the ability to documenting SOX compliance with information protection. Google Docs is one component of Google Apps and is used by approximately 20% of users according to an IDC Study. This application provides the tools to gather usage statistics relative to the Disclosure Controls (Section 302) and Internal Controls (Section 404) of SOX. In Table 4 we show the ways in which Section 302 and Section 404 reporting requirements of SOX are met by Google Docs.

The discussion so far in this section points to the fact that compliance standards require all components in the system support one or more aspects of compliance. Taking a holistic approach to compliance, the methods discussed so far are focused on each component in a larger system being compliant and the burden of proof resting with the system provider. Microsoft Corporation is trying a new approach to compliance in the cloud whereby the compliance is demonstrated at the platform level and each user who uses an application on the platform validates their application for compliance. This way the platform provider is able to provide a master compliance document and all applications are individually able to provide their fit with the platform for compliance (Microsoft, 2012). At a practical level, Microsoft Azure cloud service provides

Table 4. Google Docs support for SOX reporting requirements

SOX Section	Google Docs Support
302	CloudLock Access Management System provides file access privileges for all files in the domain for all users in an automated manner. Also, there is additional alert capability to approve access to sensitive data. IT can set access control and file sharing policies in Google Docs usage. Any deviation from the policies will result in an alert being sent to IT.
404	CloudLock Security Policy Engine will alert IT based on deviation from Acceptable Use Policies. This data will be useful in security audit reporting.

strict compliance data for clinical trials of new drugs. This is achieved by providing access to various databases developed by National Institutes of Health (NIH) using the Azure platform whereby the cloud customer could test their innovative solutions for drug discovery. Since the Azure platform is SAS 70 Type II Audit, FISMA, HIPAA and ISO 27001 certified, any application that uses the Azure platform has to provide compliance data for the application specific activities only, which the customer should be able to gather based on their use of the application. Thus, shifting the compliance requirement from the building blocks to the platform level facilitates compliance aspects on the cloud.

In many parts of the discussion on cloud computing so far we have alluded to the concern of customers about security in the cloud. This is a natural concern because the customer does not have control over the infrastructure or storage of data in the cloud. Depending on the type of service they choose such as SaaS, PaaS, or IaaS, the customer has varying levels of control on the applications that they deploy in the cloud. For this reason we raised the issue of who is liable to protect the customer data – the service provider or the customer. Earlier in this section we identified the reasoning of the provider, based on the Ponemon Institute study, that the provider does not have the necessary information to know the level of protection to be afforded different data that are stored in the cloud. This is one piece of information that the customer would need for meeting compliance requirements. However, the service provider is at an advantage when it comes to protecting centralized hardware and software since the customer may not be able to afford the level of protection that a cloud service provider could afford based on the economies of scale. In this context we highlight the role of Simple Customer Identity Management (SCIM) which is being discussed by the Internet Engineering Task Force (IETF), the agency responsible for internet standards. SCIM is focused towards large

Table 5. Summary of allowed actions for resources in SCIM

Resource	Allowed Action
User	Retrieve, Add, Modify users
Group	Retrieve, Add, Modify groups
Service Provider	Retrieve the service provider's configuration

enterprises. SCIM would help a lot in meeting compliance requirements of HIPAA, SOX, GLBA, FISMA, PCI and SAS 70 in that the organization that allows access to their data controls who would get that access. The SCIM model has three important components:

1. Service provider holds the identity information for allowing access to resources
2. Customer using SCIM protocol manages the identity data used by service provider
3. Resources are service provider managed entities that have attributes

It is clear from this model that the service provider's role is limited to managing access to resources on the cloud for users that the customer authorizes and manages. This division of responsibility is enforceable and attributable in audit. In Table 5 we summarize the actions allowed for each resource.

We have discussed several compliance aspects in this section. One of the compliance requirements deals with how secure the data would be in the cloud for any customer. Al-Aqrabi et al studied this aspect and found out the availability of Unified Threat Management (UTM) approach to protect systems and facilitate compliance. From a theoretical perspective this concept works well but in practice UTM is found to degrade service quality. Also, UTM at times becomes a bottleneck for organizations (Al-Aqrabi, 2012). Consequently UTM approach may not the right solution for businesses to meet the compliance requirements for security.

We conclude this section with the observation that in order to meet the compliance requirements for services on the cloud each customer must understand what the service provider could provide. For example, the cloud service provider would be responsible for the physical security of the cloud system and would manage the customer access restrictions set by the customer. The cloud service provider must have the ability to provide in an automated manner access to service logs and compliance audit data for each customer that requires it. The customer should work with the application vendors as to the level of compliance that is expected of the application in order to meet their own compliance requirements either for the federal laws in effect or the industry standards.

9. SUMMARY

In this chapter we have examined the compliance requirements for using cloud services by businesses both with respect to federal laws as well as industry standards. In particular, we described the main aspects of each of the federal laws related to Health Care (HIPAA and HITECH), financial services (SOX, GLBA), federal information security (FISMA) and industry standards (SAS 70 and PCI). Then we discussed in greater detail the various issues associated with compliance for services on the cloud and highlighted how sometimes the old paradigm of a party responsible for data is responsible for its protection from abuse may not be applicable when it comes to cloud services. In this context we were able to bring to the discussion the different view points from different stakeholders. Overall, compliance is important and both the federal laws and industry standards should keep up with the changes in technology in order to identify the responsible party for security and privacy of customer data.

REFERENCES

Al-Aqrabi, H., et al. (2012). Investigation of IT security and compliance challenges in security-as-a-service for cloud computing. In *Proceedings of IEEE 15ʰ International Symposium on OCS Workshops*, (pp. 124-129). IEEE.

Amazon Web Services. (2013). Retrieved from http://aws.amazon.com/

Antonopoulos, N., & Gillam, L. (2010). *Cloud computing: Principles, systems and applications*. London: Springer. doi:10.1007/978-1-84996-241-4

Armbrust, M. et al. (2010). A view of cloud computing. *Communications of the ACM, 53*(4), 50–58. doi:10.1145/1721654.1721672

Chaput, S. R., & Ringwood, K. (2010). Cloud compliance: A framework for using cloud computing in a regulated world. In *Cloud computing* (pp. 241–256). London: Springer. doi:10.1007/978-1-84996-241-4_14

Cloud Security Alliance. (2013). Retrieved from http://www.cloudsecurityalliance.org

Federal Register. (2013, January 25). *HIPAA Privacy, Security, Enforcement and Breach Notification Rules, 78*(17), 5566-5702.

FISMA. (2010). Retrieved from http://www.dhs.gov/federal-information-security-management-act-fisma

GLBA. (2006). Retrieved from http://business.ftc.gov/privacy-and-security/gramm-leach-bliley-act

Goolge Apps. (2013). Retrieved from http://www.google.com/intl/en/enterprise/apps/business/

HIPAA. (2013). Retrieved from http://www.hhs.gov/ocr/privacy/

Microsoft. (2012). *Guiding principles and architecture for addressing life science compliance in the cloud*. Redmond, WA: Microsoft.

NIST. (2006). *Guide for developing security plans for federal information systems*. Gaithersburg, MD: National Institute for Standards and Technology.

OMB. (2012). *FISMA compliance report to US congress for 2011*. Washington, DC: Office of Management and Budget.

PCI. (2013). Retrieved from https://www.pcisecuritystandards.org/security_standards

Ponemon. (2013). *Security of cloud computing users*. Ponemon Institute Study.

Ristenpart, T., Tromer, E., Schacham, H., & Savage, S. (2009). Hey, you, get off of my cloud: Exploring information leakage in third-party compute clouds. In *Proceedings of the 16th ACM Conference on Computer and Communications Security*, (pp. 199-212). ACM.

Salesforce. (2013). Retrieved from http://www.salesforce.com

SAS. (2013). Retrieved from http://sas70.com

Sengupta, S., Kaulgud, V., & Sharma, V. S. (2011). Cloud computing security – Trends and research directions. In *Proceedings of IEEE World Congress on Services*, (pp. 524-531). IEEE.

SOX. (2002). Retrieved from http://www.soxlaw.com

Yang, H., & Tate, M. (2012). A descriptive literature review and classification of cloud computing research. *Communications of AIS*, *31*(2), 35–60.

Chapter 8
Risk Management in the Cloud and Cloud Outages

S. Srinivasan
Texas Southern University, USA

ABSTRACT

Cloud computing is facilitated often through the open Internet, which is not designed for secure communications. From the cloud user perspective, access to the cloud through a Virtual Private Network (VPN) is a possibility, but this is not the default access method for all cloud users. Given this reality, the cloud service users must be prepared for risk management because they do not control the cloud hardware or the communication channels. Added to this uncertainty is the potential for cloud service outage for risk management planning. In this chapter, the authors discuss the various aspects of risk management from the cloud user perspective. In addition, they analyze some of the major cloud outages over the past five years that have resulted in loss of trust. This list includes the outages in Amazon Web Services, Google, Windows, and Rackspace.

1. INTRODUCTION

Cloud computing is designed to operate over the internet. The internet is not designed with security in mind. All cloud users when they give up control over their hardware, software and data still have the obligation to protect the security of their data.

Any loss or compromise of their data will result in major business consequences. Added to this uncertainty is the loss of access to their information systems because of outage at the cloud service providers. In the case of major providers such as Amazon Web Services, Google and Rackspace the outages are rare. By the same token, any brief outage in the availability of cloud services is a major problem for the cloud customers. Major cloud service providers build-in various layers

DOI: 10.4018/978-1-4666-5788-5.ch008

of redundancy in storage as well as computing power. Yet, sometimes they fail in their efforts to provide uninterrupted service. Over the past five years there have been several well publicized outages of cloud services. Our goal in this chapter is to analyze the risk management aspects in the cloud and connect it with how cloud outages erode trust among users.

The risk management concept requires the user to control the resources that they are trying to use and protect. The research literature discusses risk management from various perspectives. The core of cloud computing relies on resource sharing and multi-tenancy. This means that the cloud service provider such as Amazon is able to provide service to numerous customers using large servers. Major risk factors arise when there is multi-tenancy because data belonging to one customer could accidentally be accessed by an application running on another customer's virtual server. One obvious solution is to limit multi-tenancy. It is not possible for majority of cloud users. The concept of Virtual Private Cloud (VPC) provides a solution for this risk factor but it is an expensive solution. Moreover, it defeats the economies of scale that the cloud offers in keeping the cost low for many cloud users. The risk management applies both to the cloud user and the cloud provider. The cloud provider aims to bolster trust among its users by putting in place mechanisms that lead to compliance certification from external agencies such as SAS70 Type II Audit compliance, FISMA, and PCI-DSS compliance.

Gartner's report points out that a major source of risk for customers stem from Software as a Service (SaaS) application (Gartner Report, 2013a). When customers contract for this type of service they are dissatisfied with the level of guarantee on data protection that the provider is able to offer. The major risk for the cloud customer comes from the data comingling aspect. Moreover, the outages in the provider services lead to lack of trust. To overcome these concerns the cloud service provider should be able to provide

the cloud customer with an annual audit of their security practices and third party validation of their controls. Another important data that the cloud customer could use comes from the Cloud Security Alliance's recommendation for a Cloud Controls Matrix that the provider could share with the customers. The Cloud Controls Matrix contains recommended goals for risk management from several cloud customers.

2. RISK MANAGEMENT

Risk is defined as the likelihood that an event will occur that affects the ability to achieve certain goals. With this definition of risk, we can classify the risks as pertaining to system availability, data integrity, system performance and security in general. When a customer uses a cloud service their major risk is with respect to the cloud system availability. In the next section we have addressed some of these aspects to show certain metrics that the customer can evaluate about the service provider's obligations for system uptime. When the service provider is unable to maintain the level of uptime promised then it leads to multiple risks for the customer. Risk management involves having processes to handle these types of risks.

From the customer perspective, managing the risk associated with system availability involves using more than one cloud service provider. For example, the customer could use one cloud service provider for all primary functions but use another service provider for cloud backup. This way, when the main service provider's system is not up then the customer could access their data from the other service provider where the backup data is stored. Theoretically this is feasible but from a practical perspective it is more complex and expensive. The customer must have a way of disk mirroring all activities on the main service provider's system onto the backup service provider. One way to handle simultaneous storage of data among two different providers is to use a peering system. Such solutions exist but are often too costly for most organizations.

Cloud customers evaluating risks should consider four aspects with respect to risk management. These are: Avoidance, Mitigation, Sharing, and Acceptance. Avoidance requires the customer to take prudent steps to avoid the risk. With cloud computing, the choices available to the customer are either very minimal or costly. In many cases it has to do with the type of service used such as SaaS. Since most customers use SaaS in a public cloud environment the best risk management strategy is to be aware of the risks and try to mitigate those risks. The mitigation strategy is one that most customers should be able to follow. There is no single approach to risk mitigation. It depends on the nature of risk and the method has to be developed for that particular method. For example, when one has the need to share health data the mitigation strategy could be to use an alternative communication method. Given the public nature of cloud services, sharing risk is one of the best options for many customers. In this case, by explicit contract, the customer is able to share their risk in storing data with the CSP. For their part, the CSP assures the customer that their data will not be released to third party without customer consent or notification, depending on the nature of the need for data disclosure. The final risk management strategy is to accept that certain risks are essential in order for them to do business. For example, when a small or medium sized business contracts with a third party payroll service provider such as ADP, they accept the inherent risk that ADP could lose control of the customer data.

In the above paragraph we discussed four types of risks that customers face. Additional risks that organizations face when using the cloud include co-location of their data with other businesses. This process alone leads to data integrity issues because certain updates might not occur on the customer's instances on the cloud. To overcome this risk the customer could subscribe to a private cloud. Private clouds are more expensive compared to public clouds. So, managing this type of risk is not affordable for most cloud customers.

Cloud services are slowly maturing in spite of the lack of global standards. Cloud services are global in nature and so there should be global standards to provide assurances to the customers. Such a development will greatly enhance risk management for many customers. Based on our analysis of the existing cloud practices we have developed a set of recommendations below for consideration by the cloud customer community. Similar details are found in the European Report titled "Cloud Computing: Benefits, risks and recommendations for information security" (European Report, 2009) and the COSO report titled "Enterprise Risk Management for Cloud Computing" (COSO, 2012).

1. Cloud customers need guarantee that the Cloud Service Providers (CSPs) are following good security practices to mitigate risks (e.g., monitor DDOS attacks on servers)
2. Cloud provides an attractive target for attackers to have the greatest impact
3. Concentration of data in the cloud offers many governments the opportunity to access vast amounts of data easily (e.g., NSA ability to collect phone records)
4. Sound policies against governments' ability to require access to data in the cloud must be developed
5. In order to enhance customer trust, customers must be aware of such policies and assurances from CSPs against unauthorized sharing of data with governments
6. Cloud provides a great opportunity to develop scalable defense against a variety of attacks and thus enhance security
7. CSPs should be able to provide the customer a means to:
    a. Assess the risk of cloud computing
    b. Compare various cloud service offerings from a variety of providers
    c. Negotiate SLAs to meet their needs

d. Evaluate CSPs based on their compliance certifications from a legal and industry requirements perspective

8. CSPs should be required to notify customers in the event of a security breach

9. CSPs should offer end-to-end data confidentiality in the cloud

10. Customers who can afford the cost should have the ability to choose higher security levels using VPN access and Virtual Private Clouds

11. CSPs should report on incident handling and monitoring activity to build customer trust

12. Cloud service being global in nature, there should be global policies for data and privacy protection along the lines of OECD agreements

13. Global service standards must be developed to support service portability and thus avoid service lock-in

14. Cloud being multi-tenant and co-location of services, the risks include failure of storage separation, memory and routing

15. CSPs should be forthcoming with data logs on demand for customers and service uptime. Amazon has taken the lead in this effort by providing the Service Health Dashboard (AWS Dashboard, 2013)

16. Assurances on data deletion are essential for the customer because the CSP should have the ability to delete data stored in multiple locations because of the necessary redundancy practices used. Such deletion need not be immediate but should be done within a reasonable period such as 24 hours.

It should be clear to the cloud customer that they bear the ultimate responsibility for their reputation when using the cloud and so they should take prudent measures to safeguard that reputation. There is a disconnect here because surveys have shown that the CSPs do not think it is their responsibility to provide such a protection (Ponemon Institute, 2011).

3. CLOUD OUTAGES

One of the main trust builders for cloud services is the 24x7 availability of the system. Major service providers assure that the system uptime is guaranteed 99.99% of the time. In industry parlance this is known as four 9s uptime. In order to provide this level of uptime the system design will require plenty of backup and redundant processes. Table 1 highlights the possible duration of a downtime for various levels of uptime guarantee.

An analysis of the above table shows that it is extremely expensive to maintain plenty of redundant systems to provide a very high level of uptime. In spite of the customer expectation at four 9s uptime, many of the major service providers like Amazon, Google and Microsoft have suffered significant downtimes over the past three years that throw away the uptime guarantees expected. However, unscrupulous marketers tout the uptimes for some of the small niche cloud service providers at five 9s. This should be a point that cloud customers must focus on when they decide on a particular cloud service provider. The customer should not simply take the assurances of the cloud service provider for the uptime. Knowing the data from the above table, the customer should be able to validate for themselves if the cloud service provider has the resources to provide the uptime that they try to claim. One way to get this information is to find out from the cloud service provider the system downtimes that they have experienced over the preceding three years. The downtime data should include routine maintenance downtimes as well. In the rest of this section we will identify the major cloud outages over the past three years and note the main reason for the outage. This will help us develop recommendations in the next section to help the customer craft their Service Level Agreements (SLAs) with the cloud service providers.

Amazon is the largest cloud service provider in the world. The annual revenue of Amazon Web Services (AWS) is a staggering $3 billion. Accord-

Table 1. System downtime level for various uptime guarantees

System Availability Percentage	Maximum downtime Per day	Maximum downtime Per month	Maximum downtime Per year
99%	00:14:23	07:18:17	87:39:29
99.9%	00:01:26	00:43:49	08:45:56
99.99%	00:00:09	00:04:32	00:52:56
99.999%	00:00:00.9	00:00:26	00:05:26
99.9999%	00:00:00.2	00:00:03	00:00:32

Note: The above table information was adapted from data available on Wikipedia

ing to Gartner Research, Amazon's cloud service capability exceeds by five times the combined capacity of the next 14 major rivals in the field (Gartner Report, 2013b). These rivals include major niche providers such as Rackspace and Microsoft. In spite of the heavy investment in cloud services, Amazon has experienced major outages over the past three years. One of the well documented cloud outages occurred at AWS on April 21, 2011. Since Amazon provides cloud services globally, this had a major impact. One of the important lessons learned from this outage is that the cloud service provider should be able to recognize an outage when it occurs. For several hours on that day Amazon was telling their customers that the problem was not at their end and that the customers should look at the way they had configured their services. In reality, the problem occurred when one of Amazon's automatic backup systems was erroneously programmed to handle the backup. This system that is part of the popular Elastic Compute Cloud (EC2) uses what is known as Elastic Block Storage (EBS). The EBS is designed to provide high reliability by making multiple copies of data available in redundant servers. When that traffic moved to a lower bandwidth secondary network for handling the EBS, it affected both the primary and secondary networks as far as accepting customer requests for EC2 Read/Write. Net result, the system was unable to do any fresh backup and make available the data to the customers. Amazon finally restored full service after a lapse of nearly 3 days (Amazon, 2011). The total down-

time of over 65 hours clearly exceeded the uptime guarantee provided by Amazon. Consequently, Amazon offered a 10-day credit for all their use of Amazon services to all affected customers to gain their trust back. The most recent service outage at Amazon occurred on September 13, 2013 for two hours. This type of repeated outages even for the most equipped service provider shows that customers should not depend on a single cloud service provider for their services since it leads to a single point of failure.

Gmail has experienced several outages over the past five years. Gmail offers a 99.9% guarantee of uptime, also known as three 9s assurance, for its premier service for which customers pay $50 per user per year. The failures occurred in August 2008 over several days and each time the outage lasted several hours and affected millions of users. By April 17, 2013, when the latest outage occurred at Gmail, even though the outage lasted only a few minutes its impact was significant because Gmail serves over 425 million users worldwide. The takeaway for the ordinary Gmail user is that the service is highly reliable but yet Gmail does not offer even the three 9s guarantee for their free service. Gmail, which challenged Microsoft Exchange's dominance in the workplace email service, needed to be more reliable than Microsoft. Microsoft's Outlook and Hotmail services failed for 16 hours on March 14, 2013, caused by a firmware update that literally affected the temperature control in data centers.

Google provides a variety of services such as Google Talk, Google Drive and Google Apps. Outages occurred in all three of these major services. Google Talk experienced a five hour outage on July 27, 2012. Google Apps lost service for four hours on October 26, 2012. The latest outage problem for Google occurred in its Google Drive service between March 18, 2013 and March 20, 2013. Due to problems in network software this service was down for 17 hours. Google's analysis of this failure showed that its edge routers – those that connect the provider service to the internet – failed.

Microsoft experienced outages in its popular SaaS service known as Office 365 on February 1, 2013 and February 2, 2013 for a total of two hours. The problem was traced to a routine maintenance update. This was preceded by earlier outages in 2012 in the same service. Its cloud service Azure experienced an outage on February 28-29, 2012 when it failed to adequately handle the leap year calculation in its service. Azure was down on February 22, 2013 for 12 hours. When Microsoft analyzed the cause of this problem it was shocked to find out that it was caused by non-renewal of their SSL (Secure Socket Layer) certificate in a timely manner. This goes to show the importance of monitoring all aspects of a service and watch for potential failure points.

Popular social network service provider Facebook experienced a two hour service interruption on January 28, 2013. This was traced to a Denial of Service attack which puts the service provider at a disadvantage because the outage was not caused by their failure but by circumstances beyond their control. There are tools available to monitor for the Denial of Service attack but running such tools all the time will result in service latency and so the service provider would deal with the problem when it occurs.

We pointed out earlier problems with Google Drive that made the service unavailable for extended periods of time. Google introduced the Google Drive service as a direct competition to the popular Dropbox service which offered customers certain amount of free cloud storage. Dropbox experienced outages on October 26, 2012 for several hours because it depended on Google App Engine which was down for four hours that day. Another longer outage occurred at Dropbox on January 10, 2013 for 16 hours, followed by a 90 minute outage on May 30, 2013. Dropbox enjoys customer loyalty for its free service but it has a significant challenge for business services because they demand higher reliability. One such provider is SyncBlaze. The lesson learned from the Dropbox outages is that the cloud user must have an alternate provider as well, especially since Dropbox has not identified the reasons for the outages. This lack of transparency from Dropbox leads to trust erosion since the customer cannot be sure that Dropbox will be able to take adequate steps to prevent future outages.

PayPal, world's largest online payment service, had a service outage on August 3, 2009 that lasted five hours. The outage was caused by internal network problems at PayPal. The PayPal service processes $8 million worth of transactions every hour. Its customer base consists of numerous small businesses and they were all affected. One lesson learned from this experience for small businesses is to set up a backup system, be it manual or delayed processing, whereby customer payments using credit cards go through but not authorized immediately. This approach involves risk but maintains customer loyalty. Any transactions that do not get authorized can be traced back to the customers and dealt with separately. Some businesses have adopted this approach to not inconvenience their customers.

Rackspace, a niche cloud service provider in the managed hosting space, is based in San Antonio, TX. It has experienced multiple power outage problems over an extended period of time that dates back to 2007. On June 29, 2009 the company's largest data center in Dallas, TX experienced power outage for 45 minutes. It affected many of its global customers. Rackspace prides itself in providing 100% service availability via its SLAs. This should be viewed in the context of data provided in Table 1. These recurring outages have put a dent in the company's reputation as a highly dependable cloud service provider. Rackspace, ranked third among cloud service providers besides Amazon and Microsoft, focuses on hybrid cloud whereby the customer has better control over their mission critical applications by hosting them on a private cloud and others on a public cloud. This hybrid cloud approach with some minor changes provides a company a best case scenario for maintaining service despite outages at the cloud service provider. The hybrid approach mentioned above involves the organization managing some of the mission critical services behind a firewall internally.

In some instances the outages force a company to lose its reputation and customer base. This is what happened to the popular web hosting service GoDaddy. GoDaddy specializes in serving small and medium sized businesses for their web hosting needs. On September 10, 2012 it had an outage for six hours which affected many small and medium sized businesses. One month later GoDaddy decided to exit the cloud service business.

An analysis of the outages shows that some of the outages in larger service providers have a cascading effect. Often the outages experienced by Amazon Web Services resulted in problems for Dropbox since it depends on AWS for its services. Likewise, when Google Apps experienced problems it affected Dropbox because it uses Google Apps as well for its service. Similarly, the Amazon outage caused problems for Tumblr, a blog hosting platform.

In this section we focused on some of the major outages over the past five years among the various cloud service providers. In defense of cloud service providers it should be noted that the failure rate among company owned systems is much higher but they do not interrupt service for many users like a cloud outage does. We conclude this section with a summary of the major cloud outages over the past five years, many of which we discussed

above. This summary is intended to provide a quick overview of the outages, their cause and how one could insulate their business from the cloud service downtime. We have removed from this summary those outages for which the outage duration could not be determined. As is evident from the Summary, many service providers do not disclose the root cause of the problem when an incident occurs. This practice does not bode well to building trust for customers.

4. IMPACT ON CUSTOMER TRUST

In the previous section we have highlighted some of the major outages in cloud service over the past five years. Every time such an outage occurred the service provider vowed to protect against such failures in the future. However, in reality this did not happen as is evident from the Summary provided in Table 2. In the case of Amazon, the best equipped and by far the largest cloud service provider, there were recurring occurrences of failures in their East Coast Availability Zone due to Elastic Block Storage handling problems. Amazon has been most forthcoming in providing details on the causes for their outages. In a way it assures the customer that given the complexity of the systems and the scale of data handling involved such outages are not due to negligence. In every case Amazon built trust with their customer base by offering generous credits for the service failures. It implemented the Service Health Dashboard whereby the customer can monitor the uptime of the systems in the various Availability Zones. The Summary points out that Gmail experienced multiple outages over the five year period. In the case of Google, the outages have had a significant impact on the customer base because of the large number of people who depend on Google's various services such as Google Apps, Google Talk and Google Drive. The failures at Google were identified as due to network failure or programming errors during scheduled maintenance. Even though the amount of details forthcoming from Google was limited, it is sufficient for the customers to know that they have some alternatives to avoid such problems such as their premier service. With a user base of nearly 425 million customers globally, any brief outage at Google would affect a large number of users. Consequently, sharing more information on outages would help customers understand the problems and thus trust the system more. In the case of Google, their services were used not only by ordinary users but also other cloud service providers such as Dropbox and Flickr. So, any failure at Google had a cascading effect on other providers as well.

Other major service providers such as Microsoft, Facebook, Rackspace, Salesforce and Dropbox also experienced several outages over the five year period. An analysis of the outages and availability of limited information from these companies shows that they experienced power outages and their power management systems were not adequate to handle extenuating circumstances. Details provided show that in certain cases the power failures occurred by activities beyond their control such as accidental crash into their power systems by trucks. Given the millions of users for these services these companies could learn from the expertise gained by telecom companies in maintaining their service lines with minimal interruptions. In defense of these companies, it should be noted that customers should be aware that company owned systems also fail often but they do not have this much impact because the problems are isolated.

This analysis shows that a set of best practices would help build customer support for the Cloud Service Provider (CSP). We will identify next several of these recommendations.

1. Building customer trust requires making relevant data available to customers
2. Customers need on demand log data for the services they subscribe to
3. Provide customers with a list of internal employees at the CSP with network access
4. CSP obtains industry recognized compliance certifications from regulators and government
5. CSP makes available audit data of their systems
6. CSP provides data on their incident handling and disaster recovery procedures
7. CSP makes known their uptime statistics in a verifiable manner
8. CSP carries multiple certifications such as SAS 70 Type II Audit, FISMA, PCI DSS, etc
9. CSP facilitates the customer to have the ability to choose their data storage locations in order to meet their government mandated requirements. For example, Massachusetts and Nevada require cloud data to be stored within state borders.
10. Publicity about NSA PRISM program shows that government collects vast amounts of data from large cloud providers
11. European Union and Canada have specifically expressed concerns about the reach of USA PATRIOT Act whereby the US government can have access to the data they need. Both the European Union and Canada have laws against storing data in US clouds for companies in their countries.
12. Access to newer encryption technologies provide a higher level of security for customer data before they leave their control
13. Customers subscribing to Infrastructure as a Service (IaaS) will be able to support this level of encryption. Those customers subscribing to SaaS and PaaS services will not be able to support such a level of encryption.

We conclude this section with three major risk aspects that every business should evaluate. These are: provider lock-in, loss of control, and compliance. Given the current state of cloud service and the lack of global standards, users do not have too

Table 2. Summary of major cloud outages between 2008 and 2013

Date of Outage	Cloud Service Provider	Outage Duration	Cause of problem
Aug. 11, 2008	Gmail	5 hours	
Oct. 16, 2008	Gmail	30 hours	
Mar. 13, 2009	Windows Azure	22 hours	
Jun. 29, 2009	Rackspace	45 minutes	Power interruption
May 11, 2010	Amazon	1 hour	Power interruption due to external event
Apr. 21, 2011	Amazon	3 days	Automatic backup configuration
Feb. 28-29, 2012	Windows Azure	1 day	Leap year processing
Jun. 14, 2012	Amazon	6 hours	
Jun. 28, 2012	Salesforce	5 hours	Storage tier issues
Jul. 10, 2012	Salesforce	12 hours	Power interruption
Jul. 26, 2012	Windows Azure	2½ hours	
Jul. 27, 2012	Google Talk	5 hours	
Sep. 10, 2012	GoDaddy	6 hours	
Oct. 22, 2012	Amazon	6 hours	Fix for failed hardware cascaded
Oct. 26, 2012	Google Apps	4 hours	
Nov. 8, 2012	Microsoft	8 hours	Maintenance issues and network failures
Nov. 15, 2012	Microsoft	5 hours	
Jan. 10, 2013	Dropbox	16 hours	
Jan. 28, 2013	Facebook	2 hours	Denial of Service
Feb. 1-2, 2013	Microsoft Office 365	2 hours	Error in routine maintenance update
Feb. 22, 2013	Windows Azure	12 hours	
Mar. 14, 2013	Microsoft	16 hours	
Mar. 18-20, 2013	Google Drive	17 hours	Network software problem
Mar. 25, 2013	Telstra, Australia	1 day	
Apr. 17, 2013	Gmail	Less than 30 minutes	
Apr. 23, 2013	Apple iCloud	Several hours	
May 30, 2013	Dropbox	1½ hours	
Sep. 13, 2013	Amazon	2 hours	

many options when it comes to provider lock-in. Many providers use proprietary forms of storage and processing techniques. Moreover, if the user decides to move to a different service provider then they will have to port large volumes of data within a short period of time. There is cost associated with

this aspect. Depending on the bandwidth needed to transfer the data the customer should be prepared to pay for this service and this data transfer may take considerable time to transfer depending on the volume of stored data accumulated by the customer. The second and more serious risk involves the compatibility of the data when it is transferred to another service provider because of the format in which the data was stored. For this reason many customers choose a service provider and stay with the service provider for extended periods of time.

The second risk in this regard involves loss of control for the customer to some extent, depending on the type of service the customer chooses. With SaaS and PaaS the customer cedes control to the provider, not only on the hardware side but also on the software side. With IaaS, the customer retains majority of the control and according to data available over 75% of the customers fall in the non-IaaS category. With IaaS, the customer retains most of the control for the operation and storage but does not control the physical protection of the hardware. Physical security of the hardware is not a major problem in the industry and so with IaaS customers there is significant control. It is to be noted that an organization choosing the IaaS service will have considerable computing knowledge and tends to be a large company. Thus, to a major extent, loss of control is a serious risk for many businesses.

The third risk from the cloud customer perspective is with respect to their need for compliance with laws and industry standards. For example, every health care organization must be compliant with HIPAA and so it will need extensive data to show to their regulators that they are compliant with data security and access control for patient health care data. The service provider can help address this aspect by obtaining their own compliance certifications at Level II of SAS 70 which provides evidence of adequate internal controls. In the case of financial organizations, they must be compliant with both Sarbanes-Oxley Act and Gramm-Leach-Bliley Act. This will require access to log data from the service provider on a regular basis. The cloud customer must be able to gather such data on demand and not depend on the service provider to make available such data. These analysis shows that in order to minimize risks to the organization, it must work closely with the cloud service provider to obtain the necessary data.

5. SUMMARY

Cloud Computing is here to stay and many businesses will adopt cloud computing because of the convenience and cost advantage it offers. In this chapter we have raised several issues about the risk management aspects from the cloud customer perspective. We have also highlighted the many cloud outages over the last five years. An analysis of these outages shows that this problem is widespread among many of the major cloud providers like Amazon, Google and Microsoft. In spite of these outages that challenge the trust that customers place in these companies, the advantages offered by cloud services far outweigh the drawbacks. Moreover, every company's own IT departments also face such challenges when it comes to keeping their systems up all the time. Organizations should take advantage of the many resources that they have in evaluating the cloud service providers and choose the appropriate one that will meet their needs and service guarantees.

REFERENCES

Amazon. (2011). *Report on cloud outage*. Retrieved from http://aws.amazon.com/message/65648/

COSO. (2012). *Enterprise risk management for cloud computing*. Retrieved from http://www.coso.org/documents/Cloud%20Computing%20Thought%20Paper.pdf

Dashboard, A. W. S. (2013). *Service health dashboard*. Retrieved from http://status.aws.amazon.com/

European Union Report. (2009). *Cloud computing: Benefits, risks and recommendations for information security*. Retrieved from http://www.enisa.europa.eu/activities/risk-management/files/deliverables/cloud-computing-risk-assessment

Ponemon Institute. (2011). *Security of cloud computing providers study*. Ponemon Institute.

Report, G. (2013a). *Cloud contracts need more transparency to improve risk management*. Retrieved from http://www.gartner.com/newsroom/id/2567015

Report, G. (2013b). *Amazon has reached a staggering level of dominance when it comes to cloud computing*. Retrieved from http://www.businessinsider.com/amazons-aws-market-share-and-revenues-2013-8

Chapter 9
Regulatory Aspects of Cloud Computing in Business Environments

Michael Losavio
University of Louisville, USA

Pavel Pastukhov
Perm State University, Russia

Svetlana Polyakova
Perm State University, Russia

ABSTRACT

Cloud computing allows us to solve problems of information on a global scale and of a full range of tasks. Cloud computing has many advantages, but the reliability of data protection is a major concern of provider-client, industry, and governmental regulation. These information systems must comply with existing standards and anticipate new standards of information security. The legal process must distinguish who is responsible for what within a dynamically changing infrastructure significantly different from traditional models. The authors first examine the models and substance of regulation as established by service-level agreements between cloud providers, their clients, and their clients' customers. The authors discuss industry self-regulation and government regulations regarding data protection, privacy, criminal and tort law, and intellectual property law complicated by the inherent cross-jurisdictional nature of cloud computing.

INTRODUCTION

"Cloud computing" turns devices into portals to power and service all over the world all the time. It offers significant advantages in service availability and security. The issues of cloud security, trust and regulation for business are *generally* the same as with any information and informatics business. But with the benefits there are enhanced risks from the novelty of the technology, its provision and its use that may segment and distribute control of systems and data to others than owners and the needed diligence in the oversight of the provision and use of cloud services. (Harbour,

DOI: 10.4018/978-1-4666-5788-5.ch009

2010) The challenge to security and trust is maintaining useful services from anywhere all of the time in a distributed, heterogeneous environment of systems, services and users. For informatics services this is assurance that the confidentiality of their information is protected, the integrity of their data is maintained and it is available for use as needed. These reflect the on-demand power and elasticity cloud computing offers.

The initial, fundamental regulation of those engaged in cloud computing comes from internal regulation within the relationship of cloud provider and cloud user/client and the cloud client and that client's customer. In other words, a user/client uses a provider they trust to provide timely and reliable services to *their* downstream customers who, in turn, may have *their* downstream customers. If the cloud provider fails, the clients/customers fail, or, at best, take their business where greater reliability can be found in the services they need.

As with many business alliances within informatics, regulation and compliance may be first handled by the service providers themselves and, over time, may evolve as a collaborative/contractual relationship between providers and users. This may vary with the relative market power of the cloud provider and the user, especially individual consumers. When this challenge seems unmanageable, state regulation and industry self-regulation may step in to enforce appropriate levels of performance.

The role of central bodies in engaging with a broad commercial technology is seen in the widely-cited definition of cloud computing put forth by the National Institute of Standards and Technology (NIST) (US).

DEFINITION OF CLOUD COMPUTING

Cloud computing is a model for enabling ubiquitous, convenient, on-demand network access to a shared pool of configurable computing resources (e.g., networks, servers, storage, applications, *and services) that can be rapidly provisioned and released with minimal management effort or service provider interaction. This cloud model promotes availability and is composed of five essential characteristics, three service models, and four deployment models. (Mell, 2011)*

This encapsulation of essential characteristics serves to highlight the commercial and functional advantages of cloud services. The cloud's services are always available on-demand with broad network access, a pooling of resources while elastically growing or shrinking as needed with measurement and monitoring of the services provided. Service model components are the software, platforms for applications and infrastructure options. Services may be keyed to individual organizations, communities, the general public or to various combinations of these entities.

Obligations and rights relating to cloud activities may vary with the roles of those affected by them. The primary parties would be the cloud provider, that provider's client and that client's customers and clients. Each would carry with them the respective rights and obligations given by whichever respective jurisdiction(s) oversee their activities, of which there may be several. These may be defined, created or limited by statute, case law and contract. Each primary party may have rights and obligations to the other parties, as seen in Figure 1.

Figure 1. Interrelated rights and obligations of primary cloud parties

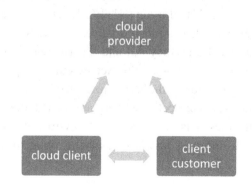

But additional parties may also include third-parties impacted by cloud operations and sovereign entities responsible for all the other parties. Third-parties without contractual relations with but affected by the activities of the three primary parties may have rights defined by statute and case law they may seek to enforce. This may come where third-parties have been injured in some way by cloud activities of the three primary parties. Sovereign entities assert power over activities that are directed towards or impact their areas of control and their citizens; this exercise of *jurisdiction* is of great significance for cloud computing and its regulation.

Hill, et al, propose a cloud computing model to implement the National Health Information Network (NHIN) for the effective, efficient and affordable use of electronic personal health information (PHI) to improve medical outcomes (Hill, 2011). They note that such information must have high-level safeguards for patient data privacy, integrity and security matched with high-levels of interconnectivity and interoperability with the many distributed, heterogeneous systems within the American health care system. They suggest a hybrid public-private cloud computing architecture would revolutionize the speedy, interoperable and secure deployment of such a network, as opposed the gradual interconnection of localized, proprietary systems.

In turn, though, this immediately raises issues with the privacy and security laws of each of the U.S. states and of the federal government. Such a system must comply with the Health Insurance Portability and Accountability Act (HIPAA) and the Health Information Technology for Economic and Clinical Health Act (HITECH) at the federal level. State laws remain diverse, but the Model State Health Privacy Act and the Turning Point Model State Public Health Act are guidance proposals to states for the harmonization of their state laws on data protection and privacy. Nonetheless, Hill notes it is "a messy legal environment in which differing privacy-preserving obligations exist." (Hill, 2007)

Activity in cloud computing embraces the entire gamut of information handling, from storage and processing to rendering and transmission. Every person holds supercomputing power in their hands. From an always-available national health information network to on-demand access to books and music, it has huge benefits. But the immense benefits provided may be matched by significant damage or injury for the failure or misuse of the cloud. How regulation may better prevent failure or misuse, or compensate for injury, will depend first on the jurisdictions that oversee the cloud, the rights of providers and users, and the engineering of the technical systems used.

Jurisdiction, Rights and Technical Systems

The wide distribution of cloud service provision and use, unrestricted by physical boundaries, opens the provider and user to the jurisdiction of many possible sets of laws. Whether laws of contract, service reliability, data protection or the many other possible laws, the particular law at issue may depend on the physical location of the provider, the provider's servers, the cloud customer, the user or the source of data being processed and where the impact of the cloud services may be directed or felt. The straightforward determination of the controlling jurisdiction for actions rendered in one location has become much more complex with the Internet; with the distributed and multi-party nature of cloud computing, this has become more complex and may give *multiple* jurisdictions power over cloud transactions. This may require parties involved in the cloud to comply with the regulations of *all* such controlling jurisdictions.

Those particular laws may define the rights and obligations of the providers, users, data subjects and third parties as to the protections of contracts, privacy, property (copyright, trade secret, trademark) and even personal injury of individuals. And there is the inevitable issue of to whom tax revenues may be owed for particular activities in the cloud.

These, in turn, may support or require technical systems for the allocation and protection of the respective rights of the parties. Parties may be obligated in performing their due diligence to assure certain technical systems are implemented and maintained to protect the rights of those involved. Failure to verify which laws apply as to whom and assure compliance with them may subject a business in the cloud to significant liability and damage to their customer relationships and a data subject to injury in their rights and persons. The diversity of jurisdictions may make it more complex for the cloud service provider or its customer to know what laws may be available to enforce respective rights, whether they be civil regulation within the business relationship or a resort to administrative or criminal process through a government.

One example of this may be seen in the Russian programming, online services and game solutions company AlternativaPlatform and some of the issues it has faced (Alternativa, 2013). AlternativaPlatform develops and supports systems for online services, particularly massive multi-player online games. It has expanded with a development collaboration in the People's Republic of China, AlternativaChina.. Its online gaming services include both its own TankI Online browser-based games and those of other developers. It online services include the RealtimeBoard browser-based MMO whiteboard for real time project collaboration. As the service provider of its own games and services it is responsible for matters relating to them; where services are provided to other service and game developers it may be responsible to those developers as well as to what those developers do through AlternativaPlatform's system. It either instance consumer-level customer satisfaction, either that of AlternativePlatform or of its developer customers, is essential to business success, expansion and survival.

AlternativaPlatform's own TankI Online will have tens of thousands of users playing online across the world. It is a straightforward battle action game with little or no objectionable content. This permits it to operate across many jurisdictions without conflicts with the many varied national laws on many varied content issues, especially those related to children's activities. This also helps mitigate risk from evolving precedent or case law standards relating to liability for gaming activity. But it must still deal with tax issues across nations where its gamers reside and play, requiring more and more from its legal staff.

A significant issue is coding misconduct within the game by player/programmers who may exploit "cheats" within the game to traffic in game tokens and other online goods. This may divert revenue away from the game operators and irritate legitimate gamers exploited or at a disadvantage to those using the illegal code. The misconduct may range from a violation of terms of service to violation of national laws for unauthorized access to the game system, injection of hostile code into programming environment and fraud. System and company resources are spent securing the system from these problems.

Resort to police powers is possible, as with other misconduct. But there are many challenges with a cloud services system. The player/programmer engaging in misconduct may be anywhere in the world. The system that is compromised may be one of several used to provide cloud services, or it may be several such systems. Efforts may be made to obscure the origin of the misconduct, such as through proxy systems. And law enforcement may not have the expertise, time or inclination to track over the Internet the source of the misconduct, especially if the target of the misconduct is in a country other than that of the origin of the misconduct.

This places a greater responsibility on the cloud service provider for self-protection through practical and technical means. It is a legal asymmetry in that the cloud service provider will often be easily subject to legal process against it but may have difficulty enforcing legal process against those that injure it. It is an additional complication for operations within cloud environments.

One very important way cloud operations address their need for self-protection is through regulation within the relationship with clients and customers, especially through generally accepted principles of contract law.

Regulation within the Relationship: Service Level Agreements

Informatics services have extended this through a comprehensive regime of contracts to detail the obligations between the parties. In cloud computing Services Level Agreements (SLAs) set out the rights and obligations of the parties. These may detail

1.   The services to be provided
2.   The availability of the services
3.   Measures of service performance
4.   The security provided as to data confidentiality and integrity and service availability
5.   Limitations on damages from failure of the cloud services
6.   User obligations in use of the cloud services, such as securing access, maintaining secure access systems to the cloud and
7.   Anything else that may impact the parties. (Patel, 2009)

SLAs are crucial, regardless of the legal jurisdiction, in setting out and defining the expectations and obligations of the parties in a cloud computing relationship. They can promote trust between the parties that might not otherwise exist and the lack of which might prohibit use of cloud services where the user is mandated to assure a level of security. (Stanko, 2012)

The particular terms of the SLA may vary with the relative negotiating power of the parties. Thus an individual consumer may be required to

accept all of the provider's SLA provisions, no matter how unfair they appear, as a condition of use. A major corporation may, in turn, be able to dictate its SLA terms to a provider.

A cloud provider may be subject to regulations or seek to a serve a customer base subject to regulations to which the provider must conform. For example, legal service providers are often subject to external mandates requiring they have in place effective and reasonable systems for preserving data confidentiality. Such customers cannot contract with a cloud provider unless that provider, in turn, assures it has effective systems in place to preserve confidentiality.

Regardless of market power, a provider's success and growth will depend on reliable services and good treatment of its customers. This is particularly true in the hyper-competitive world for online services. Any slight of a customer will appear in a weblog with minutes. The online market itself becomes self-regulating. Risk management protects both the provider and the customers.

Nonetheless, areas deemed too sensitive to leave to market effects or service sector requirements inevitably become subject to direct regulation. The key areas of external regulation presently reflect the ways in which a cloud provider's failure in certain domains injure their customers, their customers' customers and other third parties.

Regulation Outside the Relationship: Industry Self-Regulation and Government Oversight of Cloud Providers, Provider Clients and Cloud Customers

External regulation may come from governments or industry self-regulatory bodies. That regulation will focus on the outcomes and results of cloud provider operations: the storage, processing and transmittal of information. Whether via government or industry rules, regulation may be directly of the cloud provider or indirectly through regulation of the provider's clients and those clients' customers using cloud services.

For example, securities and financial instrument trading may be regulated by the U.S. Securities and Exchange Commission and by the industry's National Association of Securities Dealers. A cloud provider dealing in such services may need to assure its operations comply with those regulations so its clients and their customers would not be in violation of them. Distribution of illegal content, such as with pornography, hate speech or violent materials, may be the subject of state criminal prosecution, civil actions for damages against provider, client or customer or industry self-regulation standards for controlling such distribution.

CRIMINAL REGULATION AND RELATED CIVIL LIABILITY

The criminal laws, procedures and powers of any jurisdiction impacted by cloud activity may apply to anyone involved. Criminal regulation addresses definitions of what cloud activity constitutes a crime, the appropriate punishment for that activity and the procedures by which such activity is investigated, prosecuted and punished. Areas of criminal regulation vary significantly by jurisdiction. For example, informational conduct that damages reputation, advocates "hate" speech or is seen to disparage particular ethnic or religious groups may be prosecuted criminally in many countries but is protected noncriminal activity in the United States. Financial fraud and hacking crimes may risk punishment by significant prison sentences in the United States but only minor financial penalties in the Russian Federation. And although these may represent the independent malicious actions of parties other than the cloud provider or its client, national laws may hold the provider or client, or both, civilly liable for damages for the failure to prevent injuries caused by others using their cloud services.

Given the diverse particulars of different countries, the general schema for "traditional," pre-Internet, pre-cloud crimes may serve as a guide for areas of possible criminal regulation for cloud activity. That schema is shown in Table 1, which lists the general domains of criminal law by the nature of injury. These are then matched by definition or analogy to some modern criminal statutory regimes:

Table 1. "Traditional" crime domains and examples of cloud analogues

"Traditional" Crime Domains	Cloud Analogues
Injury to Persons and Their Rights	Statutes punishing: conduct resulting in injuries from damage or modification of data used for medical treatment or control systems; conduct defaming and damaging reputation; conduct invading the privacy rights of individuals; conduct relating to the sexual exploitation of children
Trespass of Property Rights	Statutes punishing: unauthorized access to computing systems and information; conduct that reduces or prevents the availability of data or services
Damage to Property	Statutes punishing: conduct destroying data, impacting the integrity of data, damaging systems, impacting system performance, distributing malware
Theft of Property	Statutes punishing: invasion of intellectual property rights in copyright, patent, trade secret, trademark; unauthorized use of services and system resources
Injury to Public Morals	Statutes punishing: conduct relating to materials of the sexual exploitation of children, obscene depictions of human sexual conduct, cruelty to animals
Injury to Public Order	Statutes punishing: conduct relating to materials addressing prohibited conduct, such as "hate" speech, negative depictions of ethnic groups, negative depictions of religious groups, incitement to violence, denial of "accepted" facts and other matters.

The structure of the Convention on Cybercrime of the Council of Europe ("Convention on Cybercrime") reflects another way of categorizing the criminal law regulation of cloud computing conduct. (Council of Europe, 2001) The profound impact of transnational networks for information storage, processing and transmittal - the heart of cloud computing - drove the drafting and multi-state ratification of the Convention. It is an effort to harmonize the laws in this domain and promote cross-jurisdictional cooperation. (European Convention, 1957) It defines computer-related offenses (Council of Europe, 2001) and content-related offenses (Council of Europe, 2001) where the cloud computing systems, services and output may be either a tool to accomplish a criminal act or the target of the criminal act, such as direct access to resources or to gain access elsewhere. Intellectual property offenses relating copyright infringement look to cloud computing as tool for such offenses (Council of Europe, 2001) which may be seen in cloud-based file storage and distribution systems. The Convention also covers matters similar to but outside of traditional criminal law, which it structures into five general areas. These areas and the related conduct are the misuse of devices, interference with systems, interference with data, interception of data and unauthorized access to a system. (Council of Europe, 2001) Financial and data fraud receive special attention and may be seen in the national laws of most countries, such as the United States. (Council of Europe, 2001)

National laws generally reflect these Convention's legal principles. The applicability to cloud computing follows that of generally for information conduct. A key concern caused by the technology itself is the enforceability of the laws for misconduct relating to the cloud above and beyond the practical concerns of jurisdictional power and jurisdictional will to enforce it. Cloud computing, given the possibility of activities and data distributed across many systems in many places controlled by many entities, creates special difficulties for the forensic discovery of evidence and enforcement of laws.

Dykstra and Riehl detail the potential conflict between cloud user/clients/customers expectations of a "locale" for their activities and data and the reality of cloud computing systems (Dykstra, 2012). Whether in civil or criminal investigation and discovery of electronically stored information (ESI), the cloud offers challenges in simply finding where the data/ESI needed is located, who has custody of it and who can access it all within the legal rules governing such activity. "Digital Forensics," or the finding of reliable electronically stored digital information, has "new and non-trivial challenges" such as "remotely located data, lack of control, layers of complexity and authenticity." when acting within a cloud computing environment. (Dykstra, 2012) The issues with this may develop within three general situations:

1. A crime or other misconduct injures the *cloud provider's operations* and the cloud provider seeks to act against the offending party by seeking information within its data corpus, and those of others;

2. A crime or other misconduct injures the *cloud provider's client or the client's customers*, who, in turn, seek to act against the offending party by seeking information within the cloud provider's data corpus, and

3. A crime or other misconduct injures *third parties not directly using* the cloud provider's services and they seek to act against the offending party by seeking information within the cloud provider's data corpus and those of the provider's client or the client's customer.

A cloud provider may face several different sources of costs relating to the system of justice. It must bear the costs of its efforts to seek legal redress. It may also have the costs for responding to legal process from those who see legal redress from it for alleged injuries. And even where a cloud provider or service client is innocent of injuring others, it may also face the costs of providing evidence and information in legal disputes between others where, essentially, it is a witness.

A primary difficulty may be the cost of finding and acquiring the relevant data in the cloud environment. A second, but very important issue, is the validation of the authenticity of the data found if multiple parties have access to it or to the ancillary data files regarding access and use. This may be straightforward in cases where the data is centrally tracked and logged with no outside intervention. But where there may have been unauthorized access to a system by a programmer skilled enough to also modify or forge log records and operating system files, establishing that the records are authenticate may be very difficult.

Lastly, investigation and discovery within the law creates its own new challenges to the fundamental relationship between people and with their governments. For the United States a primary limitation is that of the Fourth Amendment to the U.S. Constitution, which prohibits "unreasonable" searches by state officials. The privacy protections of the Fourth Amendment have been supplemented by various specialized statues. Ohm notes as to access to personal information on one's life, "Today's technology poses a constitutional puzzle that is different in kind, not just in degree, from the one solved only a few decades ago." (Ohm, 2011) Ohm contends that given the massive data storage capabilities of systems (and the cloud may be the most massive of all), traditional police search warrants are close to becoming like the hated "general warrants" of search used by the British against colonists leading up to the War for Independence. Functionally, if a person's entire data life is stored in a cloud system, then an order of a court permitting search of that system is a search of an entire personal history.

FINANCIAL REGULATION

Personal financial information is fundamental to an individual's ability to effectively function in contemporary commercial society, whether buying aspirin or health insurance. The use of cloud services to facility the use of financial information improves the efficiency and convenience of transactions to financial institutions, merchants and customers. But compromise of that information may reveal personal issues for someone may deprive them of access to their funds to buy what they need and may lead to errors in their credit personae and character. Such damage may then cascade into further injuries, such as inadvertent foreclosure or credit denial that may be difficult or impossible to correct. These risks have increasingly become real injuries with the rise of identity theft in financial systems itself aided by electronic commerce. This has, in turn, led to regulation of financial data systems.

A primary example is the Gramm-Leach-Bliley Act (GLBA), which requires financial institutions to protect the nonpublic personal information of their customers from improper disclosure. These obligations cover account access information, the ubiquitous Social Security Numbers of customers and other personal information. This is financial information that may be used to commit fraud through identity theft or damage someone's financial profile for malicious purposes or sheer carelessness.

GLBA requires financial institutions to, among other obligations,

1. not disclose and institute practices to assure non-disclosure of customers' covered information to or by third parties,
2. institute practices to prevent and stop unauthorized access or use of customers' information, including through non-technical fraudulent means and
3. institute practices to protect the integrity of customer data.

Cloud service providers may or may not be directly covered by GLBA. But if their customers are covered financial institutions, then the cloud provider must implement systems to assure their customers that these protections are in place. The regulatory bodies for such financial institutions periodically verify GLBA compliance by the institutions and their third-party service providers. Failure to comply by either may lead to serious financial penalties, possible loss of charters to conduct business and the possible loss of clients and customers.

An example of industry self-regulation is the credit/debit card industry's Payment Card Industry (PCI) Security Standards Council's Data Security Standards (DSS) for companies providing and using credit cards. These standards require personnel and technical practices to protect customer credit card data for breach of confidentiality and unauthorized access and notification and mitigation responses upon breach. Failure to comply may lead to financial penalties or revocation of the right to use credit cards, reducing financial viability of a business in current markets.

HEALTH INFORMATION

Efficient access to health information may be vital in an emergency. It aids in reducing costs and errors for medical services. Compromise of this information may lead to erroneous medical decisions and increased costs to a patient. Even where no direct physical injury occurs, disclosure of personal health information may impact other aspects of personal life, such as associations, decisions to extend credit or services or a otherwise affect personal and commercial relationships. It may even contribute to "medical identity theft" where one person improperly uses another person's information to access expensive medical services without paying for them.

These are some of the concerns that led to regulation of data use relating to personal health

information. One of the most important of these is the Health Insurance Portability and Accountability Act (HIPAA). HIPAA mandates the privacy and security of information that may be associated with a particular person and the provision of medical care or payment, what is called "protected health information" (PHI). It covers institutions, "entities" and organizations providing health care that process health care information for treatment or payment for that health care.

HIPAA limits the use, disclosure and sharing of PHI and requires patient consent of use or disclosure falls outside of permitted activities. PHI, for example, may be used for patient treatment, health care provider operations and to obtain payment for that treatment, but not for use by other providers of therapeutic services to solicit business. It gives a patient the right to require disclosure of their PHI and to have that information added to. Logging of certain data disclosures is required.

As with financial information under GLB, those working with personal health information covered by HIPAA must also comply with security standards assuring the confidentiality, integrity and availability of electronic protected health information. Administrative, physical and technical security standards must be implemented that cover the prevention, detection and recovery from security breaches. These expressly apply to "business associates" who provide services involving protected health information. The covered institution or entity must assure by *written contract* that the third party will adequately protect patient information in accordance with HIPAA standards.

Under HIPAA a cloud service provider must expressly incorporate HIPAA standards via express contractual guarantees of administrative, physical and technical security to assure confidentiality, integrity and availability of data. Failure to do so is an express violation by the health care provider/customer. Where implemented by contract as required, a cloud provider, at a minimum, would face loss of business and economic damages for a breach of its security obligations.

Where a contract required the cloud provider to indemnify the health care customer for damages and penalties, damages could be massive. This may happen where a massive data breach occurs or an individual data integrity breach leads to mal-treatment and injury to a patient.

Privacy and security compliance by cloud service providers has become essential given the impact from the American Recovery and Reinvestment Act of 2009, which promoted the expansion of electronic health care information technologies. This includes expanded use of cloud technologies for health care, "electronic health records" (EHR) of health care providers and "personal health records" (PHR) of individuals.

To address this expansion, the Act increased protections of the security and privacy of protected personal health information. It added breach notification to patients whose information was improperly disclosed, increased the penalties for failing to comply with the security and privacy rules, and applied them directly to *business associates*. These provisions, known as the HITECH Act, would now directly require a cloud service provider to comply with its and HIPAA's rules and be subject to compliance audits.

The HITECH Act also gives individual states the power to enforce compliance when protected health information of their state residents is collected, transmitted, stored, processed or used. For a cloud provider serving a national audience, this greatly expanded the possible regulatory authorities overseeing cloud provider operations.

Providers and their clients must still look to the state laws on privacy that may impact their operations. The Model State Health Privacy Act and the Turning Point Model State Public Health Act offer guidance to states. They do so as model legislative provisions on data protection and privacy for states that, if broadly accepted and implemented, would assure greater consistency in the law between states.

INTELLECTUAL PROPERTY

Intellectual property regulation may vary between jurisdictions, may only apply within a particular jurisdiction or may apply across jurisdictions, depending on the particular rights involved. Cloud computing distributed systems and controls bring their own issues to the protections of intellectual property rights. (Gervais, 2012) Gervais and Hindman suggest cloud computing may actually make it easier for oversight of intellectual property rights through a concentration of services while creating greater privacy challenges. They note that the forms of business models this will make possible are not yet defined but, if successful, will most likely involve intermediary parties with the cloud system.

The core intellectual property interests are copyright, patent, trademark and trade secret. Each has its own separate legal regime as created by statute and case law. Copyright protects the creative works of people set in a fixed storage medium, from software to music to video. It gives the holder of the copyright control over, among other things, the rights to copy, distribute and make derivative use of that creation. A copyright exists from the moment of creation and fixation, but is not an exclusive right to the content; other, if they independently create something, may also have copyrights. Copyright vests from the time of creation and fixation and is recognized in countries around the world.

Patent rights may be given over a new, novel and useful process or way of doing something that no one has done before and is not an obvious extension of some existing process. The patenting process is much more difficult and expensive and involves the arduous and expensive application for and examination of the proposed patent in those countries where protection is desired. But it is also a monopoly grant in that no one else may use the patented process without permission during the time granted for the patent. Nor may they export products made with the patented process to countries where the patent has issued without the permission of the patent holder.

Trademarks are rights in a particular way a product or service is named or titled as to identify it. That identification may come to be value if the product or service becomes respected for quality. Trademark rights protect others from trying to exploit the mark to sell their similar products or services by misleading people as to who actually is providing the product or service. Trade secret is a secret business process or system that gives competitive advantage to the enterprise that has it and uses it. That enterprise must take reasonable efforts to protect the secret. That includes practices such as keeping the information safe and confidential, requiring employees to sign nondisclosure agreements and implementing any needed technical security to keep the secret a secret. Examples of both may be seen in KFC's chicken restaurants: KFC, which sells Kentucky Fried Chicken, has a trademark in its logo of Colonel Sanders and a trade secret in its "11 herbs and spices" chicken recipe.

Copyright, under the Berne Convention, offers the most consistent regulation across jurisdictions. Enforcement may vary, but signatories to the Convention generally implement through local law reciprocal protections for copyrights. Of importance to cloud providers are "safe harbor" provisions in statute or case law that exempt the cloud provider from liability for copyright infringement claims for actions by others using their services as long as the provider has effective procedures to respond to claims of infringement. A cloud provider or client providing cloud services to others should verify the existence of these protections in the jurisdictions in which they operate and effect procedures to respond to claims of infringement and "take down" notices.

Patent regulation is more dependent on the jurisdictions which may have issue a patent to a particular entity. Cloud providers and clients should review the technology they use as to patent coverage and any needed licensing and *where*

that technology is implemented. As it is possible for a patent on the same technology to be issued to different entities in different countries, an implementation that would be properly licensed in one country may be infringement if, through the distributed nature of the cloud implementation, it is executed in a jurisdiction where someone else holds the patent.

Trademarks are market-specific but must be actively protected in that market or exclusive use of the mark is lost. But the Internet and cloud systems make the world the market. This may require massive world-wide effort, at least in major markets, for trademark registration and protection in the cloud. (Gutierrez 2011) Conversely, trade secrets are protected by successful efforts to maintain a secret that offers competitive advantage. It may be problematic within a cloud system as to who has the ability or responsibility to protect trade secrets, especially where a provider's client or that client's customer is implementing a trade secret technology. Cloud providers, with either trademark or trade secret, may seek to shift the entire burden and liability of these to others through the SLA; cloud users, in turn, may insist on protections from the provider.

CONCLUSION: ON THE EVOLVING LAW FOR INJURY FROM INFORMATION

Beyond express regulation by statute or contract, American law in many cases provides that where someone is injured by the fault of another, that other is liable for that injury. This principle is still evolving as it relates to information and information systems. But some examples demonstrate the immediate risks a cloud provider may face.

Assuring data integrity is an essential security service. A cloud system that suffers regular breaches of data integrity in personal health information may place a patient's life at risk. This may be true if the breach is due to inadequate protections from external attack or from internal system error. In either case the cloud provider may be liable for damages (often significant) regardless of any protective contract provisions or even if compliant with statutory law.

Similarly, the availability of critical personal health information may be a life or death issue. The failure of information availability, whether due to internal or external factors, may lead to liability for civil damages. Privacy tort damages may lie in the disclosure of personal information. Reputational damages, either of a general nature or specific to activities such as financial management, may also subject a cloud provider to liability. The compromise of intellectual property rights may also subject a cloud provider to potential liability. These are areas where risk may be mitigated by contract or statute, but where injury is to a third party those protections may not be sufficient. Some suggested conditions to ensure reliable security of cloud service may include:

1. The protection of information should be done by clearly identified, legally responsible persons - providers.
2. Primary parties should publish their policies for the processing of data and ongoing requirements for data protection.
3. The transfer of data from the customer or client to the provider's systems should to use secure protocols.
4. A provider should use or offer cryptographic methods for data safety. All data within the service should be securely encrypted. (Ganore, 2013)

There may be cultural aspects to this. For example, the information technology outsourcing represented by cloud computing has not yet received such a development in Russia as in the USA, and many executives are skeptical about the idea of transfer of IT infrastructure services to an outside expert.

There are other considerations beyond regulatory liability for those in the cloud. The impact of cloud systems goes beyond individual transactions to a broader perception of good and bad. Justice Sonja Sotomayor of the U.S. Supreme Court suggested the need to reconsider what privacy means in an era of massive third party data collection and analysis. (*United States v Jones*, 2012). Though her concern related to GPS data collection and analytics, it is equally applicable to the data and analytical power of the cloud and its use by business and government:

The net result is that ... —by making available at a relatively low cost such a substantial quantum of intimate information about any person whom the Government, in its unfettered discretion, chooses to track—may "alter the relationship between citizen and government in a way that is inimical to democratic society."

The future regulation of the cloud, as well as its financial future, will depend on how the cloud relationship between citizen and government, between provider and customer and government, evolve. It will certainly be better for all if cloud implementation looks ahead to both benefits and potential risks to people. This can promote the early engineering of the system for the maximum good and minimum of risks to the people it engages.

REFERENCES

Additional Protocol to the European Convention on Mutual Assistance in Criminal Matters, opened for signature in Strasbourg, on 17 March 1978 (ETS No. 99).

AlternativaPlatform. (n.d.). *About us*. Retrieved from http://alternativaplatform.com/en/about/

Council of Europe Convention on Cybercrime, Chapter II, Section 1, Articles 2-6, Nov. 23, 2001, ETS No. 185.

Council of Europe Convention on Cybercrime, Chapter II, Section 1, Article 7, Nov. 23, 2001, ETS No. 185

Council of Europe Convention on Cybercrime, Chapter II, Section 1, Article 8, Nov. 23, 2001, ETS No. 185.

Council of Europe Convention on Cybercrime, Chapter III, Section 1, Title 2, Nov. 23, 2001, ETS No. 185.

Council of Europe Convention on Cybercrime, Chapter III, Section 1, Title 3, Nov. 23, 2001, ETS No. 185.

Council of Europe Convention on Cybercrime, Chapter III, Section 1, Title 4, Nov. 23, 2001, ETS No. 185.

Council of Europe Convention on Cybercrime (ETS No. 185). (n.d.). Retrieved from http://conventions.coe.int/Treaty/en/Treaties/Html/185.htm

Dykstra, J., & Riehl, D. (2012). Forensic collection of electronic evidence from infrastructure-as-a-service. *Rich Journal of Law & Technology, 1.*

European Convention on Extradition, opened for signature in Paris, on 13 December 1957 (ETS No. 24)

European Convention on Mutual Assistance in Criminal Matters, opened for signature in Strasbourg, on 20 April 1959 (ETS No. 30)

Financial Services Modernization Act of 1999 (US)

Ganore, P. (2013). *Security in cloud computing.* Retrieved from http://blog.esds.co.in/

Gervais, D., & Hundman, D. (2012). Cloud control: Copyright, global memes and privacy. *Journal on Telecommunications & High Technology Law, 53,* 10.

Gutierrez, H. (2011). Peering through the cloud: The future of intellectual property and computing. *Fed. Cir. B.J., 580,* 20.

Harbour, P., & Koslov, T. (2010). Section 2 in the web 2.0 world: An expanded vision of relevant product markets. *Antitrust Law Journal, 769,* 76.

Health Insurance Portability and Accountability Act of 1994 (US)

Hill, J. et al. (2007). Law, information technology, and medical errors: Toward a national healthcare information network approach to improving patient care and reducing malpractice costs. *University of Illinois Journal of Law. Technology and Policy, 159,* 159–165.

Hill, J., Langvardt, A., Massey, A., & Rinehart, J. (2011). A proposed national health information network architecture and complementary federal preemption of state health information privacy laws. *48. American Business Law Journal,* 503. doi:10.1111/j.1744-1714.2011.01120.x

Mell, P., & Grance, T. (2011). *The NIST definition of cloud computing.* Retrieved from http://csrc.nist.gov/publications/drafts/800-145/Draft-SP-800-145_cloud-definition.pdf

Ohm, P. (2011). Massive hard drives, general warrants and the power of magistrate judges. *Virginia Law Review in Brief, 1*(8), 97.

Patel, P., Ranabahu, A., & Sheth, A. (2009). Service level agreement in cloud computing. In *Proceedings of Cloud Workshops at OOPSLA09.* Retrieved from http://knoesis.wright.edu/library/download/OOPSLA_cloud_wsla_v3.pdf

Stankov, I., Datsenka, R., & Kurbel, K. (n.d.). *Service level agreement as an instrument to enhance trust in cloud computing – An analysis of infrastructure-as-a-service providers.* Retrieved from http://aisel.aisnet.org/amcis2012/proceedings/HCIStudies/12/

United States v. Cuevas-Perez, 640 F. 3d 272, 285 (CA7 2011) (Flaum, J., concurring).

United States v. Jones, 565 U.S. ___, 132 S. Ct. 945 (2012), concurring opinion of Justice Sotomayor

18. U.S.C. § 1030 (2006) (US), Computer Fraud and Abuse Act

18. U.S.C. § 1343 (2006) (US), Fraud By Wire, Radio or Television

28. USC §1782 (2006) (US). Assistance To Foreign And International Tribunals And To Litigants Before Such Tribunals

Chapter 10
Cloud Computing Forensics

Mario A. Garcia
Texas A&M University – Corpus Christi, USA

ABSTRACT

As computer technology evolved over the last 30 years, so did the opportunity to use computers to break the law. Out of necessity, digital forensics was birthed. Computer forensics is the practice of extracting information from the digital media in order to prosecute the individuals that carried out the crime. Forensic challenges presented by cloud computing are vast and complex. If a company becomes the target of a digital criminal investigation and they are using cloud computing, some unique challenges are faced by a digital forensics examiner. The data in the cloud only represents a "snapshot" of when it was sent to the cloud. Establishing a chain of custody for the data would become difficult or impossible if its integrity and authenticity cannot be fully determined. There are also potential forensic issues when the customer or user exits a cloud application. Items subject to forensic analysis, such as registry entries, temporary files, and other artifacts are lost, making malicious activity difficult to prove. The challenges of applying forensics to a cloud environment are tied to cloud security. This chapter discusses securing a cloud environment and how that would help with the forensic analysis.

INTRODUCTION

In today's fast paced global economy people are busier now than ever before. The financial strain has forced people to do more with less. Every day people are watching more and more companies close their doors. One of the ways corporations have been able to keep their heads above water is by reverting back to an old technology made new again in Cloud computing. The concept behind Cloud computing is the ability to store ones data on a server in the datacenter "The Cloud" and retrieve it via users digital devices (PC, laptops, tablets, and smart phone). Cloud computing demand for mobile technology has increased dramatically as more and more people have begun to move away

DOI: 10.4018/978-1-4666-5788-5.ch010

from traditional desktops to using mobile devices and cloud services. Recent advances in computer communications technology and particularly Cloud computing is driving some of these changes.

A 2010 report by Gartner Consulting shows that cloud revenue will increase from 58.6 billion in 2009 to almost 150 billion in 2014 (Knipp, 2009). Cloud computing is a transformative technology that provides; on demand service, ubiquitous network access, location independent resource pooling, rapid elasticity, and pay per usage. "As the cloud continues to grow new developments in cloud computing will continue to have a significant and far reaching impact now and in the future of IT systems, networks, and applications" (Berry, 2011).

CLOUD COMPUTING

Cloud computing is the digital version of Rent-A-Center. It has burst out on the scene with many executives and cloud providers touting its ability to be flexible, on demand and responsive to changes in the operating landscape for nearly any organization. However, there are still some myths as what is exactly involved with Clouding computing. Cloud computing is defined by the National Institute of Standards and Technology as "a model for enabling convenient, on-demand network access to a shared pool of configurable computing resources that can be rapidly provisioned and released with minimal management effort or service provider interaction" (Barnes, 2010). Some of the key elements of Cloud computing includes:

- The infrastructure is owned and maintained by a third party called the Cloud Service Provider.
- Access to the cloud is provided via a subscription basis using a demand elastic pricing model in which the customer pays more if he uses more resources on the cloud. This is a major reason why many small and medium sized businesses use the cloud service because they pay for what they use.
- The services of cloud computing are delivered via the web making them platform and location agnostic. In other words, the end user needs to maintain their internet connection and all the other required services can be acquired through the internet.

Service Types

On Demand Self Service

Having on demand services requires less human interaction as well as network storage from a service provider. The key feature of this service is the ability for the cloud customer to acquire and release service capacity without human intervention from the service provider. This process enables the cloud customer to manage their computing needs for processing as well as storage on demand.

Broad Network Access

This allows data to be accessed via thin or thick client platforms and cloud based software application services. In most cases the cloud customer needs only a thin client, which they have. Because of this the benefits of cloud service is within reach of a very large segment of the business community globally.

Resource Pooling

The third party provider essentially serves multiple organizations by using pooled resources depending on the organization's need. Traditionally the server utilization rates have been rather low, around 10% of the server capacity in most cases. The cloud service provider is able to use virtualization technique and make their server capacity usable by multiple customers. In this aspect the cloud service has significantly increased the server utilization rate at the cloud service provider level.

Rapid Elasticity

Depending on an organization's needs, the capabilities can be scaled up or down to meet the organization's needs. For example, a business in US focused on tax preparation has a higher demand on their services for the period January through April middle of every year. During other periods this industry does not need the high computing capacity. Using the service elasticity feature of cloud service, companies focused on tax preparation will be able to acquire the needed resources during their peak demand times and release those resources at other times. Entertainment industry is another one where the demand elasticity is very high. Their high demand periods are around the holiday season starting in late November of each year.

Measured Service

The cloud service monitors the resource usage of the organization by reporting it to the client (Barnes, 2010). This enables the cloud service provider to charge for the services used by the client. This type of usage indicates that cloud computing is viewed by many as utility computing because that is what the customers are being charged for when using a utility such as water or electricity.

Deployment Models for Cloud Services

There are four possible deployment models for cloud computing: public, private, hybrid, and community.

Public Cloud

The cloud infrastructure is made available to the general public but is still owned by the organization selling and servicing the cloud. This is the most widely used of the four cloud models. Nearly 40% of the cloud users prefer the public cloud because of the cost advantages and the availability of a large number of service providers offering this model. According to a Gartner Research study in 2013 the public cloud offering is expected to grow from a revenue of $111 billion in 2012 to $131 billion in 2013. According to a Comp_TIA study this segment of cloud service is maturing and companies are migrating from public cloud to other forms of cloud service. This study shows that with the availability of more service providers there has been a significant movement between various public service providers among their clientele based on cost, open standards adoption, reliability issues due to system outages and higher quality of customer service. It is worth noting that Rackspace, a major cloud service provider, is focused on customer service and they have branded their customer service as Fanatical Customer Support. Amazon web service is a classic example of this type of service. They are also the leader in other types of web services as well.

Private Cloud

The cloud is operated solely for one organization; the cloud is managed by that organization or a third party vendor and the data maybe on or off the premises. The cost of managing a private cloud is much higher than that of the public cloud. Certain industry segments such as the financial sector prefer the private cloud for the security and control it offers. The overall percentage of customers preferring private cloud is about 20%. For security reasons there has been a migration from public cloud to private cloud. Salesforce.com which specializes in Customer Relationship Management (CRM) application on the cloud is one of the best examples of this type of service.

Hybrid Cloud

This model is comprised of two or more clouds (deployment models) that are bound together by proprietary technology and allows for data and application portability. (Barnes, 2010). Hybrid cloud is emerging as an efficient alternative to public cloud. Companies that are concerned about security and control are moving their sensitive applications to private cloud while continuing to use the public cloud for less sensitive applications. Current surveys show that the hybrid cloud comprises about 35% of the cloud service today. Rackspace, a leading cloud service provider with specialization in the web hosting market, is an example of this type of service provider.

Community Cloud

The data within the cloud is shared by several organizations or agencies that have similar interests; the cloud is managed by that organization or a third party vendor and the data maybe on or off the premises. Common community cloud services are in the following industries: automotive, entertainment, and health care. Even though this comprises a small segment of the cloud service market, approximately 5%, it involves some of the major companies that serve the public at large. Examples of this type of service are provided by niche providers specializing in automotive market, such as ADP and Optum Health Cloud by United Health Group for the health care market. CFN Financial Services offers the Global Financial Services Network for the financial sector.

Cloud Computing has Three Primary Delivery Types

Infrastructure-as-a-Service

On demand virtual servers and other infrastructure components. This type of cloud service requires a very high level of computing sophistication from the cloud user because the cloud service provider merely provides the computing infrastructure and the user has to configure and install all the necessary application software on these systems. It is

widely used by developers because they have the ability to test their service usability under a variety of scenarios. This accounts for nearly 18% of all cloud services. Major IaaS providers are Amazon and Rackspace.

Platform-as-a-Service

Allows organizations to develop custom applications to run on a provider's technology and infrastructure. In this case the customer chooses the platform that they need. The level of computing expertise needed by the organization to manage this type of service is less than that of IaaS. This accounts for nearly 18% of all cloud services. Major PaaS providers are Google and Microsoft

Software-as-a-Service

Applications that are hosted in another location and usually within a Community Cloud model (Barnes, 2010). This is the most widely used service in the market. It accounts for nearly 65% of all cloud services. This type of service is used by companies of all sizes but this service is the backbone for small and medium sized enterprises. Microsoft Office 365 and several email and search engine services are classic examples of this type of service.

VIRTUAL ENVIRONMENT

Cloud computing/virtualization presents many challenges to network and computer forensics. The lack of Cloud computing monitoring tools, the need for new programming methods to track transactions, as well as the skill sets of information security workers need to change to address the Cloud computing environment. Currently there are a number of obstacles to conducting a forensic investigation "in" the cloud, much less "on" the cloud. Factors like the law, court-approved methods, standard operating procedures for investigators, and the involvement of a third party – the cloud provider – and a list of others stand in the way of a modern digital forensics investigator conducting a successful investigation in a cloud environment. Part of the problem is simply the old rules of investigation don't apply. A perfect example of this is the differences between traditional hard drive forensics and mobile forensics.

The use of virtualization in Cloud computing further blurs the lines between the physical and logical when it comes to computing. Virtualization is an integral part of Cloud computing and involves the ability to separate the one to one relationship between OS and physical server that has existed till date. It enables multiple instances of different operating systems, called guest operating systems, to run on a single hardware device using a Virtual Machine Monitor or hypervisors such as VMware ESX. The VMM virtualizes the same physical Network Interface Card (NIC) for an instance of Windows as well as an instance of Linux that are running as guest OS on the same physical server. Cloud computing utilizes virtualization to homogenize and provide elasticity to the load of Cloud applications for users as demand increases and decreases. This disentanglement of the servers which run the applications on the Cloud has introduced the possibility that the application that was used by a suspect in a case could have resided on multiple virtual servers on multiple data centers. (Ko, 2011)

DILEMMA WITH FORENSICS IN THE CLOUD

One of the major dilemma with forensic in the cloud is "cloud services are especially difficult to investigate. This is because logging and data for multiple customers may be co-located and may also be spread across an ever-changing set of hosts and data centers. Therefore, if there are no contractual commitments to support specific forms of investigations then investigation and

discovery requests are likely to be impossible." (Brodkin, 2008) "With cloud computing, law enforcement does not have physical control of the media nor the network on which it resides, many users will have access to a particular cloud. How does law enforcement seize only that portion of the media where the evidence may exist? How will they know if they have gotten everything that they will need during the analysis, interpretation, documentation and presentation phases? Another challenge comes from the massive databases used in customer relationship management systems and social graphs that current forensics cannot address. At the moment, investigators rely on traditional evidence-gathering methods while documenting the steps taken by law enforcement during the seizure and examination phases. "While this approach might suffice in some cases, there is a paucity of case law specific to forensics as applied to Cloud computing." The non-localized nature of Cloud computing will also usher in a debate about jurisdiction. "One of the long-term issues related to Cloud computing are those clouds that physically exist on a foreign server. What legal jurisdiction does law enforcement have in these cases? Do they have jurisdiction at all? Will the country in question be cooperative in terms of obtaining evidence?" (Lawton, 2011)

Digital forensics for Cloud computing faces many of the same challenges as virtual forensics and network forensics. Cloud computing is utilizing computing services provided remotely over a network such as the Internet. These services are often distributed over many datacenters, spread over different physical locations, with applications and data storage spread over a distributed architecture. As with virtual forensics, one of the larger issues is trying to understand the details of how the distributed architecture is designed so an investigator can pinpoint where the data they need to collect is actually located.

Unfortunately with large Cloud computing instances such as Goggle Apps, data can be stored across multiple servers within a datacenter for speed of access, efficiency and redundancy. Many customers' data may reside on the same physical disks making a whole disk image impossible to create without violating privacy laws. This can also lead to issues of attribution. How does an investigator prove that a subject actually wrote data to a specific place when there are many people and programs writing data on the same physical disks? It's especially hard when that data is spread over multiple disks. Since an investigator might not be able to make an accurate image of the data or disks live data analysis might have to be used which can be very time consuming and increases the risk of evidence data corruption with the possibility of inadvertent data change. It would be virtually impossible to prove that data found in unallocated space or file slack as so many people would be writing to the servers.

SECURITY OF CLOUDS

The newness of cloud technology and the uncertainty of cloud computing security leaves the door wide open for unscrupulous cyber-criminals who seek to exploit every opportunity. In addition, the explosion of cloud computing comes at a time when cybercrime is rapidly increasing. A recent Ponemon report indicates that cybercrime in 2011 is up 56 percent as compared to last year. (Ponemon Institute, 2011a) The report should alarm cloud providers however, Biggs and Vidalis warn that many providers don't fully understand the issues surrounding usage of the cloud; they state: 'The inevitability that unscrupulous users will identify and exploit any weaknesses that the cloud model possesses is a stark reality. Vendors, in their quest to secure a lucrative market share may have undermined the possibilities of attack and misuse of their cloud resources.' (Biggs, 2009).

Another issue in the use of Cloud for data storage and processing is the security of the data itself. Customers are completely reliant on the Cloud Service Provider for ensuring the secure transmission, storage and backup of the data they place on the Cloud. Therefore, the customer has no control over the use of robust cryptographic algorithms for transmission or storage and no control over provider's backup and remote storage procedures. The loss of control of data raises such security issues as well as a broader issue of what to do when there is a compromise of the Cloud. Since customers would have largely outsourced the data to the provider, they would likely not have any remaining infrastructure to support migrating the data back in-house. The last issue related to Cloud intrusions is that a malicious individual that has successfully targeted another customer in the Cloud now has access to your data as well since a single exploit gives him access to nearly all Cloud data. (Barbara, 2009)

Many vendors have claimed that they have invested a lot of money to provide data security in digital and physically at their data center but are being questioned by experts about the confidentiality, integrity and availability (CIA) model on cloud computing. The security concept of confidentiality of data in the traditional setting assumes that once the data is written the medium it cannot be retrieved by a malicious individual. In Cloud computing, there is no visibility for the owner of the data as who is accessing that data since the medium is physically and logically in the control of the Cloud Service Provider.

Questions that should be considered concerning confidentiality are:

Once the users give data to a third party so therefore no control over it, the questions are: give it to who? What access to the data? Who sees it? Can it be taken and used by someone else? Who administers this? What assurance of data being confidential? Happy with a contractual warranty? If so, then what's the user resource if the contract is breached?

This loss of control of the medium also has an impact on the previously held notion of integrity.

The owner of the data cannot be sure that the data is not tampered or modified since he doesn't control the medium on which it is stored on.

Questions that should be considered concerning integrity are:

Are the users convinced about the integrity of data? Can it be tampered with? If it was, would the users be informed of this? Are the users satisfied with the isolation of data? Any chance of leakage and how it's being protected and tested?

Cloud computing provides availability of data for the owner whenever it is needed. However, this availability is ever present for all the users of the Cloud including malicious individuals. Therefore, the data doesn't go into a dormant state once the legitimate user is done with it. Instead, is still highly available, even for those who are not authorized to access it. Therefore, the availability that the Cloud offers keeps the data available for all to use, good and bad. (Biggs, 2010)

LEGAL IMPLICATIONS

One major legal challenge which is brought up continuously is the fact that Cloud, and the data within the Cloud, would likely stretch across multiple legal jurisdictions and even international boundaries. This challenges acquisition of data from the Cloud as each cooperating law enforcement agency may employ varying software packages, perhaps without hashes, to acquire data and its admissibility into a foreign court. Considering the jurisdictions involved and how the laws in each of those areas address digital data as well as physical access to Cloud infrastructure is another hurdle. Instead of using a single standardized approach, Cloud forensics may have to be crafted for each legal environment and then homogenized after all data is acquired. Also, court orders to perform computer forensics are very narrow and the inherent nature of shared data within the cloud can create legal paradoxes

in which retrieving data related a criminal case can potentially copy data of innocent third parties.

At least in the United States, this would raise privacy concerns as the data can inadvertently end up in public as e-discovery would require its release to the opposition counsel. This may contaminate the evidence to a point where it may not be admissible in court (Phillips, 2009). Along the same lines it is to be noted that many foreign governments, including Canada and the European Union nations, fear the reach of the USA PATRIOT Act whereby the US Government could access data stored within its national boundaries. Because of this reason, these governments have restricted companies headquartered in their countries from using cloud services where the data could be stored within US government reach. There is good reason to fear this type of intrusion by US government agencies such as NSA based on the recent revelations about the data gathering practices of the US government under the Prism project.

SOLUTIONS

Two recent studies conducted by Ponemon Institute in 2011 indicate that the majority of cloud computing providers believe that it is the user's responsibility to secure the cloud. Customers must have procedures and policies in place for Cloud forensics after an incident (Ponemon Institute, 2011a; Ponemon Institute, 2011b). Currently, there are no industries or government standards for forensics in the Cloud, therefore companies should have formalized procedures for forensics with their Cloud Service Provider in case of an intrusion to ensure that there is a mechanism for performing a damage assessment as well as collecting forensic evidence for possible legal proceedings.

One possible solution that is posited is to use the Cloud itself for forensics. One approach introduces a concept of Sentinels within the Cloud that can activate to assist with forensics.

These sentinels would reside in the cloud and when activated, monitor and track the movements of cyber criminals. They would monitor the data they introduce or manipulate where it is stored and the path that they cyber criminals take within the cloud. This monitoring infrastructure would be transparent to the cyber criminals and logged for forensic purposes. Therefore, the elasticity of the Cloud itself can be used to create an on demand forensic service which can then be turned off when not needed. (Fu, 2010)

Brocade Systems have provided a unique solution to our current dilemma with Cloud computing. Since sells on network devices have slowed down to a snails pace, Brocade has decided instead of having all of these boxes sit around going to waste, what if we put the networking gear at the customers site and charge him for only the ports he uses. If there is more than one customer at the site at the same classification level allow multiple user to use the same box and keep all of there traffic separated by putting them on different VLAN.

Some other proposed solutions are:

- Build in forensics when developing your cloud infrastructure
- Develop forensics tools to address the cloud environment
- Develop new SOPs for forensic investigators working in the cloud
- Have established court approved methods for working in the cloud
- Customers need to clearly communicate and define to cloud providers what they consider incidents as opposed to suspicious events.
- Customers should have prearranged lines of communication to the cloud provider's incident response team.
- Customers should ensure that the cloud provider's incident detection and analysis tools are compatible with their own systems. Proprietary formats can become huge time wasters in an investigation, par-

ticularly if it is a joint investigation with legal or government entities.
- Any sensitive data that would violate a regulation in the event of a breach should be encrypted.
- Customers should look for cloud providers that can deliver snapshots of the customer's entire virtual environment for offline analysis

CONCLUSION

Cloud computing can be both an advantage and disadvantage for an organization. The advantages of reducing hardware and system administrator costs can be a plus for any organization but the disadvantages should be carefully considered before implementing the cloud architecture. While the savings on costs may be attractive to senior management within an organization, the level of data should always come first. Although the cloud infrastructure is the latest trend in technology, it does not mean it is the best for every organization. Private companies that only need to store proprietary information can consider using the cloud technology by implementing the private cloud model to protect their data. When National Security is considered, the cloud should be a far off future project that should be considered for a small fraction of the data that is considered to be classified.

Another disadvantage that organizations must be mindful of consists of the integrity of the data when computer forensics is involved. Since the norm for a computer forensics investigator is to perform his/her computer detective skills on the logical drive or the actual computer system, what would users do when a cloud infrastructure is involved? As trends come and organizations are so quick to spend money without doing the proper research, the cloud technology should be carefully researched before making decisions that organizations may soon regret. The risk obtained with loss of data, compromised data, and availability of data is too great for cloud service providers to take lightly. The less secure these environments are the more crimes that will occur and the investigators will be helpless to stop them. Forensics of cloud environments will become futile because the lack of security measures implemented opens up the door to any cyber criminal intent on malicious activity.

REFERENCES

Barbara, J. (2009). *Cloud computing: Another digital forensic challenge*. Retrieved from http://www.forensicmag.com/article/cloud-computing-another-digital-forensic-challenge?Page=0,1

Barbara., J. (2007). *Cloud computing: Another digital challenge*. Retrieved from http://www.forensicmag.com/article/cloud-computing-another-digital-forensic-challenge?page=0,1

Barnes, F. (2010). Putting a lock on cloud-based information: Collaboration between records and it professionals before contracting with cloud-based information services will help organizations ask the right questions to ensure their information is secure. *Information Management Journal, 44*(4).

Berry, T., Reilley, D., & Wren, C. (2011). Cloud computing, pros and cons for computer forensic investigations. *International Journal Multimedia and Image Processing, 1*(1), 26–34.

Biggs, S., & Vidalis, S. (2009). *Cloud computing: The impact on digital forensic investigations*. Retrieved from http://ieeexplore.ieee.org/search/freesearchresult.jsp?newsearch=true&queryText=cloud+computing%3A+impact+on+digital+forensic+investigations&x=19&y=11

Biggs, S., & Vidalis, S. (2010). Cloud computing storms. *International Journal of Intelligent Computing Research*, *1*(1/2), 61–68.

Brodkin, J. (2008). *Gartner: Seven cloud-computing security risks*. Retrieved from http://www.networkworld.com/news/2008/070208-cloud.html

Fu, X., Ling, Z., Yu, W., & Luo, J. (2010). Cyber crime scene investigations (C2SI) through cloud computing. In *Proceedings of 2010 IEEE 30th International Conference on Distributed Computing Systems Workshops* (ICDCSW). IEEE.

Knipp, E., et al. (2009). *Predicts 2010: Application infrastructure for cloud computing*. Retrieved from http://www.gartner.com/DisplayDocument?doc_cd=172072&ref=g_BETAnoreg

Ko, R., Lee, B., & Pearson, S. (2011). Towards achieving accountability, auditability and trust in cloud computing. *Advances in Computing and Communications: Communications in Computer and Information Science, 444*(193).

Lawton, G. (2011). *Cloud computing crime poses unique forensics challenges*. Retrieved from http://searchcloudcomputing.techtarget.com/feature/Cloud-computing-crime-poses-unique-forensics-challenges

Nelson, P., & Steuart, C. (2009). *Guide to computer forensics and investigations* (4th ed.). Boston, MA: Course Technology.

Ponemon Institute. (2011a). *Second annual cost of cybercrime study world economic forum, report: Exploring the future of cloud computing, riding the next wave of technology driven transformation*. Retrieved from http://www.ponemon.org/blog/post/second-cost-of-cyber-crime-study-is-released-today

Ponemon Institute. (2011b). *Security of cloud computing providers study*. Retrieved from http://www.ca.com/~/media/Files/IndustryResearch/security-of-cloud-computing-providers-final-april-2011.pdf

Section 3
Trust Builders in the Cloud

Chapter 11
Authentication and Identity Management for Secure Cloud Businesses and Services

Bing He
Cisco Systems, Inc., USA

Tuan T. Tran
InfoBeyond Technology LLC, USA

Bin Xie
InfoBeyond Technology LLC, USA

ABSTRACT

Today, cloud-based services and applications are ubiquitous in many systems. The cloud provides undeniable potential benefits to the users by offering lower costs and simpler deployment. The users significantly reduce their system management responsibilities by outsourcing services to the cloud service providers. However, the management shift has posed significant security challenges to the cloud service providers. Security concerns are the main reasons that delay organizations from moving to the cloud. The security and efficiency of user identity management and access control in the cloud needs to be well addressed to realize the power of the cloud. In this chapter, the authors identify the key challenges and provide solutions to the authentication and identity management for secure cloud business and services. The authors first identify and discuss the challenges and requirements of the authentication and identity management system in the cloud. Several prevailing industry standards and protocols for authentication and access control in cloud environments are provided and discussed. The authors then present and discuss the latest advances in authentication and identity management in cloud, especially for mobile cloud computing and identity as a service. They further discuss how proximity-based access control can be applied for an effective and fine-grained data access control in the cloud.

DOI: 10.4018/978-1-4666-5788-5.ch011

1. INTRODUCTION

Cloud computing offers us the state of the art technique to accomplish businesses or services over the networked cloud platforms while we don't need to own or manage the corresponding infrastructure. It provides our business many benefits, such as allowing us to set up a virtual office and thus connecting to our business anywhere and anytime. Such a capability is more flexible with the even growing popularity of web-enabled devices in today's business environment (e.g., smartphones, tablets), ubiquitously accessing the business data and performing various business operations in the cloud, which again is named as cloud business. The directly benefit of cloud business is the reduced IT costs as purchasing IT system can be avoided for running our business, consequently resulting in no cost on system upgrades, system maintenance, and IT staff. The other benefit is that our business can scale up or scale down easily with less cost. In addition, the business on the cloud promotes collaboration efficiency and flexibility of business practices.

New technology brings new risks and challenges. In the cloud, security is a critical issue for cloud users and the question is that if our business data and operations are well protected. For example, the business data should be protected from various cyber attackers as well as the insiders. For any requests of accessing the cloud data, the users have to be reliably and effectively authenticated to provide a secure and seamless user experience in cloud-based services. Identity Management (IDM) refers to the policies, processes, and technologies that establish user identities and enforce rules about access to certain resources and services. In cloud environment, service providers need to identify different users for bill purpose, to grant different access to resources and information, or to analyze user's behavior to optimize the customer experience with customized service and highly relevant content. All these rely on the IDM mechanism. An IDM mechanism can authenticate users and ser-

vices based on credentials and characteristics, and protect private and sensitive information related to users and processes. Authentication is the process of verify the identity of an individual, an entity or an organization through verifying the credentials. Typically there are three type of credentials a user could provide, i.e., what you know, e.g., passwords; what you have, e.g., ID card, wrist band, etc.; and what you are, e.g., biometric identifiers including fingerprints, palmprints, retinal pattern, signature, etc. Each of them has advantages and disadvantages in different application scenarios.

In a cloud environment, service are delivered through servers that are dynamically launched or terminated, IP address are dynamically allocated and assigned, and services are dynamically started or stopped. Traditional IDM may not be sufficient in this dynamic-changing and distributed cloud computing environment. The unique security and privacy implications in cloud computing imposes special requirements to IDM in cloud computing (Rhoton, 2011; Gopalakrishnan, 2009; Takabi, 2010):

- **Multi-Tenant Cloud Environments:** The multi-tenant cloud environments can affect the privacy of identity information. In multi-tenant cloud environments, providers must separate customer identity and authentication information. While users interact with a front-end service, their identity should be protected from other services which are running in back-end.
- **Volatility of Cloud Relations:** In traditional model, IDM is based on the long-term relations of users to an organization, company or trust domain. While in could, the relationships between tenant and venders change dynamically and quickly, imposing additional challenges for cloud IDM.
- **On-Demand Provisioning and Real-Time De-Provisioning:** An appropriate authentication and IDM solution in could

need to make sure current user gain access to requested resource immediately after authentication, while discontinued user could not access to previous accessible resources. On-demand provisioning indicates the federation of user accounts without sharing prior data. Real time de-provisioning requires that a user account has to synchronize instantaneously with all participating service providers. When a deployment or service or machine is decommissioned, the IDM has to be informed so that future access to it is revoked.

- **Interoperability**: A key issue concerning IDM in clouds is interoperability drawbacks that could result from using different identity tokens and identity negotiation protocols. The identity and privilege information may need to be exchanged among different cloud based service providers, which require the interoperable format and pattern to support the transfer of access right and privileges. Authentication and IDM components should also be easily integrated with other security components in different service models, which impose further requirement on standardization.

- **Scalability**: To accommodate multi-tenant enterprise applications and global consumer-oriented services, the IDM in cloud requires the ability to scale to hundreds of millions of transactions for millions of identities and thousands of connections with short/rapid deployment cycles.

- **Efficiency and Simplicity:** IDM in cloud is supposed to be able to provide multiple levels, seamless access in a distributed multi-vendor architecture in cloud, which implies the requirement to simplify the user experience with minimum user-involved re-authentication between services and providers.

- **Architecture Specific Requirements:** Appropriate IDM mechanisms depend on different cloud architecture and service models. Among the three major categories of cloud computing services, from SaaS to PaaS to IaaS, less security reply on provider, more rely on customer. For example, one limitation with PaaS is that the complex IDM solution designed for one PaaS is rendered useless while migrating to another cloud provider. While in IaaS, customers may get more flexibility in choosing and implementing their own customized IDM schemes.

- **Law Compliance:** Due to the distributed characteristics of cloud, both the service provider and the customer may be located in different locations around the world, where different countries may have different law enforcement regarding the privacy and security. The multi-jurisdiction issue can even complicate protection measures in cloud IDM.

The purpose of this chapter is to provide a comprehensive and thoughtful insight on the cloud authentication and IDM for enabling secure cloud business. The focus of our discussion is not only the study of the authentication and IDM approaches envisioned in the academic sphere but also an investigation of the standardization and initiatives on the industry. The Trusted Cloud Initiative that was launched in 2010 by CSA (Cloud Security Alliance) and Novell includes identity management on one of its work emphasis. Identity management providers are targeting the cloud and looking to make use of federated identity methods to provide single sign on along with strong authentication if required. Based on such an observation, the discussion of this chapter starts from the federated identify management specifications with the illustration of a typical authentication procedure. Moreover, this chapter will describe the following issues:

- **Specifications for Authentication and IDM:** Several standards are discussed including OpenID, Secure Assertion Makeup Language, and OAuth. All these protocol enables the cloud service provider to authenticate a cloud user by validating the user's credentials. As the authentication is performed on the cloud over the Internet, secure communication is required to protect the message exchanged between the business users and the cloud. These protocols should be able to prevent potential cyber vulnerabilities.
- **Authentication and IDM for Mobile Cloud Computing:** With the ever growing popularity, mobile devices become an indispensable part for cloud business. The authentication and IDM ofthese mobile devices as well as the users is critical to protect the business data and other assets. The data at rest of a cloud business should be protected from unauthorized access, poison, or other attacks. TrustCube (Chow, 2010) authentication protocol is a technology to authenticate mobile users. Identity as a Service (IDaaS) provides an SOA-based architecture for identity management, authentication, authorization, and access control.
- **Proximity-Based Access Control (PBAC):** Recently, many applications utilize all proximity-based conditions for user authentication and data access to the cloud. The cloud could dynamically adjust access controls for individuals, based on the changes of the proximity-based attributes, e.g., roles, status, geographical locations, moving speeds, organizations. PBAC supports need-to-know on data access in the mobile and distributed environment. It provides the ability to securely and accurately

evaluate the organizational and geographical proximity to grant the data access with dynamic, context-aware, and risk-intelligent access control.

Specifically, in Section 2, we will cover the prevalent federated identity management in cloud computing, along with the popular identity management protocols and standards used in industry, including OpenID, OAuth, and SAML. To solve the new challenges on authentication and identity management in cloud computing, especially for the mobile cloud computing and the identity-as-a-service model, researchers have proposed a couple of new approaches and mechanisms, which will be covered in Section 3. Section 4 illustrates proximity-based access control to provide an efficient means of evaluating the proximity distance and enabling fine grained access control in a complex context. In Section 5, the future direction of the authentication and identity management in cloud computing will be discussed, and the chapter will be concluded in Section 6.

2. IDENTITY MANAGEMENT SOLUTIONS AND STANDARDS IN CLOUD

In the traditional IT architecture, the identify management is implemented and maintained by separated organizations as fragmented approaches. This fragmented IDM approach has several problems as described below (Rhoton, 2011):

1. **Burden for Customers:** Users have to register at each individual security domains of service providers (like websites), and remember multiple usernames and passwords.
2. **Burden on Service Providers:** Each service provider need to implement and maintain their own identity management system, which incur considerable amount of work

and financial cost, which may be put into the core competency of the company.

3. **Risk of Leak:** The burden on user lead to weak password or reuse of credentials across security domains, which increase the risk that more sensitive information compromised when the credentials are leaked. Especially, the existing password-based authentication has an inherited limitation and poses significant leak risks.

4. **Difficulty to Comply with Regulations:** Different countries impose different regulations on the identity management and privacy protection, which imply sophisticated IDM system, and set an obstacle for small business with limited resource to enter the market.

By using cloud services, users can easily access their personal information and make it available to various services across the Internet. Single sign-on (SSO) is a preferable property of access control of multiple related, independent systems, in which a user's single authentication ticket, or token, is trusted across multiple software systems or even organizations. With this property, a user logs in once and gains access to all systems without being prompted to log in again at each of them. SSO reduces the burden of users to remember different user name and password pairs, simplifies the authentication process among multiple providers and thus provides a better user experience. The Cloud Security Alliance recommends cloud provider to provide stronger authentication mechanism and also allow users to use third party identity management and single signon platforms. SSO today has become prevailing in cloud security, and the security of the deployed SSO mechanisms becomes essential to security of cloud service. In enterprise, SSO usually relies on the Microsoft active directory. In cloud, it will be preferable to have the widely accepted user store to implement the SSO, which lead to the need for federated identity management (FIM). As the key solution to SSO in cloud computing, feder-

ated identity is becoming the dominant trend in identity management of cloud environment today. OAuth, OpenID, SAML are three main concepts in cloud authentication and federated environment, providing user centric and transparent federated identity in cloud applications.

2.1. Federated Identity Management Architecture

In traditional security architecture, each company/enterprise maintain their own directory services such as Microsoft Active Directory or other similar products based on LDAP (Lightweight Directory Access Protocol) to provide LDAP based authentication for users / customers through a single identity. While a user may need to maintain separate credentials for each system/companies to get services. Federated identity management (FIM) is a mechanism that can be implemented among multiple enterprises that allows subscribers use the same identification data to obtain access to the networks of all enterprises in the group. The use of such a system is also called identity federation. Federation refers to the establishment of business agreements, cryptographic trust, and user identifiers or attributes across security and policy domains to enable more seamless cross-domain business interactions (OASIS, 2005).

The main idea behind the federated identity management is it separates the identity provider and the service provider. Federated identity allows identity to be shared among multiple service providers, and/or one service provider may rely on multiple identity providers to get the identity and authentication service. A diagram illustrate the federated identity management schema is as in Figure 1.

As illustrated in Figure 1, there are three roles in a federated identity management architecture scheme, i.e., the customers, service providers and identity providers. The customers are the end users, which could be a person, a business, or a software entity. Customer may have multiple identity profiles

Figure 1. Federated identity management architecture (Shin, 2003)

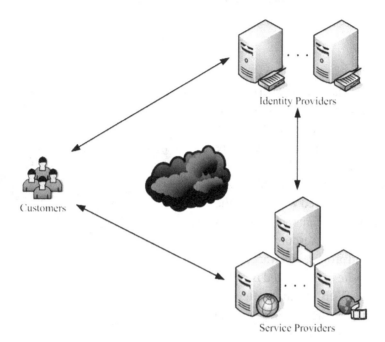

maintained by different identity providers based on user's habit, credibility, type of service, and so on. Identity providers could cooperate among themselves if they have permission to do so from the profile's owner, i.e., the consumer. The service providers provide the services to the customers. By retrieving relevant identity profiles from the identity providers, service providers may provide customers with highly relevant information and customized services.

Federated Identity Management allows a user to use same login credential data (such as user name, password or other identification method like biometrics) to get authenticated to multiple services, is the key technology to provide the Single Sign-on (SSO) in Cloud. With FIM one user only need to register with one identity provider and gain services form multiple service providers who are in the agreement circle of the federated identity management with the registered identity provider. Identity federation offers economic advantages, as well as operation convenience, to

both service providers and their customers. FIM allows companies to keep their own directories and securely exchange information among them. With FIM, multiple companies can share a customer's information from one or multiple identity providers, with resultant cost savings and consolidation of resources.

In order for FIM to be effective, the partners must build a relationship of mutual trust, and able to exchange user information in a uniform way or follow some agreed protocols. One sample of the standard to exchange FIM information is the Security Assertion Markup Language (SAML), which allows a way to identify and authenticate a user. Authorization messages among partners in an FIM system can be transmitted using SAML or similar XML standards. Besides SAML, popular technologies used for federated logon include OAuth and OpenID, as well as proprietary standards. OpenID and OAuth are widely used in consumer market, and SAML-based federations are more prevalent in enterprise market such as education, government, and corporate intranets.

2.2. OpenID

One widely used authentication approach for web Single Sign on is OpenID, which provides an authentication method that uses single identification to access multiple websites and resources. There are three major parties in the OpenID framework, i.e., user, relaying party and identity provider. The provider that customer registered with called the OpenID provider (OP) and obtains a uniqueOpenID identity, which is a uniform resource identifier (URI) that the user would provide when accessing a Web site, and the website being visited is called the relying party (RP). With OpenID, after the user registering with one OP, the obtained OpenID identity could be used to sign on to other web sites accepting OpenID authentication.

To utilize the benefits of the OpenID, the end-user need to first register with OpenID Identity provider, and obtains an OpenID, which is a URI for this particular user with this OpenID provider, such as bob.openidprovider.org. During the authentication, the OpenID framework provides the cryptographic substructure to prove that a user owns the URL he/she use to log in. OpenID standards provide a framework for the secure communications between these three parties. In a typical OpenID authentication scenario in which the registered user (who owns his OpenID URI) is requesting access to an OpenID supported website, following steps happen as illustrated in Figure 2.

1. User visits the website who is the relying party of OpenID, such as NPR website.
2. The relaying party provides the user the OpenID login option by refers the user to the OpenID provider.
3. The user authenticate with the OpenID identity provider via providing security credentials such as passwords, or biometrics information.

Figure 2. OpenID authentication

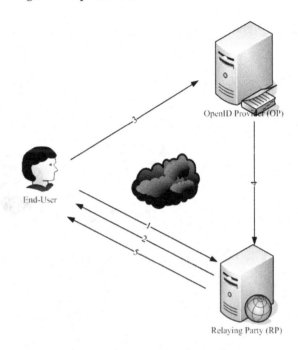

4. The Identity Provider will authenticate the user and provide the authentication result to the relaying party directly after the authentication is done.
5. When the relaying party gets the authentication confirmation from the identity provider, it will grant the user with access without asking any authentication credentials.

One benefit of OpenID is that you only need to remember one pair of username and password. Also, OpenID provides another level of security that you only need to give the credentials (such as user name and password) to the OpenID provider; the relaying party (i.e., the website that the user is visiting) only got to know you are who you say you are, while it will not know your credentials (i.e., password). Thus, you don't need to worry about an insecure website may compromise your identity.

The OpenID authentication protocol was originally developed by Brad Fitzpatrick in May 2005 (OpenIdwiki, n.d.). Currently the OpenID

Foundation, which is a non-profit organization incorporated in the United States, commits to enabling, promoting and protecting OpenID protocols and technologies. The latest version of OpenID is 2.0, which was announced in 2007. OpenID authentication service have been provided and supported by multiple large websites. The major OpenID providers include Google, Yahoo, AOL, PayPal, VeriSign, etc. As of December 2009, approximately 9 million sites support OpenID and over 1 billion OpenID enabled accounts have been established (OpenIdwiki, n.d.).

2.3. Security Assertion Markup Language (SAML)

The Security Assertion Markup Language (SAML) is another approach for providing the Single Sign-on service. SAML is an XML-based framework for communicating user authentication, entitlement, and attribute information, and allows business entities to make assertions regarding the identity, attributes, and entitlements of an individual user to other entities, such as a partner company or another enterprise application (OASIS, 2005). It was developed and supported by the Security Services Technical Committee of the open standards consortium, Organization for the Advancement of Structured Information Standards (OASIS). Prior to SAML, there was no XML-based standard that enabled exchange of security information between a security system (such as an authentication authority) and an application that trusts the security system. SAML provides a standard XML representation for specifying this information and interoperable ways to exchange and obtain it.

Similar to OpenID, there are three entities in the SAML architecture, i.e., customer, service provider and identity provider. The service provider provides the service to customer, i.e., the end user. Customer is end-user, who is requesting the service from the service provider. The identity provider is responsible to maintain the user pro-

Figure 3. SAML

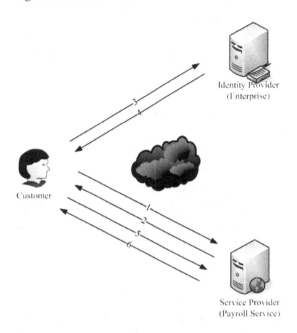

file and provide the authentication mechanism. Service provider will grant the user requested service based on the authentication result from identity provider.

One example of SAML is as illustrated in Figure 3, in which a payroll company provides payroll service to employee of an employer company. The employer maintains the employee's account information and subscribes the payroll service provided by the payroll company. Each individual employee is the customer, who already have their profile established and account registered with the identity provider.

1. The user attempts to access the service provider, i.e., the payroll company, to request the payroll service, e.g., query the paycheck and direct deposit of this month.
2. The service provider, i.e., the payroll company, generates a SAML authentication request and sends it over to the employee.
3. The user/customer will be redirected to the identity provider's authentication portal, i.e., the employer's website along with the

SAML request generated by the service provider, i.e., the payroll service company. The identity provider decodes the SAML request and authenticates the user based on its authentication mechanism, such as asking user to provide user name and password, or checking for valid session cookies, etc.

4. Once the authentication is done, the identity provider generates a SAML response for this particular user and signs it with public key, and sends it back to the customer.

5. The customer forwards the receivedSAML authentication response to the service provider.

6. The service provider decodes the SAML response using its private key. If the authentication is successful, the payroll company will grant the user access to the requested service, and the user logins into the payroll service successfully.

By utilization of SAML, the costs to maintain and develop proprietary SSO are reduced. Similar to OpenID, SAML simplifies the user authentication by allowing user only register and authenticate at the identify provider to access multiple service providers. Also, one service provider could provide services to users managed by multiple identity providers. Due to all authentications is located at the identity provider, the cost to maintain user information is reduced, particularly for service provider. The identity provider could customize the authentication methods per its preference. Another benefit for the service provider is since it replies on the identity provider to take the responsibility to maintain the identity, which also take the risk of information disclosure.

Even both able to provide Single Sign-on, SAML have some advantages compared with OpenD. OpenID is mainly targeted for web SSO, while SAML is more flexible and not limited to Web SSO. Besides commonly found among Web services management and security vendors,

SAML support also appears in major application server products. Interoperability is another huge advantage of SAML over proprietary SSO mechanisms, which require the Identity Provider (IdP) and Service Provider (SP) to both implement the same software. For an enterprise, proprietary SSO means each new SSO partnership requires new and different software implementation. With SAML, a single SAML implementation can support SSO connections with many different federation partners. Some large organizations and companies with their own proprietary SSO implementations have been able to utilize SAML for Internet SSO with Software-as-a-Service (SaaS) applications and other external service providers.

SAML is a flexible and extensible standard designed to be used and customized if necessary by other standards/protocols. By defining standardized mechanisms for the communication of security and identity information between partners, SAML will be able to provide federated identity, and enable the cross-domain transactions (OASIS, 2005). The latest SAML 2.0, which was approved in 2005, demonstrates a key progress towards convergence in the federated identity management standards. The Liberty Alliance, an industry group formed to promote federated-identity standards, has adopted SAML as part of its application framework. An alternative specification called WS-Security which is proposed by Microsoft and IBM, also have adopted SAML as a technological underpinning. Shibboleth (Internet2) project, which is an open-source project that provides Single Sign-On capabilities, also utilize SAML as the underlying standard. As the gold standard for federated identity, SAML has been broadly implemented by all major Web access management vendors such as Entrust, IBM, Microsoft, Novell, Ping Identity, SAP, Siemens, RSA Security, and NEC etc. Several companies have adopted SAML as the standards to exchange the user authentication information, including

American Express, Boeing, General Motor, and Proctor and Gamble.

2.4. OAuth

Commonly known as an authorization protocol, OAuth provides another way to authorize a third-party (called consumer) to access their private data stored in another website (called provider), without disclosing user's credentials associated with the provider to the third-party service site. There are three entities in OAuth, i.e., the user, provider and consumer. User have private resource located at the provider, and would like the consumer to access these resource without disclosing the authentication credentials to the consumer. Contrast to the OpenID, in which customers will be required to provide OpenID credentials (e.g., user name and password) to identity provider, in OAuth, users are asked to login to the consumer website once, and then user grant the consumer website the access to services provided by other service providers, and they user doesn't need to provide any further authentication to visit other websites. Similar to the OpenID, OAuth simplifies the way that user to access multiple different website with one login credentials.

A typical scenario of OAuth is as illustrated in Figure 4. User (let's say Tom) has some photos stored in an online photo storage store, e.g., Flickr. He wants to have it printed out by another printing service company, e.g., Jane's printing store, with portal janesprint.com. By using OAuth, Tom may grant the printing service store to access to his photos stored in Flickr, while without disclosure his user name and password with Flickr to the printing service store. In this scenario, Tom is the user, Flickr is the provider, and the printing service store (i.e., janesprint.com) is the consumer. In the OAuth scheme, the provider website, i.e., Jane's printing store in the example, not the end user, need to request access to the photo storage website, e.g., Flickr. During the authorization process, the printing service website (i.e., janesprint.com)

Figure 4. OAuth Authorization

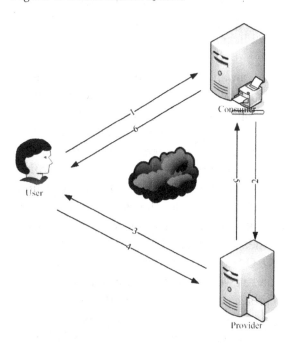

will be the customer to the access photo storage website (i.e., Flickr).

1. Tom initially requests the printing store to access the photos stored in Flickr under Tom's account.
2. Printing store will request a Request token from Flickr.
3. Tom will be redirected to the Flickr authorization URL, asked to provide authentication information to authenticate.
4. Tom authenticate with the provider, i.e., Flickr here by providing requested authentication credentials. After authentication is successful, Tom will immediately request Flickr to grant access to the Consumer, i.e., the printing store, for his photos.
5. Flickr notify access is granted by issuing token to consumer marked as User-authorized. For now on, printing store could access Tom's photos in Flickr.

6. Printing store will confirm with user that it has gotten the access to Tom's photo in Flickr.

As an approach to provide Single Sign-on, OAuth provides a simplified way to grant third-party applications to access customer's private data. OAuth doesn't disclose authentication credentials, e.g. passwords, to third-party applications, and can cancel at any time with any app they have granted permission to. OAuth didn't limit how the provider authenticate the user, in which the authentication methods could be password, biometric identifier, physical token or even OpenID. OAuth could be used in enterprises and the cloud as well. Enterprises are able to useOAuth to protect the APIs they offer their partners and customers as well as internal clients in their own private cloud. For instance, Salesforce have used OAuth to protect the APIs they offer up to their enterprise customers (PingIdentity).

OAuth was first developed in 2006 during Twitter OpenID implementation, and the OAuth Core 1.0 final draft was released in 2007 (OAuthSite, 2007). In April 2010, OAuth 1.0 Protocol was formally published as RFC 5849. The latest version of OAuth 2.0 Framework was published as RFC649 in Oct 2012, along with Bearer Token Usage as RFC 6750. Even though it focuses on client developer simplicity, OAuth 2.0 is also explicitly designed to support a variety of different client types such as web applications, desktop applications, mobile phones, and living room devices (OAuthwiki, 2012). OAuth 2.0 is not backward compatible with OAuth 1.0. Almost all the major Internet companies like Facebook, Google, and Microsoft support OAuth. Because OAuth 2.0 is more like a framework rather than a defined protocol, any OAuth 2.0 implementation is unlikely to naturally be interoperable with any other OAuth 2.0 implementation. Companies provide their own API for customers to develop their OAuth application. For example, Flickr,

Salesforce, and Twitter all provide many APIs for their OAuth application.

3. CHALLENGES AND ADVANCES OF AUTHENTICATION AND IDENTITY MANAGEMENT IN CLOUD

Even cloud vendors provided various cloud products with the authentication and identity management schemes based on these industry standards, there are still many challenges need to be faced in implementing a robust and secure cloud service platform, especially when cloud computing is combined with mobile networks. Identity management also start to be provided as an independent cloud service, i.e., the Identity as a Service, which imply more requirements on the reliability, scalability and efficiency.

3.1. Challenges and Issues

In cloud computing environment, SSO-oriented approaches such as OpenId or SAML offer seamless service accesses across the service providers. However, the current approaches have several issues:

- **Privacy-Preserving:** Interoperability allows the users seamlessly access the services and resources across the service providers. However, it also poses significant issues ranging from the use of different identity tokens and different identity negotiation protocols to the use of different names for identity attributes. In addition, users should be able to control on which personal information is disclosed and how the information is used by different service providers to reduce the risk of identity theft and fraud.
- **Authentication "Bottle-Neck":** Traditional SSO approaches implement asymmetric encryption technique which

results in a significant increase of computation load on both service provider and identity provider. In addition, when identity is provided by a third party IdP, the authentication request is redirected out of the cloud federation (to the identity provider), it has a higher chance of security breach. Alternatively, when identity is provided by cloud's identity management system (IMS), rather than a third party IdP, IMS has to verify a large amount of users' credentials and session information, significantly increasing the service latency.

- **Security for Mobile Cloud Computing:** Mobile cloud computing (MCC) becomes animportant domain in the development of IT as well as commerce and industry fields. The paradigm of MCC allows mobile users to store their data and performs intensive processing functions on centralized-powerful computing platforms in the clouds. However, the architecture of the MCC, an integration of two different fields, i.e., cloud computing and mobile networks, creates many technical challenges such as low transmission bandwidth, connection availability, network heterogeneity, load balancing, and system security.

3.2. Latest Advances in Authentication and IDM

To overcome the issues of the current approaches, some advanced techniques have been proposed in (Ahn, 2009; Bertino, 2009; Nunez, 2012). In particular, the work of Ahn et al (Ahn, 2009) proposed a user-centric based IDM approach to handle private and critical identity attributes. Such an approach lets users control their digital identities and takes away the complexity of IDM from the SPs. Additionally, the proposed approach allows the users to have fine-grained control on their credentials in response to an authentication or attribute request. It provides users more rights and responsibility over their identity information.

Alternatively, the work of Bertino et al (Bertino, 2009) proposed privacy-preserving multi-factor identity attribute verification protocol supporting a matching technique based on look-up tables, dictionaries, and ontology mapping techniques to match cloud SPs and client vocabularies. Particularly, the proposed protocol implements aggregate zero-knowledge proofs of knowledge (AgZKPK) cryptographic protocol which allows clients to prove with a single interactive proof the knowledge of multiple identity attributes without the need to provide them in clear forms. The multi-factor authentication protocol is carried out in two steps. In the first step, the SP matches the identity attributes in the client vocabulary with its own attributes to obtain identity verification policy. Basically, an identity verification policy consists of a set of identity attributes that the user must prove to be known. In the second step, the user performs the AgZKPK protocol to prove to the SP that its knowledge of the matched identity attributes without revealing their values.

In a different approach, the work of Nunez et al, (Nunez, 2012) demonstrated how a privacy-preserving IDM system can be implemented using the OpenID protocol and proxy re-encryption technique. In particular, the proposed scheme allows an IdP to provide attributes to other parties without being able to read their values in an efficient way; thus, preserving the users' privacy with respect to the IdP. In other words, the IdP can serve as an identity source but it learns nothing about the users' information. In addition, the work of Spantzel et al (Spantzel, 2005) showed a flexible and privacy-preserving scheme which enables a user to establish a unique identifier and complex identity attributes in a federation. Importantly, the proposed scheme relaxes the dependence on PKI for user authentication, which currently is the "bottle-neck" of several trust management solutions.

In a different avenue, the work of Kimet al. (Kim, 2010) proposed Chord for Cloud (C4C) framework, a peer-to-peer (P2P) based scheme, for balancing processing load among the computing nodes within the cloud. Particularly, the proposed C4C decreases the number of authentication request sent to the IdPs and balances the authentication processing within the federated environments. In another work, Ahn et al. (Ahn, 2011) proposed a user authentication platform using provisioning. Particularly, the proposed platform architecture analyzes user information and authenticates the user based on its profile. The advantage of this approach is that the user authentication process required by the SP can be omitted if the user has prior used other cloud computing services.

3.3. Authentication and IDM for Mobile Cloud Computing

Basically, mobile cloud computing (MCC) is built from the traditional cloud computing infrastructure to provide advanced services to mobile users. Although MCC potentially brings several benefits to the mobile users, it also creates additional technical challenges due to the unique characteristics of the mobile networks and mobile devices. We start with the system architecture of the MCC.

- **System Architecture**: The architecture of MCC is illustrated in Figure 5. Generally, the MCC architecture consists of two main components, i.e., mobile networks and cloud service providers, which are connected via the Internet. The mobile users (MUs) interact with a cloud service provider using either native mobile applications or embedded browser applications. The native mobile applications are developed based on programming language-supported mobile platform with a set of application programming interfaces (APIs), provided by the SPs. Differently, the embedded browser applications are devel-

oped from the standard web development languages such as HTML and Javascript. Typically, the MUs are connected to the mobile network via a wireless link (e.g., over WiFi or cellular carrier). The MU's request and information (e.g., ID and location, etc.) are transmitted to the mobile network services (MNS) where the authentication, authorization, and accounting (AAA) will be performed. Once validated, the MU's request will be relayed to the SPs via the Internet. The cloud controllers of the SPs play as gateways which receive and process the MUs' requests. Once users' credentials are verified, the cloud controllers utilize the back-end cloud services to provide requested services to the MUs.

- **Advantages of MCC**: MCC is a promising solution for mobile applications by offering several benefits:
  - **Extending battery lifetime**: MCC can significantly extend the battery lifetime of mobile devices by off-loading computational and processing to the cloud service providers. In fact, substantial performance improvements are obtained, depending on the transmission scenarios, for example, about 45% (Rudenko, 1998) and 41% (Kremer, 2001) energy savings can be achieved in large-scale numerical computations and image processing, respectively.
  - **Providing large data storage space and high processing capability**: MCC enables mobile users to store and access large amount of data on the cloud via wireless networks to address the issues of limited storage capacity of mobile devices. For example, Amazon S3 supports large file storage services (Amazon S3, 2013; Flickr, 2013; Shozu, n.d.). On the other hand, intensive computations

can also be supported by clouds such as multimedia services (Garcia, 2011; Li, 2010) to mobile devices. In these cases, all the complex calculations are quickly performed on the clouds.

○ **Improving reliability**: Data in the clouds is usually stored in multiple servers that reduce the chance of data loss or failures. In addition, the clouds can provide mobile users with security services such as virus scanning, malicious code detection, and authentication (Oberheide, 2008).

• **Security Challenges of MCC**: There are several security and privacy issues in the MCC which are inherited from the current cloud service providers such as data replication, consistency, scalability, unreliability, portability, trust, and network security (Zissis, 2012). In addition, the mobile devices in MCC are resource-limited; thus, the security algorithms proposed for the cloud computing environments cannot be directly implemented on the mobile devices. It requires a lightweight security framework which can be run on the resources-limited mobile devices with minimum communication and processing overhead. Furthermore, it is difficult to achieve a secure end-to-end communication channel from the cloud service provider to the mobile device due to the vulnerable wireless link between the mobile network and mobile device.The existing secure routing protocols can be used to protect the communication channels between the mobile devices and the clouds; however, they cannot be applied directly onto the mobile devices due to their energy inefficiency (Ren, 2011). In what follows, we will discuss an efficient authentication scheme for the MCC.

• **An efficient authentication technique for MCC**: To address the existing issues

of the MCC, Chow et al (Chow, 2010) proposed an authentication framework for the MCC environments.In particular,the proposed framework, an integration of the TrustCube (Song, 2009) and implicit authentication (Jakobsson, 2009), offers a practical and efficient way for authentication in the MCC.The high-level system architecture of the proposed framework is illustrated in Figure 6. The authentication process is carried out as follows:

1. Tom, as a mobile cloud user, initially requests a service on the cloud service provider.
2. Upon receiving the request, the cloud service provider redirects the request to the integrated authentication (IA) service with the details of the request.
3. Tom is asked to provide credentials for service authentication by the IA service.
4. Tom authenticates with the IA by providing requested authentication credentials.
5. The IA service retrieves the policy for the access request, extracts the information that needs to be collected, and send an inquiry to the implicit authentication (ImA) server via a trusted network connection (TNC) protocol.
6. The ImA server processes the inquiry, generates a report, and sends it back to the IA service.
7. The IA service applies the authentication rule in the policy and determines the authentication result which is sent to the service provider.
8. If the authentication rules are satisfied, the requested service is returned to the mobile user.

Noting that in this architecture, prior to the authentication process, the cloud service providers need to register a policy for each request type

Figure 5. Mobile cloud computing (MCC) architecture

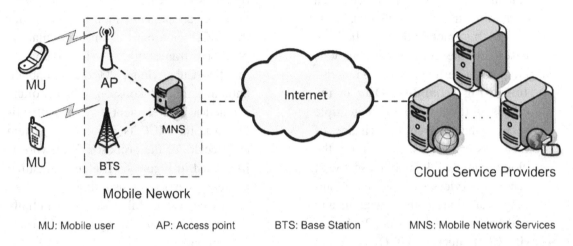

MU: Mobile user   AP: Access point   BTS: Base Station   MNS: Mobile Network Services

Figure 6. TrustCube authentication protocol

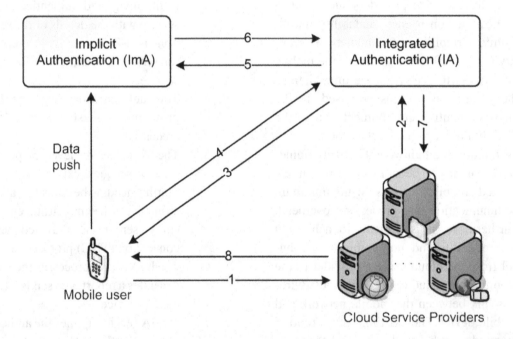

with the IA service. The policy basically contains the access request (e.g., money transaction, web-page access, etc.), the information to be collected from the client mobile device, and a rule to generate the authentication result. Furthermore, during the normal operation of the mobile device, it periodically sends reports to the ImA containing the data which is then used to track the user's

behavior and support authentication requests. The performance of the proposed scheme is dependent on the IA service to identify legitimate users. As the number of users increases, the "bottle-neck" effect will degrade the system performance. To avoid this issue, several instances of IAs may be deployed within cloud on demand (Khan, 2013).

Figure 7. SOA-Based shared and reusable services

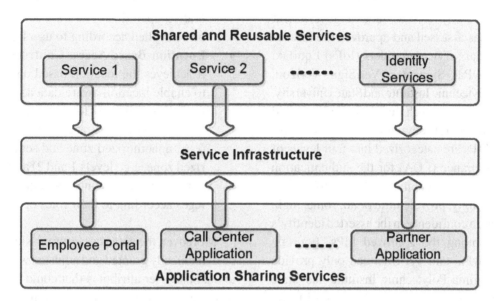

3.4 Identity as a Service (IDaaS)

Identity as a service (IDaaS) is the terminology used to describe the management of identity, authorization, authorization access control, etc. in the cloud services. The aims of IDaaS are not only to enable SSO convenience to the end users but also to reduce the heavy burden of identity management of the users and enterprises. IDaaS can provide identity services in a consistent and reusable way for application developments and application runtime environments. Typically, IDaaS takes the functionality of an identity management and makes a set of identity services available in a Service-Oriented Architecture (SOA) environment as illustrated in Figure 7 (Oracle, 2010).

In this architecture, IDaaS provides several identity-related services such as:

- **Identity Provider:** a service that provides access to identity profile data.
- **Authentication:** a service that provides identity authentication capabilities.
- **Role Provider:** a service that provides roles and role memberships

- **Authorization:** a service that supports entitlement modeling and fine-grained authorization.
- **Provisioning:** a service that supports administration of identity and access management (IAM) context.
- **Audit:** a service that provides all identity events.

There are multiple benefits that could be provided by IDaaS:

- Reduce system complexity by leveraging critical identity data across business parties and removing the management/replication challenges.
- Increase security by providing centralized policy management and a controls framework that can dynamically mitigate risks.
- Create a flexible, adaptable, integrated platform on which to build applications
- Makes new types of de-perimeterised, identity-based business functionality viable.

The Identity, Credential and Access Management (ICAM), a U.S. federal government initiative, has assessed and approved the following credential service providers (IdPs) Equifax, Google, PayPal, Symantec, VeriSign, Verizon, Virginia Polytechnic Institute and State University, and Wave Systems, such that they can be trusted and used by federal Relying Parties (RPs). Typically, the IdPs are categorized into four levels of identity assurance (LOA) for the authentication of electronic transaction. The LOA1 to LOA4, correspondingly, provide little or no, some, high, and very high confidence in the asserted identity's validity. Among the approved IdPs, Equifax, Google, PayPal and VeriSign can only provide LOA1, Virginia Polytechnic Institute and State University can provide both LOA1 and LOA2, and Symantec and Verizon can provide LOA1, LOA2, and non-PKI LOA3.

4. PROXIMITY-BASED ACCESS CONTROL

Recently, the cloud data access moves the access control towards intelligent systems to achieve fine grained access capabilities. Proximity-Based Access Control (PBAC) provides such fine grained data access on the cloud:

- **Attribute-Based Access Control (ABAC):** Attributes are sets of properties that can be used to describe all the entities that must be considered for authorization purposes. ABAC provides dynamic access to the data information for users with appropriate data attributes while prohibiting access to the requestors who do not meet the attribute expressed criteria. In addition, it needs efficient and flexible revocation of the attributes for access control to achieve dynamic data access control.
- **Role-Based Access Control (RBAC):** It advocates the personalized data access, ac-

cording to users' roles during their collaborative operations. The data access should be controlled according to users' roles.

- **Location-Based Access Control (LBAC):** It achieves the location based data service to enable location-aware data access or information delivery to users. Approaches mostly divide the granted area into zones (e.g., unauthorized zone and scaled authorized zone, e.g., levels 1 and 2) and the data consumers in the zone have different privileges according to their roles of an event.

Moreover, the data access permissions should be dynamically granted and adjusted with respect to data and user attributes that could be defined from the aspects of organizational relationships, geographic features, business roles, and others. For facilitating collaborative service, for example, a doctor should have more detailed information of a patient when he/she is approaching the operational room while sharing necessary information with his/her team members to collaborate better. Furthermore, the doctor on the operational chain of patient service should exchange the service information, in accordance with their operational proximity to improve their collaborative efficiency. In other words, an access control mechanism is required to provide data or resources to doctor on a need-to-know basis for the patient to ensure assured information delivery and sharing. The need-to-know considers not only the data properties but also the collaborators on the team from the following aspects:

- **Organizational Proximity:** The organizational relationships among a team in the chain of operations are fundamental to providing access control such that the operations are collaboratively conducted to accomplish a service or a mission.
- **Geographic Proximity:** It considers the geographic attributes as a key aspect for need-to-know when the users are located

at a specific location site that is a factor of sharing data.

- **Operational Proximity:** The data attributes allow teams to share the data if they perform similar operations.

In a complex and dynamic context, all of these aspects can be considered as "joint attributes" for "dynamic decision" of data access. It allows all partners to share the information they need, when they need it, in a form they can understand and act on with confidence, and protects information against those who should not have it. Therefore, the authentication and data access control should quantify:

- **Quantification of the Proximity:** It is to effectively quantify the organizational proximity, location proximity, and operation proximity, i.e., how to measure the proximity distance. Consequently, the data system provides data to right persons while the others are prohibited from data access.

- **Quantification of Locations:** Some approaches (e.g., GPS) are able to evaluate the geographical proximity. GPS should be considered with the data access policy while preventing attacks of forging location claims. It is to ensure a requestor car-

ries his/her locations for authentication for data access.

- **Integration of all Accessing Factors:** The data access should integrate the individual roles, data attributes, organizational relations, locations, and operations in a unified form to create standard form of data access to facilitate collaborative service.

Figure 8 illustrate the location-based authentication by evaluating the geographical proximity. The geographic proximity is normally measured by distance that is the physical distance between two locations. The access control is conducted over an accessing granted area **A** that could be the place of the event or operations. This area **A** can be further divided into non-overlapping smaller zeros if necessary and each zone has different data access policies. In the mobile environment, the data requests have to continuously validate their locations and the data access policies are dynamically adjusted with respect to their moving locations. Figure 8(a) and (b)show two typical scenarios:

- **WLAN Mode:** In this mode, the data requestor is able to receive referring beacons or other signals in the access granted area **A**. These beacons are broadcast by references. A set of references can be located

Figure 8. Location-based data access

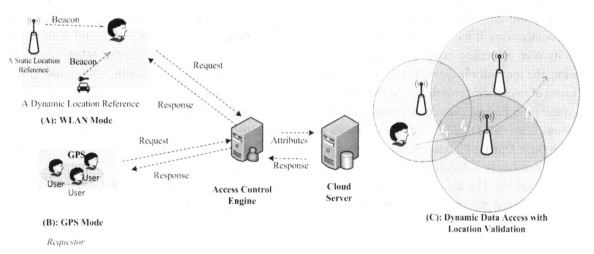

around **A**. The references are wireless devices and each one has its coverage. The reference can be securely located by a secure network access. The reference could be:

○ **Static Reference:** The location is fixed in the beacon.

○ **Dynamic Reference:** The location keeps changing over the time.

• **GPS Mode:** GPS mode uses GPS signal to locate a user. It has no reference that is connected to the data access engine. Therefore, all data users are localized independently by GPS from the data access engine. Due to lack reliable reference, the location could be fraud and the data access engine is usually unable to directly validate GPS authenticity.

For both modes, the authentication allows the data requestors to securely provide its location information to the data access engine. On the other hand, the data access engine validates the users' identities along with their locations. In the WLAN, the access points are the references and their locations are known by the data access engine. The data requestor performs a remote authentication process to validate identities and its locations by using the knowledge of the references.

Figure 8(c) shows the mobility of the data requestors and the WLAN references (e.g., the access points). The data requestor accesses the data by presenting the fresh beacons from the references during it movements. Each reference has its own signaling coverage. During some period, the requestor is located in the overlapped domain of reference's coverage. The data request, in some time period, cansimultaneously present beacons from these three references as shown in Figure 8(c). During the movement, the data accessing privileges is accordingly changed based on the locations. The data request cannot access the data when it moves out the coverage of all WLAN references.

5. FUTURE DIRECTIONS AND TRENDS

Currently multiple standard bodies (e.g., CSA, W3C, etc.) and companies are proposing and maintain independent identity management standards, which make the management and integration of identities in cloud more complicated, especially for the scenarios that enterprise cloud and public cloud need communication and synchronization. In many scenarios, the current approaches are not secure, reliable, and robust enough to support the integration of mobile devices for use in the business systems. The question, for example, is who should have access to business systems from the application on the mobile platform, and how they will securely gain access to the tactical information. If answered well, these systems will give business users unprecedented capabilities on business management and operational controls. If answered poorly, the adversary could have unprecedented access to the business system, resulting in various vulnerabilities on business operations.

There are many challenges in securing the business systems and some of them are:

• **Verifying the User Identity:** Some businesses or services require that the users' identity should be verified before they access the sensitive data on a portable device. The authentication of the user identity verification could occur at two levels. The security on the mobile device level protects the device, apps, and data at the mobile platform. On the other hand, the security on the system level protects the business system and the data in transmit or data-at-rest. An easy, reliable, and flexible user identification scheme should be obtained by differentiating users in the business systems.

• **Accessing Polices and Control:** Access policies on the business data information should be enforced by role-based or other strategies. Security and privacy should be achieved to prevent unauthorized access on any sensitive information in the business system. On the other hand, the access control should include the secure process for re-authentication, granting new users, or new capabilities, revoking a user or capabilities in the business system.

- **Flexible Access Control Architectures:** Both centralized and decentralized architecture are needed to conduct the access control algorithms.

Considering the above challenges, the sensitive data in mobile phones or other device used for accessing cloud business should be strongly protected. For example, the personal identify code should become invalid once the code is leaked. These vulnerabilities on the traditional user authentication motivate researcher to develop more reliable user authentication to improve the security mechanisms of the user authentication for the devices in the business system. In addition, the traditional access control maintains the access polices in terms of users, i.e., individually applying the accessing polices to each user. In such a case, the business system is fallible due to very high complexity on maintaining the accessing policies on the cloud business. Therefore, a fine-grained access control is required for access control in a secure, flexible, and reliable fashion. The privacy should be achieved to prevent unauthorized access on any sensitive information.

6. CONCLUSION

Access control in the cloud is a complex problem in attempt to provide need-to-know information in a massive and distributed environment. In this book chapter, the challenges and requirements of the authentication and identity management in cloud computing are discussed. The prevailing industry standards and protocols including OpenID, OAuth, SAML, are outlined. To meet the requirement of the authentication and identity management in cloud environment, the latest advances are introduced, especially for the mobile cloud computing, and Identity as a Service model. Proximity-based access control is introduced as an effective way to provide fine grained data access. In the end, the future research directions and trends of authentication and identity management in cloud security are discussed.

REFERENCES

Ahn, G., Ko, M., & Shehab, M. (2009). Privacy-enhanced user-centric identity management. In *Proceedings of the IEEE International Conference on Communications* (ICC'09). IEEE.

Ahn, H., Chang, H., Jang, C., & Choi, E. (2011). User authentication platform using provisioning in cloud computing environment. *Advanced Communication and Networking Communications in Computer and Information Science*, 132-138.

Amazon S3. (2013). Retrieved from http://aws.amazon.com/s3

Bertino, E., Paci, F., & Ferrini, R. (2009). Privacy-preserving digital identity management for cloud computing. *IEEE Computer Society Data Engineering Bulletin*, *32*(1), 21–27.

Chow, R., et al. (2010). Authentication in the clouds: A framework and its application to mobile users. In *Proceedings of the ACM Cloud Computing Security Workshop* (CCSW '10). Chicago: ACM.

Flickr. (2013). Retrieved from http://www.flickr.com

Garcia, A., & Kalva, H. (2011). Cloud transcoding for mobile video content delivery. In *Proceedings of the IEEE International Conference on Consumer Elecronics* (ICCE). IEEE.

Gopalakrishnan, A. (2009). Cloud computing identity management. *SETLabs Briefings*, 7(7), 45–54.

IdPs. (n.d.). Retrieved from http://www.idmanagement.gov/pages.cfm/page/ICAM-TrustFramework-IDP

Jakobsson, M., Shi, E., Golle, P., & Chow, R. (2009). Implicit authentication for mobile devices. In *Proceedings of the 4th USENIX Workshop on Hot Topics in Security* (HotSec). USENIX.

Khan, A., Kiah, M., Khan, S., & Madani, S. (2013). Towards secure mobile cloud computing: A survey. *Future Generation Computer Systems*, 29(5), 1278–1299. doi:10.1016/j.future.2012.08.003

Kim, I., Pervez, Z., Khattak, A., & Lee, S. (2010). Chord based identity management for e-healthcare cloud applications. In *Proceedings of the 10th IEEE/IPSJ Annual International Symposium on Applications and the Internet*. IEEE.

Kremer, U., Hicks, J., & Rehg, J. (2001). A compilation framework for power and energy management on mobile computers. In *Proceedings of the 14th International Conference on Languages and Compilers for Parallel Computing* (LCPC'01). LCPC.

Li, L., Li, X., Youxia, S., & Wen, L. (2010). Research on mobile multimedia broadcasting service integration based on cloud computing. In *Proceedings of the IEEE International Conference on Multimedia Technology* (ICMT). IEEE.

Nunez, D., Agudo, I., & Lopez, J. (2012). Integrating OpenID with proxy re-encryption to enhance privacy in cloud-based identity services. In *Proceedings of IEEE 4th International Conference on Cloud Computing Technology and Science* (CloudCom). IEEE.

OASIS. (2005). *SAML V2.0 executive overview*. Retrieved from https://www.oasis-open.org/

OAuthSite. (2007). Retrieved from http://oauth.net/

OAuthwiki. (2012). Retrieved from http://en.wikipedia.org/wiki/OAuth

Oberheide, J., Veeraraghavan, K., Cooke, E., Flinn, J., & Jahanian, F. (2008). Virtualized in-cloud security services for mobile devices. In *Proceedings of the 1st Workshop on Virtualization in Mobile Computing* (MobiVirt). MobiVirt.

OpenIdwiki. (n.d.). Retrieved from http://en.wikipedia.org/wiki/OpenID

Oracle. (2010). *Identity federation whitepaper*. Retrieved from http://www.oracle.com/technetwork/middleware/id-mgmt/overview/idm-tech-wp-11g-r1-154356.pdf

PingIdentity. (n.d.). Retrieved from https://www.pingidentity.com/resource-center/oauth-essentials.cfm

Ren, W., Yu, L., Gao, R., & Xiong, F. (2011). Lightweight and compromise resilient storage outsourcing with distributed secure accessibility in mobile cloud computing. *Tsinghua Science & Technology Report*, 16(5), 520–528. doi:10.1016/S1007-0214(11)70070-0

Rhoton, J., & Haukioja, R. (2011). *Cloud computing architected: Solution design handbook*. Recursive Press.

Rudenko, A., Reiher, P., Popek, G., & Kuenning, G. (1998). Saving portable computer battery power through remote process execution. *ACM SIGMOBILE Mobile Computing and Communications Review*, 2(1), 19–26. doi:10.1145/584007.584008

Shin, S. (2003). *Secure web services: The upcoming web services security schemes should help drive web services forward*. Retrieved from http://www.javaworld.com/javaworld/jw-03-2003/jw-0321-wssecurity.html

Shozu. (n.d.). Retrieved from http://www.shozu.com/portal/index.do

Song, Z., Molina, J., Lee, S., Kotani, S., & Masuoka, R. (2009). TrustCube: An infrastructure that builds trust in client. In *Proceedings of the 1st International Conference on Future of Trust in Computing*, (pp. 68-79). Academic Press.

Spantzel, A., Squicciarini, A., & Bertino, E. (2005). Establishing and protecting digital identity in federation systems. In *Proceedings of the ACM Workshop on Digital Identity Management'05* (DIM'05), (pp. 11-19). ACM.

Takabi, H., Joshi, J., & Ahn, G. (2010). Security and privacy challenges in cloud computing environments. *IEEE Security & Privacy, 8*(6), 24–31. doi:10.1109/MSP.2010.186

Zissis, D., & Lekkas, D. (2012). Addressing cloud computing security issues. *Future Generation Computer Systems, 28*(3), 583–592. doi:10.1016/j.future.2010.12.006

Chapter 12
Green Cloud Computing:
Site Selection of Data Centers

Haibo Wang
Texas A&M International University, USA

Da Huo
Central University of Finance and Economics, China

ABSTRACT

This chapter considers the data center site selection problem in cloud computing with extensive reviews on site selection decision models. The factors considered in the site selection include economic, environmental, and social issues. After discussing the environmental impact of data centers and its social implications, the authors present a nonlinear multiple criteria decision-making model with green computing criteria and solve the problem by using a variable neighborhood search heuristic. The proposed model and solution methodology can be applied to other site selection problems to address the environmental awareness, and the results illustrate both the robustness and attractiveness of this solution approach.

1. INTRODUCTION

Cloud computing, also known as on-demand or utility computing, was introduced by Amazon in 2006. It allows firms and individuals to obtain computing power and software applications over the Internet, avoiding the expense of purchasing and maintaining their own hardware and software. Data accessed by the firms and individuals are permanently stored on powerful servers in the massive remote data center and updated over the Internet by its users. While the cost of computing is reduced for users, the availability of cloud computing relies on a number of remote data centers around the country or even all over the world for the large service providers of cloud computing. According to Emerson Network company(Lee & Kim, 1993), there were about 500,000 data centers around the world in 2011 and the number has been increasing dramatically in recent years due to the growing demand of cloud computing and social

DOI: 10.4018/978-1-4666-5788-5.ch012

network media. These data centers provide critical computing infrastructure for millions of users around the world at the cost not only of capital but also of environmental impact. Baker reported these new data centers built by Google cost an average of $600 million each and the electric bills at each of these data centers run more than $20 million a year (Lenk & Rao, 1993). Some IT analyst pointed out the cost of power consumption in the data center might exceed the cost of hardware in the future (Sneide, 1995).

The decision on the data center location has direct impact on the performance of cloud computing and the criteria to evaluate the decision involve economic, environmental and social issues. Therefore, the data center site selection problems are important but hard to model. There are key environmental variables should be considered in the decision of data center construction (Liang & Wang, 1993):

1. Suitable physical space
2. Proximity to high-capacity Internet connections
3. Affordable electricity or other alternative energy resources

In terms of physical space, the geographical condition, climate and weather, energy-saving natural features and safety are the main factors in the decision making process.

Most of the early models dealt with the site selection for data centers with the economic criteria where cheap land and tax incentive were important. However, the size of early data centers was moderately small and the power consumptions of the servers were relative low due to the processors and applications. The main purpose for early data centers was to provide internet access and to be shared by a number of organizations. This type of data centers was also known as an Internet data center (IDC). IDC obtained popularity during the dot.com booming. High level availability is the key concern for building an IDC. There are

four levels of data centers according to the level of availability where level 1 has 99.671% availability and level 4 has 99.995% availability(ADC Telecommunications, 2006). Higher levels of data centers require more power to run the servers and clusters with well-designed cooling systems in the facility. Redundancy plays an important role in maintaining high levels of availability, which requires more accurate estimations of power consumption during the upfront planning. In the meantime, the design of cooling system evolved over the past decade based on the configuration of hardware. The low level data center concerns the use of adequate cooling equipment and the high level data center involves the design and structure of raised-floor system (Karki & Patankar, 2006). The design of air flow in the high level data center can reduce the long term power consumption and the cold-hot rack/shelf placement in the data center can be managed through the job queuing systems.

The recent development of distributed computing enables the creation of large size data centers, while the computational intensive applications in cloud computing require powerful processors which produce lots of heat during the computation and command extra cooling system. The environmental impact of large size data centers to cloud computing platform attracted lots of attention and green computing is the key to the problem.

The new green computing driven models presented in recent literature consider hardware configurations, software applications, network communication, and environmental resources for the data center energy management problem. The decision on processor configuration plays an important role on power efficiency including the type of the processors and the utilization of the processors. Servers and clusters are key components in data centers for cloud computing. In most data centers, servers are configured as clusters to carry out high performance computing jobs. Various cluster configuration lead to different power efficiencies and they are well reported in the literature.

In general, the objectives of site selection problems are to maximize or minimize the criteria or attributes including cost, profit, revenue, travel distance, service, waiting time, coverage, and even market share. Therefore, the site selection problems have been defined as multiple objective decision making (MODM) or multiple attribute decision making (MADM). In the literature, both types of problems come together as Multiple Criteria Decision Making (MCDM). The site selection problem in the business environment can be represented by various linear MCDM models under the assumption of independent variables, which is readily solved by standard approaches such as the Analytic Hierarchy Process (AHP) and Goal programming (GP). A survey of AHP is given by (Vaidya & Kumar, 2006) and a survey of Goal programming is given by (Moon-Kyu, 2012). In addition, a few comprehensive books have been written to discuss the site selection problems and interested readers can refer to these books to learn about specific models and applications (Church & Murray, 2009; Daskin, 1995; Handler & Mirchandani, 1979; Love, Morris, & Wesolowsky, 1988). However, in real world practice, most site selection system problems contain interdependent criteria, which can best be represented by a nonlinear discrete objective function. Conventional mathematical programming approaches are sometimes limited in directly solving site selection problems with interdependent criteria. Methods reported in the literature to solve these problems include the application of a combination of artificial intelligence, evolutionary computation, system dynamics and heuristic algorithms such as genetic algorithm and ant colony (Grover & Srinivasan, 1992; Kaplan & Glass, 1995; Kauffman, 1993). Other approaches using chaos theory, fuzzy algorithm, and morphological analysis are also reported in the literature (Hayles, 1991; Hoepfner & Mata, 1993; Ritchey, 2006). Most site selection problems rely on the Geographical information systems (GIS) for data and information resources. The characteristics of candidate sites are provided

by GIS in terms of land use, land cover, proximity to roads, seismicity, soil, presence of water, distance to transmission grid, population density, and various infrastructure layers. The site selection problem models are classified based on these characteristics provided by GIS as environmental variables and other characteristics such as capacity, customer demand, financial uncertainty and firm strategy as internal variables. These models are also classified as stochastic or deterministic based on the nature of the problems. If the problem concerns the continuous space, the stochastic approach can accommodate uncertainty. On the other hand, for the problem concerning the discrete network described by travel distance or cost, the deterministic approach provides the best solution based on the objectives such as lowest cost, minimum distance and et al. Table 1 describes some examples of site selection models for the real-world problems as follows:

In the data center site selection problem, both AHP and GP approaches are reported (Kamiyama, 2013; Lent, 2012). Other solution methods such as nearest neighborhood (Rahman, Alhajj, & Barker, 2008), fuzzy set theory (Awasthi, Chauhan, & Goyal, 2011) are implemented in the decision process of data center site selection. Research also discussed the data placement issues related to the data center site selection (Yuan, Yang, Liu, & Chen, 2010). Unfortunately, research on decision support related to the data center location issues has lagged behind the fast growth of the data centers.

2. GREEN COMPUTING METRICS

Energy use associated with data centers in the United States has seen an unprecedented increase after the dot.com boom in the 90's. With the rising cost of energy, the huge volume of energy consumption has become a major challenge in cloud computing development. The green computing initiatives have been adopted by the service pro-

Table 1. Site selection models in the real world problems

Model Class	Criteria	Solution Method(s)	Real World Problems
Deterministic Stochastic	Dealing with cost: • Total Set Up Cost • Fixed Cost • Operating Cost Demand Coverage: • Travel Distance • Waiting Time • Responsiveness • Site Capacity Profit maximization: • Net Profit • Return of Capital • Revenue • Asset Value • Product value Service Effectiveness: • Accessibility • Service Level • Downtime • Efficiency	Deterministic: • AHP • Ant Colony • Branch-and-Bound • Data Envelope Analysis • Generalized Expansion Method • Genetic Algorithm • Goal Programming • Hershberger Algorithm • Karush-Kuhn-Tucker • Lagrangian Algorithm • Particle Swarm • Scatter Search • Simulated Annealing • Tabu Search	• Agriculture • ATM banking • Conservation Planning • Critical infrastructure protection • Distribution System • Energy • Government and Education • Health Care • Manufacturing • Retailing Business • Supply Chain Management • Transportation • Waste Management
	Environmental and social Issues: • Risk • Energy Cost • Land Use • Construction Cost • Noise • Quality Of Life • Pollution • Crisis	Stochastic: • Bayesian Network • Chaos Theory • Fuzzy algorithm • Fuzzy Set Theory • Markov Process • Morphological Analysis • Neural Network • Simulation	

viders of cloud computing in the past few years to find innovative approaches on reducing resource consumption and environmental impact. There are five areas of green computing technologies reported in the literature(Zhu, Sun, & Hu, 2012): green cloud/grid computing, green data centers, green communications and networks, virtual resources management and green metrics and IT lessons. In each area, performance metrics have been proposed and recommended by private and public organizations(Rivoire, Shah, Ranganatban, Kozyrakis, & Meza, 2007). The list of metrics is presented in Table 2 as follows:

(Shehabi et al., 2011) pointed out the locations of data centers have a greater effect on energy efficiency and should be carefully evaluated using the metrics in Table 2.

3. MULTIPLE CRITERIA DECISION MAKING IN SITE SELECTION

In general business site selection problems, a Decision Maker (DM) is often faced with choosing a subset of alternatives from a bigger set. MCDM has been studied in a number of fields and a survey on the theory and practice of this process can be found in (Stewart, 1992). Linear MCDM models are often used to address these problems under the assumption of independent criteria.

In the linear MCDM model, only independent criteria are satisfied; however, in business decision making, these criteria are usually at least in part conflicting. If an alternative is selected in conjunction with other alternatives, it has different effects on a specific criterion. In this case,

Table 2. Green computing metrics classification

Metrics	References
Power Usage Effectiveness	(Loper & Parr, 2007)
Work Load Balancing	(Jung, Hundewale, & Zelikovsky, 2005),
Data Center Effectiveness and Productivity	(Brill, 2007)
Carbon Emission Measurement	(Recker, Rosemann, & Gohar, 2011)
Energy Saving Mechanical Design	(Shehabi, Masanet, Price, Horvath, & Nazaroff, 2011)
Infrastructure Overhead	(Taheri & Zomaya, 2012)
Server Energy Performance	(Gandhi, Gupta, Harchol-Balter, & Kozuch, 2010)
Hardware Overhead	(Taheri & Zomaya, 2012)
Hardware Utilization Ratio	(Taheri & Zomaya, 2012)

these criteria are interdependent. Thus, selected alternatives have *interactive* effects on different criteria. Often a DM uses a simple weighted linear function to rank alternatives, and selects the top few alternatives. Such an approach may not make full use of interdependence among the alternatives. Not considering *interdependencies* among alternatives can lead to an undesirable outcome. In fact, the decision process involving interdependent multiple criteria are more complex than the simple independent alternatives, and some researchers have reported a few methods such as fuzzy set theory and hybrid MCDM to address this issue. Table 3 presents the summary of solution algorithms in MCDM.

3.1 New Modeling Approach for Data Center Site Selection Problem with Green Computing Criteria

It is commonly known that data center power consumption cause not only economic and environment issues, but also there are social implications connected to global warming. According to Katz (2009), most of the energy as much as 80% to 90% will be wasted by the data center. The energy cost and energy efficiency are critical issues to the data center management and cloud computing providers. There are benefits to building data centers that take advantage of hydroelectric power generation rather than coal-fired power plants. Reduction of the daily commute distance for the employees can also be considered as an environment-friendly factor. Each of these business practices are con-

Table 3. Summary of solution algorithms in MCDM

MCDM Model	References	Solution Algorithm
Fuzzy MCDM	(Ekmekçioğlu, Kaya, & Kahraman, 2010)	AHP
Multi-objective	(Xifeng, Ji, & Peng, 2013)	Constrain Programming
Fuzzy Random Variables	(Wen & Kang, 2011)	Simulation and Genetic Algorithm
P-median	(Brimberg & Drezner, 2013)	Genetic Algorithm, Tabu Search, Simulated Annealing
Multi-attribute	(Hon, Guh, Wang, & Lee, 1996)	AHP Genetic Algorithm and AHP

sidered as green computing. We consider Green computing is the key criterion in the selection of a data center site.

A data center consists of vast, immaculate warehouses filled with row upon row of computers that allow fast access from the users. The data center plays an important role in cloud computing applications in addition to online search functions. Service providers need to build a number of data centers in order to provide fast access to their customers. In the Data Center Site Selection problem (DCSS problem), the objective is to identify the best locations among a large number of potential sites based on the criteria, which are economic and social criteria in this case. In the factors on data center construction used by service providers, three key green computing criteria for success have been identified: (1) *infrastructure such as cheap, abundant hydro-electric power resource, fiber optic backbone, and excess water capacity to keep the server computers cool; (2) asset values such as lots of inexpensive and inarable land; (3) accessibility such as proximity to other existing data centers and user population.* The DCSS problem can be defined by interdependencies among alternatives. To present the new model for DCSS, we will present a case study in next section.

3.2 A Case Study of Data Center Site Selection

For an illustration, we consider the following example on the DCSS problem for a large technology company to select two sites in eight different states in the USA for new data centers and with no more than one new data center to be built in each state. Some candidate sites have interdependent criteria. For example, building a new fiber optic backbone connecting a data center in North Carolina (site 1) and a data center in South Carolina (site 2) that could serve both sites; There are a number of hydro power plants near both sites which provide low cost of electricity with less air pollution and plenty of water way in both states; if both sites

are selected, savings in the infrastructure investment will be obtained but with an increase on the land expense. If both sites are selected, there is an increase of 10% on the infrastructure investment criterion and negative 5% on the asset value criterion. Similarly, if a data center in Oklahoma (site 3) and a data center in Iowa (site 4) are simultaneously selected, we can take advantage of low cost of the land. In that case, a positive property value of 15% is estimated when it comes to asset value criterion. If a data center in Texas (site 5) and a data center in Florida (site 6) are simultaneously selected, there is an increase of land expense but with a payoff benefit of closer to other existing data centers and user population with better available Internet infrastructure. In that case, an increase of 40% on accessibility criteria, negative 10% on assets values and positive 35% on infrastructure. If a data center in California (site 7) and a data center in Washington (site 8) are selected simultaneously, there is saving in infrastructure with the most wired communities in the country but the land expense should be included in the consideration, which will lead to 25% increase in infrastructure, 20% increase in accessibility, and 15% decrease on assets values. While considering the green computing criteria on the potential sites for data center in eight different states, Table 4 presents the data of normalized consequences of eight feasible sites as follows:

IF- infrastructure; AV-Asset Value; AC- Accessibility

We have adopted the following notations through this paper:

$S=\{a^1,....,a^n\}$ is a set of alternatives in data center sites

$a^i,(i=1,...,n)$ is alternative i

$G=\{1,...,q\}$ is a set of criteria based on green computing

e^i_k is effect of alternative i on criterion k in data center site

Table 4. Normalized consequences of eight feasible sites

Criteria		Alternatives							
		a^1	a^2	a^3	a^4	a^5	a^6	a^7	a^8
Name	*Weights*	SC	NC	OK	IA	TX	FL	CA	WA
IF	0.35	0.75	0.60	0.40	0.55	0.81	0.75	0.60	0.75
AV	0.23	0.60	0.85	0.65	0.30	0.54	0.30	0.45	0.40
AC	0.42	0.65	0.55	0.30	0.25	0.85	0.85	0.85	0.95
	Payoff	0.67	0.64	0.42	0.37	0.76	0.69	0.67	0.75

F_k is a set of alternatives that if selected together have some positive or negative effect on criterion k of green computing

$l(F_k)$ is the amount of effect (positive or negative) of an *interacting* set F_k on criterion k of green computing

w_k is the weight associated with criterion k

$p(F)$ is the total payoff benefits of a subset of alternatives data center locations $F \subseteq N$

x_i is equal to 1 if alternative a^i is selected and 0 otherwise.

We consider 8 alternatives $N=\{1, 2, 3, 4, 5, 6, 7, 8\}$ and 3 criteria $G=\{1, 2, 3\}$ as in Table 3. Alternative a^1 has effects of $e^1_1=0.75$, $e^1_2=0.60$, and $e^1_3=0.65$ on criterion 1, 2, and 3 while alternative a^2 has effects of $e^2_1=0.60$, $e^2_2=0.85$, and $e^2_3=0.55$. Weights of three green computing related criteria are $w=(w_1, w_2, w_3) = (0.35, 0.23, 0.42)$.. Considering criterion 1 there are three interacting alternatives, $F_1=(a^1,a^2)$, $F_2=\{a^5, a^6\}$, and $F_3=\{a^7, a^8\}$, with interaction effects of $l(\{a^1,a^2\})=0.10$, $l\{a^5,a^6\})=0.35$, and $l(\{a^7,a^8\})=0.25$. If no *interdependencies* are considered among the alternatives, then the business payoff benefit value is defined as a simple additive function; for example, for $F=\{a^i,a^j\}$ we have

$$p(a^i,a^j) = p(a^i) + p(a^j) = \sum_{k=1}^{3} w_k e^i_k + \sum_{k=1}^{3} w_k e^j_k$$

(1)

In this case, considering all possible set of 2 alternatives and selecting a subset with the largest payoff benefit without interdependencies, we have optimal solution as $p(a^5, a^8) = 0.76 + 0.75 = 1.51$, which are the states of Texas and Washington. To consider *interdependencies* between alternatives and taking into account positive and negative effects, a new *dynamic weight* is assigned to each criterion based on its interaction with other alternatives in the selected subset when applied to an alternative.

Table 5 presents all subsets of two alternatives and the associated weights of each criterion, and the payoff benefit of the selected subset of alternatives. In Table 4, subset (a^5,a^8) obviously is no longer the optimal solution, as we have $p(a^5, a^8) = 1.51$,. However, the subset (a^5,a^6) has the largest payoff benefit of $p(a^5, a^6) = 1.92$, which is optimal.

The level of *dynamism* for each weight will increase if the interdependencies among alternatives on different criteria are high. To consider the interdependencies among alternatives represents the practical nature of the problem, calculating the dynamic weight is very time consuming. The number of subsets is exponential due to the calculation of weights for all subset of alternatives

In the DCSS problem, if we want to find any subset of alternatives with largest payoff benefit, then we can formulate the DCSS problem by a nonlinear integer programming model as follows:

Table 5. Calculation of business payoff benefit with dynamic weight for alternatives when interdependencies are considered

2 alternatives (a^i,a^j)	w_1	w_2	w_3	$p(a^i,a^j)$
1, 2	0.35(1+0.10)=0.39	0.23(1-0.05)=0.22	0.42	1.34
1, 3	0.35	0.23	0.42	1.09
1, 4	0.35	0.23	0.42	1.04
1, 5	0.35	0.23	0.42	1.44
1,6	0.35	0.23	0.42	1.36
1,7	0.35	0.23	0.42	1.34
1,8	0.35	0.23	0.42	1.43
2, 3	0.35	0.23	0.42	1.05
2, 4	0.35	0.23	0.42	1.00
2, 5	0.35	0.23	0.42	1.40
2, 6	0.35	0.23	0.42	1.33
2,7	0.35	0.23	0.42	1.31
2,8	0.35	0.23	0.42	1.39
3, 4	0.35	0.23(1+0.15)=0.2645	0.42	0.81
3, 5	0.35	0.23	0.42	1.18
3,6	0.35	0.23	0.42	1.10
3,7	0.35	0.23	0.42	1.09
3,8	0.35	0.23	0.42	1.10
4, 5	0.35	0.23	0.42	1.13
4,6	0.35	0.23	0.42	1.06
4,7	0.35	0.23	0.42	1.04
4,8	0.35	0.23	0.42	1.12
5,6	0.35(1+0.35)= 0.47	0.23(1-0.10)=0.21	0.42(1+0.40)=0.59	**1.92**
5,7	0.35	0.23	0.42	1.44
5,8	0.35	0.23	0.42	1.51
6,7	0.35	0.23	0.42	1.36
6,8	0.35	0.23	0.42	1.44
7,8	0.35(1+0.25)=0.44	0.23(1-0.15)=0.20	0.42(1+0.2)=0.50	1.66

$$\max \sum_{i \in N} x_i \left[\sum_{k \in G} w_k e_k^i \right] + \sum_{k \in G} \sum_{F_k \in N} \left(w_k \left[1\left(F_k\right)\right] \left[\sum_{i \in F_k} e_k^i \right] \right) \prod_{i \in F_k} x_i^?$$

s.t.

$$\sum_{i \in n} x_i = m, x_i \in \left\{ 0,1 \right\}$$

To illustrate the optimization problem, we use the DCSS example presented above.

Max $0.67x_1 + 0.64x_2 + 0.42x_3 + 0.37x_4 + 0.76x_5 + 0.69x6 + 0.67x_7 + 0.75x_8 + 0.35(0.10)(0.75 + 0.60)x_1x_2 - 0.23(0.05)(0.60 + 0.85)x_1x_2 + 0.23(0.15)(0.65 + 0.30)x_3x_4 + 0.35(0.35)(0.81 + 0.75)x_5x_6 - 0.23(0.10)(0.54 + 0.30)x_5x_6 +$

$0.42(0.40)(0.85 + 0.85)x_5x_6 + 0.25(0.35)(0.60 + 0.75)x_7x_8 - 0.23(0.15)(0.45 + 0.40)x_7x_8 + 0.42(0.20)(0.85 + 0.95)x_7x_8$ (3)

s.t.

$x_1 + x_2 + x_3 + x_4 + x_5 + x_6 + x_7 + vx_8 = 2$

$x_i \in \{0,1\}$

Simplifying the above formulation we get:

$Max\ 0.67x_1 + 0.64x_2 + 0.42x_3 + 0.37x_4 + 0.76x_5 + 0.69x6 + 0.67x_7 + 0.75x_8 + 0.031x_1x_2 + 0.033x_3x_4 + 0.46x_5x_6 + 0.24x_7x_8$ (4)

s.t.

$x_1 + x_2 + x_3 + x_4 + x_5 + x_6 + x_7 + x_8 = 2$

$x_i \in \{0,1\}$

The objective function (4) is a standard constrained binary quadratic programming problem (CBQP). There are many solution methods to solve CBQP readily including genetic algorithms [90], Tabu Search [91], greedy algorithms [92] and particle swarm optimization [93]. A survey on constrained binary quadratic programming problem is found in ([94] ref).

In the DCSS problem, if there are more than two data centers to be built simultaneously and there are interdependent criteria among alternative candidate sites, the objective function is no longer the CBQP but nonlinear programming with cubic, quartic, even quintic terms. Therefore the problem-oriented methods are limited useful to solve these nonlinear programming problems with high order variables. This chapter proposes a variable neighborhood search algorithm as follows:

Step 1. Set initial solution for objective function with the first two variables with value of 1, get ($x_1 = 1$, $x_2 = 1$, $x_3 = 0$, $x_4 = 0$, $x_5 = 0$, $x_6 = 0$, $x_7 = 0$, $x_8 = 0$), denote x*(1, 1, 0, 0, 0, 0, 0, 0), compute f(x*)=1.31.

Step 2. Change the value of one of the variables (x_1, x_2, x_3, x_4, x_5, x_6, x_7, x_8) from 0 to 1 if it is 0 in the initial solution, otherwise change from 1 to 0 and keep the rest of the variable unchanged, create a list of new candidate solutions f(x*) as in Table 6. If one of the new candidate solutions is an improved solution, which is also the best solution found so far, return to **Step 2**. If none of the candidate solutions is improved solution, set L=1 and x*(L) as the set of solution found so far. Then move to **Step 3**.

In Table 6, solution x*(1, 0, 0, 0, 1, 0, 0, 0) is the best one among four solutions that are improvement from the initial solution. Then we go back to **Step 2** and create a new list of candidate solutions based on improved solutions.

Step 3. Change L=L+1 variables at a time and evaluate each solution. If an improved solution is found, set the solution as best solution found. Go back to **Step 2**. If no improved solution is found

Table 6. Candidate solutions from a variable neighbourhood search heuristic Step 2

The value of x*	The value of f(x*)
(1, 0, 1, 0, 0, 0, 0, 0)	1.089
(1, 0, 0, 1, 0, 0, 0, 0)	1.04
(1, 0, 0, 0, 1, 0, 0, 0)	1.4382
(1, 0, 0, 0, 0, 1, 0, 0)	1.362
(1, 0, 0, 0, 0, 0, 1, 0)	1.344
(1, 0, 0, 0, 0, 0, 0, 1)	1.427

and L is small than the maximum value for L, then go back to **Step 3**; otherwise, stop. The best solution in the list is the optimal solution.

The above algorithm was coded by a visual Fortran compiler and used to solve the sample problem. The result obtained gives the objective function value of 1.92 for assignments $x_5 = x_6 = 1$ and $x_1 = x_2 = x_3 = x_4 = x_7 = x_8 = 0$, which means two data centers to be built in Texas and Florida with the best payoff benefits based on the selection criteria.

4. SUMMARY

This chapter discusses approaches on modeling the DCSS problems considering the green computing criteria. However, the modeling results are discussed without considering mechanical designs of different levels of data centers. In addition, the climate conditions and other environmental variables are considerably important to operational effectiveness. More empirical data should be collected and analyzed to provide better decision support.

The computational results of the presented case study show that interdependence between a pair of alternatives within the criteria should be recognized in order to achieve more accurate results and better solutions in the decision making process.

The DCSS problem with more selection criteria often is associated with more complicated interrelated variables. While the computational testing reported in the case study was carried out on the DCSS problems with interdependence between two alternatives, which is represented by a quadric objective function, it is noted that this approach is not restricted to such cases and can be readily applied to more than two alternatives with more selection criteria such as climate conditions. The model and its solution approach are designed to accommodate more criteria and

alternatives which can be represented by variables in the cubic, quartic, even quantic terms.

The green cloud computing not only promotes the social responsibility of information technology, but also brings huge financial incentive for the business. There are tremendously potential efficiency improvements in the data center operations such as different temperature set-points for different applications to balance the cost of energy and computational efficiency.

REFERENCES

Awasthi, A., Chauhan, S. S., & Goyal, S. K. (2011). A multi-criteria decision making approach for location planning for urban distribution centers under uncertainty. *Mathematical and Computer Modelling, 53*(1–2), 98-109. doi: http://dx.doi.org/10.1016/j.mcm.2010.07.023

Brill, K. G. (2007). *Data center energy efficiency and productivity*. Santa Fe, NM: The Uptime Institute. Retrieved from www. uptimeinstitute. org/symp_pdf/(TUI3004C)DataCenterEnergyEfficiency.pdf

Brimberg, J., & Drezner, Z. (2013). A new heuristic for solving the p-median problem in the plane. *Computers & Operations Research, 40*(1), 427-437. doi: http://dx.doi.org/10.1016/j.cor.2012.07.012

Carlsson, C. (1982). Tackling an MCDM-problem with the help of some results from fuzzy set theory. *European Journal of Operational Research, 10*(3), 270–281. doi:10.1016/0377-2217(82)90226-0

Carlsson, C., & Fuller, R. (1995). Multiple criteria decision making: The case for interdependence. *Computers & Operations Research, 22*(3), 251–260. doi:10.1016/0305-0548(94)E0023-Z

Carlsson, C., & Fuller, R. (1996). Fuzzy multiple criteria decision making: Recent developments. *Fuzzy Sets and Systems*, *78*(2), 139–153. doi:10.1016/0165-0114(95)00165-4

Church, R. L., & Murray, A. T. (2009). *Business site selection, location analysis and GIS*. New York: Wiley.

Daskin, M. S. (1995). *Network and discrete location: Models, algorithms, and applications*. New York: Wiley Interscience. doi:10.1002/9781118032343

Ekmekçioğlu, M., Kaya, T., & Kahraman, C. (2010). Fuzzy multicriteria disposal method and site selection for municipal solid waste. *Waste Management (New York, N.Y.)*, *30*(8–9), 1729–1736. doi:10.1016/j.wasman.2010.02.031 PMID:20303733

Gandhi, A., Gupta, V., Harchol-Balter, M., & Kozuch, M. A. (2010). Optimality analysis of energy-performance trade-off for server farm management. *Performance Evaluation*, *67*(11), 1155–1171. doi:10.1016/j.peva.2010.08.009

Grover, R., & Srinivasan, V. (1992). Evaluating the multiple effects of retail promotions on. *JMR, Journal of Marketing Research*, *29*(1), 76. doi:10.2307/3172494

Handler, G. Y., & Mirchandani, P. B. (1979). *Location on networks: Theory and algorithms*. Cambridge, MA: MIT Press.

Hayles, N. K. (1991). Introduction: Complex dynamics in literature and science. In N. K. Hayles (Ed.), *Chaos and order: Complex dynamics in literature and science* (pp. 1–36). Chicago: Univ. Chicago Press.

Hoepfner, G. K., & Mata, F. (1993). A multi-criteria decision analysis methodology for selection of a preferred residence based on physical attributes. *Computers & Industrial Engineering*, *25*(1-4), 365–368. doi:10.1016/0360-8352(93)90297-B

Hon, C.-C., Guh, Y.-Y., Wang, K.-M., & Lee, E. S. (1996). Fuzzy multiple attributes and multiple hierarchical decision making. *Computers & Mathematics with Applications (Oxford, England)*, *32*(12), 109–119. doi:10.1016/S0898-1221(96)00211-8

Jung, S., Hundewale, N., & Zelikovsky, A. (2005). *Energy efficiency of load balancing in MANET routing protocols*. Paper presented at the Software Engineering, Artificial Intelligence, Networking and Parallel/Distributed Computing, 2005 and First ACIS International Workshop on Self-Assembling Wireless Networks. SNPD/SAWN 2005. New York, NY.

Kamiyama, N. (2013). Designing data center network by analytic hierarchy process. *Computer Networks*, *57*(3), 658–667. doi:10.1016/j.comnet.2012.10.009

Kaplan, D., & Glass, L. (1995). *Understanding nonlinear dynamics*. New York: Springer-Verlag. doi:10.1007/978-1-4612-0823-5

Karki, K. C., & Patankar, S. V. (2006). Airflow distribution through perforated tiles in raised-floor data centers. *Building and Environment*, *41*(6), 734–744. doi:10.1016/j.buildenv.2005.03.005

Kauffman, S. A. (1993). *The origins of order: Self-organization and selection in evolution*. Oxford, UK: Oxford University Press.

Lee, Y.-H., & Kim, S. (1993). Neural network applications for scheduling jobs on parallel machines. *Proceedings of the 21st International Conference on Computers and Industrial Engineering*, *25*(1-4), 227.

Lenk, P. J., & Rao, A. G. (1993). Nonstationary conditional trend analysis: An application to scanner panel data. *JMR, Journal of Marketing Research*, *30*(3), 288. doi:10.2307/3172882

Lent, R. (2012). A model for network server performance and power consumption. *Sustainable Computing: Informatics and Systems*. http://dx.doi.org/10.1016/j.suscom.2012.03.004

Liang, G.-S., & Wang, M.-J. J. (1993). Evaluating human reliability using fuzzy relation. *Microelectronics and Reliability*, *33*(1), 63–80. doi:10.1016/0026-2714(93)90046-2

Loper, J., & Parr, S. (2007). Energy efficiency in data centers: A new policy frontier. *Environmental Quality Management*, *16*(4), 83–97. doi:10.1002/tqem.20144

Love, R., Morris, J., & Wesolowsky, G. (1988). *Facility location: Models and methods*. Amsterdam: North-Holland.

Moon-Kyu, L. (2012). A storage assignment policy in a man-on-board automated storage retrieval system. *International Journal of Production Research*, *30*(10), 2281.

Önüt, S., Efendigil, T., & Soner Kara, S. (2010). A combined fuzzy MCDM approach for selecting shopping center site: An example from Istanbul, Turkey. *Expert Systems with Applications*, *37*(3), 1973–1980. doi:10.1016/j.eswa.2009.06.080

Ostermark, R. (1997). Temporal interdependence in fuzzy MCDM problems. *Fuzzy Sets and Systems*, *88*(1), 69–79. doi:10.1016/S0165-0114(96)00046-2

Rahman, R. M., Alhajj, R., & Barker, K. (2008). Replica selection strategies in data grid. *Journal of Parallel and Distributed Computing*, *68*(12), 1561–1574. doi:10.1016/j.jpdc.2008.07.013

Rajabi, S., Hipel, K. W., & Kilgour, D. M. (1995). *Multiple criteria decision making under interdependence of actions - Systems, man and cybernetics*. Paper presented at the IEEE International Conference on Systems, Man and Cybernetics --Intelligent Systems for the 21st Century. New York, NY.

Recker, J., Rosemann, M., & Gohar, E. R. (2011). *Measuring the carbon footprint of business processes*. Paper presented at the Business Process Management Workshops. New York, NY.

Ritchey, T. (2006). Problem structuring using computer-aided morphological analysis. *The Journal of the Operational Research Society*, *57*(7), 792–801. doi:10.1057/palgrave.jors.2602177

Rivoire, S., Shah, M. A., Ranganatban, P., Kozyrakis, C., & Meza, J. (2007). Models and metrics to enable energy-efficiency optimizations. *Computer*, *40*(12), 39–48. doi:10.1109/MC.2007.436

Shehabi, A., Masanet, E., Price, H., Horvath, A., & Nazaroff, W. W. (2011). Data center design and location: Consequences for electricity use and greenhouse-gas emissions. *Building and Environment*, *46*(5), 990–998. doi:10.1016/j.buildenv.2010.10.023

Sneide, G. A. (1995). A study of factors in office site selection using discrete choice models. *Transportation Research Part A, Policy and Practice*, *29*(1), 79–80. doi:10.1016/0965-8564(95)90286-4

Stewart, T. J. (1992). A critical survey on the status of multiple criteria decision making theory and practice. *Omega*, *20*(5-6), 569–586. doi:10.1016/0305-0483(92)90003-P

Taheri, J., & Zomaya, A. Y. (2012). Energy efficiency metrics for data centers. *Energy Efficient Distributed Computing Systems*, *88*, 245. doi:10.1002/9781118342015.ch9

Teixeira, J. C., & Antunes, A. P. (2008). A hierarchical location model for public facility planning. *European Journal of Operational Research*, *185*(1), 92–104. doi:10.1016/j.ejor.2006.12.027

Telecommunications, A. D. C. (2006). *Data center standards overview. TIA-942*. Author.

Vaidya, O. S., & Kumar, S. (2006). Analytic hierarchy process: An overview of applications. *European Journal of Operational Research*, *169*, 1–29. doi:10.1016/j.ejor.2004.04.028

Wen, M., & Kang, R. (2011). Some optimal models for facility location–allocation problem with random fuzzy demands. *Applied Soft Computing*, *11*(1), 1202–1207. doi:10.1016/j.asoc.2010.02.018

Xifeng, T., Ji, Z., & Peng, X. (2013). A multi-objective optimization model for sustainable logistics facility location. *Transportation Research Part D, Transport and Environment*, *22*, 45–48. doi:10.1016/j.trd.2013.03.003

Yuan, D., Yang, Y., Liu, X., & Chen, J. (2010). A data placement strategy in scientific cloud workflows. *Future Generation Computer Systems*, *26*(8), 1200–1214. doi:10.1016/j.future.2010.02.004

Zhu, R., Sun, Z., & Hu, J. (2012). Special section: Green computing. *Future Generation Computer Systems*, *28*(2), 368–370. doi:10.1016/j.future.2011.06.011

Chapter 13
Leveraging Cloud Technology for Rural Healthcare in India

Girish Suryanarayana
Siemens Corporate Research and Technologies, India

Roshan Joseph
Siemens Corporate Research and Technologies, India

Sabishaw Bhaskaran
Siemens Corporate Research and Technologies, India

Amarnath Basu
Siemens Corporate Research and Technologies, India

ABSTRACT

Cloud technology is used for a variety of purposes in order to handle large volumes of data. This chapter explores a rural healthcare project in India in which cloud technology was introduced in order to store and share large volumes of data. This project benefits from cloud technology because of the ability to store patients' full health history on the cloud and access them wherever services are provided. The impetus for this project originated with the fact that many hospitals maintained their proprietary information systems, and thus, patient history was unavailable to physicians outside of that system. The search engine used in this project is called Indexer, which can search a vast collection of records stored in the cloud and help with the diagnosis. The solution developed supports multi-tenancy of data and uses the Azure platform. The project has taken adequate precautions to protect the data. This project is not focused on privacy protection per se but on saving lives.

1. INTRODUCTION

Kala, a poor widow in her early forties living in a village in the heart of South India, wakes up one night with chest pain. It is night time and she does not want to disturb her children, so she bears the pain silently. The pain is accompanied with heavy sweating. Just as she ponders how to counter the pain, it starts reducing and disappears in about 20-25 minutes. The next morning, she visits the local primary healthcare center (PHC) and narrates her experience to the physician. Kala and the physician are both unaware that her family has had a history of heart problems. The care provider being a general physician attributes her

DOI: 10.4018/978-1-4666-5788-5.ch013

chest pain to stomach indigestion and recommends some pain killers and medication for indigestion.

Kala returns home and being the sole bread-winner of her family returns to work immediately. But she experiences a similar chest pain three months later. In spite of their meager earnings, the alarmed family members decide that Kala should be taken to a small hospital in a nearby town. At the hospital, she is immediately referred for an ECG examination by the out-patient department (OPD) physician. The ECG report shows an abnormal heart rhythm and is sent back to the referring physician at the hospital. The general physician does not have access to Kala's past medical reports; fortunately, he can read the ECG report just enough to decipher that Kala needs to be immediately referred to the hospital's cardiology center as an emergency case.

The cardiologist, Dr. John, at the cardiology center also does not have access to Kala's past medical reports, allergy information, and previous procedures that she has undergone. Because of trauma, Kala is unable to communicate critical information about her past medical history to Dr. John. In the absence of this data, he has to take a calculated risk and recommends a coronary angiography. This is followed by a PCI (Percutaneous Coronary Intervention) as the patient is found to very unstable and at high ischemic risk. Fortunately for Kala, the risk taken by Dr. John pays off and she recovers. But this expensive treatment brings Kala and her family virtually on the streets. Being an unskilled laborer, Kala does not have any medical insurance that can bear the expense of her medical care. It should be also be pointed out that often Government hospitals in small towns do not have the needed infrastructure to support advanced cardiac procedures. Kala meets this medical expense by mortgaging the only piece of land she owns. And, it will take years for her and her family to pay back the loans.

Throughout this process, the doctors who examined Kala did not have access to the complete clinical history of the patient. This lack of medical data handicapped the cardiac specialist from preparing a patient centric treatment plan. Moreover, lack of expert advice at the initial stage delayed the diagnosis and treatment. This delay could have led to further complications and even fatality! In fact, availability of expert advice at the initial stage could have addressed Kala's cardiovascular disease via oral medication and diet guidance. This would have also helped avoid the expensive treatment that Kala had to eventually undergo.

This scenario highlights the value of past medical data in diagnosis and treatment. If the general physician at the PHC had been aware of Kala's family and her medical history, he would have been able to provide better and faster treatment in the initial stages.

Next, let us look at a different scenario and see things from the perspective of Dr. Ram, a well-known cardiologist working in a tertiary care hospital in a tier-2 city in India. He has worked hard to achieve success in his life and is now reaping the benefits by attracting a large number of patients who only want to be treated by him. In a country like India where physician to patient ratio is very poor, a successful physician finds himself beset with more patients to treat and a more hectic schedule.

Of late, Dr. Ram is spending more time at work. A larger number of patients and with increased expectations are approaching him both at his home and as well in the hospital looking for a cure to their medical problems. The outpatient consulting, the ward rounds, and the surgery (both planned and emergency cases) consume the major portion of his time during the day. As the number of patients increase, the number of surgeries he needs to perform increases, and consequently, Dr. Ram finds himself busy with surgery at the hospital until late in the night.

Over time, Dr. Ram gradually starts to suffer from "physician burnout" which can be equated to loss of enthusiasm for work, feelings of cynicism, and a low sense of personal accomplishment.

Though patient care is his priority, he starts wondering whether he is able to actually provide the quality care that his patients need and expect from him. Serving a larger number of patients implies a reduction in the amount of time he could spend with them discussing their problems. This also leads to decision making with partial information or even in some cases no information about their past details. This can lead to medical errors which are considered as one of the leading causes of death in cardiac care. Dr Ram has always approached patient care with passion and compassion but his heavy work load makes him prone to mistakes. As a specialist in cardiology he doesn't want to make mistakes that can lead to serious problems or even death of a patient.

His other responsibilities also suffer. For instance, he is unable to pursue any of his research interests. He also finds it difficult to take out time to mentor the junior physicians working under him. On the one hand, he wants to build a professional team of physicians to support him in his work, but on the other hand his schedule makes it difficult for him to invest the necessary time and effort for the same. Further, as a specialist, he needs to constantly keep abreast of the latest trends in his field and needs to regularly attend conferences organized by his medical fraternity. This involves lot of travel and preparation and he makes it a point to regularly attends these conferences and interact with his colleagues from different other healthcare organizations. All these activities can contribute to sleep deprivation and make time management a challenge.

Let's take a detour here and look at healthcare organizations in India. A typical healthcare organization consists of various diagnostics laboratories and clinical departments. The process of providing care at such a facility involves multiple administrative and clinical cycles. Embedded in this overall process are multiple diagnostic and therapeutic cycles which can proceed (depending on the nature of the case) in parallel or sequentially at several laboratories and clinical departments.

This process of care providing generates a lot of structured and unstructured data which includes diagnostic images, lab reports, clinical observations, reports, and medication prescriptions.

Most of this data today is generated and maintained within a number of IT systems that are used for the purposes of diagnosis, workflow automation, and storage. Often these systems are owned and managed by different (and in many cases autonomous) clinical departments within a healthcare organization. A report by PriceWaterhouseCoopers (PriceWaterhouseCoopers, 2007) states that the large number of patients in India has motivated healthcare organizations to invest rapidly and heavily in Healthcare Information Technologies. However, this has resulted in a set of non-interoperable systems which can potentially lead to critical medical information becoming isolated in silos thus posing a challenge to the interchange of information across care providers.

In order to provide higher quality care but at a lower cost, this information across different systems and data sources must be available across clinical departments. The availability of a holistic view of patients' lab, diagnostic, and therapeutic documentation across care teams is essential for accurate and cost effective clinical care. Along with a patient's current lab and diagnostic data past health data can be vital in making accurate clinical decisions. Hence, data from a patient's previous visits also needs to be available across care providers for more effective treatment and positive outcomes.

With this context, if we go back to Dr. Ram's example, one can imagine the difficulty he must undergo to access patient data available in multiple systems that lack viable common interfaces. The problem is heightened when he knows that relevant medical data exists somewhere but is not sure about its actual location. Since having a partial view of a patient's medical data can adversely impact his decision-making, he may have to depend on his past experience or allocate resources to get to the data he needs and expend additional time, energy and effort in the process. This can reduce the effectiveness of care as well as cause undue delays in the treatment delivery for patients. Further, if past medical data is not easily accessible, he may have to ask the patient to repeat a particular test. This can pose a health risk and involves unnecessary resource usage. To better illustrate this, consider the case of a patient who has already undergone a chest X-RAY for a medical condition in one of his recent visits. If this chest image were to not be accessible to the physician, when the patient next visits the healthcare center, he would prescribe another chest X-Ray for the patient. This would expose the patient to preventable repeated ionizing radiation. Additionally, it would lead to un-necessary consumption of resource (in this case the X-RAY machine) which can hold up other needy patients.

These problems are more accentuated in a developing country like India, where a large number of patients need to be provided efficient and affordable care within the constraints of available resources. Often, the physician to patient ratio is really low and this means that a physician needs to make a choice between treating a large number of patients and the quality of care he can provide. Thus, it is not surprising sometimes to see physicians in India asking patients to meet another care provider or postpone the visitation to another day. Similarly, there are also cases when a physician has compromised on the quality of care in order to not disappoint a large number of patients awaiting care delivery.

India also suffers from a large number of poor patients. Unlike developed markets, more than 80% Indians do not have medical insurance and have to pay for medical expenses on their own. In fact, cost of healthcare treatment is one of the main reasons for people without medical insurance, going into debt. In this context, when physicians ask patients to repeat tests because past medical records are not available, it imposes an unnecessary additional financial burden on the poor patients.

2. ELECTRONIC MEDICAL RECORD

To address the above challenges and to facilitate the seamless sharing of complex medical data across departments, a standards-compliant Electronic Medical Record (EMR) is a promising solution. An EMR provides the ability to easily record and transmit medical information in a clear, predictable and secure fashion across different providers (Hristidi, 2007). However, the main shortcoming of an EMR system is that it is quite expensive. It also requires significant effort and investment to integrate it with a hospital's IT systems. It turns out that these shortcomings have limited EMR adoption even in developed countries and is the reason why governments in development countries offer subsidies to encourage its adoption. An example would be the HITECH provisions of American Recovery and Reinvestment Act 2009 in USA (ARRA USA, 2009).

To support an EMR-based approach, the varied health IT systems need to adopt and follow certain standards. However, as we have discussed earlier in this chapter, cost is a big factor in the Indian context; thus, hospitals and clinics would be hesitant to replace their existing IT systems with standards-compliant IT systems. Therefore, in spite of its benefits in the long run, an EMR-based approach is infeasible for Indian healthcare organizations in the medium term.

3. ORGANIZATIONAL BACKGROUND

Before we delve into the solution space, it is relevant to give a brief background about Siemens Corporate Research and Technologies, India (RTC IN) since it helps understand our solution approach. RTC IN is the research wing of Siemens and works on innovating and developing business-relevant technologies across different domains to meet the needs of people worldwide. One such domain is healthcare where an acute need of data integration across healthcare entities is felt especially in the Indian context. RTC IN's objective in this context is to investigate how affordable high-quality healthcare can be delivered in developing countries so that a large number of patients can be served efficiently and effectively in India. RTC IN's goal is to leverage new technologies to build architectures and solutions that provide affordable data management and access in the healthcare domain.

4. REQUIREMENTS STEMMING FROM THE INDIAN CONTEXT

This section lists the technical requirements stemming from the requirements and constraints of the Indian context. A detailed mapping of the requirements to the architectural decisions can be found in (Bhaskaran, 2013).

- How can we avoid the need to repeat unnecessary diagnostic procedures? As already described earlier, this not only poses a health risk but also financially burdens poor patients. This requires the need for a solution that can connect to and search existing IT systems for requested patient data.
- How can we enable a physician to treat a large number of patients per day via supporting faster decision making? This requires that our solution should be able to identify and retrieve clinically-relevant medical data quickly.
- How can we support physicians to easily search and locate patient data? This is a critical requirement since there can be a lot of unstructured textual data. This requires that our solution should support free-text search (like a standard internet search engine), clinical vocabulary, and advanced queries using search operators. It also requires data to be indexed appropriately in order to facilitate correct search results.

- How can we manage large volumes of medical data? As a large number of patients are treated, a large volume of medical data is generated. This requires the solution to scale as the data grows over time.
- How can we ensure that the results returned are comprehensive? Since medical data can be critical to clinical decision making, the solution should be able to communicate with and query all existing data sources (as well as newly added ones in the future). The search results should be reliable and should include the most recently updated medical data as well, all listed in a chronological order under a patient header.
- How can we create an affordable solution? Since healthcare centers will pass on cost of their infrastructure to poor patients, it is important that the solution be simple, inexpensive, and be flexible and extensible to work with newer IT systems that may be deployed in the future.

Towards addressing the above requirements, our approach leveraged well-known information retrieval techniques and consisted of the following steps -

- extract content from broad types of medical data available in different, disparate information systems
- use it to create an indexed collection of medical data, and
- provide an interface to query the indexed collection and retrieve relevant content from the search results.

5. UNIFYING ACCESS TO DISPARATE DISTRIBUTED DATA

In this section, we describe the architecture of the solution that was adopted to address the technical requirements mentioned in the previous section.

Figure 1. Overview of healthcare search engine

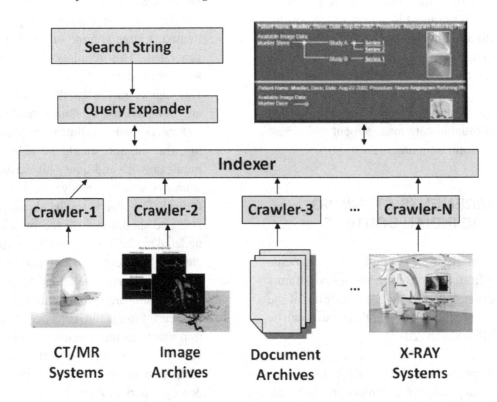

Figure 1 provides an overview of the Healthcare Search Engine that we designed to address our technical requirements. The Healthcare Search Engine offers a Google-like search interface for medical data and can be used by clinicians to look up information they want. A clinician has to first login to the solution. Once he is authenticated, he enters a search string in the search box of the user interface. The clinician's input is received by the Query Expander module which analyzes it and expands it so as to improve the effectiveness of the search. This is because typically in the medical domain, multiple terms may represent the same medical artifact or condition. For instance, "heart attack" is more properly known as "myocardial infarction" in the medical domain.

Once the clinician's search query is analyzed and expanded, it is then passed to the Indexer. The Indexer is the cornerstone of the Healthcare Search Engine and maintains an index of the medical data that is gleaned from various medical data stores across departmental IT systems via crawlers at regular intervals. The Indexer uses the input search query to iterate through the vast medical data index and identify relevant medical data. This is then returned to the user interface so that it can be displayed for the clinician's perusal. As in standard web search engines, the Healthcare Search Engine can be configured to present a user-desired view of medical data.

The architecture of the Healthcare Search Engine follows a Client-Server style. The Client runs in a web browser and offers search interface to clinicians. A web interface for the client allows users to use different kinds of devices such as PCs and mobile devices (supporting different platforms and browsers) to access the Healthcare Search Engine. To control and regulate access to the Healthcare Search Engine, an access control mechanism is employed. The Server part of the

Figure 2. Server layers of healthcare search engine

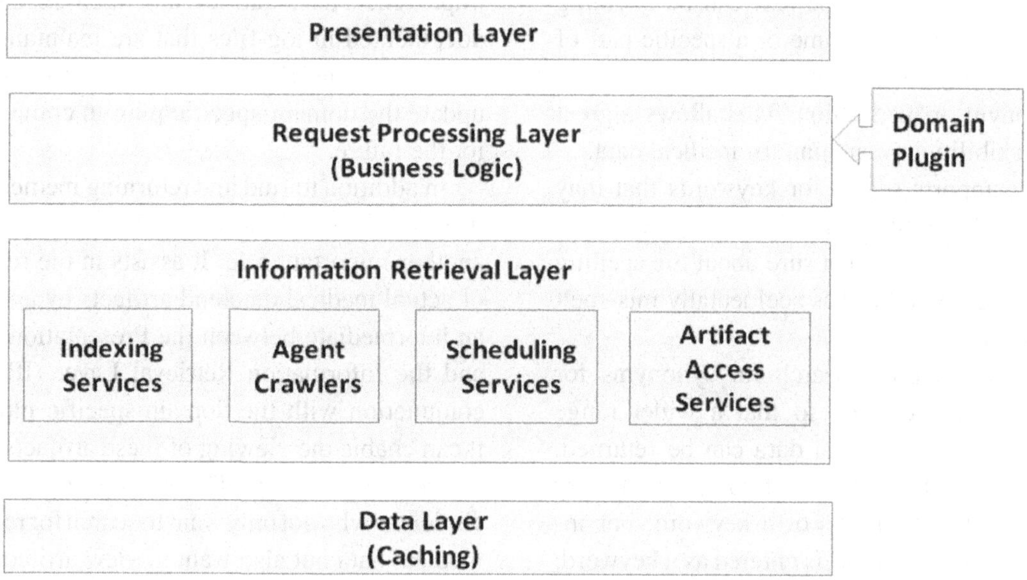

Healthcare Search Engine follows a layered architectural style and consists of four logical layers (see Figure 2). Each layer builds upon the services provided by the layers below it. We describe these layers starting from the top.

5.1. Presentation Layer

This layer is responsible for facilitating users to search for medical data using free text search. Users are not expected to have full knowledge of the medical domain or the structure of the medical data to retrieve information. The user interface is similar to that of Google's search interface. That means a user can just enter a search string in the UI to look up medical data. A skilled user can refine the query using operators such as AND, OR, LIKE etc.

Query results are displayed in a tree view fashion with a patient's name as the root node and the relevant artifacts and studies of that patient as the child nodes. Each search result also indicates the location where that particular artifact is located. This can help in the quick retrieval of actual medi-

cal data. It is also possible to integrate domain-specific artifact viewers with the Healthcare Search Engine so that medical artifacts such as images and videos that have been retrieved by clicking on a search link can be played in the Client. Finally, if a search result contains a series of images, a representative thumbnail image is displayed for that series of images. The Presentation Layer also includes an Admin UI that enables an administrator to configure, control, and monitor the scheduling of data crawls.

5.2. Request Processing Layer (RPL)

As the name indicates, this layer is responsible for processing the search strings that have been entered by users in the Healthcare Search Engine user interface. This layer is akin to a business logic layer since it embeds the domain-specific logic to identify medical artifacts and data that are relevant to the keywords in the search string. This layer plays a very important role in ensuring that the correct and relevant results are returned to the user and offers the following features towards that end:

- It supports free text-based search where the keywords in the text can be anything from a patient's name or a specific part of the body to a particular procedure or acronym or medication. This allows a great flexibility in searching for medical data.

- It supports search for keywords that may have been mis-spelt. This is very helpful in case the user is not sure about the spelling of a keyword or has accidentally mis-spelt . a keyword.

- It also support search for synonyms for keywords entered so that a wider range of relevant medical data can be returned. Further, it supports searching for different grammatical forms of a keyword. For instance, if a "noun" is entered as a keyword, the query will include search for the "adjective", "verb" and "adverb" form of the "noun" as well.

- It supports operators such as AND and OR between keywords in the search string. This allows a user to specialize the search results that he wants.

It should be mentioned that this layer also ensures that the search results cover a wider conceptual scope than the search query while still being relevant. This is to ensure that all relevant data is located in response to a specific query. For instance, a query for "angiogram" should return results limited to cardiology, and "heart failure" should include results related to "heart attack" and "myocardial infarction", and "coronary artery disease".

The domain-specific plug-in components play an important role in supporting such a concept-based search. They help resolve medical acronyms, map one clinical phrase to another, and spell-check keywords. As a result of this, the search space may be enlarged or reduced depending upon the specific query issued by the user. It is important for the Healthcare Search Engine to constantly monitor and learn from user interactions so that the quality of search results can be constantly improved. Thus, queries and their results are documented in log files that are maintained on the Server, and these are used to appropriately update the domain-specific plug-in components for the future.

In addition to find and returning medical data in response to user queries, the RPL also performs another important role. It assists in the retrieval of actual medical data and artifacts by acting as an intermediate between the Presentation Layer and the Information Retrieval Layer (IRL). In conjunction with the domain-specific plug-ins, it can enable the viewing of these artifacts using external applications. This can be very useful to clinicians who not only want to search for relevant medical data but also want to view artifacts that may be in proprietary formats.

5.3. Information Retrieval Layer (IRL)

The Information Retrieval Layer is responsible for retrieving the data requested in response to search queries. For this, IRL components crawl data sources to get medical data, create index information for this data, and facilitate access to artifacts such as images, videos, reports and clinical notes. The IRL consists of four components namely the Agent Crawlers, the Indexing Service, the Scheduling Service, and the Artifact Access Service. These components are described below.

5.3.1. Agent Crawlers

Agent Crawlers are responsible for "crawling" medical data sources and extracting medical data from those sources so that they can be indexed. Crawlers are monitored and managed by the Scheduling Service. Each crawler runs as a separate process. Further, a crawler's access to data sources is restricted to only reading data. This is done in order to prevent changes to medical data by the crawlers which would compromise the reliability of medical data and artifacts. In order to crawl multiple data sources simultaneously, it is possible to have multiple crawlers executing concurrently.

Each crawler has an associated configuration file that contains rules and data templates that guide how medical artifacts should be crawled. When an agent crawls through a medical artifact, it collects the contents of the artifact and passes it to the Indexing Service. If an irrecoverable error is encountered during this process, the agent notifies the scheduler of the same. Additionally, while crawling medical images, an agent creates thumbnails of the image which help provide an insight into the image dataset associated with a search result. A thumbnail helps to provide a pointer to the entire image series, and helps a clinician decide which image series to view based on the thumbnails shown.

5.3.2. Indexing Service

The Indexing Service is responsible for creating index information for the medical data retrieved by the crawlers. Specifically, based on the artifact contents received from the crawlers, the Indexing Service invokes Lucene to create a corresponding virtual document for each artifact. A virtual document contains elements from the original artifact that are important for indexing. These include patient identifiers, clinical terms, title, contents, URL and so on.

The index information created by Lucene is then stored in an internal repository. When queries are received from the request processing layer, these queries are executed on the internal repository using Lucene to identify relevant artifacts.

An interesting question that arises here is the semantic relationship between portions of medical data that is retrieved by Agent Crawlers and sent to the Indexing Service. For instance, what happens if two data sources have different medical data for a patient named "Anand Krishnan" who is 58 years old and hails from Kochi. Are these two different patients who merely happen to have the

same name and demographic information or are they indeed one and the same patient?

The resolution of these issues is beyond the scope of the Healthcare Search Engine; however, it should be mentioned that there are various approaches to resolve this and the Healthcare Search Engine can easily integrate any of these approaches. One such approach is the adoption of an Enterprise-wide Master Patient Index which can be leveraged by the Indexing Service component to improve the accuracy of search results.

5.3.3. Scheduling Service

The Scheduling Service is responsible for controlling and monitoring the crawl jobs. It runs as a back-end process and allows an administrator to monitor and manage the crawl jobs via the user interface in the Presentation Layer. A configuration file containing the crawl jobs, the associated crawlers and the various crawling parameters (such as data source information and the crawl schedule) acts as input to the Scheduling Service.

Crawlers supply regular status updates to the Scheduling Service. This is used by the Scheduling Service to maintain the state of each crawl job so that this can be viewed by an administrator via the Presentation Layer.

Our solution supports two modes of crawls that can be specified while configuring a crawl job. A *batch* crawl job has a start date-time and an end date-time. The Scheduling Service breaks up this interval into manageable sub-intervals (depending on the throughput of the site) and schedules the job accordingly. The Scheduling Service can also insert delays between each object handled within this sub-interval. This is done primarily to minimize the load on the source systems due to crawling. Batch crawl is used for bulk indexing, typically required when a new system is introduced into the search domain.

The other mode is called a delta crawl job. As the name suggests, it is concerned with updating a previously generated index that was created from a data source. A delta crawl job will crawl the data source and only look up that medical data that has been added or modified since the previous crawl and add this to the index. For a delta crawl job, the Scheduling Serving uses a pre-configured re-crawl interval to schedule the crawl. Our experience is that these re-crawl jobs do not exert much load on the source systems due to crawling. This is because most corrections to the data happen within a few days after the data is created and it is easily possible to identify a safe window for the delta crawl.

5.3.4. Artifact Access Service

The Artifact Access Service is responsible for providing access to and viewing medical artifacts. When a user clicks on a particular result returned by a search query, the Artifact Access Service connects to the data source wherein the artifact is stored and retrieves it. It leverages external applications such as a DICOM viewer to facilitate the viewing of the artifact in the user interface. In order to avoid unnecessary retrievals of the same artifact in the future, a copy of the artifact is cached in the Data Layer.

5.4. Data Layer

The Data Layer is responsible for maintaining a time-bound cache for thumbnails and image data. It also provides a mechanism to insert and read thumbnails and image data from the cache.

Figure 3 shows the physical deployment of various components in different nodes with separate process boundary marked using dotted lines. Data Source 1...Data Source N represent original data repositories that store medical information. Agent crawlers A_1...A_N crawl the respective data sources. Scheduler can be a separate process running either in the same machine or can run independently in a separate machine; however, it should be in the same network in order to communicate with the crawlers. The Web Server is a Tomcat server

and hosts most of the search related components. Figure 4 shows the component level decomposition of the system.

6. HEALTHCARE SEARCH ENGINE DEPLOYMENT

We have deployed our web-based search solution in the cardiac specialty of a mid-range healthcare organization in India. Our objective was to provide practitioners seamless access to healthcare data (including medical images and other non-image data) that is lying in disparate information systems in the Cardiology Department of this healthcare organization. The team of cardiologists at this department completes approximately 6000 cardiac procedures per year.

The department's infrastructure consists of three X-ray Angiography machines, four Ultrasound scanners for stress echo, one cardiac-PACS (Picture Archiving and Communication System) solution for local medical image management, another enterprise grade PACS solution which is used across the organization owned by Radiology, 4-5 Reporting and Imaging workstations, proprietary Cardiology Information System (CIS) with relational database, and Nuclear Medicine imaging equipment.

Each cardiac procedure generates data that is on an average about 100MB in size. This translates into roughly 1.2TB of image data and 5GB of textual data per year within the Cardiology Department.

6.1. Benefits of the Deployed Solution

Our interaction, post-deployment of the Healthcare Search Engine, with the staff of the Cardiology Department revealed that our solution proved to be very beneficial to them. We include here some of the quotes uttered by the staff members.

Figure 3. Deployment view

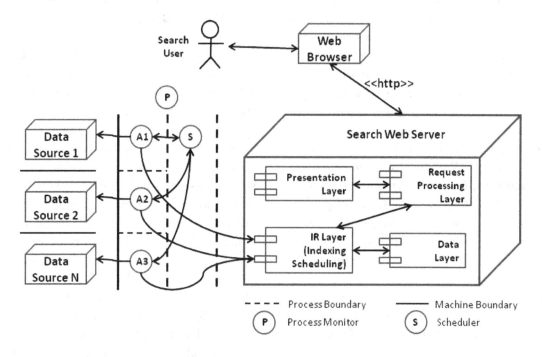

Figure 4. Component view

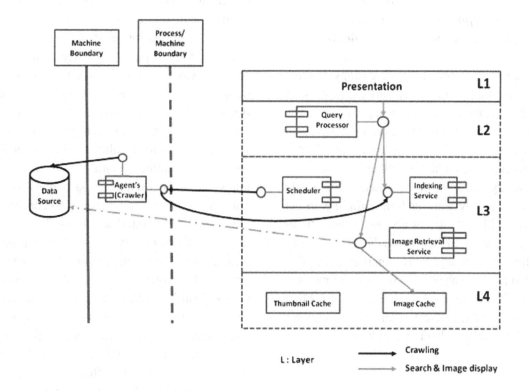

(Cardiologist 1) We have found that using the Healthcare Search Engine, we can easily and quickly find out about data that is lying in different systems across the department. This has allowed us as well as encouraged widespread sharing and access of medical data which was not possible previously.

(Cardiologist 2) Since there is a web interface, I can easily access all the data I need during patient consultations with a few clicks from a web browser on my PC. This allows me to make more informed clinical decisions than previously possible. In the end, I am able to treat more patients per day as well as provide high quality care at the same time.

(Cardiologist 3) Due to the Healthcare Search Engine solution, my efficiency has increased and I am able to save 20-30 mins per OPD day.

(Cardiologist 4) Because of this solution, I can now access details of past cases that have been done at the Department. This is quite helpful in guiding the care for patients in the future.

Due to our solution, the Cardiology Department was able to achieve a significant increase in outpatient handling with its existing resources. The advantage of this was that the existing resources at the Department could be utilized more efficiently. This is very significant in the context of a developing country like India since patients who would have to regularly wait for long durations to get quality healthcare are now able to get faster treatment. This can help them avoid the repercussions stemming from delayed care. Another benefit that resulted from the access to a wider set of medical data was the avoidance of unnecessary tests that puts additional financial burden on poor patients as well as subjects them to health risks.

6.2. Challenges of the Deployed Solution

Interactions with the members of the Cardiac Department also revealed some limitations of our solution. The first was regarding the storage of the growing index information. As new medical artifacts and data are created in the IT systems every day, the index information starts to grow rapidly. In the absence of a scalable solution for storing this index information, it is quite likely that an administrator may delete some of the index files to allocate more space in the machine. If index information is lost, it is a great setback to the Healthcare Search Engine because some relevant past medical data may not show up when clinicians issue search requests. This will impact the anticipated benefits of the Healthcare Search Engine. Thus, an effective solution to manage the growing index information is required. One solution to this is to scale up the hardware resources, but this would negatively impact the affordability factor of our solution.

Another limitation arises if our existing solution were to be applied to a different deployment scenario. Consider the case where the cardiology department of the super specialty hospital scales out to a chain of satellite health centers. This scenario is very common in India. In such a case, we could install the Healthcare Search Engine at each of the satellite health centers. This would allow all medical data at a particular site to be consolidated; however, there is no consolidated view across ALL satellite centers. Thus, if a patient were to visit a different site in the future, his past medical data (such as reports and test results) generated at a previous site would not be shown by the Healthcare Search Engine at the current site. A solution to limitation is to deploy a Wide Area Network infrastructure and make medical data available across sites. However, this would involve a huge cost and effort which healthcare organizations in India are reluctant to invest.

The Head of the Cardiology department also said the following – *"If this solution was to be taken to the cloud, it can reduce the hardware cost plus maintenance hassles for the hospital. However we do not have such system installed here right now. There is huge scope for cost reduction through taking the whole search engine in cloud."* What is evident from this above quote is that hospital management is aware of the burgeoning costs of maintaining a plethora of IT systems in hospitals, and see potential in disruptive technologies to reduce these costs.

7. HEALTHCARE DATA CLOUD

The limitations of the Healthcare Search Engine mentioned in the previous section combined with the inputs from the Head of the Cardiology Department were the key motivation towards taking our solution to the cloud. As we started exploring with a cloud-based approach, we realized that the above limitations could be easily addressed with a cloud-based solution.

First, because broadband-based internet connectivity is ubiquitous in India, each of the satellite health centers could be connected to the cloud via internet and could therefore upload medical data to the cloud without significant cost overhead. Such a solution could address the need for a consolidated view of patient data across sites in an affordable way without employing an expensive enterprise-wide WAN infrastructure.

Second, cloud offers elastic storage; this means, that as a client's storage needs increase, the cloud can easily offer more storage capacity to him. This can be leveraged to address the problem of storing voluminous index information.

For our healthcare data cloud solution, we have utilized MS Azure, which provides an integrated platform as a service (PaaS), as our preferred cloud provider and built our solution on top of it. Since the platform is readily offered by the

cloud vendor, it has allowed us to roll out the new solution quickly.

7.1 Keyword Search in Healthcare Data Cloud

We list below some of the architectural decisions with respect to the search and retrieval of medical data that we have made while developing the Healthcare Data Cloud.

- Crawlers will run on premise at the hospital. They will crawl the data stores and generate index information.
- The generated index information is uploaded via a gateway machine to the MS Azure cloud storage. This storage also stores cache data that includes thumbnails, images, reports etc. as shown in Figure 5.
- Users of the Healthcare Data Cloud can be either outside or inside the Enterprise Network and can issue search requests through a location-independent front-end interface. Search results are displayed in the user interface.
- The application functionality is divided among the Web Role and Worker Roles provided by MS Azure.
- The Web Role instance serves the front-end application that receives user specified search requests and displays search results.
- The Worker Role instance receives artifact content from the crawlers that are located in the hospital premises, creates index information, and suitably updates the index files in the MS Azure cloud storage.
- Crawlers directly upload relevant thumbnails to the MS Azure cloud storage.

As more users start to use this solution and more IT systems are integrated into the solution, a scale-out strategy is needed. We indicate our strategy in Figure 6. To support more users, more web roles can be created to serve their requests.

Figure 5. Healthcare data cloud architecture

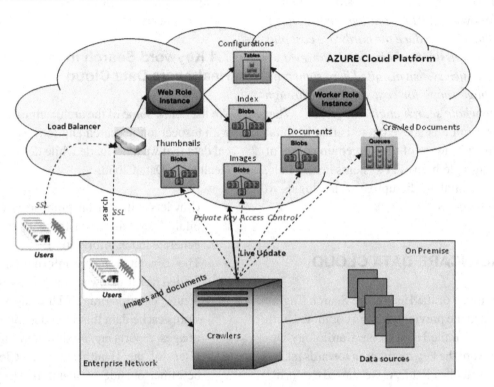

Similarly, as more data sources are integrated into our system, the number of crawlers increases. Since the same crawler cannot be used for crawling different types of data sources, we need different types of crawlers that need to be customized. As the number of crawlers increases, the data crawled by them increases. This increasing load can be handled by creating more worker roles that parse this data and create index information.

7.2 Security considerations for Healthcare Data Cloud

Most discussions today about cloud computing in healthcare quickly converge to how security and privacy concerns will be addressed. It is becoming increasingly clear that an essential step for the success of healthcare in the cloud domain is an in-depth understanding and effective administration of security and privacy (Jansen, 2011;

Johnson, 2009; Squicciarini, 2010; Gellman, 2009; Kaufman, 2009).

In this context, we realized that moving portions of our Healthcare Search Engine to a public cloud exposed certain vulnerabilities that needed to be properly addressed. Realizing the importance of these concerns for our Healthcare Data Cloud, we adopted a systematic approach to study and mitigate these concerns.

First, we performed a detailed threat analysis. Our goal here was to find out what were the assets that needed protection, under what situation and environment, and from whom. Next, we determined the various strategies and tactics that we could employ to protect the important assets from various threats. In the case of Healthcare Data Cloud, the asset that primarily needed to be protected was the medical data. This data needed to be secured while it was in transit from the clinical sites to the Cloud. It also needed to be secured while it was at rest within the Cloud.

Figure 6. Scale-out strategy for healthcare data cloud

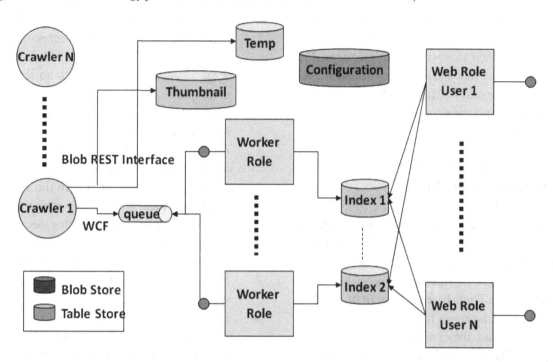

We list below some of the key design decisions that we made to ensure the security of the Healthcare Data Cloud. These are based on the best practices for security in Windows Azure (Azure Security, 2013).

- To ensure the security of data in transit, we used the Transport Layer Security protocol with mutual authentication as shown in Figure 5.
- In order to secure data at rest within the cloud, we relied on MS Azure's protected storage mechanism.
- In order to protect all the keys that are used in on-premise and cloud environment, we used certificate stores with appropriate password protection.
- We used a claim-based identity mechanism to protect the Healthcare Data Cloud application against unauthorized access. Specifically, the Active Directory Federation Services (ADFS) has been used

for the claim-based identity mechanism. This reuses the identity management and access control policies already in existence at the hospital. The advantage of using ADFS is that once a user logs into his PC, he does not have to enter his authentication information again while using the Healthcare Data Cloud search application.

- The Access Control Service provided by MS Azure is used to validate the claims submitted by a user. This ensures that only genuine clinicians authenticated by their healthcare organization can use the Healthcare Data Cloud application.
- Keys are periodically rotated to maintain good security on the data. This means that the application uses a key only for a certain period of time, and then switches to a new key. This restricts the damage that can be caused if a key is compromised.

It should be pointed out that encryption mechanisms and security-related technologies constitute only half of the security measures. The other half is the adherence to good secure practices. For instance, a user may have a strong password, but if he leaves the password on a sticky note attached to his computer monitor, his computer can be easily compromised.

7.3 Supporting Multi-Tenancy Architecture

In the course of the development of the Healthcare Data Cloud, we could envision that the solution could be configured to support multi-tenancy. The advantages of multi-tenancy in cloud are well-known. Clients have the benefit of avoiding capital expenditure on hardware, software, and service. Instead, they only need to pay for what they use. The cloud provider has the benefit that the same application can be used for more than one client without any additional cost.

Figure 7 illustrates our vision of multi-tenancy for the Healthcare Data Cloud using MS Azure. In Figure 7, clients A, B, and C represent three different healthcare organizations that are using the same Healthcare Data Cloud solution. While each client has a separate storage account, the other components such as Web Role and Worker Role are reused across the three healthcare organizations. The growth in the number of users across these organizations can be handled by creating more Web Role and Worker Role instances.

The main concern with such a multi-tenant architecture is to ensure the security and privacy of the data belonging to a healthcare organization. It is critical that data uploaded by one organization is not visible to other organizations. This requires the following additional design decisions on top of the existing Healthcare Data Cloud.

- The Web Role acts as the access point for the external world; specifically, it receives search requests issued by the user. For se-

curity reasons, it is therefore important to ensure that a Web Role does not directly access the Azure storage to execute queries. Thus, in our solution, Web Roles write requests as messages to an intermediate queue (see Figure 7).

- Messages in the queue are read by a Worker Role instance. This Worker Role instance is completely trusted and is allowed access to the Azure storage in accordance with the privileges associated with the security token provided in each user request. This Worker Role instance executes the queries on the Azure storage and inserts the results back into the queue for the Web Role to pick up and display to the user via a client web browser.

- Each healthcare organization has a separate MS Azure storage account. This is to ensure a hard separation between multiple healthcare organizations.

- To restrict access to patient data belonging to a healthcare organization from users belonging to other healthcare organizations, each organization is assigned a separate storage key.

- For auditing purposes, all transactions between the Web Role and Worker Role are logged. These can be very helpful to monitor any unusual or abnormal accesses that happen in the system.

8. HEALTHCARE DATA CLOUD DEPLOYMENT

We have deployed our Healthcare Data Cloud at one of the largest multi super special hospital in India. This hospital specializes in cardiac care and has three satellite health care centers. The heart-care institute at this hospital consists of a large highly qualified team of cardiologists providing round-the-clock help to patients with a wide spectrum of cardiac diseases.

Figure 7. Cloud-based multi-tenant architecture

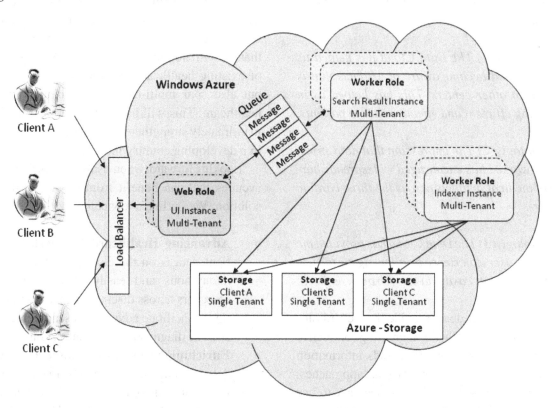

The super specialty hospital also has several advanced diagnostic imaging technologies including Cardiac MRI, PET scan, CT scan and 3D echocardiography. Further, it has several Cardiac Catheterization Labs each of which handles 5-6 procedures every day. The institute performs roughly 15,000 cardiac procedures a year and a corresponding number of medical artifacts are generated in all these catheterization labs. In comparison to catheterization labs, the 10 echo labs handle three times more the number of procedures (approximately 45,000) like echocardiograph, cardiac stress tests etc. Each of these cardiac care centers is equipped with Cardiac PACS for the image management. However, the radiology PACS at the main specialty center has not been integrated with any of the cardiology PACS systems.

The hospital uses an in-house Cardiac Information System which has been deployed at each of the satellite centers. This system handles workflows such as report generation, visit tracking, etc. However, the Cardiac Information Systems across sites have not been integrated to present a consolidated view of patient-centric medical data.

Our interactions with the hospital management has revealed that prior to the deployment of our Healthcare Data Cloud solution, there was a pressing need to have a search facility that can be used to identify and access the data lying in different systems. The hospital management has reported that our solution is beginning to play an important role in decision making and impacting the outcome of treatment. They anticipate that continued use of our solution will significantly improve the overall clinical care performance of the hospital. The management also sees a network effect; as clinicians start to use our cloud-based solution and derive value from it, their awareness increases and attracts more clinicians to use the system.

We include specific quotes from three cardiologists:

(Cardiologist 1) The Data Cloud has helped us to search and become aware of artifacts that is present in other centers. This has helped us in providing efficient and effective care to patients.

(Cardiologist 2) The impression that data stores are networked has encouraged widespread sharing of medical artifacts across the three cardiac centers.

(Cardiologist 3) The Data Cloud has provided me a positive user experience by allowing me to view medical artifacts easily via the web browser itself.

Based on the feedback provided by the cardiologists, we believe that there is increasing confidence that our cloud-based solution finds information faster than previously used manual approaches. Further, they find the web interface easy to use and also appreciate the fact that they can view medical artifacts in their web browser itself.

9. CONCLUSION

As patient data and artifacts become increasingly available and accessible across a healthcare enterprise, the main benefits that emerge include -

- Increased opportunity for improving healthcare delivery and outcomes
- New opportunities for inter-disciplinary teams of experts and researchers to work together to develop tools for improving healthcare
- Better experience and higher quality care for patients compared to what is existing today

We believe that we have only just started to tap the potential of having healthcare data in a cloud.

As more healthcare organizations and the community at large start to become more comfortable with the use of cloud computing, we anticipate that it will not only encourage the migration of existing healthcare applications to the cloud but also spur multi-dimensional innovation in healthcare. This will have a far-reaching impact in ultimately strengthening the healthcare system in a developing country like India.

Looking forward, we envisage several potential avenues that can benefit from our cloud-based solution. We outline a few below.

- **Advancing Healthcare Research:** If patient data is on the cloud, it can be made anonymous and easily shared with researchers across disciplines and communities to facilitate advanced research in areas such as diagnostics and pharmacology.
- **Enriching Medical Education:** If patient data is on the cloud, it can be made anonymous and shared with medical students and researchers to facilitate their skill development and learning towards creating high-quality professionals.
- **Efficient Pooling of Available Resources:** If past medical data is made available on the cloud, a large pool of well-trained radiologists available in metro cities can be efficiently used to support the remote interpretation and consultation of cases from remote areas of the country where skilled physicians are lacking.
- **Promoting Healthcare Analytics:** The availability of data on the cloud can help support advanced healthcare analytics that will lead to improved outcomes and efficient and effective healthcare delivery.

10. A PARTING THOUGHT

We want to share two clear messages that arise from our work.

- **Right to Live Over Right for Privacy:** Everyone today is worried about the privacy and security of healthcare data if it were to be moved to a public cloud. We believe that the apprehensions today for moving data or applications to the cloud are more due to a psychological mindset prevalent in society than the lack of actual capable technologies for security and privacy in the cloud context. In a country like India, where there are a large number of poor patients who need to be urgently provided quality healthcare, the right to live should take precedence over right for privacy. It is more important to treat patients and save lives.

- **Technology Can Compensate for Lack of Capital:** A consistent constraint during our journey has been the cost and affordability of the solutions. Since the increased cost of infrastructure eventually translates to expensive healthcare, it is extremely important to deploy low-cost solutions in developing countries like India. Towards this, we have found that disruptive technologies like Cloud Computing can be leveraged to create novel, yet affordable solutions. We believe such technologies are extremely relevant and urgently needed to solve key problems in emerging economies.

ACKNOWLEDGMENT

We thank Sreenivasan Narayanan of Siemens Medical Solutions USA Inc. for sponsoring the work and providing valuable suggestions.

REFERENCES

ARRA USA. (2009). *American recovery and reinvestment act 2009 in USA*. Retrieved from http://www.recovery.gov/Pages/default.aspx

Azure Security. (2013). *Windows Azure security guidance*. Retrieved from http://www.windowsazure.com/en-us/develop/net/best-practices/security/

Bhaskaran, S., Suryanarayana, G., Basu, A., & Joseph, R. (2013). *Cloud-enabled search for disparate healthcare data: A case study*. Paper presented at IEEE Cloud Computing for Emerging Markets. Bangalore, India.

Hristidis, V., Farfán, F., Burke, R. P., Rossi, A. F., & White, J. A. (2007). *Information discovery on electronic medical records*. Paper presented at NSF Symposium on Next Generation of Data Mining and Cyber-Enabled Discovery for Innovation (NGDM). New York, NY.

Jansen, W., & Grance, T. (2011). *Guidelines on security and privacy in public cloud computing (NIST Special Publication 800-144)*. Washington, DC: NIST.

Johnson, M. E. (2009). Data hemorrhages in the health-care sector. In *Financial cryptography and data security*. Berlin: Springer-Verlag. doi:10.1007/978-3-642-03549-4_5

Kaufman, L. M. (2009). Data security in the world of cloud computing. *IEEE Security and Privacy*, 7(4), 61–64. doi:10.1109/MSP.2009.87

PriceWaterhouseCoopers. (2007). *Healthcare in India: Emerging market report 2007*. Retrieved from http://www.pwc.com/en_GX/gx/healthcare/pdf/emerging-market-report-hc-in-india.pdf

Squicciarini, A., Sundareswaran, S., & Dan, L. (2010). *Preventing information leakage from indexing in the cloud*. Paper presented at IEEE 3rd International Conference on Cloud Computing (CLOUD). New York, NY.

Gellman, R. (2009). *Privacy in the clouds: Risks to privacy and confidentiality from cloud computing*. Paper presented at World Privacy Forum. New York, NY.

Chapter 14
Organizational Control Related to Cloud

Sathish A. Kumar
Coastal Carolina University, USA

ABSTRACT

Cloud computing is touted as the next big thing in the Information Technology (IT) industry, which is going to impact the businesses of any size. Yet, the security issue continues to pose a big threat. Lack of transparency in the infrastructure and platforms causes distrust among users, and the users are reluctant to store information on the cloud. This undermines the potential of cloud computing and has proved to be a big barrier in the realization of the potential of cloud computing and its widespread adoption. The big paradigm shifts in the technology has not been reflected on the methods used to secure the technology. When an organization builds the infrastructure for cloud computing, security and privacy controls should be kept in mind from the holistic security perspective. It is also critical that the organization monitor and adapt controls to determine the success of cloud computing in dealing with the security and reliability issues relating to the cloud. From an organizational control perspective, the authors suggest an independent governing body to mediate between the cloud provider and the user, with the control framework that they have developed to fulfill their responsibilities of protecting the cloud environment.

1. INTRODUCTION

National Institute of Standards and Technology (NIST) defines cloud computing as a computing model for enabling ubiquitous, convenient, on-demand network access to a shared pool of configurable computing resources (e.g., networks, servers, storage, applications, and services) (Mell, 2011). These services can be rapidly provisioned and released with minimal management effort or service provider interaction. NIST also defines that the cloud computing can be achieved through three service models: *Software as a Service (SaaS), Platform as a Service (PaaS) and Infrastructure as a Service (IaaS)*. Cloud computing can be

DOI: 10.4018/978-1-4666-5788-5.ch014

implemented by the four deployment models: *Private Cloud, Community Cloud, Public Cloud and Hybrid Cloud.*

Cloud Computing is widely considered as the next big thing in IT evolution, and is getting rapid adoption in the industry. This emerging paradigm allows an organization to reduce costs and develop highly scalable solutions (Armbrust, 2009). Cloud promises customers with the benefits of a more convenient way of provisioning IT resources at a faster speed and with a lower cost, compared to traditional IT processes and systems. Cloud Computing provides the following important features (Sarna, 2011):

- **Availability:** Services of Cloud Computing are ubiquitous and can be accessed from anywhere and by anyone just by signing in. Due to high availability, large amount of data can be uploaded and retrieved from the cloud. This data can be accessed from any devices - laptops, desktops, mobile phones, tablets etc.
- **Scalability:** Depending upon number of users logged in or the amount of data accessed, the number of servers can be increased or decreased in order to handle the demand through regular monitoring of the systems. The scaling is done with the help of Virtualization. Virtualization is achieved with the help of hypervisors such as VMware vSphere, Citrix XenServer etc.
- **Low Cost:** Small companies and startup companies that are in the early stages of their inception find cloud computing a very efficient way to set up the Infrastructure. This is due to Infrastructure as a Service (IaaS) offered by Cloud Computing which provides an infrastructure to companies. Therefore the companies need not set up the infrastructure themselves. They can just get a monthly or annual subscription of a Cloud Server on a pay-what-you-use basis. That way the businesses don't need

a huge IT investment upfront and can scale their IT budget up and down based on the business demand. All these advantages seem to be very enticing and as a result cloud computing has become very popular in recent years. Due to this, more and more IT resources, such as software, platform and infrastructure are available on the cloud and subsequently, it results in more risk factors. There are more attackers that have become active, for example active Denial of Service (DoS) attacks on the cloud providers such as Amazon, Yahoo and Google. Thus, Cloud computing has proved to be a very promising field with many benefits but the major problem that remains is of security and compliance with regulations regarding privacy.

Users generally do not rely on cloud service providers on whether their data will remain secure or not. Cloud service providers are reluctant to provide information about how they keep the data and geographical locations of their data centers. This is very obvious as it helps them keep the data safe and away from the eyes of the attackers. This in turn causes distrust among the users as they do not know where their data is and whether it is secured or not. They cannot just blindly trust the techniques used by cloud service providers without actually knowing them. As a result, users are hesitant to put their valuable and confidential data on the cloud as it may reduce the confidentiality of their data and may result in their private data becoming public. This is resulting in undermining the potential of cloud computing and making its growth slow down a little.

Cloud service providers try to provide cloud services with built-in security features. They try to build a cloud infrastructure that can withstand any sort of failure whether it is technical, logical or physical. However, there are many factors that can harm the security and reliability of the Cloud infrastructure despite of taking all the necessary steps. There are generally categorized in the following three layers, in which an organization takes control of the security. These are as follows:

- **Physical Layer:** The physical layer of security encompasses many factors.
  1. **Data Center:** This deals with the geographical location of the data center. Locations are chosen in such a way that they are not prone to natural or man-made disasters. No data center will be successful in withstanding severe earthquakes, cyclones, volcanic eruptions etc. and it is best to keep the data center in a place that is less vulnerable to be affected by these factors. Also, location of data centers is kept confidential so that it does not fall prey to external attacks.
  2. **Biometric Scanning:** There are methods such as finger-print scan or retina-scan which allow only selected employees to enter the data center. There are usually very few people that are allowed physical entry inside the area where the data is actually stored.
  3. **Building:** The buildings are generally designed to be a data center from the start. They are built in such a way that they can withstand fires. There are cameras all around the place and alarms that go off in case of emergency. Employees and security guards are present in the data center 24x7.
- **Logical Layer:** Logical Layer of security deals with the design of the network that is used for providing cloud services. The network is kept secured with the help of firewalls, anti-virus and intrusion detection systems. Companies that provide cloud services do not want to compromise with the quality of the software used, since it would harm their reputation and affect their business. The hypervisors are generally of high

standards and these systems are centrally managed and protected.

- **Methodology Layer:** This layer is concerned with the security method used at local level in a cloud service provider and it may differ from one organization to another. The main concept of this layer is to assure that various other aspects of security is taken care of. The password that every employee has is made to be very secure and difficult to crack as opposed to some preposterous passwords like "1234" which do not really help in making the system secure. The environment inside a data center is generally very secure and only a few trusted staff members are allowed to make significant changes in the system. The cloud service providers try to give the tasks to trusted staff members instead of outsourcing the tasks.

Organizations are playing a vital role in determining the course of Cloud Computing. If the security and privacy issues continue to remain, then future of Cloud Computing might be in danger. We have to find solutions and controls to the security, privacy and reliability problems in order to make cloud computing a trustworthy paradigm.

2. LITERATURE REVIEW

As we discussed earlier, the main concern in cloud computing is of security and the security issues in cloud computing remain the only obstacle that may prevent its widespread adoption. As more and more data is being migrated to the cloud, there have been more attacks, such as Denial of Service and Authentication attacks. For example, the increase of Internet-capable devices creates opportunities for remote hacking and data leakage. More cloud adopters have been at the receiving end of cloud infrastructure security incidents as compared to traditional IT infrastructure security events. These security incidents and data breaches can have financial consequences on a corporate organization (Glisson, 2006). Despite the decrease in the cost of data breaches in the last year, data breaches are still reported to have cost British and German organizations on average between \$2.7 million and \$4.4 million (Ponemon Institute, 2012). In addition to the economic and financial troubles, security breaches and threats can lead to damaged reputations, loss of customers, delayed software releases and a reduction in investor confidence (Glisson, 2006).

2.1 Role of Users

The customers also play an important role in determining the course of cloud computing. Cloud adopters need to trust the cloud providers and understand that until the technology is fully matured, that cloud computing customers will need to understand the fundamental principles of security (Willcocks, 2012). Reed and Bennett (2010) provide key guidelines on how to make best use of secure cloud services and a concise guide to cloud computing. The key points of their discussion are:

- The biggest risk that the technology faces today is Users.
- Shadow IT is an on-going risk and generally introduced by such employees who have no concerns beyond their own role in considering the risks involved in the solution provided.
- Experienced teams often roll out new technologies, but there still exists the risk when traditional security practices are ignored or adapted to the new environment.
- Attackers will always go after the valuable things and it may not be money itself.
- A single security standard is unlikely to save you.

2.2 Deployment of Security

Compared to traditional IT environment, security deployed at every level in the cloud environment must be different while considering the security needs for each level. Subashini and Kavitha (2011) highlighted security issues applicable to various layers of the cloud computing environment while noting that security needs will vary for each delivery model. The biggest threat to the cloud environment that exists today is of unauthorized access. The users put their confidential data on the cloud hoping that their data will remain safe but due to unauthorized access, the confidentiality of the data is undermined. As a result, users are reluctant to migrate their data to the cloud. Chow et al., (2009) think that this is a concern because traditional in-house authorization and authentication framework that were employed previously cannot be extended to the cloud environment and would probably need some modification to be compatible to the services of cloud computing.

The way each cloud service provider deploys the cloud is different from one to another. Therefore, the techniques followed by them are significantly different. For example, as per Cloud Security Alliance Guide (2009), Amazon's AWS EC2 infrastructure, as an example, includes vendor responsibility with respect to security and privacy lies only at the physical security, environmental security, and virtualization security level. The user is responsible for security controls at the operating system, applications, and data level. As an example of how the cloud service providers differ from one another, Salesforce.com's Customer Relationship management (CRM) is a SaaS offering and provides entire service to the user. Hence the provider is not only responsible for the physical and environmental security controls, but it must also address the security controls on the infrastructure, the applications, and the data.

2.3 Cloud Computing vs. Outsourcing

In traditional outsourcing, service providers are commissioned to handle data, system and process actively for the user according to the organization's mandate. However, cloud computing has a self-service nature, where users pay for pre-packaged IT resources made available by the cloud providers, using which they process data or other jobs on their own in a self-service fashion. In such cases, the users use infrastructure/resources supplied by the provider, and don't need to own them. Unlike outsourcing, service providers who act actively, cloud providers can be considered as agents who help users to process data and perform other jobs. Cloud providers can, at most, store data passively that the users decide to store on the provider's infrastructure, which is readily retrieval as and when needed.

Shared infrastructure/environments and economies of scale are what drive the public cloud computing providers instead of tailor-made infrastructure to fit the needs of every customer. Though customization of the service is possible in some cases, it would cost additional time/money.

The organization exercises better control over the service provider in traditional outsourcing due to the body of knowledge related to process and systems. Due to one size fit all nature and type of service in the cloud, it's often seen that organization lose control on the cloud providers and struggle with the use of resources on the cloud

2.4 Security Issues

Per our literature review, common security issues that arise in cloud computing can be classified broadly into six areas:

2.4.1 Infrastructure

This concern is mainly related to the physical security provided by the cloud service provider. For example, security of the data centers provisioned by the cloud service providers would fall under infrastructure area. This concerns the amount of surveillance that exists inside the data center. There must be enough security guards and cameras present so as to reduce the risk of external intrusion or attacks. Cohen (2012) states that from physical security perspective, the security issues might be more vulnerable in cloud computing as compared to traditional in-house security techniques. Moreover, this security control must be consistent across all the cloud providers. Cloud provider should ensure that the data center security is well-planned out and this might just alleviate the security risks which are larger as it is.

2.4.2 Data

With more and more organizations moving to cloud and storing their data in the cloud, there is more data available than there ever has been before. Therefore the surface area of the attacks is also larger. Unauthorized data access is a common attack that occurs frequently. These attacks undermine the trust of the users and they feel that their data is insecure. Users also raise other issues that might be possible with the type of data security provided by cloud providers. These include the security of Application Program Interfaces (API) provided by them. Users would want to know whether the software used and the machines present are reliable and the way in which they are used, be sufficient to ensure data security.

2.4.3 Access

Users are generally concerned about who can access their data. Jansen and Grance (2011) stated that one of the biggest concerns for an organization, considering the adoption of cloud computing, is preventing unauthorized access to data resources. It has been demonstrated that the unauthorized access of data compromises the confidentiality of the data stored access (Vascellaro, 2009). Cloud computing promises availability i.e. users can access the same data from any device. Questions is would this impact security? If there would be any unauthorized access of someone's data, it will not be from the same device that the user uses to access it but from a remote location and obviously from a different device. In that case, it is essential to ensure that the user is genuine. Therefore, a default device should be assigned to a user by the cloud provider and if the user tries to access the data from another device, one would need to give proper verification and authentication in order to prove his identity. Google follows the location based access technique but not all the cloud providers follow this Jansen and Grance (2011). Hence an organization should ensure all the providers consistently follow these controls.

2.4.4 Availability

To ensure availability to all the users, that try to access their account or data, the cloud service must scale itself according to the number of users. The number of servers increases or decreases to keep up with the traffic. This scalability feature is performed either automatically by the cloud providers' servers through knowledge learning or manually by prompting the administrator to do this. This however, will not ensure that a cloud can handle any amount of traffic that comes its way. This raises another issue that in case of huge traffic caused by DoS attacks, the cloud might just collapse and for that time the users will not be able to access their data.

2.4.5 Compliance

Several organizations such as SAS 70 and ISO 27001 put forth regulations from the security audits, operation traceability and data location perspective. Cloud providers are supposed to follow these rules & regulations in order to ensure security of the cloud. Users need to be completely aware of what all rules and regulations are fol-

lowed by their cloud provider. There have been many instances such as the case of Google Docs in March 2009, where full security and data safety audit reports were not made public and data integrity was allegedly compromised by improper access (Vascellaro, 2009).

2.5 Solutions Proposed in Literature

There are few organizational control perspective solutions proposed to the security problem of cloud computing proposed in the literature. Organizational control will help to manage the overall services of the cloud service provider and in return, reduce the security and reliability issues of cloud computing. The cloud computing governance model by Guo, Song and Song (2010) addresses requirements and objectives of service, policy, security, risk and compliance management in cloud computing and supplements detailed descriptions and important information on the required system design. Their main contribution lies in the development of an architecture for Risk and Compliance Management (RCM), which focuses on controlling of services and policies (compliance regulations) by means of monitoring cloud computing Services. An overview of RCM in Cloud Computing is provided by Chaput and Ringwood (2010). They discuss different types of RCM regulations like laws and industry regulations affecting the adoption of Cloud Computing. Four key features discussed are security methods like data classification, access control, authentication and authorization, risk management methods like business impact analysis and business continuity, certifications and auditing standards.

In the territory of compliance management, Matthews et al. (2009) propose virtual machine contracts, which extend the open virtual machine format. These electronic contracts describe and formalize technical requirements such as firewall rules, transport protocols, source and destination addresses as well as source and destination ports, to configure the virtual machines for a particular network segment. Kamara and Lauter (2010) present methods and architectures for the encryption of cloud storage. One objective is to secure storage services for regulatory compliance by encrypting the data on- premise to avoid access to the data by a third party. They argue that this approach reduces the legal exposure and in return reduces the risk factors. Brandic et al. (2010) provides an extension of Service Level Agreements (SLA) with regard to compliance issues. They introduce Compliance Level Agreements (CLA) and develop a detailed architecture for compliance management in Cloud Computing.

The security risks in cloud computing can be reduced by specifically outlining the attacks and threats which may be considered as malicious. Ristenpart et al. (2009) believes that security guidelines are also needed to address and mitigate risks associated with hypervisor-level attacks including cross-virtualization attacks. An insecure hypervisor can allow a malicious user to gain access to data stored in virtual machines hosted on a vulnerable hypervisor. Standards and guidelines can specify how the organization accomplishes a Virtual Machine Image (VMI) (PCI Security Standards Council, 2011). Wei et al. (2009) suggest that a framework is developed to manage VMI creation, storage and destruction procedures. This framework is likely to contain controls such as filters to remove sensitive information from an image prior to publishing and a mechanism to track changes performed on a specific image to mitigate malicious image modification.

Another organizational control is punishment, which is carried out to reduce the undesirable behavior of employees such as non-compliance to the safety regulations and rules. Punishment is generally considered as a very effective way to produce behavior change. As a management tool within organizations, punishment is defined as "the application of a negative consequence to, or the withdrawal of a positive consequence from, an employee" (Trevino, 1992). Merhi and Ahluwalia (2013) state that some employees in general tend to repeat actions that do not produce negative outcomes and prefer to avoid those actions that lead to negative actions; thus reducing likelihood of punishment. The rationale behind this argument is that punishment creates an anxiety in minds of employees which forces them to change their behaviors towards organizational policies.

3. ORGANIZATIONAL CONTROL

There is a need for the cloud providers to hide some security related information, as they need to keep all the information about the security procedures confidential in order to minimize any security breaches. However, the lack of transparency results in the cloud customers losing trust on the cloud providers. As a result, customers are reluctant to store their valuable data on the cloud, which undermines the potential of cloud computing.

Our approach to solve this is by formation of a governing body which will act as an interface between the cloud providers and cloud end users and provide organizational control. The governing body in our framework is unique compared to the existing infrastructure due to the following reasons: This governing body will be an independent unit and will not be influenced by any of the two entities involved. It will be responsible for any and every actions that take place inside the cloud environment. Various cloud providers will need to register themselves to the governing body and then that body will assess all the procedures and methodologies involved in the technology.

In general, this Governing Body will be responsible for risk assessment & management, security performance evaluation, policy, audit and compliance with respect to the deployment of cloud layer. The Governing Body will not be limited to just assessing the conditions. It will also provide solutions and alternatives to the customers in case of any issues that takes place in the cloud

Figure 1. Organizational control through governing body

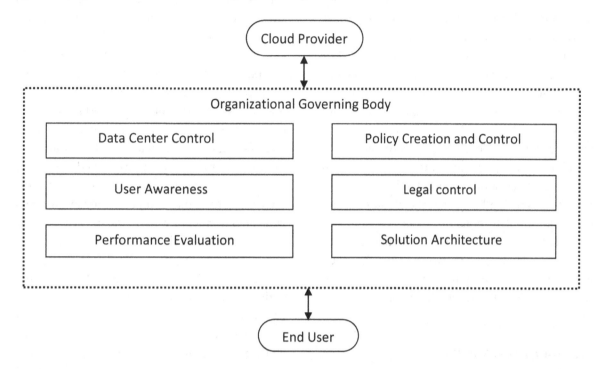

environment whether it is due to technology failure or any external factors.

As shown in Figure 1, the governing body is an interface that provides formal control and governance between cloud provider and customer, to ensure that there is a smooth working and a well-coordinated system. The governing body will be responsible for the following functionalities that the cloud provider cannot provide on their own.

3.1 Data Center Control

Governing body will be responsible for the happenings inside the cloud environment. By migrating applications to the cloud, the risk factors increase. The traditional data control methods need to be modified in order to cope with the security and privacy challenges associated with the cloud environment. The entity that is at most risk inside the cloud environment is data center. The data center is a centralized location, where the entire customer's data is stored. Hence, cloud provid-

ers need to ensure that no security breaches take place inside the data center. To achieve this, the governing body should continuously monitor the possible security related threats and the products/solutions available to counter those threats, procure and implement them. For instance, some of the solutions include data replication facilities with hot site disaster recovery service. The governing body would need to ensure that the data centers are safe and secure and that all the data that resides inside it, must be backed up to ensure the business continuity incase disaster happens. Disaster recovery and business continuity is one thing that every cloud provider promises. However, to ensure it gets implemented and operates in a right manner, there needs to be a centralized authority to get them implemented.

3.2 Policy Creation and Control

The security features that are included in the cloud environment are very important to determine the level of security present in the cloud. The security policy that will be drafted by the governing body will be responsible for all the layers of the security features that will be included in the cloud. For example, the security policy shall specify the use of firewalls and anti-virus, type of virtualization and the hyper-visor used to achieve the secure cloud functionality. It is to be noted that the above features may vary depending upon the budget of the cloud provider, which in turn will reflect in the use and adoption of that cloud. We suggest that the governing board and the cloud provider would jointly determine the security features to be included. Only an outline of the features will be discussed between the two and once the cloud is deployed, the governing body would validate to see if all the features discussed before have been implemented.

3.3 User Awareness

The governing body will need to go through all the procedures and methods that a cloud provider follows in order to gain information about the security features of the cloud. The governing body needs to filter and provide information to users in such a way that the users are aware of the security features and at the same time, no confidential information is leaked. Our automated control framework ensures that based on triggers, central body convey right information at right time to right parties involved in the environment in an automated fashion. This will ensure removal of the lack of transparency in security features so that users are able to trust the cloud providers.

3.4 Legal Control

There are a number of jurisdictions and laws that apply to cloud computing. Laws vary from place to place and generally the data centers of a cloud provider are located in different countries or may be different continents. To gain knowledge and abide by all the laws of different location can be very difficult to cope with. For example US Patriot Act can be applied to foreign organizations that use U.S based cloud provider. Per US Patriot Act the Governmental authorities only may access cloud data pursuant to the Patriot Act to (i) "obtain foreign intelligence information not concerning a United States person" or (ii) "protect against international terrorism or clandestine intelligence activities". Even a single law broken may affect the organization in many different ways. These laws and jurisdiction vary from geographical locations to the methods involved in the cloud computing and allowing the personnel to enter or work in the facility. Complying with all the jurisdiction and laws is a very time consuming job and may reflect in the efficiency of the cloud. Therefore, by letting the governing body take care of all the legal matters, the cloud provider can really think about making the cloud safe, secure and efficient. This will also ensure that all the jurisdictions and laws are followed.

3.5 Performance Evaluation

One of the parameters to evaluate the performance of the cloud is the number of security breaches and attacks to determine the performance of the cloud. Governing body should assess the performance of the cloud environment based on the security parameters and draft a report that will determine the efficiency of the cloud. This will help users in determining what all security features are being ignored by the cloud provider and help them make decisions by providing the right choices. The performance evaluation of the providers would motivate the good providers to increase their trust score with the governing body, compared to those providers who can try to negatively affect the organization. This will also help the governing body to rank the providers based on the provider's trust score. The cloud providers will also benefit from this evaluation, as they will get to know the limitations and the disadvantages in their implementation of security controls in the cloud computing environment.

With the performance evaluation functionality, the factors that caused attacks and threats will be removed and the cloud will be safe and reliable.

3.6 Solution Architecture

The governing body shall not only be responsible for the policy, monitoring, evaluation and legal controls but also responsible for providing solutions to the customers. For example, following are some of the problem samples that the governing body shall be responsible for providing solutions: a) Customers lost their data or are unable to access their data due to the occurrence of mishaps in the cloud environment. b) If a Cloud Provider goes bankrupt or due to some other factors and decides to shut down some of the data centers, many users' data will be at risk. At that point of time, the governing body will be responsible for providing alternative solutions to the users. The solution might range from migrating the data to some other cloud or giving all the data back to the user so that they can manage it themselves. This results in tighter organizational control for the resources, which is the governing body's mandate.

In a large organization that caters to the needs of millions of customers, there could be many unsatisfied customers, who often file legal complaints or threaten to damage the reputation of the organization in some way or the other. Disputes and conflicts may also arise between two or more cloud providers, due to the disagreement over the issues. Disputes in IT industry are very common and there have been a number of incidents where some company adopted someone else's ideas to develop their own product. For instance, recently Microsoft sued Salesforce.com for the cloud computing patent infringement. In this case, the governing body will make sure that the conflicts and disputes are solved through our framework. This is done with the help of threat index that we introduced in our framework. The threat index is computed by the security parameters, of which conflicts and disputes are part of it.

Thus the governing body provides organizational control to the cloud environment by keeping track of all the activities going on and providing solutions as and when required. By establishing a central body, cloud computing will become organized and managed by ensuring right information is conveyed at right time to right parties. This will also eliminate the lack of transparency that exists between the user and the cloud provider.

4. ORGANIZATION CONTROL FRAMEWORK

The functionalities that were discussed earlier can be achieved by our framework, as shown in Figure 2. Security parameters indicated in Figure 2 include technical, legal and policy parameters. In this framework, Threat Index (TI) calculates the vulnerability of a cloud environment based data center to threats and attacks. This threat index is calculated based on the parameters from cloud based data center security control, legal control, policy control perspectives. By calculating the threat index, performance trend of a cloud provider can be identified and communicated to the user. Threat Index can be calculated over a specified period of time and that can be compared with the benchmark index thresholds obtained with the help of historical training. Historical training is done by collection of data, with and without attacks, with and without legal control, with and without policy control over a long period of time. The comparison of the index threshold with the threat index helps the organization to gain knowledge of the current security, policy and legal trends. This will help the organization and the cloud provider to increase or decrease the controls from technical, legal and policy perspective with the help of solution architecture framework. It will also help them pointing out the methodologies that are flawed, if any, and help them improve it in order to increase the reliability of the cloud.

Figure 2. Organization control framework for cloud services

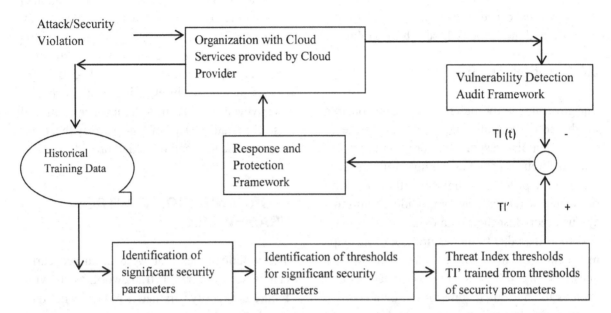

5. SUMMARY AND CONCLUSION

Cloud computing is purported to be the future of the IT industry. Cloud computing marks a true paradigm shift in how the computing would happen in the future and cloud computing is likely to have the same impact on IT industry that foundries have had on the manufacturing industry. However, one thing that proves to be the biggest obstacle in its course is security issue.

Security issues vary from physical and legal level involving data centers and geographical locations to methodological level involving the policy and logic used in deploying the cloud to technical level involving the technology involved in implementing the cloud. This has prevented cloud computing from its widespread adoption.

From an organizational control perspective, we provided an automated control framework comprised of independent governing body that will mediate between the cloud provider and the user. Governing body will be responsible for ensuring the security of cloud based data center, implementation of a secure policy & control, increase the user awareness about security methods deployed, handling the legal matters, resolution of disputes, evaluation of performance and providing solutions for the end user. We have described a framework, which computes threat index based on the security parameters, that the governing body could apply to fulfill their responsibilities and use in the planning the implementation of the security policy to keep the organization in control from the cloud computing security and privacy issues.

ACKNOWLEDGMENT

The author wishes to thank Harshit Srivastava for his contributions to this chapter.

REFERENCES

Armbrust, M., Fox, A., Griffith, R., Joseph, A. D., Katz, R., & Konwinski, A. ... Zaharia, M. (2009). *Above the clouds: A Berkeley view of cloud computing* (Technical Report No. UCB/EECS-2009-28). Berkeley, CA: University of California.

Brandic, I., Dustdar, S., Anstett, T., Schumm, D., Leymann, F., & Konrad, R. (2010). Compliant cloud computing (C3), architecture and language support for user-driven compliance management in clouds. In *Proceedings of the 3rd International Conference on Cloud Computing*. IEEE.

Chaput, S. R., & Ringwood, K. (2010). Cloud compliance: A framework for using cloud computing in a regulated world. In N. Antonopoulos, & L. Gillam (Eds.), *Cloud computing principles systems and applications*. Berlin: Springer. doi:10.1007/978-1-84996-241-4_14

Chow, R., Golle, P., Jakobsson, M., Shi, E., Staddon, J., Masuoka, R., & Molina, J. (2009). Controlling data in the cloud: Outsourcing computation without outsourcing control. In *Proceedings of the 2009 ACM Workshop on Cloud Computing Security*. Chicago: ACM.

Cloud Security Alliance. (2009). Retrieved from https://www.cloudsecurityalliance.org/csaguide.pdf

Cohen, M. (2012, January 17). Forecasting the first steps of cloud adoption. *eWeek*, 1–3.

Glisson, W. B., McDonald, A., & Welland, R. (2006). Web engineering security: A practitioner's perspective. In *Proceedings of the 6th International Conference on Web Engineering*. Palo Alto, CA: ACM.

Guo, Z., Song, M., & Song, J. (2010). A governance model for cloud computing. In *Proceedings of the International Conference on Management and Service Science*. IEEE.

Jansen, W., & Grance, T. (2011). *Guidelines on security and privacy in public cloud computing (NIST Technical Report- SP 800-144)*. Washington, DC: NIST.

Kamara, S., & Lauter, K. (2010). Cryptographic cloud storage. In *Proceedings of the 1st Workshop on RealLife Cryptographic Protocols and Standardization*. Academic Press.

Matthews, J., Garfinkel, T., Hoff, C., & Wheeler, J. (2009). Virtual machine contracts for datacenter and cloud computing environments. In *Proceedings of the 1st Workshop on Automated Control for Datacenters and Clouds* (ACDC 09), (pp. 25-30). ACDC.

Mell, P., & Grance, T. (2011). *The NIST definition of cloud computing, September 2011 (NIST Special Publication 800-145)*. Washington, DC: NIST.

Merhi, M. I., & Ahluwalia, P. (2013). Information security policies compliance: The role of organizational punishment. In *Proceedings of the Nineteenth Americas Conference on Information Systems*. Chicago, IL: ACM.

PCI Security Standards Council. (2011). *Information supplement: PCI DSS virtualization guidelines*. PCI.

Ponemon Institute. (2012). *The 2011 cost of data breach study: Global*. Symantec.

Reed, G. B. (2010). *Silver clouds, dark linings: A concise guide to cloud computing*. Upper Saddle River, NJ: Prentice Hall.

Ristenpart, T., Tromer, E., Shacham, H., & Savage, S. (2009). Hey, you, get off of my cloud: Exploring information leakage in third-party compute clouds. In *Proceedings of the 16th ACM Conference on Computer and Communications Security*. Chicago, IL: ACM.

Sarna, D. E. Y. (2011). *Implementing and developing cloud computing applications*. Boca Raton, FL: CRC Press, Taylor & Francis Group.

Subashini, S., & Kavitha, V. (2011). A survey on security issues in service delivery models of cloud computing. *Journal of Network and Computer Applications*. doi:10.1016/j.jnca.2010.07.006

Szefer, J., & Lee, R. B. (2011). A case for hardware protection of guest VMs from compromised hypervisors in cloud computing. In *Proceedings of Distributed Computing Systems Workshops (ICDCSW)*. IEEE.

Trevino, L. K. (1992). The social effects of punishment in organizations: A justice perspective. *Academy of Management Review*, *17*(4), 647–676.

Vascellaro, J. E. (2010). *Article*. Retrieved from http://blogs.wsj.com/digits/2009/03/08/1214/

Wei, J., Zhang, X., Ammons, G., Bala, V., & Ning, P. (2009). Managing security of virtual machine images in a cloud environment. In *Proceedings of 2009 ACM Workshop on Cloud Computing Security*. ACM.

Willcocks, L., Venters, W., Whitley, E., & Hindle, J. (2012). *Cloud on the landscape: Problems and challenges in the new IT outsourcing landscape: From innovation to cloud services*. London: Palgrave Macmillan Publisher.

Related References

To continue our tradition of advancing information science and technology research, we have compiled a list of recommended IGI Global readings. These references will provide additional information and guidance to further enrich your knowledge and assist you with your own research and future publications.

Aalmink, J., von der Dovenmühle, T., & Gómez, J. M. (2013). Enterprise tomography: Maintenance and root-cause-analysis of federated erp in enterprise clouds. In P. Ordóñez de Pablos, H. Nigro, R. Tennyson, S. Gonzalez Cisaro, & W. Karwowski (Eds.), *Advancing information management through semantic web concepts and ontologies* (pp. 133–153). Hershey, PA: Information Science Reference.

Abu, S. T., & Tsuji, M. (2011). The development of ICT for envisioning cloud computing and innovation in South Asia. [IJIDE]. *International Journal of Innovation in the Digital Economy, 2*(1), 61–72. doi:10.4018/jide.2011010105

Abu, S. T., & Tsuji, M. (2012). The development of ICT for envisioning cloud computing and innovation in South Asia. In I. Management Association (Ed.), Grid and cloud computing: Concepts, methodologies, tools and applications (pp. 453-465). Hershey, PA: Information Science Reference. doi: doi:10.4018/978-1-4666-0879-5.ch207

Abu, S. T., & Tsuji, M. (2013). The development of ICT for envisioning cloud computing and innovation in South Asia. In I. Oncioiu (Ed.), *Business innovation, development, and advancement in the digital economy* (pp. 35–47). Hershey, PA: Business Science Reference. doi:10.4018/978-1-4666-2934-9.ch003

Adams, R. (2013). The emergence of cloud storage and the need for a new digital forensic process model. In K. Ruan (Ed.), *Cybercrime and cloud forensics: Applications for investigation processes* (pp. 79–104). Hershey, PA: Information Science Reference.

Adeyeye, M. (2013). Provisioning converged applications and services via the cloud. In D. Kanellopoulos (Ed.), *Intelligent multimedia technologies for networking applications: Techniques and tools* (pp. 248–269). Hershey, PA: Information Science Reference.

Aggarwal, A. (2013). A systems approach to cloud computing services. In A. Bento, & A. Aggarwal (Eds.), *Cloud computing service and deployment models: Layers and management* (pp. 124–136). Hershey, PA: Business Science Reference.

Ahmed, K., Hussain, A., & Gregory, M. A. (2013). An efficient, robust, and secure SSO architecture for cloud computing implemented in a service oriented architecture. In X. Yang, & L. Liu (Eds.), *Principles, methodologies, and service-oriented approaches for cloud computing* (pp. 259–282). Hershey, PA: Business Science Reference. doi:10.4018/978-1-4666-2854-0.ch011

Ahuja, S. P., & Mani, S. (2013). Empirical performance analysis of HPC benchmarks across variations in cloud computing. [IJCAC]. *International Journal of Cloud Applications and Computing, 3*(1), 13–26. doi:10.4018/ijcac.2013010102

Ahuja, S. P., & Rolli, A. C. (2011). Survey of the state-of-the-art of cloud computing. [IJCAC]. *International Journal of Cloud Applications and Computing, 1*(4), 34–43. doi:10.4018/ijcac.2011100103

Ahuja, S. P., & Rolli, A. C. (2013). Survey of the state-of-the-art of cloud computing. In S. Aljawarneh (Ed.), *Cloud computing advancements in design, implementation, and technologies* (pp. 252–262). Hershey, PA: Information Science Reference.

Ahuja, S. P., & Sridharan, S. (2012). Performance evaluation of hypervisors for cloud computing. [IJCAC]. *International Journal of Cloud Applications and Computing, 2*(3), 26–67. doi:10.4018/ijcac.2012070102

Akyuz, G. A., & Rehan, M. (2013). A generic, cloud-based representation for supply chains (SC's). [IJCAC]. *International Journal of Cloud Applications and Computing, 3*(2), 12–20. doi:10.4018/ijcac.2013040102

Al-Aqrabi, H., & Liu, L. (2013). IT security and governance compliant service oriented computing in cloud computing environments. In X. Yang, & L. Liu (Eds.), *Principles, methodologies, and service-oriented approaches for cloud computing* (pp. 143–163). Hershey, PA: Business Science Reference. doi:10.4018/978-1-4666-2854-0.ch006

Al-Zoube, M., & Wyne, M. F. (2012). Building integrated e-learning environment using cloud services and social networking sites. In Q. Jin (Ed.), *Intelligent learning systems and advancements in computer-aided instruction: Emerging studies* (pp. 214–233). Hershey, PA: Information Science Reference.

Alam, N., & Karmakar, R. (2014). Cloud computing and its application to information centre. In S. Dhamdhere (Ed.), *Cloud computing and virtualization technologies in libraries* (pp. 63–76). Hershey, PA: Information Science Reference.

Alhaj, A., Aljawarneh, S., Masadeh, S., & Abu-Taieh, E. (2013). A secure data transmission mechanism for cloud outsourced data. [IJCAC]. *International Journal of Cloud Applications and Computing, 3*(1), 34–43. doi:10.4018/ijcac.2013010104

Alharbi, S. T. (2012). Users' acceptance of cloud computing in Saudi Arabia: An extension of technology acceptance model. [IJCAC]. *International Journal of Cloud Applications and Computing, 2*(2), 1–11. doi:10.4018/ijcac.2012040101

Ali, S. S., & Khan, M. N. (2013). ICT infrastructure framework for microfinance institutions and banks in Pakistan: An optimized approach. [IJOM]. *International Journal of Online Marketing, 3*(2), 75–86. doi:10.4018/ijom.2013040105

Aljawarneh, S. (2011). Cloud security engineering: Avoiding security threats the right way. [IJCAC]. *International Journal of Cloud Applications and Computing, 1*(2), 64–70. doi:10.4018/ijcac.2011040105

Aljawarneh, S. (2013). Cloud security engineering: Avoiding security threats the right way. In S. Aljawarneh (Ed.), *Cloud computing advancements in design, implementation, and technologies* (pp. 147–153). Hershey, PA: Information Science Reference.

Alshattnawi, S. (2013). Utilizing cloud computing in developing a mobile location-aware tourist guide system. [IJAPUC]. *International Journal of Advanced Pervasive and Ubiquitous Computing, 5*(2), 9–18. doi:10.4018/japuc.2013040102

Alsmadi, I. (2013). Software development methodologies for cloud computing. In K. Buragga, & N. Zaman (Eds.), *Software development techniques for constructive information systems design* (pp. 110–117). Hershey, PA: Information Science Reference. doi:10.4018/978-1-4666-3679-8.ch006

Anand, V. (2013). Survivable mapping of virtual networks onto a shared substrate network. In X. Yang, & L. Liu (Eds.), *Principles, methodologies, and service-oriented approaches for cloud computing* (pp. 325–343). Hershey, PA: Business Science Reference. doi:10.4018/978-1-4666-2854-0.ch014

Antonova, A. (2013). Green, sustainable, or clean: What type of IT/IS technologies will we need in the future? In P. Ordóñez de Pablos (Ed.), *Green technologies and business practices: An IT approach* (pp. 151–162). Hershey, PA: Information Science Reference.

Ardissono, L., Bosio, G., Goy, A., Petrone, G., Segnan, M., & Torretta, F. (2011). Collaboration support for activity management in a personal cloud environment. [IJDST]. *International Journal of Distributed Systems and Technologies, 2*(4), 30–43. doi:10.4018/jdst.2011100103

Ardissono, L., Bosio, G., Goy, A., Petrone, G., Segnan, M., & Torretta, F. (2013). Collaboration support for activity management in a personal cloud environment. In N. Bessis (Ed.), *Development of distributed systems from design to application and maintenance* (pp. 199–212). Hershey, PA: Information Science Reference.

Argiolas, M., Atzori, M., Dessì, N., & Pes, B. (2012). Dataspaces enhancing decision support systems in clouds. [IJWP]. *International Journal of Web Portals, 4*(2), 35–55. doi:10.4018/jwp.2012040103

Arinze, B., & Anandarajan, M. (2012). Factors that determine the adoption of cloud computing: A global perspective. In M. Tavana (Ed.), *Enterprise Information Systems and Advancing Business Solutions: Emerging Models* (pp. 210–223). Hershey, PA: Business Science Reference. doi:10.4018/978-1-4666-1761-2.ch012

Arinze, B., & Sylla, C. (2012). Conducting research in the cloud. In L. Chao (Ed.), *Cloud computing for teaching and learning: Strategies for design and implementation* (pp. 50–63). Hershey, PA: Information Science Reference. doi:10.4018/978-1-4666-0957-0.ch004

Arshad, J., Townend, P., & Xu, J. (2011). An abstract model for integrated intrusion detection and severity analysis for clouds. [IJCAC]. *International Journal of Cloud Applications and Computing, 1*(1), 1–16. doi:10.4018/ijcac.2011010101

Arshad, J., Townend, P., & Xu, J. (2013). An abstract model for integrated intrusion detection and severity analysis for clouds. In S. Aljawarneh (Ed.), *Cloud computing advancements in design, implementation, and technologies* (pp. 1–17). Hershey, PA: Information Science Reference.

Arshad, J., Townend, P., Xu, J., & Jie, W. (2012). Cloud computing security: Opportunities and pitfalls. [IJGHPC]. *International Journal of Grid and High Performance Computing, 4*(1), 52–66. doi:10.4018/jghpc.2012010104

Baars, T., & Spruit, M. (2012). Designing a secure cloud architecture: The SeCA model. [IJISP]. *International Journal of Information Security and Privacy, 6*(1), 14–32. doi:10.4018/jisp.2012010102

Bai, X., Gao, J. Z., & Tsai, W. (2013). Cloud scalability measurement and testing. In S. Tilley, & T. Parveen (Eds.), *Software testing in the cloud: Perspectives on an emerging discipline* (pp. 356–381). Hershey, PA: Information Science Reference.

Baldini, G., & Stirparo, P. (2014). A cognitive access framework for security and privacy protection in mobile cloud computing. In J. Rodrigues, K. Lin, & J. Lloret (Eds.), *Mobile networks and cloud computing convergence for progressive services and applications* (pp. 92–117). Hershey, PA: Information Science Reference.

Balduf, S., Balke, T., & Eymann, T. (2012). Cultural differences in managing cloud computing service level agreements. In I. Management Association (Ed.), Grid and cloud computing: Concepts, methodologies, tools and applications (pp. 1237-1263). Hershey, PA: Information Science Reference. doi: doi:10.4018/978-1-4666-0879-5.ch512

Banerjee, S., Sing, T. Y., Chowdhury, A. R., & Anwar, H. (2013). Motivations to adopt green ICT: A tale of two organizations. [IJGC]. *International Journal of Green Computing, 4*(2), 1–11. doi:10.4018/jgc.2013070101

Barreto, J., Di Sanzo, P., Palmieri, R., & Romano, P. (2013). Cloud-TM: An elastic, self-tuning transactional store for the cloud. In D. Kyriazis, A. Voulodimos, S. Gogouvitis, & T. Varvarigou (Eds.), *Data intensive storage services for cloud environments* (pp. 192–224). Hershey, PA: Business Science Reference. doi:10.4018/978-1-4666-3934-8.ch013

Belalem, G., & Limam, S. (2011). Fault tolerant architecture to cloud computing using adaptive checkpoint. [IJCAC]. *International Journal of Cloud Applications and Computing, 1*(4), 60–69. doi:10.4018/ijcac.2011100105

Belalem, G., & Limam, S. (2013). Fault tolerant architecture to cloud computing using adaptive checkpoint. In S. Aljawarneh (Ed.), *Cloud computing advancements in design, implementation, and technologies* (pp. 280–289). Hershey, PA: Information Science Reference.

Ben Belgacem, M., Abdennadher, N., & Niinimaki, M. (2012). Virtual EZ grid: A volunteer computing infrastructure for scientific medical applications. [IJHCR]. *International Journal of Handheld Computing Research*, *3*(1), 74–85. doi:10.4018/jhcr.2012010105

Bhatt, S., Chaudhary, S., & Bhise, M. (2013). Migration of data between cloud and non-cloud datastores. In A. Ionita, M. Litoiu, & G. Lewis (Eds.), *Migrating legacy applications: Challenges in service oriented architecture and cloud computing environments* (pp. 206–225). Hershey, PA: Information Science Reference.

Biancofiore, G., & Leone, S. (2014). Google apps as a cloud computing solution in Italian municipalities: Technological features and implications. In S. Leone (Ed.), *Synergic integration of formal and informal e-learning environments for adult lifelong learners* (pp. 244–274). Hershey, PA: Information Science Reference.

Bibi, S., Katsaros, D., & Bozanis, P. (2012). How to choose the right cloud. In I. Management Association (Ed.), Grid and cloud computing: Concepts, methodologies, tools and applications (pp. 1530-1552). Hershey, PA: Information Science Reference. doi: doi:10.4018/978-1-4666-0879-5.ch701

Bibi, S., Katsaros, D., & Bozanis, P. (2012). How to choose the right cloud. In X. Liu, & Y. Li (Eds.), *Advanced design approaches to emerging software systems: Principles, methodologies and tools* (pp. 219–240). Hershey, PA: Information Science Reference.

Bitam, S., Batouche, M., & Talbi, E. (2012). A bees life algorithm for cloud computing services selection. In S. Ali, N. Abbadeni, & M. Batouche (Eds.), *Multidisciplinary computational intelligence techniques: Applications in business, engineering, and medicine* (pp. 31–46). Hershey, PA: Information Science Reference. doi:10.4018/978-1-4666-1830-5.ch003

Bittencourt, L. F., Madeira, E. R., & da Fonseca, N. L. (2014). Communication aspects of resource management in hybrid clouds. In H. Mouftah, & B. Kantarci (Eds.), *Communication infrastructures for cloud computing* (pp. 409–433). Hershey, PA: Information Science Reference.

Bonelli, L., Giudicianni, L., Immediata, A., & Luzzi, A. (2013). Compliance in the cloud. In D. Kyriazis, A. Voulodimos, S. Gogouvitis, & T. Varvarigou (Eds.), *Data intensive storage services for cloud environments* (pp. 109–131). Hershey, PA: Business Science Reference. doi:10.4018/978-1-4666-3934-8.ch008

Boniface, M., Nasser, B., Surridge, M., & Oliveros, E. (2012). Securing real-time interactive applications in federated clouds. In I. Management Association (Ed.), Grid and cloud computing: Concepts, methodologies, tools and applications (pp. 1822-1835). Hershey, PA: Information Science Reference. doi: doi:10.4018/978-1-4666-0879-5.ch806

Boukhobza, J. (2013). Flashing in the cloud: Shedding some light on NAND flash memory storage systems. In D. Kyriazis, A. Voulodimos, S. Gogouvitis, & T. Varvarigou (Eds.), *Data intensive storage services for cloud environments* (pp. 241–266). Hershey, PA: Business Science Reference. doi:10.4018/978-1-4666-3934-8.ch015

Bracci, F., Corradi, A., & Foschini, L. (2014). Cloud standards: Security and interoperability issues. In H. Mouftah, & B. Kantarci (Eds.), *Communication infrastructures for cloud computing* (pp. 465–495). Hershey, PA: Information Science Reference.

Brown, A. W. (2013). Experiences with cloud technology to realize software testing factories. In S. Tilley, & T. Parveen (Eds.), *Software testing in the cloud: Perspectives on an emerging discipline* (pp. 1–27). Hershey, PA: Information Science Reference.

Calcavecchia, N. M., Celesti, A., & Di Nitto, E. (2012). Understanding decentralized and dynamic brokerage in federated cloud environments. In M. Villari, I. Brandic, & F. Tusa (Eds.), *Achieving federated and self-manageable cloud infrastructures: Theory and practice* (pp. 36–56). Hershey, PA: Business Science Reference. doi:10.4018/978-1-4666-1631-8.ch003

Calero, J. M., König, B., & Kirschnick, J. (2012). Cross-layer monitoring in cloud computing. In H. Rashvand, & Y. Kavian (Eds.), *Using cross-layer techniques for communication systems* (pp. 328–348). Hershey, PA: Information Science Reference. doi:10.4018/978-1-4666-0960-0.ch014

Cardellini, V., Casalicchio, E., & Silvestri, L. (2012). Service level provisioning for cloud-based applications service level provisioning for cloud-based applications. In A. Pathan, M. Pathan, & H. Lee (Eds.), *Advancements in distributed computing and internet technologies: Trends and issues* (pp. 363–385). Hershey, PA: Information Science Publishing.

Cardellini, V., Casalicchio, E., & Silvestri, L. (2012). Service level provisioning for cloud-based applications service level provisioning for cloud-based applications. In I. Management Association (Ed.), Grid and cloud computing: Concepts, methodologies, tools and applications (pp. 1479-1500). Hershey, PA: Information Science Reference. doi: doi:10.4018/978-1-4666-0879-5.ch611

Carlin, S., & Curran, K. (2013). Cloud computing security. In K. Curran (Ed.), *Pervasive and ubiquitous technology innovations for ambient intelligence environments* (pp. 12–17). Hershey, PA: Information Science Reference.

Carlton, G. H., & Zhou, H. (2011). A survey of cloud computing challenges from a digital forensics perspective. [IJITN]. *International Journal of Interdisciplinary Telecommunications and Networking, 3*(4), 1–16. doi:10.4018/jitn.2011100101

Carlton, G. H., & Zhou, H. (2012). A survey of cloud computing challenges from a digital forensics perspective. In I. Management Association (Ed.), Grid and cloud computing: Concepts, methodologies, tools and applications (pp. 1221-1236). Hershey, PA: Information Science Reference. doi: doi:10.4018/978-1-4666-0879-5.ch511

Carlton, G. H., & Zhou, H. (2013). A survey of cloud computing challenges from a digital forensics perspective. In M. Bartolacci, & S. Powell (Eds.), *Advancements and innovations in wireless communications and network technologies* (pp. 213–228). Hershey, PA: Information Science Reference.

Carpen-Amarie, A., Costan, A., Leordeanu, C., Basescu, C., & Antoniu, G. (2012). Towards a generic security framework for cloud data management environments. [IJDST]. *International Journal of Distributed Systems and Technologies, 3*(1), 17–34. doi:10.4018/jdst.2012010102

Casola, V., Cuomo, A., Villano, U., & Rak, M. (2012). Access control in federated clouds: The cloudgrid case study. In M. Villari, I. Brandic, & F. Tusa (Eds.), *Achieving Federated and Self-Manageable Cloud Infrastructures: Theory and Practice* (pp. 395–417). Hershey, PA: Business Science Reference. doi:10.4018/978-1-4666-1631-8. ch020

Casola, V., Cuomo, A., Villano, U., & Rak, M. (2013). Access control in federated clouds: The cloudgrid case study. In I. Management Association (Ed.), IT policy and ethics: Concepts, methodologies, tools, and applications (pp. 148-169). Hershey, PA: Information Science Reference. doi: doi:10.4018/978-1-4666-2919-6.ch008

Celesti, A., Tusa, F., & Villari, M. (2012). Toward cloud federation: Concepts and challenges. In M. Villari, I. Brandic, & F. Tusa (Eds.), *Achieving federated and self-manageable cloud infrastructures: Theory and practice* (pp. 1–17). Hershey, PA: Business Science Reference. doi:10.4018/978-1-4666-1631-8.ch001

Chaka, C. (2013). Virtualization and cloud computing: Business models in the virtual cloud. In A. Loo (Ed.), *Distributed computing innovations for business, engineering, and science* (pp. 176–190). Hershey, PA: Information Science Reference.

Chang, J. (2011). A framework for analysing the impact of cloud computing on local government in the UK. [IJCAC]. *International Journal of Cloud Applications and Computing, 1*(4), 25–33. doi:10.4018/ijcac.2011100102

Chang, J. (2013). A framework for analysing the impact of cloud computing on local government in the UK. In S. Aljawarneh (Ed.), *Cloud computing advancements in design, implementation, and technologies* (pp. 243–251). Hershey, PA: Information Science Reference.

Chang, J., & Johnston, M. (2012). Cloud computing in local government: From the perspective of four London borough councils. [IJCAC]. *International Journal of Cloud Applications and Computing, 2*(4), 1–15. doi:10.4018/ijcac.2012100101

Chang, K., & Wang, K. (2012). Efficient support of streaming videos through patching proxies in the cloud. [IJGHPC]. *International Journal of Grid and High Performance Computing, 4*(4), 22–36. doi:10.4018/jghpc.2012100102

Chang, R., Liao, C., & Liu, C. (2013). Choosing clouds for an enterprise: Modeling and evaluation. [IJEEI]. *International Journal of E-Entrepreneurship and Innovation*, *4*(2), 38–53. doi:10.4018/ijeei.2013040103

Chang, V., De Roure, D., Wills, G., & Walters, R. J. (2011). Case studies and organisational sustainability modelling presented by cloud computing business framework. [IJWSR]. *International Journal of Web Services Research*, *8*(3), 26–53. doi: doi:10.4018/jwsr.2011070102

Chang, V., Li, C., De Roure, D., Wills, G., Walters, R. J., & Chee, C. (2011). The financial clouds review. [IJCAC]. *International Journal of Cloud Applications and Computing*, *1*(2), 41–63. doi:10.4018/ijcac.2011040104

Chang, V., Li, C., De Roure, D., Wills, G., Walters, R. J., & Chee, C. (2013). The financial clouds review. In S. Aljawarneh (Ed.), *Cloud computing advancements in design, implementation, and technologies* (pp. 125–146). Hershey, PA: Information Science Reference.

Chang, V., Walters, R. J., & Wills, G. (2012). Business integration as a service. [IJCAC]. *International Journal of Cloud Applications and Computing*, *2*(1), 16–40. doi:10.4018/ijcac.2012010102

Chang, V., & Wills, G. (2013). A University of Greenwich case study of cloud computing: Education as a service. In D. Graham, I. Manikas, & D. Folinas (Eds.), *E-logistics and e-supply chain management: Applications for evolving business* (pp. 232–253). Hershey, PA: Business Science Reference. doi:10.4018/978-1-4666-3914-0.ch013

Chang, V., Wills, G., Walters, R. J., & Currie, W. (2012). Towards a structured cloud ROI: The University of Southampton cost-saving and user satisfaction case studies. In W. Hu, & N. Kaabouch (Eds.), *Sustainable ICTs and management systems for green computing* (pp. 179–200). Hershey, PA: Information Science Reference. doi:10.4018/978-1-4666-1839-8.ch008

Chang, Y., Lee, Y., Juang, T., & Yen, J. (2013). Cost evaluation on building and operating cloud platform. [IJGHPC]. *International Journal of Grid and High Performance Computing*, *5*(2), 43–53. doi:10.4018/jghpc.2013040103

Chao, L. (2012). Cloud computing solution for internet based teaching and learning. In L. Chao (Ed.), *Cloud computing for teaching and learning: Strategies for design and implementation* (pp. 210–235). Hershey, PA: Information Science Reference. doi:10.4018/978-1-4666-0957-0.ch015

Chao, L. (2012). Overview of cloud computing and its application in e-learning. In L. Chao (Ed.), *Cloud computing for teaching and learning: Strategies for design and implementation* (pp. 1–16). Hershey, PA: Information Science Reference. doi:10.4018/978-1-4666-0957-0.ch001

Chauhan, S., Raman, A., & Singh, N. (2013). A comparative cost analysis of on premises IT infrastructure and cloud-based email services in an Indian business school. [IJCAC]. *International Journal of Cloud Applications and Computing*, *3*(2), 21–34. doi:10.4018/ijcac.2013040103

Chen, C., Chao, H., Wu, T., Fan, C., Chen, J., Chen, Y., & Hsu, J. (2011). IoT-IMS communication platform for future internet. [IJARAS]. *International Journal of Adaptive, Resilient and Autonomic Systems*, *2*(4), 74–94. doi:10.4018/jaras.2011100105

Chen, C., Chao, H., Wu, T., Fan, C., Chen, J., Chen, Y., & Hsu, J. (2013). IoT-IMS communication platform for future internet. In V. De Florio (Ed.), *Innovations and approaches for resilient and adaptive systems* (pp. 68–86). Hershey, PA: Information Science Reference.

Chen, C. C. (2013). Cloud computing in case-based pedagogy: An information systems success perspective. [IJDTIS]. *International Journal of Dependable and Trustworthy Information Systems*, *2*(3), 1–16. doi:10.4018/jdtis.2011070101

Cheney, A. W., Riedl, R. E., Sanders, R., & Tashner, J. H. (2012). The new company water cooler: Use of 3D virtual immersive worlds to promote networking and professional learning in organizations. In I. Management Association (Ed.), *Organizational learning and knowledge: Concepts, methodologies, tools and applications* (pp. 2848-2861). Hershey, PA: Business Science Reference. doi: doi:10.4018/978-1-60960-783-8.ch801

Chiang, C., & Yu, S. (2013). Cloud-enabled software testing based on program understanding. In S. Tilley, & T. Parveen (Eds.), *Software testing in the cloud: Perspectives on an emerging discipline* (pp. 54–67). Hershey, PA: Information Science Reference.

Chou, Y., & Oetting, J. (2011). Risk assessment for cloud-based IT systems. [IJGHPC]. *International Journal of Grid and High Performance Computing*, 3(2), 1–13. doi:10.4018/jghpc.2011040101

Chou, Y., & Oetting, J. (2012). Risk assessment for cloud-based IT systems. In I. Management Association (Ed.), Grid and cloud computing: Concepts, methodologies, tools and applications (pp. 272-285). Hershey, PA: Information Science Reference. doi: doi:10.4018/978-1-4666-0879-5.ch113

Chou, Y., & Oetting, J. (2013). Risk assessment for cloud-based IT systems. In E. Udoh (Ed.), *Applications and developments in grid, cloud, and high performance computing* (pp. 1–14). Hershey, PA: Information Science Reference.

Cohen, F. (2013). Challenges to digital forensic evidence in the cloud. In K. Ruan (Ed.), *Cybercrime and cloud forensics: Applications for investigation processes* (pp. 59–78). Hershey, PA: Information Science Reference.

Cossu, R., Di Giulio, C., Brito, F., & Petcu, D. (2013). Cloud computing for earth observation. In D. Kyriazis, A. Voulodimos, S. Gogouvitis, & T. Varvarigou (Eds.), *Data intensive storage services for cloud environments* (pp. 166–191). Hershey, PA: Business Science Reference. doi:10.4018/978-1-4666-3934-8.ch012

Costa, J. E., & Rodrigues, J. J. (2014). Mobile cloud computing: Technologies, services, and applications. In J. Rodrigues, K. Lin, & J. Lloret (Eds.), *Mobile networks and cloud computing convergence for progressive services and applications* (pp. 1–17). Hershey, PA: Information Science Reference.

Creaner, G., & Pahl, C. (2013). Flexible coordination techniques for dynamic cloud service collaboration. In G. Ortiz, & J. Cubo (Eds.), *Adaptive web services for modular and reusable software development: Tactics and solutions* (pp. 239–252). Hershey, PA: Information Science Reference.

Crosbie, M. (2013). Hack the cloud: Ethical hacking and cloud forensics. In K. Ruan (Ed.), *Cybercrime and cloud forensics: Applications for investigation processes* (pp. 42–58). Hershey, PA: Information Science Reference.

Curran, K., Carlin, S., & Adams, M. (2012). Security issues in cloud computing. In L. Chao (Ed.), *Cloud computing for teaching and learning: Strategies for design and implementation* (pp. 200–208). Hershey, PA: Information Science Reference. doi:10.4018/978-1-4666-0957-0.ch014

Dahbur, K., & Mohammad, B. (2011). Toward understanding the challenges and countermeasures in computer anti-forensics. [IJCAC]. *International Journal of Cloud Applications and Computing*, 1(3), 22–35. doi:10.4018/ijcac.2011070103

Dahbur, K., Mohammad, B., & Tarakji, A. B. (2011). Security issues in cloud computing: A survey of risks, threats and vulnerabilities. [IJCAC]. *International Journal of Cloud Applications and Computing*, 1(3), 1–11. doi:10.4018/ijcac.2011070101

Dahbur, K., Mohammad, B., & Tarakji, A. B. (2012). Security issues in cloud computing: A survey of risks, threats and vulnerabilities. In I. Management Association (Ed.), Grid and cloud computing: Concepts, methodologies, tools and applications (pp. 1644-1655). Hershey, PA: Information Science Reference. doi: doi:10.4018/978-1-4666-0879-5.ch707

Dahbur, K., Mohammad, B., & Tarakji, A. B. (2013). Security issues in cloud computing: A survey of risks, threats and vulnerabilities. In S. Aljawarneh (Ed.), *Cloud computing advancements in design, implementation, and technologies* (pp. 154–165). Hershey, PA: Information Science Reference.

Daim, T., Britton, M., Subramanian, G., Brenden, R., & Intarode, N. (2012). Adopting and integrating cloud computing. In E. Eyob, & E. Tetteh (Eds.), *Customer-oriented global supply chains: Concepts for effective management* (pp. 175–197). Hershey, PA: Information Science Reference. doi:10.4018/978-1-4666-0246-5.ch011

Davis, M., & Sedsman, A. (2012). Grey areas: The legal dimensions of cloud computing. In C. Li, & A. Ho (Eds.), *Crime prevention technologies and applications for advancing criminal investigation* (pp. 263–273). Hershey, PA: Information Science Reference. doi:10.4018/978-1-4666-1758-2.ch017

De Coster, R., & Albesher, A. (2013). The development of mobile service applications for consumers and intelligent networks. In I. Lee (Ed.), *Mobile services industries, technologies, and applications in the global economy* (pp. 273–289). Hershey, PA: Information Science Reference.

De Filippi, P. (2014). Ubiquitous computing in the cloud: User empowerment vs. user obsequity. In J. Pelet, & P. Papadopoulou (Eds.), *User behavior in ubiquitous online environments* (pp. 44–63). Hershey, PA: Information Science Reference.

De Silva, S. (2013). Key legal issues with cloud computing: A UK law perspective. In A. Bento, & A. Aggarwal (Eds.), *Cloud computing service and deployment models: Layers and management* (pp. 242–256). Hershey, PA: Business Science Reference.

Deed, C., & Cragg, P. (2013). Business impacts of cloud computing. In A. Bento, & A. Aggarwal (Eds.), *Cloud computing service and deployment models: Layers and management* (pp. 274–288). Hershey, PA: Business Science Reference.

Deng, M., Petkovic, M., Nalin, M., & Baroni, I. (2013). Home healthcare in cloud computing. In M. Cruz-Cunha, I. Miranda, & P. Gonçalves (Eds.), *Handbook of research on ICTs and management systems for improving efficiency in healthcare and social care* (pp. 614–634). Hershey, PA: Medical Information Science Reference. doi:10.4018/978-1-4666-3990-4.ch032

Desai, A. M., & Mock, K. (2013). Security in cloud computing. In A. Bento, & A. Aggarwal (Eds.), *Cloud computing service and deployment models: Layers and management* (pp. 208–221). Hershey, PA: Business Science Reference.

Deshpande, R. M., Patle, B. V., & Bhoskar, R. D. (2014). Planning and implementation of cloud computing in NIT's in India: Special reference to VNIT. In S. Dhamdhere (Ed.), *Cloud computing and virtualization technologies in libraries* (pp. 90–106). Hershey, PA: Information Science Reference.

Dhamdhere, S. N., & Lihitkar, R. (2014). The university cloud library model and the role of the cloud librarian. In S. Dhamdhere (Ed.), *Cloud computing and virtualization technologies in libraries* (pp. 150–161). Hershey, PA: Information Science Reference.

Di Martino, S., Ferrucci, F., Maggio, V., & Sarro, F. (2013). Towards migrating genetic algorithms for test data generation to the cloud. In S. Tilley, & T. Parveen (Eds.), *Software testing in the cloud: Perspectives on an emerging discipline* (pp. 113–135). Hershey, PA: Information Science Reference.

Di Sano, M., Di Stefano, A., Morana, G., & Zito, D. (2013). FSaaS: Configuring policies for managing shared files among cooperating, distributed applications. [IJWP]. *International Journal of Web Portals*, *5*(1), 1–14. doi:10.4018/jwp.2013010101

Dippl, S., Jaeger, M. C., Luhn, A., Shulman-Peleg, A., & Vernik, G. (2013). Towards federation and interoperability of cloud storage systems. In D. Kyriazis, A. Voulodimos, S. Gogouvitis, & T. Varvarigou (Eds.), *Data intensive storage services for cloud environments* (pp. 60–71). Hershey, PA: Business Science Reference. doi:10.4018/978-1-4666-3934-8.ch005

Distefano, S., & Puliafito, A. (2012). The cloud@home volunteer and interoperable cloud through the future internet. In M. Villari, I. Brandic, & F. Tusa (Eds.), *Achieving federated and self-manageable cloud infrastructures: Theory and practice* (pp. 79–96). Hershey, PA: Business Science Reference. doi:10.4018/978-1-4666-1631-8.ch005

Djoleto, W. (2013). Cloud computing and ecommerce or ebusiness: "The now it way" – An overview. In *Electronic commerce and organizational leadership: perspectives and methodologies* (pp. 239–254). Hershey, PA: Business Science Reference. doi:10.4018/978-1-4666-2982-0.ch010

Dollmann, T. J., Loos, P., Fellmann, M., Thomas, O., Hoheisel, A., Katranuschkov, P., & Scherer, R. (2011). Design and usage of a process-centric collaboration methodology for virtual organizations in hybrid environments. [IJIIT]. *International Journal of Intelligent Information Technologies*, *7*(1), 45–64. doi:10.4018/jiit.2011010104

Dollmann, T. J., Loos, P., Fellmann, M., Thomas, O., Hoheisel, A., Katranuschkov, P., & Scherer, R. (2013). Design and usage of a process-centric collaboration methodology for virtual organizations in hybrid environments. In V. Sugumaran (Ed.), *Organizational efficiency through intelligent information technologies* (pp. 45–64). Hershey, PA: Information Science Reference.

Dreher, P., & Vouk, M. (2012). Utilizing open source cloud computing environments to provide cost effective support for university education and research. In L. Chao (Ed.), *Cloud computing for teaching and learning: Strategies for design and implementation* (pp. 32–49). Hershey, PA: Information Science Reference. doi:10.4018/978-1-4666-0957-0.ch003

Drum, D., Becker, D., & Fish, M. (2013). Technology adoption in troubled times: A cloud computing case study. [JCIT]. *Journal of Cases on Information Technology, 15*(2), 57–71. doi:10.4018/jcit.2013040104

Dunaway, D. M. (2013). Creating virtual collaborative learning experiences for aspiring teachers. In R. Hartshorne, T. Heafner, & T. Petty (Eds.), *Teacher education programs and online learning tools: Innovations in teacher preparation* (pp. 167–180). Hershey, PA: Information Science Reference.

Dykstra, J. (2013). Seizing electronic evidence from cloud computing environments. In K. Ruan (Ed.), *Cybercrime and cloud forensics: Applications for investigation processes* (pp. 156–185). Hershey, PA: Information Science Reference.

El-Refaey, M., & Rimal, B. P. (2012). Grid, SOA and cloud computing: On-demand computing models. In I. Management Association (Ed.), *Grid and cloud computing: Concepts, methodologies, tools and applications* (pp. 12-51). Hershey, PA: Information Science Reference. doi: doi:10.4018/978-1-4666-0879-5.ch102

El-Refaey, M., & Rimal, B. P. (2012). Grid, SOA and cloud computing: On-demand computing models. In N. Preve (Ed.), *Computational and data grids: Principles, applications and design* (pp. 45–85). Hershey, PA: Information Science Reference.

Elnaffar, S., Maamar, Z., & Sheng, Q. Z. (2013). When clouds start socializing: The sky model. [IJEBR]. *International Journal of E-Business Research, 9*(2), 1–7. doi:10.4018/jebr.2013040101

Elwood, S., & Keengwe, J. (2012). Microbursts: A design format for mobile cloud computing. [IJICTE]. *International Journal of Information and Communication Technology Education, 8*(2), 102–110. doi:10.4018/jicte.2012040109

Emeakaroha, V. C., Netto, M. A., Calheiros, R. N., & De Rose, C. A. (2012). Achieving flexible SLA and resource management in clouds. In M. Villari, I. Brandic, & F. Tusa (Eds.), *Achieving federated and self-manageable cloud infrastructures: Theory and practice* (pp. 266–287). Hershey, PA: Business Science Reference. doi:10.4018/978-1-4666-1631-8.ch014

Etro, F. (2013). The economics of cloud computing. In A. Bento, & A. Aggarwal (Eds.), *Cloud computing service and deployment models: Layers and management* (pp. 296–309). Hershey, PA: Business Science Reference.

Ezugwu, A. E., Buhari, S. M., & Junaidu, S. B. (2013). Virtual machine allocation in cloud computing environment. [IJCAC]. *International Journal of Cloud Applications and Computing, 3*(2), 47–60. doi:10.4018/ijcac.2013040105

Fauzi, A. H., & Taylor, H. (2013). Secure community trust stores for peer-to-peer e-commerce applications using cloud services. [IJEEI]. *International Journal of E-Entrepreneurship and Innovation, 4*(1), 1–15. doi:10.4018/jeei.2013010101

Ferguson-Boucher, K., & Endicott-Popovsky, B. (2013). Forensic readiness in the cloud (FRC): Integrating records management and digital forensics. In K. Ruan (Ed.), *Cybercrime and cloud forensics: Applications for investigation processes* (pp. 105–128). Hershey, PA: Information Science Reference.

Ferraro de Souza, R., Westphall, C. B., dos Santos, D. R., & Westphall, C. M. (2013). A review of PACS on cloud for archiving secure medical images. [IJPHIM]. *International Journal of Privacy and Health Information Management, 1*(1), 53–62. doi:10.4018/ijphim.2013010104

Firdhous, M., Hassan, S., & Ghazali, O. (2013). Statistically enhanced multi-dimensional trust computing mechanism for cloud computing. [IJMCMC]. *International Journal of Mobile Computing and Multimedia Communications, 5*(2), 1–17. doi:10.4018/jmcmc.2013040101

Formisano, C., Bonelli, L., Balraj, K. R., & Shulman-Peleg, A. (2013). Cloud access control mechanisms. In D. Kyriazis, A. Voulodimos, S. Gogouvitis, & T. Varvarigou (Eds.), *Data intensive storage services for cloud environments* (pp. 94–108). Hershey, PA: Business Science Reference. doi:10.4018/978-1-4666-3934-8.ch007

Frank, H., & Mesentean, S. (2012). Efficient communication interfaces for distributed energy resources. In E. Udoh (Ed.), *Evolving developments in grid and cloud computing: Advancing research* (pp. 185–196). Hershey, PA: Information Science Reference. doi:10.4018/978-1-4666-0056-0.ch013

Gallina, B., & Guelfi, N. (2012). Reusing transaction models for dependable cloud computing. In H. Yang, & X. Liu (Eds.), *Software reuse in the emerging cloud computing era* (pp. 248–277). Hershey, PA: Information Science Reference. doi:10.4018/978-1-4666-0897-9.ch011

Garofalo, D. A. (2013). Empires of the future: Libraries, technology, and the academic environment. In E. Iglesias (Ed.), *Robots in academic libraries: Advancements in library automation* (pp. 180–206). Hershey, PA: Information Science Reference. doi:10.4018/978-1-4666-3938-6.ch010

Gebremeskel, G. B., He, Z., & Jing, X. (2013). Semantic integrating for intelligent cloud data mining platform and cloud based business intelligence for optimization of mobile social networks. In V. Bhatnagar (Ed.), *Data mining in dynamic social networks and fuzzy systems* (pp. 173–211). Hershey, PA: Information Science Reference. doi:10.4018/978-1-4666-4213-3.ch009

Gentleman, W. M. (2013). Using the cloud for testing NOT adjunct to development. In S. Tilley, & T. Parveen (Eds.), *Software testing in the cloud: Perspectives on an emerging discipline* (pp. 216–230). Hershey, PA: Information Science Reference.

Ghafoor, K. Z., Mohammed, M. A., Abu Bakar, K., Sadiq, A. S., & Lloret, J. (2014). Vehicular cloud computing: Trends and challenges. In J. Rodrigues, K. Lin, & J. Lloret (Eds.), *Mobile networks and cloud computing convergence for progressive services and applications* (pp. 262–274). Hershey, PA: Information Science Reference.

Giannakaki, M. (2012). The "right to be forgotten" in the era of social media and cloud computing. In C. Akrivopoulou, & N. Garipidis (Eds.), *Human rights and risks in the digital era: Globalization and the effects of information technologies* (pp. 10–24). Hershey, PA: Information Science Reference. doi:10.4018/978-1-4666-0891-7.ch002

Gillam, L., Li, B., & O'Loughlin, J. (2012). Teaching clouds: Lessons taught and lessons learnt. In L. Chao (Ed.), *Cloud computing for teaching and learning: Strategies for design and implementation* (pp. 82–94). Hershey, PA: Information Science Reference. doi:10.4018/978-1-4666-0957-0.ch006

Gonsowski, D. (2013). Compliance in the cloud and the implications on electronic discovery. In K. Ruan (Ed.), *Cybercrime and cloud forensics: Applications for investigation processes* (pp. 230–250). Hershey, PA: Information Science Reference.

Gonzalez-Sanchez, J., Conley, Q., Chavez-Echeagaray, M., & Atkinson, R. K. (2012). Supporting the assembly process by leveraging augmented reality, cloud computing, and mobile devices. [IJCBPL]. *International Journal of Cyber Behavior, Psychology and Learning, 2*(3), 86–102. doi:10.4018/ijcbpl.2012070107

Gopinath, R., & Geetha, B. (2013). An e-learning system based on secure data storage services in cloud computing. [IJITWE]. *International Journal of Information Technology and Web Engineering, 8*(2), 1–17. doi:10.4018/jitwe.2013040101

Gossin, P. C., & LaBrie, R. C. (2013). Data center waste management. In P. Ordóñez de Pablos (Ed.), *Green technologies and business practices: An IT approach* (pp. 226–235). Hershey, PA: Information Science Reference.

Goswami, V., Patra, S. S., & Mund, G. B. (2012). Performance analysis of cloud computing centers for bulk services. [IJCAC]. *International Journal of Cloud Applications and Computing, 2*(4), 53–65. doi:10.4018/ijcac.2012100104

Goswami, V., & Sahoo, C. N. (2013). Optimal resource usage in multi-cloud computing environment. [IJCAC]. *International Journal of Cloud Applications and Computing, 3*(1), 44–57. doi:10.4018/ijcac.2013010105

Gräuler, M., Teuteberg, F., Mahmoud, T., & Gómez, J. M. (2013). Requirements prioritization and design considerations for the next generation of corporate environmental management information systems: A foundation for innovation. [IJITSA]. *International Journal of Information Technologies and Systems Approach, 6*(1), 98–116. doi:10.4018/jitsa.2013010106

Grieve, G. P., & Heston, K. (2012). Finding liquid salvation: Using the cardean ethnographic method to document second life residents and religious cloud communities. In N. Zagalo, L. Morgado, & A. Boa-Ventura (Eds.), *Virtual worlds and metaverse platforms: New communication and identity paradigms* (pp. 288–305). Hershey, PA: Information Science Reference.

Grispos, G., Storer, T., & Glisson, W. B. (2012). Calm before the storm: The challenges of cloud computing in digital forensics. [IJDCF]. *International Journal of Digital Crime and Forensics, 4*(2), 28–48. doi:10.4018/jdcf.2012040103

Grispos, G., Storer, T., & Glisson, W. B. (2013). Calm before the storm: The challenges of cloud computing in digital forensics. In C. Li (Ed.), *Emerging digital forensics applications for crime detection, prevention, and security* (pp. 211–233). Hershey, PA: Information Science Reference. doi:10.4018/978-1-4666-4006-1.ch015

Guster, D., & Lee, O. F. (2011). Enhancing the disaster recovery plan through virtualization. [JITR]. *Journal of Information Technology Research, 4*(4), 18–40. doi:10.4018/jitr.2011100102

Hanawa, T., & Sato, M. (2013). D-Cloud: Software testing environment for dependable distributed systems using cloud computing technology. In S. Tilley, & T. Parveen (Eds.), *Software testing in the cloud: Perspectives on an emerging discipline* (pp. 340–355). Hershey, PA: Information Science Reference.

Hardy, J., Liu, L., Lei, C., & Li, J. (2013). Internet-based virtual computing infrastructure for cloud computing. In X. Yang, & L. Liu (Eds.), *Principles, methodologies, and service-oriented approaches for cloud computing* (pp. 371–389). Hershey, PA: Business Science Reference. doi:10.4018/978-1-4666-2854-0.ch016

Hashizume, K., Yoshioka, N., & Fernandez, E. B. (2013). Three misuse patterns for cloud computing. In D. Rosado, D. Mellado, E. Fernandez-Medina, & M. Piattini (Eds.), *Security engineering for cloud computing: Approaches and tools* (pp. 36–53). Hershey, PA: Information Science Reference.

Hassan, Q. F., Riad, A. M., & Hassan, A. E. (2012). Understanding cloud computing. In H. Yang, & X. Liu (Eds.), *Software reuse in the emerging cloud computing era* (pp. 204–227). Hershey, PA: Information Science Reference. doi:10.4018/978-1-4666-0897-9.ch009

Hasselmeyer, P., Katsaros, G., Koller, B., & Wieder, P. (2012). Cloud monitoring. In M. Villari, I. Brandic, & F. Tusa (Eds.), *Achieving federated and self-manageable cloud infrastructures: Theory and practice* (pp. 97–116). Hershey, PA: Business Science Reference. doi:10.4018/978-1-4666-1631-8.ch006

Hertzler, B. T., Frost, E., Bressler, G. H., & Goehring, C. (2011). Experience report: Using a cloud computing environment during Haiti and Exercise24. [IJISCRAM]. *International Journal of Information Systems for Crisis Response and Management, 3*(1), 50–64. doi:10.4018/jiscrm.2011010104

Hertzler, B. T., Frost, E., Bressler, G. H., & Goehring, C. (2013). Experience report: Using a cloud computing environment during Haiti and Exercise24. In M. Jennex (Ed.), *Using social and information technologies for disaster and crisis management* (pp. 52–66). Hershey, PA: Information Science Reference. doi:10.4018/978-1-4666-2788-8.ch004

Ho, R. (2013). Cloud computing and enterprise migration strategies. In A. Loo (Ed.), *Distributed computing innovations for business, engineering, and science* (pp. 156–175). Hershey, PA: Information Science Reference.

Hobona, G., Jackson, M., & Anand, S. (2012). Implementing geospatial web services for cloud computing. In I. Management Association (Ed.), Grid and cloud computing: Concepts, methodologies, tools and applications (pp. 615-636). Hershey, PA: Information Science Reference. doi: doi:10.4018/978-1-4666-0879-5.ch305

Hochstein, L., Schott, B., & Graybill, R. B. (2011). Computational engineering in the cloud: Benefits and challenges. [JOEUC]. *Journal of Organizational and End User Computing, 23*(4), 31–50. doi:10.4018/joeuc.2011100103

Hochstein, L., Schott, B., & Graybill, R. B. (2013). Computational engineering in the cloud: Benefits and challenges. In A. Dwivedi, & S. Clarke (Eds.), *Innovative strategies and approaches for end-user computing advancements* (pp. 314–332). Hershey, PA: Information Science Reference.

Honarvar, A. R. (2013). Developing an elastic cloud computing application through multi-agent systems. [IJ-CAC]. *International Journal of Cloud Applications and Computing, 3*(1), 58–64. doi:10.4018/ijcac.2013010106

Hossain, S. (2013). Cloud computing terms, definitions, and taxonomy. In A. Bento, & A. Aggarwal (Eds.), *Cloud computing service and deployment models: Layers and management* (pp. 1–25). Hershey, PA: Business Science Reference.

Hudzia, B., Sinclair, J., & Lindner, M. (2013). Deploying and running enterprise grade applications in a federated cloud. In I. Association (Ed.), *Supply chain management: Concepts, methodologies, tools, and applications* (pp. 1350–1370). Hershey, PA: Business Science Reference.

Hung, S., Shieh, J., & Lee, C. (2011). Migrating android applications to the cloud. [IJGHPC]. *International Journal of Grid and High Performance Computing, 3*(2), 14–28. doi:10.4018/jghpc.2011040102

Hung, S., Shieh, J., & Lee, C. (2013). Migrating android applications to the cloud. In E. Udoh (Ed.), *Applications and developments in grid, cloud, and high performance computing* (pp. 307–322). Hershey, PA: Information Science Reference.

Islam, S., Mouratidis, H., & Weippl, E. R. (2013). A goal-driven risk management approach to support security and privacy analysis of cloud-based system. In D. Rosado, D. Mellado, E. Fernandez-Medina, & M. Piattini (Eds.), *Security engineering for cloud computing: Approaches and tools* (pp. 97–122). Hershey, PA: Information Science Reference.

Itani, W., Kayssi, A., & Chehab, A. (2013). Hardware-based security for ensuring data privacy in the cloud. In D. Rosado, D. Mellado, E. Fernandez-Medina, & M. Piattini (Eds.), *Security engineering for cloud computing: Approaches and tools* (pp. 147–170). Hershey, PA: Information Science Reference.

Jackson, A., & Weiland, M. (2013). Cloud computing for scientific simulation and high performance computing. In X. Yang, & L. Liu (Eds.), *Principles, methodologies, and service-oriented approaches for cloud computing* (pp. 51–70). Hershey, PA: Business Science Reference. doi:10.4018/978-1-4666-2854-0.ch003

Jaeger, M. C., & Hohenstein, U. (2013). Content centric storage and current storage systems. In D. Kyriazis, A. Voulodimos, S. Gogouvitis, & T. Varvarigou (Eds.), *Data intensive storage services for cloud environments* (pp. 27–46). Hershey, PA: Business Science Reference. doi:10.4018/978-1-4666-3934-8.ch003

James, J. I., Shosha, A. F., & Gladyshev, P. (2013). Digital forensic investigation and cloud computing. In K. Ruan (Ed.), *Cybercrime and cloud forensics: Applications for investigation processes* (pp. 1–41). Hershey, PA: Information Science Reference.

Jena, R. K. (2013). Green computing to green business. In P. Ordóñez de Pablos (Ed.), *Green technologies and business practices: An IT approach* (pp. 138–150). Hershey, PA: Information Science Reference.

Jeyarani, R., & Nagaveni, N. (2012). A heuristic meta scheduler for optimal resource utilization and improved QoS in cloud computing environment. [IJCAC]. *International Journal of Cloud Applications and Computing, 2*(1), 41–52. doi:10.4018/ijcac.2012010103

Jeyarani, R., Nagaveni, N., & Ram, R. V. (2011). Self adaptive particle swarm optimization for efficient virtual machine provisioning in cloud. [IJIIT]. *International Journal of Intelligent Information Technologies, 7*(2), 25–44. doi:10.4018/jiit.2011040102

Jeyarani, R., Nagaveni, N., & Ram, R. V. (2013). Self adaptive particle swarm optimization for efficient virtual machine provisioning in cloud. In V. Sugumaran (Ed.), *Organizational efficiency through intelligent information technologies* (pp. 88–107). Hershey, PA: Information Science Reference.

Jeyarani, R., Nagaveni, N., Sadasivam, S. K., & Rajarathinam, V. R. (2011). Power aware meta scheduler for adaptive VM provisioning in IaaS cloud. [IJCAC]. *International Journal of Cloud Applications and Computing, 1*(3), 36–51. doi:10.4018/ijcac.2011070104

Jeyarani, R., Nagaveni, N., Sadasivam, S. K., & Rajarathinam, V. R. (2013). Power aware meta scheduler for adaptive VM provisioning in IaaS cloud. In S. Aljawarneh (Ed.), *Cloud computing advancements in design, implementation, and technologies* (pp. 190–204). Hershey, PA: Information Science Reference.

Jiang, J., Huang, X., Wu, Y., & Yang, G. (2013). Campus cloud storage and preservation: From distributed file system to data sharing service. In X. Yang, & L. Liu (Eds.), *Principles, methodologies, and service-oriented approaches for cloud computing* (pp. 284–301). Hershey, PA: Business Science Reference. doi:10.4018/978-1-4666-2854-0.ch012

Jing, S. (2012). The application exploration of cloud computing in information technology teaching. [IJA-PUC]. *International Journal of Advanced Pervasive and Ubiquitous Computing*, 4(4), 23–27. doi:10.4018/japuc.2012100104

Johansson, D., & Wiberg, M. (2012). Conceptually advancing "application mobility" towards design: Applying a concept-driven approach to the design of mobile IT for home care service groups. [IJACI]. *International Journal of Ambient Computing and Intelligence*, 4(3), 20–32. doi:10.4018/jaci.2012070102

Jorda, J., & M'zoughi, A. (2013). Securing cloud storage. In D. Rosado, D. Mellado, E. Fernandez-Medina, & M. Piattini (Eds.), *Security engineering for cloud computing: Approaches and tools* (pp. 171–190). Hershey, PA: Information Science Reference.

Juiz, C., & Alexander de Pous, V. (2014). Cloud computing: IT governance, legal, and public policy aspects. In I. Portela, & F. Almeida (Eds.), *Organizational, legal, and technological dimensions of information system administration* (pp. 139–166). Hershey, PA: Information Science Reference.

Kaisler, S. H., Money, W., & Cohen, S. J. (2013). Cloud computing: A decision framework for small businesses. In A. Bento, & A. Aggarwal (Eds.), *Cloud computing service and deployment models: Layers and management* (pp. 151–172). Hershey, PA: Business Science Reference.

Kanamori, Y., & Yen, M. Y. (2013). Cloud computing security and risk management. In A. Bento, & A. Aggarwal (Eds.), *Cloud computing service and deployment models: Layers and management* (pp. 222–240). Hershey, PA: Business Science Reference.

Karadsheh, L., & Alhawari, S. (2011). Applying security policies in small business utilizing cloud computing technologies. [IJCAC]. *International Journal of Cloud Applications and Computing*, 1(2), 29–40. doi:10.4018/ijcac.2011040103

Karadsheh, L., & Alhawari, S. (2013). Applying security policies in small business utilizing cloud computing technologies. In S. Aljawarneh (Ed.), *Cloud computing advancements in design, implementation, and technologies* (pp. 112–124). Hershey, PA: Information Science Reference.

Kaupins, G. (2012). Laws associated with mobile computing in the cloud. [IJWNBT]. *International Journal of Wireless Networks and Broadband Technologies*, 2(3), 1–9. doi:10.4018/ijwnbt.2012070101

Kemp, M. L., Robb, S., & Deans, P. C. (2013). The legal implications of cloud computing. In A. Bento, & A. Aggarwal (Eds.), *Cloud computing service and deployment models: Layers and management* (pp. 257–272). Hershey, PA: Business Science Reference.

Khan, N., Ahmad, N., Herawan, T., & Inayat, Z. (2012). Cloud computing: Locally sub-clouds instead of globally one cloud. [IJCAC]. *International Journal of Cloud Applications and Computing*, 2(3), 68–85. doi:10.4018/ijcac.2012070103

Khan, N., Noraziah, A., Ismail, E. I., Deris, M. M., & Herawan, T. (2012). Cloud computing: Analysis of various platforms. [IJEEI]. *International Journal of E-Entrepreneurship and Innovation*, 3(2), 51–59. doi:10.4018/jeei.2012040104

Khansa, L., Forcade, J., Nambari, G., Parasuraman, S., & Cox, P. (2012). Proposing an intelligent cloud-based electronic health record system. [IJBDCN]. *International Journal of Business Data Communications and Networking*, 8(3), 57–71. doi:10.4018/jbdcn.2012070104

Kierkegaard, S. (2012). Not every cloud brings rain: Legal risks on the horizon. In M. Gupta, J. Walp, & R. Sharman (Eds.), *Strategic and practical approaches for information security governance: Technologies and applied solutions* (pp. 181–194). Hershey, PA: Information Science Reference. doi:10.4018/978-1-4666-0197-0.ch011

Kifayat, K., Shamsa, T. B., Mackay, M., Merabti, M., & Shi, Q. (2013). Real time risk management in cloud computation. In D. Rosado, D. Mellado, E. Fernandez-Medina, & M. Piattini (Eds.), *Security engineering for cloud computing: Approaches and tools* (pp. 123–145). Hershey, PA: Information Science Reference.

King, T. M., Ganti, A. S., & Froslie, D. (2013). Towards improving the testability of cloud application services. In S. Tilley, & T. Parveen (Eds.), *Software testing in the cloud: Perspectives on an emerging discipline* (pp. 322–339). Hershey, PA: Information Science Reference.

Kipp, A., Schneider, R., & Schubert, L. (2013). Encapsulation of complex HPC services. In C. Rückemann (Ed.), *Integrated information and computing systems for natural, spatial, and social sciences* (pp. 153–176). Hershey, PA: Information Science Reference.

Kldiashvili, E. (2012). The cloud computing as the tool for implementation of virtual organization technology for ehealth. [JITR]. *Journal of Information Technology Research, 5*(1), 18–34. doi:10.4018/jitr.2012010102

Kldiashvili, E. (2013). Implementation of telecytology in georgia for quality assurance programs. [JITR]. *Journal of Information Technology Research, 6*(2), 24–45. doi:10.4018/jitr.2013040102

Kosmatov, N. (2013). Concolic test generation and the cloud: deployment and verification perspectives. In S. Tilley, & T. Parveen (Eds.), *Software testing in the cloud: Perspectives on an emerging discipline* (pp. 231–251). Hershey, PA: Information Science Reference.

Kotamarti, R. M., Thornton, M. A., & Dunham, M. H. (2012). Quantum computing approach for alignment-free sequence search and classification. In S. Ali, N. Abbadeni, & M. Batouche (Eds.), *Multidisciplinary computational intelligence techniques: Applications in business, engineering, and medicine* (pp. 279–300). Hershey, PA: Information Science Reference. doi:10.4018/978-1-4666-1830-5.ch017

Kremmydas, D., Petsakos, A., & Rozakis, S. (2012). Parametric optimization of linear and non-linear models via parallel computing to enhance web-spatial DSS interactivity. [IJDSST]. *International Journal of Decision Support System Technology, 4*(1), 14–29. doi:10.4018/jdsst.2012010102

Krishnadas, N., & Pillai, R. R. (2013). Cloud computing diagnosis: A comprehensive study. In X. Yang, & L. Liu (Eds.), *Principles, methodologies, and service-oriented approaches for cloud computing* (pp. 1–18). Hershey, PA: Business Science Reference. doi:10.4018/978-1-4666-2854-0.ch001

Kübert, R., & Katsaros, G. (2011). Using free software for elastic web hosting on a private cloud. [IJCAC]. *International Journal of Cloud Applications and Computing, 1*(2), 14–28. doi:10.4018/ijcac.2011040102

Kübert, R., & Katsaros, G. (2013). Using free software for elastic web hosting on a private cloud. In S. Aljawarneh (Ed.), *Cloud computing advancements in design, implementation, and technologies* (pp. 97–111). Hershey, PA: Information Science Reference.

Kumar, P. S., Ashok, M. S., & Subramanian, R. (2012). A publicly verifiable dynamic secret sharing protocol for secure and dependable data storage in cloud computing. [IJCAC]. *International Journal of Cloud Applications and Computing, 2*(3), 1–25. doi:10.4018/ijcac.2012070101

Lasluisa, S., Rodero, I., & Parashar, M. (2013). Software design for passing sarbanes-oxley in cloud computing. In C. Rückemann (Ed.), *Integrated information and computing systems for natural, spatial, and social sciences* (pp. 27–42). Hershey, PA: Information Science Reference.

Lasluisa, S., Rodero, I., & Parashar, M. (2014). Software design for passing sarbanes-oxley in cloud computing. In I. Management Association (Ed.), Software design and development: Concepts, methodologies, tools, and applications (pp. 1659-1674). Hershey, PA: Information Science Reference. doi: doi:10.4018/978-1-4666-4301-7.ch080

Lee, W. N. (2013). An economic analysis of cloud: "Software as a service" (saas) computing and "virtual desktop infrastructure" (VDI) models. In A. Bento, & A. Aggarwal (Eds.), *Cloud computing service and deployment models: Layers and management* (pp. 289–295). Hershey, PA: Business Science Reference.

Levine, K., & White, B. A. (2011). A crisis at hafford furniture: Cloud computing case study. [JCIT]. *Journal of Cases on Information Technology, 13*(1), 57–71. doi:10.4018/jcit.2011010104

Levine, K., & White, B. A. (2013). A crisis at Hafford furniture: Cloud computing case study. In M. Khosrow-Pour (Ed.), *Cases on emerging information technology research and applications* (pp. 70–87). Hershey, PA: Information Science Reference.

Li, J., Meng, L., Zhu, Z., Li, X., Huai, J., & Liu, L. (2013). CloudRank: A cloud service ranking method based on both user feedback and service testing. In X. Yang, & L. Liu (Eds.), *Principles, methodologies, and service-oriented approaches for cloud computing* (pp. 230–258). Hershey, PA: Business Science Reference. doi:10.4018/978-1-4666-2854-0.ch010

Liang, T., Lu, F., & Chiu, J. (2012). A hybrid resource reservation method for workflows in clouds. [IJGHPC]. *International Journal of Grid and High Performance Computing, 4*(4), 1–21. doi:10.4018/jghpc.2012100101

Lorenz, M., Rath-Wiggins, L., Runde, W., Messina, A., Sunna, P., & Dimino, G. et al. (2013). Media convergence and cloud technologies: Smart storage, better workflows. In D. Kyriazis, A. Voulodimos, S. Gogouvitis, & T. Varvarigou (Eds.), *Data intensive storage services for cloud environments* (pp. 132–144). Hershey, PA: Business Science Reference. doi:10.4018/978-1-4666-3934-8.ch009

M., S. G., & G., S. K. (2012). An enterprise mashup integration service framework for clouds. *International Journal of Cloud Applications and Computing (IJCAC), 2*(2), 31-40. doi:10.4018/ijcac.2012040103

Maharana, S. K., P., G. P., & Bhati, A. (2012). A study of cloud computing for retinal image processing through MATLAB. [IJCAC]. *International Journal of Cloud Applications and Computing, 2*(2), 59–69. doi:10.4018/ijcac.2012040106

Maharana, S. K., Mali, P. B., & Prabhakar, G., J, S., & Kumar, V. (2011). Cloud computing applied for numerical study of thermal characteristics of SIP. [IJCAC]. *International Journal of Cloud Applications and Computing, 1*(3), 12–21. doi:10.4018/ijcac.2011070102

Maharana, S. K., Mali, P. B., & Prabhakar, G. J, S., & Kumar, V. (2013). Cloud computing applied for numerical study of thermal characteristics of SIP. In S. Aljawarneh (Ed.), Cloud computing advancements in design, implementation, and technologies (pp. 166-175). Hershey, PA: Information Science Reference. doi: doi:10.4018/978-1-4666-1879-4.ch012

Maharana, S. K., & Prabhakar, P. G., & Bhati, A. (2013). A study of cloud computing for retinal image processing through MATLAB. In I. Association (Ed.), Image processing: Concepts, methodologies, tools, and applications (pp. 101-111). Hershey, PA: Information Science Reference. doi: doi:10.4018/978-1-4666-3994-2.ch006

Mahesh, S., Landry, B. J., Sridhar, T., & Walsh, K. R. (2011). A decision table for the cloud computing decision in small business. [IRMJ]. *Information Resources Management Journal, 24*(3), 9–25. doi:10.4018/irmj.2011070102

Mahesh, S., Landry, B. J., Sridhar, T., & Walsh, K. R. (2013). A decision table for the cloud computing decision in small business. In M. Khosrow-Pour (Ed.), *Managing information resources and technology: Emerging Applications and theories* (pp. 159–176). Hershey, PA: Information Science Reference. doi:10.4018/978-1-4666-3616-3.ch012

Marquezan, C. C., Metzger, A., Pohl, K., Engen, V., Boniface, M., Phillips, S. C., & Zlatev, Z. (2013). Adaptive future internet applications: Opportunities and challenges for adaptive web services technology. In G. Ortiz, & J. Cubo (Eds.), *Adaptive web services for modular and reusable software development: Tactics and solutions* (pp. 333–353). Hershey, PA: Information Science Reference.

Marshall, P. J. (2012). Cloud computing: Next generation education. In L. Chao (Ed.), *Cloud computing for teaching and learning: Strategies for design and implementation* (pp. 180–185). Hershey, PA: Information Science Reference. doi:10.4018/978-1-4666-0957-0.ch012

Martinez-Ortiz, A. (2012). Open cloud technologies. In L. Vaquero, J. Cáceres, & J. Hierro (Eds.), *Open source cloud computing systems: Practices and paradigms* (pp. 1–17). Hershey, PA: Information Science Reference. doi:10.4018/978-1-4666-0098-0.ch001

Massonet, P., Michot, A., Naqvi, S., Villari, M., & Latanicki, J. (2013). Securing the external interfaces of a federated infrastructure cloud. In I. Management Association (Ed.), IT policy and ethics: Concepts, methodologies, tools, and applications (pp. 1876-1903). Hershey, PA: Information Science Reference. doi: doi:10.4018/978-1-4666-2919-6.ch082

Mavrogeorgi, N., Gogouvitis, S. V., Voulodimos, A., & Alexandrou, V. (2013). SLA management in storage clouds. In D. Kyriazis, A. Voulodimos, S. Gogouvitis, & T. Varvarigou (Eds.), *Data intensive storage services for cloud environments* (pp. 72–93). Hershey, PA: Business Science Reference. doi:10.4018/978-1-4666-3934-8.ch006

Mehta, H. K. (2013). Cloud selection for e-business a parameter based solution. In K. Tarnay, S. Imre, & L. Xu (Eds.), *Research and development in e-business through service-oriented solutions* (pp. 199–207). Hershey, PA: Business Science Reference.

Mehta, H. K., & Gupta, E. (2013). Economy based resource allocation in IaaS cloud. [IJCAC]. *International Journal of Cloud Applications and Computing*, 3(2), 1–11. doi:10.4018/ijcac.2013040101

Miah, S. J. (2012). Cloud-based intelligent DSS design for emergency professionals. In S. Ali, N. Abbadeni, & M. Batouche (Eds.), *Multidisciplinary computational intelligence techniques: Applications in business, engineering, and medicine* (pp. 47–60). Hershey, PA: Information Science Reference. doi:10.4018/978-1-4666-1830-5.ch004

Miah, S. J. (2013). Cloud-based intelligent DSS design for emergency professionals. In I. Association (Ed.), *Data mining: Concepts, methodologies, tools, and applications* (pp. 991–1003). Hershey, PA: Information Science Reference.

Mikkilineni, R. (2012). Architectural resiliency in distributed computing. [IJGHPC]. *International Journal of Grid and High Performance Computing*, 4(4), 37–51. doi:10.4018/jghpc.2012100103

Millham, R. (2012). Software asset re-use: Migration of data-intensive legacy system to the cloud computing paradigm. In H. Yang, & X. Liu (Eds.), *Software reuse in the emerging cloud computing era* (pp. 1–27). Hershey, PA: Information Science Reference. doi:10.4018/978-1-4666-0897-9.ch001

Mircea, M. (2011). Building the agile enterprise with service-oriented architecture, business process management and decision management. [IJEEI]. *International Journal of E-Entrepreneurship and Innovation*, 2(4), 32–48. doi:10.4018/jeei.2011100103

Modares, H., Lloret, J., Moravejosharieh, A., & Salleh, R. (2014). Security in mobile cloud computing. In J. Rodrigues, K. Lin, & J. Lloret (Eds.), *Mobile networks and cloud computing convergence for progressive services and applications* (pp. 79–91). Hershey, PA: Information Science Reference.

Moedjiono, S., & Mas'at, A. (2012). Cloud computing implementation strategy for information dissemination on meteorology, climatology, air quality, and geophysics (MKKuG). [JITR]. *Journal of Information Technology Research*, 5(3), 71–84. doi:10.4018/jitr.2012070104

Moiny, J. (2012). Cloud based social network sites: Under whose control? In A. Dudley, J. Braman, & G. Vincenti (Eds.), *Investigating cyber law and cyber ethics: Issues, impacts and practices* (pp. 147–219). Hershey, PA: Information Science Reference.

Moreno, I. S., & Xu, J. (2011). Energy-efficiency in cloud computing environments: Towards energy savings without performance degradation. [IJCAC]. *International Journal of Cloud Applications and Computing*, 1(1), 17–33. doi:10.4018/ijcac.2011010102

Moreno, I. S., & Xu, J. (2013). Energy-efficiency in cloud computing environments: Towards energy savings without performance degradation. In S. Aljawarneh (Ed.), *Cloud computing advancements in design, implementation, and technologies* (pp. 18–36). Hershey, PA: Information Science Reference.

Muñoz, A., Maña, A., & González, J. (2013). Dynamic security properties monitoring architecture for cloud computing. In D. Rosado, D. Mellado, E. Fernandez-Medina, & M. Piattini (Eds.), *Security engineering for cloud computing: Approaches and tools* (pp. 1–18). Hershey, PA: Information Science Reference.

Mvelase, P., Dlodlo, N., Williams, Q., & Adigun, M. O. (2011). Custom-made cloud enterprise architecture for small medium and micro enterprises. [IJCAC]. *International Journal of Cloud Applications and Computing*, 1(3), 52–63. doi:10.4018/ijcac.2011070105

Mvelase, P., Dlodlo, N., Williams, Q., & Adigun, M. O. (2012). Custom-made cloud enterprise architecture for small medium and micro enterprises. In I. Management Association (Ed.), Grid and cloud computing: Concepts, methodologies, tools and applications (pp. 589-601). Hershey, PA: Information Science Reference. doi: doi:10.4018/978-1-4666-0879-5.ch303

Mvelase, P., Dlodlo, N., Williams, Q., & Adigun, M. O. (2013). Custom-made cloud enterprise architecture for small medium and micro enterprises. In S. Aljawarneh (Ed.), *Cloud computing advancements in design, implementation, and technologies* (pp. 205–217). Hershey, PA: Information Science Reference.

Naeem, M. A., Dobbie, G., & Weber, G. (2014). Big data management in the context of real-time data warehousing. In W. Hu, & N. Kaabouch (Eds.), *Big data management, technologies, and applications* (pp. 150–176). Hershey, PA: Information Science Reference.

Ofosu, W. K., & Saliah-Hassane, H. (2013). Cloud computing in the education environment for developing nations. [IJITN]. *International Journal of Interdisciplinary Telecommunications and Networking, 5*(3), 54–62. doi:10.4018/jitn.2013070106

Oliveros, E., Cucinotta, T., Phillips, S. C., Yang, X., Middleton, S., & Voith, T. (2012). Monitoring and metering in the cloud. In D. Kyriazis, T. Varvarigou, & K. Konstanteli (Eds.), *Achieving real-time in distributed computing: From grids to clouds* (pp. 94–114). Hershey, PA: Information Science Reference.

Orton, I., Alva, A., & Endicott-Popovsky, B. (2013). Legal process and requirements for cloud forensic investigations. In K. Ruan (Ed.), *Cybercrime and cloud forensics: Applications for investigation processes* (pp. 186–229). Hershey, PA: Information Science Reference.

Pakhira, A., & Andras, P. (2013). Leveraging the cloud for large-scale software testing – A case study: Google Chrome on Amazon. In S. Tilley, & T. Parveen (Eds.), *Software testing in the cloud: Perspectives on an emerging discipline* (pp. 252–279). Hershey, PA: Information Science Reference.

Pal, K., & Karakostas, B. (2013). The use of cloud computing in shipping logistics. In D. Graham, I. Manikas, & D. Folinas (Eds.), *E-logistics and e-supply chain management: Applications for evolving business* (pp. 104–124). Hershey, PA: Business Science Reference. doi:10.4018/978-1-4666-3914-0.ch006

Pal, S. (2013). Cloud computing: Security concerns and issues. In A. Bento, & A. Aggarwal (Eds.), *Cloud computing service and deployment models: Layers and management* (pp. 191–207). Hershey, PA: Business Science Reference.

Pal, S. (2013). Storage security and technical challenges of cloud computing. In D. Kyriazis, A. Voulodimos, S. Gogouvitis, & T. Varvarigou (Eds.), *Data intensive storage services for cloud environments* (pp. 225–240). Hershey, PA: Business Science Reference. doi:10.4018/978-1-4666-3934-8.ch014

Palanivel, K., & Kuppuswami, S. (2014). A cloud-oriented reference architecture to digital library systems. In S. Dhamdhere (Ed.), *Cloud computing and virtualization technologies in libraries* (pp. 230–254). Hershey, PA: Information Science Reference.

Paletta, M. (2012). Intelligent clouds: By means of using multi-agent systems environments. In L. Chao (Ed.), *Cloud computing for teaching and learning: Strategies for design and implementation* (pp. 254–279). Hershey, PA: Information Science Reference. doi:10.4018/978-1-4666-0957-0.ch017

Pallot, M., Le Marc, C., Richir, S., Schmidt, C., & Mathieu, J. (2012). Innovation gaming: An immersive experience environment enabling co-creation. In M. Cruz-Cunha (Ed.), *Handbook of research on serious games as educational, business and research tools* (pp. 1–24). Hershey, PA: Information Science Reference. doi:10.4018/978-1-4666-0149-9.ch001

Pankowska, M. (2011). Information technology resources virtualization for sustainable development. [IJAL]. *International Journal of Applied Logistics, 2*(2), 35–48. doi:10.4018/jal.2011040103

Pankowska, M. (2013). Information technology resources virtualization for sustainable development. In Z. Luo (Ed.), *Technological solutions for modern logistics and supply chain management* (pp. 248–262). Hershey, PA: Business Science Reference. doi:10.4018/978-1-4666-2773-4.ch016

Parappallil, J. J., Zarvic, N., & Thomas, O. (2012). A context and content reflection on business-IT alignment research. [IJITBAG]. *International Journal of IT/Business Alignment and Governance, 3*(2), 21–37. doi:10.4018/jitbag.2012070102

Parashar, V., Vishwakarma, M. L., & Parashar, R. (2014). A new framework for building academic library through cloud computing. In S. Dhamdhere (Ed.), *Cloud computing and virtualization technologies in libraries* (pp. 107–123). Hershey, PA: Information Science Reference.

Pendyala, V. S., & Holliday, J. (2012). Cloud as a computer. In X. Liu, & Y. Li (Eds.), *Advanced design approaches to emerging software systems: Principles, methodologies and tools* (pp. 241–249). Hershey, PA: Information Science Reference.

Petruch, K., Tamm, G., & Stantchev, V. (2012). Deriving in-depth knowledge from IT-performance data simulations. [IJKSR]. *International Journal of Knowledge Society Research, 3*(2), 13–29. doi:10.4018/jksr.2012040102

Philipson, G. (2011). A framework for green computing. [IJGC]. *International Journal of Green Computing, 2*(1), 12–26. doi:10.4018/jgc.2011010102

Philipson, G. (2013). A framework for green computing. In K. Ganesh, & S. Anbuudayasankar (Eds.), *International and interdisciplinary studies in green computing* (pp. 12–26). Hershey, PA: Information Science Reference.

Phythian, M. (2013). The 'cloud' of unknowing – What a government cloud may and may not offer: A practitioner perspective. [IJT]. *International Journal of Technoethics, 4*(1), 1–10. doi:10.4018/jte.2013010101

Pym, D., & Sadler, M. (2012). Information stewardship in cloud computing. In I. Management Association (Ed.), Grid and cloud computing: Concepts, methodologies, tools and applications (pp. 185-202). Hershey, PA: Information Science Reference. doi: doi:10.4018/978-1-4666-0879-5.ch109

Pym, D., & Sadler, M. (2012). Information stewardship in cloud computing. In S. Galup (Ed.), *Technological applications and advancements in service science, management, and engineering* (pp. 52–69). Hershey, PA: Business Science Reference. doi:10.4018/978-1-4666-1583-0.ch004

Qiu, J., Ekanayake, J., Gunarathne, T., Choi, J. Y., Bae, S., & Ruan, Y. … Tang, H. (2013). Data intensive computing for bioinformatics. In I. Management Association (Ed.), Bioinformatics: Concepts, methodologies, tools, and applications (pp. 287-321). Hershey, PA: Medical Information Science Reference. doi: doi:10.4018/978-1-4666-3604-0.ch016

Rabaey, M. (2012). A public economics approach to enabling enterprise architecture with the government cloud in Belgium. In P. Saha (Ed.), *Enterprise architecture for connected e-government: Practices and innovations* (pp. 467–493). Hershey, PA: Information Science Reference. doi:10.4018/978-1-4666-1824-4.ch020

Rabaey, M. (2013). A complex adaptive system thinking approach of government e-procurement in a cloud computing environment. In P. Ordóñez de Pablos, J. Lovelle, J. Gayo, & R. Tennyson (Eds.), *E-procurement management for successful electronic government systems* (pp. 193–219). Hershey, PA: Information Science Reference.

Rabaey, M. (2013). Holistic investment framework for cloud computing: A management-philosophical approach based on complex adaptive systems. In A. Bento, & A. Aggarwal (Eds.), *Cloud computing service and deployment models: Layers and management* (pp. 94–122). Hershey, PA: Business Science Reference.

Rak, M., Ficco, M., Luna, J., Ghani, H., Suri, N., Panica, S., & Petcu, D. (2012). Security issues in cloud federations. In M. Villari, I. Brandic, & F. Tusa (Eds.), *Achieving federated and self-manageable cloud infrastructures: Theory and practice* (pp. 176–194). Hershey, PA: Business Science Reference. doi:10.4018/978-1-4666-1631-8.ch010

Ramanathan, R. (2013). Extending service-driven architectural approaches to the cloud. In R. Ramanathan, & K. Raja (Eds.), *Service-driven approaches to architecture and enterprise integration* (pp. 334–359). Hershey, PA: Information Science Reference. doi:10.4018/978-1-4666-4193-8.ch013

Ramírez, M., Gutiérrez, A., Monguet, J. M., & Muñoz, C. (2012). An internet cost model, assignment of costs based on actual network use. [IJWP]. *International Journal of Web Portals, 4*(4), 19–34. doi:10.4018/jwp.2012100102

Rashid, A., Wang, W. Y., & Tan, F. B. (2013). Value co-creation in cloud services. In A. Lin, J. Foster, & P. Scifleet (Eds.), *Consumer information systems and relationship management: Design, implementation, and use* (pp. 74–91). Hershey, PA: Business Science Reference. doi:10.4018/978-1-4666-4082-5.ch005

Ratten, V. (2012). Cloud computing services: Theoretical foundations of ethical and entrepreneurial adoption behaviour. [IJCAC]. *International Journal of Cloud Applications and Computing, 2*(2), 48–58. doi:10.4018/ijcac.2012040105

Ratten, V. (2013). Exploring behaviors and perceptions affecting the adoption of cloud computing. [IJIDE]. *International Journal of Innovation in the Digital Economy, 4*(3), 51–68. doi:10.4018/jide.2013070104

Ravi, V. (2012). Cloud computing paradigm for indian education sector. [IJCAC]. *International Journal of Cloud Applications and Computing, 2*(2), 41–47. doi:10.4018/ijcac.2012040104

Rawat, A., Kapoor, P., & Sushil, R. (2014). Application of cloud computing in library information service sector. In S. Dhamdhere (Ed.), *Cloud computing and virtualization technologies in libraries* (pp. 77–89). Hershey, PA: Information Science Reference.

Reich, C., Hübner, S., & Kuijs, H. (2012). Cloud computing for on-demand virtual desktops and labs. In L. Chao (Ed.), *Cloud computing for teaching and learning: strategies for design and implementation* (pp. 111–125). Hershey, PA: Information Science Reference. doi:10.4018/978-1-4666-0957-0.ch008

Rice, R. W. (2013). Testing in the cloud: Balancing the value and risks of cloud computing. In S. Tilley, & T. Parveen (Eds.), *Software testing in the cloud: Perspectives on an emerging discipline* (pp. 404–416). Hershey, PA: Information Science Reference.

Ruan, K. (2013). Designing a forensic-enabling cloud ecosystem. In K. Ruan (Ed.), *Cybercrime and cloud forensics: Applications for investigation processes* (pp. 331–344). Hershey, PA: Information Science Reference.

Sabetzadeh, F., & Tsui, E. (2011). Delivering knowledge services in the cloud. [IJKSS]. *International Journal of Knowledge and Systems Science, 2*(4), 14–20. doi:10.4018/jkss.2011100102

Sabetzadeh, F., & Tsui, E. (2013). Delivering knowledge services in the cloud. In G. Yang (Ed.), *Multidisciplinary studies in knowledge and systems science* (pp. 247–254). Hershey, PA: Information Science Reference.

Saedi, A., & Iahad, N. A. (2013). Future research on cloud computing adoption by small and medium-sized enterprises: A critical analysis of relevant theories. [IJANTTI]. *International Journal of Actor-Network Theory and Technological Innovation, 5*(2), 1–16. doi:10.4018/jantti.2013040101

Saha, D., & Sridhar, V. (2011). Emerging areas of research in business data communications. [IJBDCN]. *International Journal of Business Data Communications and Networking, 7*(4), 52–59. doi: doi:10.4018/ijbdcn.2011100104

Saha, D., & Sridhar, V. (2013). Platform on platform (PoP) model for meta-networking: A new paradigm for networks of the future. [IJBDCN]. *International Journal of Business Data Communications and Networking, 9*(1), 1–10. doi:10.4018/jbdcn.2013010101

Sahlin, J. P. (2013). Cloud computing: Past, present, and future. In X. Yang, & L. Liu (Eds.), *Principles, methodologies, and service-oriented approaches for cloud computing* (pp. 19–50). Hershey, PA: Business Science Reference. doi:10.4018/978-1-4666-2854-0.ch002

Salama, M., & Shawish, A. (2012). Libraries: From the classical to cloud-based era. [IJDLS]. *International Journal of Digital Library Systems, 3*(3), 14–32. doi:10.4018/jdls.2012070102

Sánchez, C. M., Molina, D., Vozmediano, R. M., Montero, R. S., & Llorente, I. M. (2012). On the use of the hybrid cloud computing paradigm. In M. Villari, I. Brandic, & F. Tusa (Eds.), *Achieving federated and self-manageable cloud infrastructures: Theory and practice* (pp. 196–218). Hershey, PA: Business Science Reference. doi:10.4018/978-1-4666-1631-8.ch011

Sasikala, P. (2011). Architectural strategies for green cloud computing: Environments, infrastructure and resources. [IJCAC]. *International Journal of Cloud Applications and Computing, 1*(4), 1–24. doi:10.4018/ijcac.2011100101

Sasikala, P. (2011). Cloud computing in higher education: Opportunities and issues. [IJCAC]. *International Journal of Cloud Applications and Computing, 1*(2), 1–13. doi:10.4018/ijcac.2011040101

Sasikala, P. (2011). Cloud computing towards technological convergence. [IJCAC]. *International Journal of Cloud Applications and Computing, 1*(4), 44–59. doi:10.4018/ijcac.2011100104

Sasikala, P. (2012). Cloud computing and e-governance: Advances, opportunities and challenges. [IJCAC]. *International Journal of Cloud Applications and Computing, 2*(4), 32–52. doi:10.4018/ijcac.2012100103

Sasikala, P. (2012). Cloud computing in higher education: Opportunities and issues. In I. Management Association (Ed.), Grid and cloud computing: Concepts, methodologies, tools and applications (pp. 1672-1685). Hershey, PA: Information Science Reference. doi: doi:10.4018/978-1-4666-0879-5.ch709

Sasikala, P. (2012). Cloud computing towards technological convergence. In I. Management Association (Ed.), Grid and cloud computing: Concepts, methodologies, tools and applications (pp. 1576-1592). Hershey, PA: Information Science Reference. doi: doi:10.4018/978-1-4666-0879-5.ch703

Sasikala, P. (2013). Architectural strategies for green cloud computing: Environments, infrastructure and resources. In S. Aljawarneh (Ed.), *Cloud computing advancements in design, implementation, and technologies* (pp. 218–242). Hershey, PA: Information Science Reference.

Sasikala, P. (2013). Cloud computing in higher education: Opportunities and issues. In S. Aljawarneh (Ed.), *Cloud computing advancements in design, implementation, and technologies* (pp. 83–96). Hershey, PA: Information Science Reference.

Sasikala, P. (2013). Cloud computing towards technological convergence. In S. Aljawarneh (Ed.), *Cloud computing advancements in design, implementation, and technologies* (pp. 263–279). Hershey, PA: Information Science Reference.

Sasikala, P. (2013). New media cloud computing: Opportunities and challenges. [IJCAC]. *International Journal of Cloud Applications and Computing, 3*(2), 61–72. doi:10.4018/ijcac.2013040106

Schrödl, H., & Wind, S. (2013). Requirements engineering for cloud application development. In A. Bento, & A. Aggarwal (Eds.), *Cloud computing service and deployment models: Layers and management* (pp. 137–150). Hershey, PA: Business Science Reference.

Sclater, N. (2012). Legal and contractual issues of cloud computing for educational institutions. In L. Chao (Ed.), *Cloud computing for teaching and learning: Strategies for design and implementation* (pp. 186–199). Hershey, PA: Information Science Reference. doi:10.4018/978-1-4666-0957-0.ch013

Sen, J. (2014). Security and privacy issues in cloud computing. In A. Ruiz-Martinez, R. Marin-Lopez, & F. Pereniguez-Garcia (Eds.), *Architectures and protocols for secure information technology infrastructures* (pp. 1–45). Hershey, PA: Information Science Reference.

Shah, B. (2013). Cloud environment controls assessment framework. In I. Management Association (Ed.), IT policy and ethics: Concepts, methodologies, tools, and applications (pp. 1822-1847). Hershey, PA: Information Science Reference. doi: doi:10.4018/978-1-4666-2919-6.ch080

Shah, B. (2013). Cloud environment controls assessment framework. In S. Tilley, & T. Parveen (Eds.), *Software testing in the cloud: Perspectives on an emerging discipline* (pp. 28–53). Hershey, PA: Information Science Reference.

Shang, X., Zhang, R., & Chen, Y. (2012). Internet of things (IoT) service architecture and its application in e-commerce. [JECO]. *Journal of Electronic Commerce in Organizations, 10*(3), 44–55. doi:10.4018/jeco.2012070104

Shankararaman, V., & Kit, L. E. (2013). Integrating the cloud scenarios and solutions. In A. Bento, & A. Aggarwal (Eds.), *Cloud computing service and deployment models: Layers and management* (pp. 173–189). Hershey, PA: Business Science Reference.

Sharma, A., & Maurer, F. (2013). A roadmap for software engineering for the cloud: Results of a systematic review. In X. Wang, N. Ali, I. Ramos, & R. Vidgen (Eds.), *Agile and lean service-oriented development: Foundations, theory, and practice* (pp. 48–63). Hershey, PA: Information Science Reference.

Sharma, A., & Maurer, F. (2014). A roadmap for software engineering for the cloud: Results of a systematic review. In I. Management Association (Ed.), Software design and development: Concepts, methodologies, tools, and applications (pp. 1-16). Hershey, PA: Information Science Reference. doi: doi:10.4018/978-1-4666-4301-7.ch001

Sharma, S. C., & Bagoria, H. (2014). Libraries and cloud computing models: A changing paradigm. In S. Dhamdhere (Ed.), *Cloud computing and virtualization technologies in libraries* (pp. 124–149). Hershey, PA: Information Science Reference.

Shawish, A., & Salama, M. (2013). Cloud computing in academia, governments, and industry. In X. Yang, & L. Liu (Eds.), *Principles, methodologies, and service-oriented approaches for cloud computing* (pp. 71–114). Hershey, PA: Business Science Reference. doi:10.4018/978-1-4666-2854-0.ch004

Shebanow, A., Perez, R., & Howard, C. (2012). The effect of firewall testing types on cloud security policies. [IJSITA]. *International Journal of Strategic Information Technology and Applications*, 3(3), 60–68. doi:10.4018/jsita.2012070105

Sheikhalishahi, M., Devare, M., Grandinetti, L., & Incutti, M. C. (2012). A complementary approach to grid and cloud distributed computing paradigms. In I. Management Association (Ed.), Grid and cloud computing: Concepts, methodologies, tools and applications (pp. 1929-1942). Hershey, PA: Information Science Reference. doi: doi:10.4018/978-1-4666-0879-5.ch811

Sheikhalishahi, M., Devare, M., Grandinetti, L., & Incutti, M. C. (2012). A complementary approach to grid and cloud distributed computing paradigms. In N. Preve (Ed.), *Computational and data grids: Principles, applications and design* (pp. 31–44). Hershey, PA: Information Science Reference.

Shen, Y., Li, Y., Wu, L., Liu, S., & Wen, Q. (2014). Cloud computing overview. In Y. Shen, Y. Li, L. Wu, S. Liu, & Q. Wen (Eds.), *Enabling the new era of cloud computing: Data security, transfer, and management* (pp. 1–24). Hershey, PA: Information Science Reference.

Shen, Y., Li, Y., Wu, L., Liu, S., & Wen, Q. (2014). Main components of cloud computing. In Y. Shen, Y. Li, L. Wu, S. Liu, & Q. Wen (Eds.), *Enabling the new era of cloud computing: Data security, transfer, and management* (pp. 25–50). Hershey, PA: Information Science Reference.

Shen, Y., Yang, J., & Keskin, T. (2014). Impact of cultural differences on the cloud computing ecosystems in the USA and China. In Y. Shen, Y. Li, L. Wu, S. Liu, & Q. Wen (Eds.), *Enabling the new era of cloud computing: Data security, transfer, and management* (pp. 269–283). Hershey, PA: Information Science Reference.

Shetty, S., & Rawat, D. B. (2013). Cloud computing based cognitive radio networking. In N. Meghanathan, & Y. Reddy (Eds.), *Cognitive radio technology applications for wireless and mobile ad hoc networks* (pp. 153–164). Hershey, PA: Information Science Reference. doi:10.4018/978-1-4666-4221-8.ch008

Shi, Z., & Beard, C. (2014). QoS in the mobile cloud computing environment. In J. Rodrigues, K. Lin, & J. Lloret (Eds.), *Mobile networks and cloud computing convergence for progressive services and applications* (pp. 200–217). Hershey, PA: Information Science Reference.

Shuster, L. (2013). Enterprise integration: Challenges and solution architecture. In R. Ramanathan, & K. Raja (Eds.), *Service-driven approaches to architecture and enterprise integration* (pp. 43–66). Hershey, PA: Information Science Reference.

Siahos, Y., Papanagiotou, I., Georgopoulos, A., Tsamis, F., & Papaioannou, I. (2012). An architecture paradigm for providing cloud services in school labs based on open source software to enhance ICT in education. [IJCEE]. *International Journal of Cyber Ethics in Education*, 2(1), 44–57. doi:10.4018/ijcee.2012010105

Simon, E., & Estublier, J. (2013). Model driven integration of heterogeneous software artifacts in service oriented computing. In A. Ionita, M. Litoiu, & G. Lewis (Eds.), *Migrating legacy applications: Challenges in service oriented architecture and cloud computing environments* (pp. 332–360). Hershey, PA: Information Science Reference.

Singh, J., & Kumar, V. (2013). Compliance and regulatory standards for cloud computing. In R. Khurana, & R. Aggarwal (Eds.), *Interdisciplinary perspectives on business convergence, computing, and legality* (pp. 54–64). Hershey, PA: Business Science Reference. doi:10.4018/978-1-4666-4209-6.ch006

Singh, V. V. (2012). Software development using service syndication based on API handshake approach between cloud-based and SOA-based reusable services. In H. Yang, & X. Liu (Eds.), *Software reuse in the emerging cloud computing era* (pp. 136–157). Hershey, PA: Information Science Reference. doi:10.4018/978-1-4666-0897-9. ch006

Smeitink, M., & Spruit, M. (2013). Maturity for sustainability in IT: Introducing the MITS. [IJITSA]. *International Journal of Information Technologies and Systems Approach*, 6(1), 39–56. doi:10.4018/jitsa.2013010103

Smith, P. A., & Cockburn, T. (2013). Socio-digital technologies. In *Dynamic leadership models for global business: Enhancing digitally connected environments* (pp. 142–168). Hershey, PA: Business Science Reference. doi:10.4018/978-1-4666-2836-6.ch006

Sneed, H. M. (2013). Testing web services in the cloud. In S. Tilley, & T. Parveen (Eds.), *Software testing in the cloud: Perspectives on an emerging discipline* (pp. 136–173). Hershey, PA: Information Science Reference.

Solomon, B., Ionescu, D., Gadea, C., & Litoiu, M. (2013). Geographically distributed cloud-based collaborative application. In A. Ionita, M. Litoiu, & G. Lewis (Eds.), *Migrating legacy applications: Challenges in service oriented architecture and cloud computing environments* (pp. 248–274). Hershey, PA: Information Science Reference.

Song, W., & Xiao, Z. (2013). An infrastructure-as-a-service cloud: On-demand resource provisioning. In X. Yang, & L. Liu (Eds.), *Principles, methodologies, and service-oriented approaches for cloud computing* (pp. 302–324). Hershey, PA: Business Science Reference. doi:10.4018/978-1-4666-2854-0.ch013

Sood, S. K. (2013). A value based dynamic resource provisioning model in cloud. [IJCAC]. *International Journal of Cloud Applications and Computing*, 3(1), 1–12. doi:10.4018/ijcac.2013010101

Sotiriadis, S., Bessis, N., & Antonopoulos, N. (2012). Exploring inter-cloud load balancing by utilizing historical service submission records. [IJDST]. *International Journal of Distributed Systems and Technologies*, 3(3), 72–81. doi:10.4018/jdst.2012070106

Soyata, T., Ba, H., Heinzelman, W., Kwon, M., & Shi, J. (2014). Accelerating mobile-cloud computing: A survey. In H. Mouftah, & B. Kantarci (Eds.), *Communication infrastructures for cloud computing* (pp. 175–197). Hershey, PA: Information Science Reference.

Spyridopoulos, T., & Katos, V. (2011). Requirements for a forensically ready cloud storage service. [IJDCF]. *International Journal of Digital Crime and Forensics*, 3(3), 19–36. doi:10.4018/jdcf.2011070102

Spyridopoulos, T., & Katos, V. (2013). Data recovery strategies for cloud environments. In K. Ruan (Ed.), *Cybercrime and cloud forensics: Applications for investigation processes* (pp. 251–265). Hershey, PA: Information Science Reference.

Srinivasa, K. G., S., H. R., H., M. K., & Venkatesh, N. (2012). MeghaOS: A framework for scalable, interoperable cloud based operating system. [IJCAC]. *International Journal of Cloud Applications and Computing*, 2(1), 53–70. doi:10.4018/ijcac.2012010104

Stantchev, V., & Stantcheva, L. (2012). Extending traditional IT-governance knowledge towards SOA and cloud governance. [IJKSR]. *International Journal of Knowledge Society Research*, 3(2), 30–43. doi:10.4018/jksr.2012040103

Stantchev, V., & Tamm, G. (2012). Reducing information asymmetry in cloud marketplaces. [IJHCITP]. *International Journal of Human Capital and Information Technology Professionals*, 3(4), 1–10. doi:10.4018/jhcitp.2012100101

Steinbuß, S., & Weißenberg, N. (2013). Service design and process design for the logistics mall cloud. In X. Yang, & L. Liu (Eds.), *Principles, methodologies, and service-oriented approaches for cloud computing* (pp. 186–206). Hershey, PA: Business Science Reference. doi:10.4018/978-1-4666-2854-0.ch008

Stender, J., Berlin, M., & Reinefeld, A. (2013). XtreemFS: A file system for the cloud. In D. Kyriazis, A. Voulodimos, S. Gogouvitis, & T. Varvarigou (Eds.), *Data intensive storage services for cloud environments* (pp. 267–285). Hershey, PA: Business Science Reference. doi:10.4018/978-1-4666-3934-8.ch016

Sticklen, D. J., & Issa, T. (2011). An initial examination of free and proprietary software-selection in organizations. [IJWP]. *International Journal of Web Portals, 3*(4), 27–43. doi:10.4018/jwp.2011100103

Sun, Y., White, J., Gray, J., & Gokhale, A. (2012). Model-driven automated error recovery in cloud computing. In I. Management Association (Ed.), Grid and cloud computing: Concepts, methodologies, tools and applications (pp. 680-700). Hershey, PA: Information Science Reference. doi: doi:10.4018/978-1-4666-0879-5.ch308

Sun, Z., Yang, Y., Zhou, Y., & Cruickshank, H. (2014). Agent-based resource management for mobile cloud. In J. Rodrigues, K. Lin, & J. Lloret (Eds.), *Mobile networks and cloud computing convergence for progressive services and applications* (pp. 118–134). Hershey, PA: Information Science Reference.

Sutherland, S. (2013). Convergence of interoperability of cloud computing, service oriented architecture and enterprise architecture. [IJEEI]. *International Journal of E-Entrepreneurship and Innovation, 4*(1), 43–51. doi:10.4018/jeei.2013010104

Takabi, H., & Joshi, J. B. (2013). Policy management in cloud: Challenges and approaches. In D. Rosado, D. Mellado, E. Fernandez-Medina, & M. Piattini (Eds.), *Security engineering for cloud computing: Approaches and tools* (pp. 191–211). Hershey, PA: Information Science Reference.

Takabi, H., & Joshi, J. B. (2013). Policy management in cloud: Challenges and approaches. In I. Management Association (Ed.), IT policy and ethics: Concepts, methodologies, tools, and applications (pp. 814-834). Hershey, PA: Information Science Reference. doi: doi:10.4018/978-1-4666-2919-6.ch037

Takabi, H., Joshi, J. B., & Ahn, G. (2013). Security and privacy in cloud computing: Towards a comprehensive framework. In X. Yang, & L. Liu (Eds.), *Principles, methodologies, and service-oriented approaches for cloud computing* (pp. 164–184). Hershey, PA: Business Science Reference. doi:10.4018/978-1-4666-2854-0.ch007

Takabi, H., Zargar, S. T., & Joshi, J. B. (2014). Mobile cloud computing and its security and privacy challenges. In D. Rawat, B. Bista, & G. Yan (Eds.), *Security, privacy, trust, and resource management in mobile and wireless communications* (pp. 384–407). Hershey, PA: Information Science Reference.

Teixeira, C., Pinto, J. S., Ferreira, F., Oliveira, A., Teixeira, A., & Pereira, C. (2013). Cloud computing enhanced service development architecture for the living usability lab. In R. Martinho, R. Rijo, M. Cruz-Cunha, & J. Varajão (Eds.), *Information systems and technologies for enhancing health and social care* (pp. 33–53). Hershey, PA: Medical Information Science Reference. doi:10.4018/978-1-4666-3667-5.ch003

Thimm, H. (2012). Cloud-based collaborative decision making: Design considerations and architecture of the GRUPO-MOD system. [IJDSST]. *International Journal of Decision Support System Technology, 4*(4), 39–59. doi:10.4018/jdsst.2012100103

Thomas, P. (2012). Harnessing the potential of cloud computing to transform higher education. In L. Chao (Ed.), *Cloud computing for teaching and learning: Strategies for design and implementation* (pp. 147–158). Hershey, PA: Information Science Reference. doi:10.4018/978-1-4666-0957-0.ch010

T.M. K., & Gopalakrishnan, S. (2014). Green economic and secure libraries on cloud. In S. Dhamdhere (Ed.), Cloud computing and virtualization technologies in libraries (pp. 297-315). Hershey, PA: Information Science Reference. doi: doi:10.4018/978-1-4666-4631-5.ch017

Toka, A., Aivazidou, E., Antoniou, A., & Arvanitopoulos-Darginis, K. (2013). Cloud computing in supply chain management: An overview. In D. Graham, I. Manikas, & D. Folinas (Eds.), *E-logistics and e-supply chain management: Applications for evolving business* (pp. 218–231). Hershey, PA: Business Science Reference. doi:10.4018/978-1-4666-3914-0.ch012

Torrealba, S. M., Morales P., M., Campos, J. M., & Meza S., M. (2013). A software tool to support risks analysis about what should or should not go to the cloud. In D. Rosado, D. Mellado, E. Fernandez-Medina, & M. Piattini (Eds.) Security engineering for cloud computing: Approaches and tools (pp. 72-96). Hershey, PA: Information Science Reference. doi: doi:10.4018/978-1-4666-2125-1.ch005

Trivedi, M., & Suthar, V. (2013). Cloud computing: A feasible platform for ICT enabled health science libraries in India. [IJUDH]. *International Journal of User-Driven Healthcare*, *3*(2), 69–77. doi:10.4018/ijudh.2013040108

Truong, H., Pham, T., Thoai, N., & Dustdar, S. (2012). Cloud computing for education and research in developing countries. In L. Chao (Ed.), *Cloud computing for teaching and learning: Strategies for design and implementation* (pp. 64–80). Hershey, PA: Information Science Reference. doi:10.4018/978-1-4666-0957-0.ch005

Tsirmpas, C., Giokas, K., Iliopoulou, D., & Koutsouris, D. (2012). Magnetic resonance imaging and magnetic resonance spectroscopy cloud computing framework. [IJRQEH]. *International Journal of Reliable and Quality E-Healthcare*, *1*(4), 1–12. doi:10.4018/ijrqeh.2012100101

Turner, H., White, J., Reed, J., Galindo, J., Porter, A., Marathe, M., et al. (2013). Building a cloud-based mobile application testbed. In I. Management Association (Ed.), IT policy and ethics: Concepts, methodologies, tools, and applications (pp. 879-899). Hershey, PA: Information Science Reference. doi: doi:10.4018/978-1-4666-2919-6.ch040

Turner, H., White, J., Reed, J., Galindo, J., Porter, A., & Marathe, M. et al. (2013). Building a cloud-based mobile application testbed. In S. Tilley, & T. Parveen (Eds.), *Software testing in the cloud: Perspectives on an emerging discipline* (pp. 382–403). Hershey, PA: Information Science Reference.

Tusa, F., Paone, M., & Villari, M. (2012). CLEVER: A cloud middleware beyond the federation. In M. Villari, I. Brandic, & F. Tusa (Eds.), *Achieving federated and self-manageable cloud infrastructures: Theory and practice* (pp. 219–241). Hershey, PA: Business Science Reference. doi:10.4018/978-1-4666-1631-8.ch012

Udoh, E. (2012). Technology acceptance model applied to the adoption of grid and cloud technology. [IJGHPC]. *International Journal of Grid and High Performance Computing*, *4*(1), 1–20. doi:10.4018/jghpc.2012010101

Vannoy, S. A. (2011). A structured content analytic assessment of business services advertisements in the cloud-based web services marketplace. [IJDTIS]. *International Journal of Dependable and Trustworthy Information Systems*, *2*(1), 18–49. doi:10.4018/jdtis.2011010102

Vaquero, L. M., Cáceres, J., & Morán, D. (2011). The challenge of service level scalability for the cloud. [IJCAC]. *International Journal of Cloud Applications and Computing*, *1*(1), 34–44. doi:10.4018/ijcac.2011010103

Vaquero, L. M., Cáceres, J., & Morán, D. (2013). The challenge of service level scalability for the cloud. In S. Aljawarneh (Ed.), *Cloud computing advancements in design, implementation, and technologies* (pp. 37–48). Hershey, PA: Information Science Reference.

Venkatraman, R., Venkatraman, S., & Asaithambi, S. P. (2013). A practical cloud services implementation framework for e-businesses. In K. Tarnay, S. Imre, & L. Xu (Eds.), *Research and development in e-business through service-oriented solutions* (pp. 167–198). Hershey, PA: Business Science Reference.

Venkatraman, S. (2013). Software engineering research gaps in the cloud. [JITR]. *Journal of Information Technology Research*, *6*(1), 1–19. doi:10.4018/jitr.2013010101

Vijaykumar, S., Rajkarthick, K. S., & Priya, J. (2012). Innovative business opportunities and smart business management techniques from green cloud TPS. [IJABIM]. *International Journal of Asian Business and Information Management*, *3*(4), 62–72. doi:10.4018/jabim.2012100107

Wang, C., Lam, K. T., & Kui Ma, R. K. (2012). A computation migration approach to elasticity of cloud computing. In J. Abawajy, M. Pathan, M. Rahman, A. Pathan, & M. Deris (Eds.), *Network and traffic engineering in emerging distributed computing applications* (pp. 145–178). Hershey, PA: Information Science Reference. doi:10.4018/978-1-4666-1888-6.ch007

Wang, D., & Wu, J. (2014). Carrier-grade distributed cloud computing: Demands, challenges, designs, and future perspectives. In H. Mouftah, & B. Kantarci (Eds.), *Communication infrastructures for cloud computing* (pp. 264–281). Hershey, PA: Information Science Reference.

Wang, H., & Philips, D. (2012). Implement virtual programming lab with cloud computing for web-based distance education. In L. Chao (Ed.), *Cloud computing for teaching and learning: Strategies for design and implementation* (pp. 95–110). Hershey, PA: Information Science Reference. doi:10.4018/978-1-4666-0957-0.ch007

Warneke, D. (2013). Ad-hoc parallel data processing on pay-as-you-go clouds with nephele. In A. Loo (Ed.), *Distributed computing innovations for business, engineering, and science* (pp. 191–218). Hershey, PA: Information Science Reference.

Wei, Y., & Blake, M. B. (2013). Adaptive web services monitoring in cloud environments. [IJWP]. *International Journal of Web Portals*, 5(1), 15–27. doi:10.4018/jwp.2013010102

White, S. C., Sedigh, S., & Hurson, A. R. (2013). Security concepts for cloud computing. In X. Yang, & L. Liu (Eds.), *Principles, methodologies, and service-oriented approaches for cloud computing* (pp. 116–142). Hershey, PA: Business Science Reference. doi:10.4018/978-1-4666-2854-0.ch005

Williams, A. J. (2013). The role of emerging technologies in developing and sustaining diverse suppliers in competitive markets. In I. Association (Ed.), *Enterprise resource planning: Concepts, methodologies, tools, and applications* (pp. 1550–1560). Hershey, PA: Business Science Reference. doi:10.4018/978-1-4666-4153-2.ch082

Williams, A. J. (2013). The role of emerging technologies in developing and sustaining diverse suppliers in competitive markets. In J. Lewis, A. Green, & D. Surry (Eds.), *Technology as a tool for diversity leadership: Implementation and future implications* (pp. 95–105). Hershey, PA: Information Science Reference.

Wilson, L., Goh, T. T., & Wang, W. Y. (2012). Big data management challenges in a meteorological organisation. [IJEA]. *International Journal of E-Adoption*, 4(2), 1–14. doi:10.4018/jea.2012040101

Wu, R., Ahn, G., & Hu, H. (2012). Towards HIPAA-compliant healthcare systems in cloud computing. [IJCMAM]. *International Journal of Computational Models and Algorithms in Medicine*, 3(2), 1–22. doi:10.4018/jcmam.2012040101

Xiao, J., Wang, M., Wang, L., & Zhu, X. (2013). Design and implementation of C-iLearning: A cloud-based intelligent learning system. [IJDET]. *International Journal of Distance Education Technologies*, 11(3), 79–97. doi:10.4018/jdet.2013070106

Xing, R., Wang, Z., & Peterson, R. L. (2011). Redefining the information technology in the 21st century. [IJSITA]. *International Journal of Strategic Information Technology and Applications*, 2(1), 1–10. doi:10.4018/jsita.2011010101

Xu, L., Huang, D., Tsai, W., & Atkinson, R. K. (2012). V-lab: A mobile, cloud-based virtual laboratory platform for hands-on networking courses. [IJCBPL]. *International Journal of Cyber Behavior, Psychology and Learning*, 2(3), 73–85. doi:10.4018/ijcbpl.2012070106

Xu, Y., & Mao, S. (2014). Mobile cloud media: State of the art and outlook. In J. Rodrigues, K. Lin, & J. Lloret (Eds.), *Mobile networks and cloud computing convergence for progressive services and applications* (pp. 18–38). Hershey, PA: Information Science Reference.

Xu, Z., Yan, B., & Zou, Y. (2013). Beyond hadoop: Recent directions in data computing for internet services. In S. Aljawarneh (Ed.), *Cloud computing advancements in design, implementation, and technologies* (pp. 49–66). Hershey, PA: Information Science Reference.

Yan, Z. (2014). Trust management in mobile cloud computing. In *Trust management in mobile environments: Autonomic and usable models* (pp. 54–93). Hershey, PA: Information Science Reference.

Yang, D. X. (2012). QoS-oriented service computing: Bringing SOA into cloud environment. In X. Liu, & Y. Li (Eds.), *Advanced design approaches to emerging software systems: Principles, methodologies and tools* (pp. 274–296). Hershey, PA: Information Science Reference.

Yang, H., Huff, S. L., & Tate, M. (2013). Managing the cloud for information systems agility. In A. Bento, & A. Aggarwal (Eds.), *Cloud computing service and deployment models: Layers and management* (pp. 70–93). Hershey, PA: Business Science Reference.

Yang, M., Kuo, C., & Yeh, Y. (2011). Dynamic rightsizing with quality-controlled algorithms in virtualization environments. [IJGHPC]. *International Journal of Grid and High Performance Computing, 3*(2), 29–43. doi:10.4018/jghpc.2011040103

Yang, X. (2012). QoS-oriented service computing: Bringing SOA into cloud environment. In I. Management Association (Ed.), Grid and cloud computing: Concepts, methodologies, tools and applications (pp. 1621-1643). Hershey, PA: Information Science Reference. doi: doi:10.4018/978-1-4666-0879-5.ch706

Yang, Y., Chen, J., & Hu, H. (2012). The convergence between cloud computing and cable TV. [IJTD]. *International Journal of Technology Diffusion, 3*(2), 1–11. doi:10.4018/jtd.2012040101

Yassein, M. O., Khamayseh, Y. M., & Hatamleh, A. M. (2013). Intelligent randomize round robin for cloud computing. [IJCAC]. *International Journal of Cloud Applications and Computing, 3*(1), 27–33. doi:10.4018/ijcac.2013010103

Yau, S. S., An, H. G., & Buduru, A. B. (2012). An approach to data confidentiality protection in cloud environments. [IJWSR]. *International Journal of Web Services Research, 9*(3), 67–83. doi:10.4018/jwsr.2012070104

Yu, W. D., Adiga, A. S., Rao, S., & Panakkel, M. J. (2012). A SOA based system development methodology for cloud computing environment: Using uhealthcare as practice. [IJEHMC]. *International Journal of E-Health and Medical Communications, 3*(4), 42–63. doi:10.4018/jehmc.2012100104

Yu, W. D., & Bhagwat, R. (2011). Modeling emergency and telemedicine heath support system: A service oriented architecture approach using cloud computing. [IJEHMC]. *International Journal of E-Health and Medical Communications, 2*(3), 63–88. doi:10.4018/jehmc.2011070104

Yu, W. D., & Bhagwat, R. (2013). Modeling emergency and telemedicine health support system: A service oriented architecture approach using cloud computing. In J. Rodrigues (Ed.), *Digital advances in medicine, e-health, and communication technologies* (pp. 187–213). Hershey, PA: Medical Information Science Reference. doi:10.4018/978-1-4666-2794-9.ch011

Yuan, D., Lewandowski, C., & Zhong, J. (2012). Developing a private cloud based IP telephony laboratory and curriculum. In L. Chao (Ed.), *Cloud computing for teaching and learning: Strategies for design and implementation* (pp. 126–145). Hershey, PA: Information Science Reference. doi:10.4018/978-1-4666-0957-0.ch009

Yuvaraj, M. (2014). Cloud libraries: Issues and challenges. In S. Dhamdhere (Ed.), *Cloud computing and virtualization technologies in libraries* (pp. 316–338). Hershey, PA: Information Science Reference.

Zaman, M., Simmers, C. A., & Anandarajan, M. (2013). Using an ethical framework to examine linkages between "going green" in research practices and information and communication technologies. In B. Medlin (Ed.), *Integrations of technology utilization and social dynamics in organizations* (pp. 243–262). Hershey, PA: Information Science Reference.

Zapata, B. C., & Alemán, J. L. (2013). Security risks in cloud computing: An analysis of the main vulnerabilities. In D. Rosado, D. Mellado, E. Fernandez-Medina, & M. Piattini (Eds.), *Security engineering for cloud computing: Approaches and tools* (pp. 55–71). Hershey, PA: Information Science Reference.

Zapata, B. C., & Alemán, J. L. (2014). Security risks in cloud computing: An analysis of the main vulnerabilities. In I. Management Association (Ed.), Software design and development: Concepts, methodologies, tools, and applications (pp. 936-952). Hershey, PA: Information Science Reference. doi: doi:10.4018/978-1-4666-4301-7.ch045

Zardari, S., Faniyi, F., & Bahsoon, R. (2013). Using obstacles for systematically modeling, analysing, and mitigating risks in cloud adoption. In I. Mistrik, A. Tang, R. Bahsoon, & J. Stafford (Eds.), *Aligning enterprise, system, and software architectures* (pp. 275–296). Hershey, PA: Business Science Reference.

Zech, P., Kalb, P., Felderer, M., & Breu, R. (2013). Threatening the cloud: Securing services and data by continuous, model-driven negative security testing. In S. Tilley, & T. Parveen (Eds.), *Software testing in the cloud: Perspectives on an emerging discipline* (pp. 280–304). Hershey, PA: Information Science Reference.

Zhang, F., Cao, J., Cai, H., & Wu, C. (2011). Provisioning virtual resources adaptively in elastic compute cloud platforms. [IJWSR]. *International Journal of Web Services Research*, 8(3), 54–69. doi:10.4018/jwsr.2011070103

Zhang, G., Li, C., Xue, S., Liu, Y., Zhang, Y., & Xing, C. (2012). A new electronic commerce architecture in the cloud. [JECO]. *Journal of Electronic Commerce in Organizations*, 10(4), 42–56. doi:10.4018/jeco.2012100104

Zhang, J., Yao, J., Chen, S., & Levy, D. (2011). Facilitating biodefense research with mobile-cloud computing. [IJSSOE]. *International Journal of Systems and Service-Oriented Engineering*, 2(3), 18–31. doi:10.4018/jssoe.2011070102

Zhang, J., Yao, J., Chen, S., & Levy, D. (2013). Facilitating biodefense research with mobile-cloud computing. In D. Chiu (Ed.), *Mobile and web innovations in systems and service-oriented engineering* (pp. 318–332). Hershey, PA: Information Science Reference.

Zheng, S., Chen, F., Yang, H., & Li, J. (2013). An approach to evolving legacy software system into cloud computing environment. In X. Yang, & L. Liu (Eds.), *Principles, methodologies, and service-oriented approaches for cloud computing* (pp. 207–229). Hershey, PA: Business Science Reference. doi:10.4018/978-1-4666-2854-0.ch009

Zhou, J., Athukorala, K., Gilman, E., Riekki, J., & Ylianttila, M. (2012). Cloud architecture for dynamic service composition. [IJGHPC]. *International Journal of Grid and High Performance Computing*, 4(2), 17–31. doi:10.4018/jghpc.2012040102

Compilation of References

Ahn, G., Ko, M., & Shehab, M. (2009). Privacy-enhanced user-centric identity management. In *Proceedings of the IEEE International Conference on Communications (ICC'09)*. IEEE.

Ahn, H., Chang, H., Jang, C., & Choi, E. (2011). User authentication platform using provisioning in cloud computing environment. *Advanced Communication and Networking Communications in Computer and Information Science*, 132-138.

Al-Aqrabi, H., et al. (2012). Investigation of IT security and compliance challenges in security-as-a-service for cloud computing. In *Proceedings of IEEE 15th International Symposium on OCS Workshops*, (pp. 124-129). IEEE.

AlternativaPlatform. (n.d.). *About us*. Retrieved from http://alternativaplatform.com/en/about/

Altnam, D. (2012). *Three reasons private clouds are winning over the business world*. Retrieved December 2012 from http://www.business2community.com/tech-gadgets/three-reasons-private-clouds-are-winning-over-the-business-world-0362241

Amazon S3. (2013). Retrieved from http://aws.amazon.com/s3

Amazon Web Services, Cloud Computing: Compute, Storage, Database. (n.d.). Retrieved April 2013 from http://aws.amazon.com/

Amazon Web Services. (2013). Retrieved from http://aws.amazon.com/

Amazon. (2011). *Report on cloud outage*. Retrieved from http://aws.amazon.com/message/65648/

Amazon. (2013). *Amazon web services*. Retrieved from http://aws.amazon.com/

Antonopoulos, N., & Gillam, L. (2010). *Cloud computing: Principles, systems and applications*. London: Springer. doi:10.1007/978-1-84996-241-4

App. Engine & Google Developers. (n.d.). Retrieved April 2013 from https://developers.google.com/appengine/

Archer, J., Boheme, A., Cullinarie, D., Puhlmann, N., Kurtz, P., & Reavis, J. (2010). Top threats to cloud computing. *Cloud Security Alliance*. Retrieved from http://www.cloudsecurityalliance.org/topthreats

Armbrust, M., Fox, A., Griffith, R., Joseph, A. D., Katz, R., & Konwinski, A. … Zaharia, M. (2009). *Above the clouds: A Berkeley view of cloud computing* (Technical Report No. UCB/EECS-2009-28). Berkeley, CA: University of California.

Armbrust, M. et al. (2010). A view of cloud computing. *Communications of the ACM, 53*(4), 50–58. doi:10.1145/1721654.1721672

Armstrong, D., & Djemame, K. (2009). *Towards quality of service in the cloud*. Paper presented at the 25th UK Performance Engineering Workshop. Leeds, UK.

ARRA USA. (2009). *American recovery and reinvestment act 2009 in USA*. Retrieved from http://www.recovery.gov/Pages/default.aspx

Awasthi, A., Chauhan, S. S., & Goyal, S. K. (2011). A multi-criteria decision making approach for location planning for urban distribution centers under uncertainty. *Mathematical and Computer Modelling, 53*(1–2), 98–109. doi: http://dx.doi.org/10.1016/j.mcm.2010.07.023

AWS Security and Compliance Center. (n.d.). Retrieved April 2013 from http://aws.amazon.com/security/

Azure Security. (2013). *Windows Azure security guidance.* Retrieved from http://www.windowsazure.com/en-us/develop/net/best-practices/security/

Backend as a Service. (n.d.). Retrieved December 2012 from http://en.wikipedia.org/wiki/Backend_as_a_service

Barbara, J. (2009). *Cloud computing: Another digital forensic challenge.* Retrieved from http://www.forensicmag.com/article/cloud-computing-another-digital-forensic-challenge?Page=0,1

Barbara., J. (2007). *Cloud computing: Another digital challenge.* Retrieved from http://www.forensicmag.com/article/cloud-computing-another-digital-forensic-challenge?page=0,1

Barnes, F. (2010). Putting a lock on cloud-based information: Collaboration between records and it professionals before contracting with cloud-based information services will help organizations ask the right questions to ensure their information is secure. *Information Management Journal, 44*(4).

Beal, V. (2012). *The difference between server and desktop virtualization?* Retrieved March 2013 from http://www.webopedia.com/DidYouKnow/Computer_Science/difference_between_server_and_desktop_virtualization.html

Berners-Lee, T. (2009). *Program integration across application and organizational boundaries.* Retrieved April 2013 from http://www.w3.org/DesignIssues/WebServices.html

Berry, T., Reilley, D., & Wren, C. (2011). Cloud computing, pros and cons for computer forensic investigations. *International Journal Multimedia and Image Processing, 1*(1), 26–34.

Bertino, E., Paci, F., & Ferrini, R. (2009). Privacy-preserving digital identity management for cloud computing. *IEEE Computer Society Data Engineering Bulletin, 32*(1), 21–27.

Biddick, M. (2011). *Cloud storage: Changing dynamics beyond services.* Retrieved December 2012 from http://reports.informationweek.com/abstract/24/7534/Storage-Server/research-cloud-storage.html

Biggs, S., & Vidalis, S. (2009). *Cloud computing: The impact on digital forensic investigations.* Retrieved from http://ieeexplore.ieee.org/search/freesearchresult.jsp?newsearch=true&queryText=cloud+computing%3A+impact+on+digital+forensic+investigations&x=19&y=11

Biggs, S., & Vidalis, S. (2010). Cloud computing storms. *International Journal of Intelligent Computing Research, 1*(1/2), 61–68.

Bishop, M. (2005). *Introduction to computer security.* Reading, MA: Addison-Wesley Professional.

Biswas, S. (2011). *Quotes about cloud computing (and some background information on them).* Retrieved December 2012 from http://www.cloudtweaks.com/2011/03/quotes-about-cloud-computing-and-some-background-information-on-them/

Blanquer, I., Hernández, V., Segrelles, D., & Torres, E. (2008). A supporting infrastructure for evaluating QoS-specific activities in SOA-based grids. *Distributed and Parallel Systems,* 167–178.

BlueKrypt. (2013). Retrieved from http://www.keylength.com/en/

Bort, J. (2012). *Larry Ellison just took on Amazon with a new cloud service.* Retrieved December 2012 from http://www.businessinsider.com/larry-ellison-just-took-on-amazon-with-a-new-cloud-service-2012-9

Bosworth, S., Kabay, M., & Whyne, E. (2009). *Computer security handbook.* Hoboken, NJ: Wiley.

Brandic, I., Dustdar, S., Anstett, T., Schumm, D., Leymann, F., & Konrad, R. (2010). Compliant cloud computing (C3), architecture and language support for user-driven compliance management in clouds. In *Proceedings of the 3rd International Conference on Cloud Computing.* IEEE.

Brill, K. G. (2007). *Data center energy efficiency and productivity.* Santa Fe, NM: The Uptime Institute. Retrieved from www.uptimeinstitute.org/symp_pdf/(TUI3004C)DataCenterEnergyEfficiency.pdf

Brimberg, J., & Drezner, Z. (2013). A new heuristic for solving the p-median problem in the plane. *Computers & Operations Research, 40*(1), 427-437. doi: http://dx.doi.org/10.1016/j.cor.2012.07.012

Brodkin, J. (2008). *Gartner: Seven cloud-computing security risks*. Retrieved from http://www.networkworld.com/news/2008/070208-cloud.html

Butler, B. (2012). *Are community cloud services the next hot thing?* Retrieved December 2012 from http://www.networkworld.com/news/2012/030112-are-community-cloud-services-the-256869.html

Buyya, R., Yeo, C., Venugopal, S., Broberg, J., & Brandic, I. (2009). Cloud computing and emerging IT platforms: Vision, hype, and reality for delivering computing as the 5th utility. *Future Generation Computer Systems, 25*(6), 599–616. doi:10.1016/j.future.2008.12.001

Cao, B., & Li, B. (2009). A service-oriented QoS-assured and multi-agent cloud computing architecture. *Cloud Computing, 5531*, 644–649. doi:10.1007/978-3-642-10665-1_66

Carlsson, C. (1982). Tackling an MCDM-problem with the help of some results from fuzzy set theory. *European Journal of Operational Research, 10*(3), 270–281. doi:10.1016/0377-2217(82)90226-0

Carlsson, C., & Fuller, R. (1995). Multiple criteria decision making: The case for interdependence. *Computers & Operations Research, 22*(3), 251–260. doi:10.1016/0305-0548(94)E0023-Z

Carlsson, C., & Fuller, R. (1996). Fuzzy multiple criteria decision making: Recent developments. *Fuzzy Sets and Systems, 78*(2), 139–153. doi:10.1016/0165-0114(95)00165-4

CASHRUN. (2010). *The importance of PCI DSS compliance*. Retrieved from http://www.cashrun.com/1038/the-importance-of-pci-dss-compliance

Catteddu, D. (2010). Cloud computing: Benefits, risks and recommendations for information security. *Web Application Security, 72*, 17. doi:10.1007/978-3-642-16120-9_9

Catteddu, D., & Hogben, G. (2009). *Cloud computing risk assessment*. Greece: European Network and Information Security Agency.

Chaput, S. R., & Ringwood, K. (2010). Cloud compliance: A framework for using cloud computing in a regulated world. In *Cloud computing* (pp. 241–256). London: Springer. doi:10.1007/978-1-84996-241-4_14

Chen, Y., Paxson, V., & Katz, R. (2010). *What's new about cloud computing security?* (Master's thesis). UC Berkeley, Berkeley, CA. Retrieved from www.eecs.berkeley.edu/Pubs/TechRpts/2010/EECS-2010-5.pdf

Chernicoff, D. (2012). *A less than merry Christmas for Netflix*. Retrieved December 2012 from http://www.zdnet.com/a-less-than-merry-christmas-for-netflix-7000009187/

Chow, R., et al. (2010). Authentication in the clouds: A framework and its application to mobile users. In *Proceedings of the ACM Cloud Computing Security Workshop* (CCSW '10). Chicago: ACM.

Chow, R., Golle, P., Jakobsson, M., Shi, E., Staddon, J., Masuoka, R., & Molina, J. (2009). Controlling data in the cloud: Outsourcing computation without outsourcing control. In *Proceedings of the 2009 ACM Workshop on Cloud Computing Security*. Chicago: ACM.

CHUBB Group of Insurance Companies. (2011). *Fore-Front portfolio 3.0 cyber security insurance*. Author.

Chunawala, Q. S. (n.d.). *Early batch-oriented operating systems, in what on earth is a mainframe-the sum and substance of a mainframe*. Retrieved April 2013 from http://www.mainframe360.com

Chunlin, L., & Layuan, L. (2006). QoS based resource scheduling by computational economy in computational grid. *Information Processing Letters, 98*(3). doi:10.1016/j.ipl.2006.01.002

Church, R. L., & Murray, A. T. (2009). *Business site selection, location analysis and GIS*. New York: Wiley.

CISCO. (n.d.). *Privacy and security compliance journey-cisco systems*. Retrieved from http://www.cisco.com/web/about/doing_business/legal/privacy_compliance/index.html

Cloud Computing Digest. (2013). *Thirteen cloud service providers to watch in 2013*. Author.

Cloud Harmony: Benchmarking the Cloud. (2001). Retrieved June 27, 2011, from http://cloudharmony.com

Cloud Security Alliance. (2009). Retrieved from https://www.cloudsecurityalliance.org/csaguide.pdf

Cloud Security Alliance. (2013). Retrieved from http://www.cloudsecurityalliance.org

Cloud Security Alliance. (2013). *The notorious nine: Cloud computing top threats in 2013.* Retrieved March 2013 from http://www.cloudsecurityalliance.org/top-threats

Cohen, M. (2012, January 17). Forecasting the first steps of cloud adoption. *eWeek*, 1–3.

Conroy, S. P. (2011). *History of virtualization.* Retrieved March 2013 from http://www.everythingvm.com/content/history-virtualization

COSO. (2012). *Enterprise risk management for cloud computing.* Retrieved from http://www.coso.org/documents/Cloud%20Computing%20Thought%20Paper.pdf

Council of Europe Convention on Cybercrime (ETS No. 185). (n.d.). Retrieved from http://conventions.coe.int/Treaty/en/Treaties/Html/185.htm

Council of Europe Convention on Cybercrime, Chapter II, Section 1, Article 7, Nov. 23, 2001, ETS No. 185

Council of Europe Convention on Cybercrime, Chapter II, Section 1, Article 8, Nov. 23, 2001, ETS No. 185.

Council of Europe Convention on Cybercrime, Chapter II, Section 1, Articles 2-6, Nov. 23, 2001, ETS No. 185.

Council of Europe Convention on Cybercrime, Chapter III, Section 1, Title 2, Nov. 23, 2001, ETS No. 185.

Council of Europe Convention on Cybercrime, Chapter III, Section 1, Title 3, Nov. 23, 2001, ETS No. 185.

Council of Europe Convention on Cybercrime, Chapter III, Section 1, Title 4, Nov. 23, 2001, ETS No. 185.

Cyber-InsuranceMetrics. (n.d.). *Cyber-insurance metrics and impact on cyber-security.* Retrieved from http://www.whitehouse.gov/files/documents/cyber/ISA%20-%20Cyber-Insurance%20Metrics%20and%20Impact%20on%20Cyber-Security.pdf

CyberSecIndex. (2011). *New index measures cyberspace safety, the index of cyber security.* Retrieved from http://www.cybersecurityindex.org/

Dashboard, A. W. S. (2013). *Service health dashboard.* Retrieved from http://status.aws.amazon.com/

Daskin, M. S. (1995). *Network and discrete location: Models, algorithms, and applications.* New York: Wiley Interscience. doi:10.1002/9781118032343

Deb, K., Pratap, A., Agarwal, S., & Meyarivan, T. (2002). A fast and elitist multiobjective genetic algorithm: NSGA-II. *IEEE Transactions on Evolutionary Computation, 6*(2). doi:10.1109/4235.996017

Diaz, A. (2011). *Service level agreements in the cloud: Who cares?* Wired Cloudline. Retrieved from http://www.wired.com/cloudline/2011/12/service-level-agreements-in-the-cloud-who-cares/

Dierks, T., & Rescorla, E. (2008). *RFC 5246 - The transport layer security (TLS) protocol version 1.2.* RFC.

Dines, R. (2012). *How Amazon ruined my Christmas.* Retrieved December 2012 from http://www.zdnet.com/how-amazon-ruined-my-christmas-7000009215/?s_cid=rSINGLE

Dinucci, D. (1999, April). Fragmented future. *Print Magazine*, 220-222.

DoD. (2011). *Cyber security operations centre initial guidance.* Retrieved from http://etherealmind.com/wp-content/uploads/2011/04/Cloud_Computing_Security_Considerations-1.pdf

Dokras, S. et al. (2009). *The role of security in trustworthy cloud computing.* RSA Security Inc.

Durillo, J. J., & Nebro, A. J. (2006). jMetal: A Java framework for multi-objective optimization. Academic Press.

Dykstra, J., & Riehl, D. (2012). Forensic collection of electronic evidence from infrastructure-as-a-service. *Rich Journal of Law & Technology, 1.*

Ekmekçioğlu, M., Kaya, T., & Kahraman, C. (2010). Fuzzy multicriteria disposal method and site selection for municipal solid waste. *Waste Management (New York, N.Y.), 30*(8–9), 1729–1736. doi:10.1016/j.wasman.2010.02.031 PMID:20303733

Email as a Service (EaaS). (n.d.). Retrieved December 2012 from http://www.gsa.gov/portal/content/112223?utm_source=FAS&utm_medium=print-radio&utm_term=eaas&utm_campaign=shortcuts

EMC Solutions Group. (2012). *Big data-as-a-service: A marketing and technology perspective.* Retrieved December 2012 from http://www.emc.com/collateral/software/white-papers/h10839-big-data-as-a-service-perspt.pdf

EuroCloud. (2011). Retrieved from http://www.euro-cloud.org

Europa. (n.d.). *Summaries of EU legislation.* Retrieved from http://europa.eu/legislation_summaries/information_society/data_protection/ l14012_en.htm

European Convention on Extradition, opened for signature in Paris, on 13 December 1957 (ETS No. 24), European Convention on Mutual Assistance in Criminal Matters, opened for signature in Strasbourg, on 20 April 1959 (ETS No. 30), Additional Protocol to the European Convention on Mutual Assistance in Criminal Matters, opened for signature in Strasbourg, on 17 March 1978 (ETS No. 99),

European Union Report. (2009). *Cloud computing: Benefits, risks and recommendations for information security.* Retrieved from http://www.enisa.europa.eu/activities/risk-management/files/deliverables/cloud-computing-risk-assessment

Farber, D. (2008). Cloud computing on the horizon. *CNET News.* Retrieved from http://news.cnet.com/8301-13953_3-9977517-80.html

Farber, D. (2008). *Oracle's Ellison nails cloud computing.* Retrieved December 2012 from http://news.cnet.com/8301-13953_3-10052188-80.html

Federal Register. (2013, January 25). *HIPAA Privacy, Security, Enforcement and Breach Notification Rules, 78*(17), 5566-5702.

FedRAMP. (2012). *Concept of operations (CONOPS).* Retrieved from http://www.gsa.gov/graphics/staffoffices/FedRAMP_CONOPS.pdf

Fielding, R. (2000). *Architectural styles and the design of network-based software architectures.* (doctoral Dissertation).

Financial Services Modernization Act of 1999 (US)

FISMA. (2010). Retrieved from http://www.dhs.gov/federal-information-security-management-act-fisma

Fitzpatrick, B. W., & Lueck, J. J. (2010). The case against data lock-in. *Communications of the ACM, 53*(11), 42–46. doi:10.1145/1839676.1839691

Flickr. (2013). Retrieved from http://www.flickr.com

Fortinet. (2006). *Simplified GLBA compliance for community banks using fortinet hardware, software and partner services* (Whitepaper WPR127-0806-R1). Retrieved from http://www.fortinet.com/doc/whitepaper/GLBA-Compliance.pdf

Fu, X., Ling, Z., Yu, W., & Luo, J. (2010). Cyber crime scene investigations (C2SI) through cloud computing. In *Proceedings of 2010 IEEE 30th International Conference on Distributed Computing Systems Workshops* (ICDCSW). IEEE.

Gandhi, A., Gupta, V., Harchol-Balter, M., & Kozuch, M. A. (2010). Optimality analysis of energy-performance trade-off for server farm management. *Performance Evaluation, 67*(11), 1155–1171. doi:10.1016/j.peva.2010.08.009

Ganore, P. (2013). *Security in cloud computing.* Retrieved from http://blog.esds.co.in/

Gantz, J. (2011). *Extracting value from chaos.* Retrieved December 2012 from http://www.emc.com/digital_universe

Garcia, A., & Kalva, H. (2011). Cloud transcoding for mobile video content delivery. In *Proceedings of the IEEE International Conference on Consumer Elecronics* (ICCE). IEEE.

GDPdU. (2002). *Principles of data access and auditing of digital documents.* Retrieved from http://www.avendata.de/downloads/e-GDPdU.pdf

Gellman, R. (2009). *Privacy in the clouds: Risks to privacy and confidentiality from cloud computing.* Paper presented at World Privacy Forum. New York, NY.

Gervais, D., & Hundman, D. (2012). Cloud control: Copyright, global memes and privacy. *Journal on Telecommunications & High Technology Law, 53,* 10.

Getov, V. (2012). Security as a service in smart clouds – Opportunities and concerns. In *Proceedings of the IEEE 36th Annual Computer Software and Applications Conference* (COMPSAC), (pp. 373-379). IEEE.

Getting, B. (2007). *Basic definitions: Web 1.0, web 2.0, web 3.0.* Retrieved March 2013 from http://www.practicalecommerce.com/articles/464-Basic-Definitions-Web-1-0-Web-2-0-Web-3-0

Ghatak, A. (2012). *Cloud insurance for ramping up cloud adoption.* TechRepublic Blog. Retrieved from http://www.techrepublic.com/blog/datacenter/cloud-insurance-for-ramping-up-cloud-adoption/5606

Giallonardo, E., & Zimeo, E. (2007). More semantics in QoS matching. In *Proceedings of IEEE Inter. Conf. Service-Oriented Computing and Applications* (pp. 163–171). Newport Beach, CA: IEEE.

GLBA. (2006). Retrieved from http://business.ftc.gov/privacy-and-security/gramm-leach-bliley-act

Glisson, W. B., McDonald, A., & Welland, R. (2006). Web engineering security: A practitioner's perspective. In *Proceedings of the 6th International Conference on Web Engineering.* Palo Alto, CA: ACM.

GoGrid Cloud Hosting. (2010). *The cloud pyramid: Cloud infrastructure.* Retrieved from http://pyramid.gogrid.com/cloud-infrastructure/

Goldberg, R. P. (1973). *Architectural principles for virtual computer systems.* National Technical Information Service (NIST), U.S. Department of Commerce. Retrieved from http://www.dtic.mil/cgi-bin/GetTRDoc?AD=AD772809&Location=U2&doc=GetTRDoc.pdf

Google Chrome Team. (2010). *20 things I learned about browsers and the web.* Retrieved December 2012 from http://www.20thingsilearned.com/en-US

Google Cloud Platform. (n.d.). Retrieved April 2013 from https://cloud.google.com/

Google, Inc. (2012). *Google app. engine – The platform for your next great idea.* Retrieved December 2012 from https://cloud.google.com/files/GoogleAppEngine.pdf

Google's Approach to IT Security. (n.d.). Retrieved April 2013 from https://cloud.google.com/files/Google-CommonSecurity-WhitePaper-v1.4.pdf

Gopalakrishnan, A. (2009). Cloud computing identity management. *SETLabs Briefings, 7*(7), 45–54.

Grid Computing Info Center. (n.d.). Retrieved December 2012 from http://gridcomputing.com

Grid Computing. (n.d.). Retrieved December 2012 from http://en.wikipedia.org/wiki/Grid_computing

Grover, R., & Srinivasan, V. (1992). Evaluating the multiple effects of retail promotions on. *JMR, Journal of Marketing Research, 29*(1), 76. doi:10.2307/3172494

Grush, M. (2011). *A community cloud strategy for the education enterprise.* Retrieved December 2012 from http://campustechnology.com/articles/2011/09/08/a-community-cloud-strategy-for-the-education-enterprise.aspx

Guo, Z., Song, M., & Song, J. (2010). A governance model for cloud computing. In *Proceedings of the International Conference on Management and Service Science.* IEEE.

Gutierrez, H. (2011). Peering through the cloud: The future of intellectual property and computing. *Fed. Cir. B.J., 580,* 20.

Hadley, M., Nielsen, H., Mendelsohn, N., Gudgin, M., & Moreau, J. (2003). *SOAP version 1.2 part 1: Messaging framework.* Retrieved from http://www.w3.org/TR/2003/REC-soap12-part1-20030624/

Handler, G. Y., & Mirchandani, P. B. (1979). *Location on networks: Theory and algorithms.* Cambridge, MA: MIT Press.

Harbour, P., & Koslov, T. (2010). Section 2 in the web 2.0 world: An expanded vision of relevant product markets. *Antitrust Law Journal, 769,* 76.

Harnik, D., Pinkas, B., & Shulman-Peleg, A. (2010). Side channels in cloud services: Deduplication in cloud storage. *IEEE Security & Privacy, 8*(6), 40–47. doi:10.1109/MSP.2010.187

Hasan, R., Winslett, M., & Sion, R. (2007). *Requirements of secure storage systems for healthcare.* Stony Brook, NY: Network Security and Applied Cryptography Lab. doi:10.1007/978-3-540-75248-6_12

Hayles, N. K. (1991). Introduction: Complex dynamics in literature and science. In N. K. Hayles (Ed.), *Chaos and order: Complex dynamics in literature and science* (pp. 1–36). Chicago: Univ. Chicago Press.

Heart, T., Tsur, N., & Pliskin, N. (2010). Software-as-a-service vendors: Are they ready to successfully deliver? *Global Sourcing of Information Technology and Business Processes, 55*, 151–184. doi:10.1007/978-3-642-15417-1_9

Hess, K., & Newman, A. (2010). *Practical virtualization solutions: Virtualization from the trenches.* Upper Saddle River, NJ: Prentice Hall/Pearson Education.

Hill, J. et al. (2007). Law, information technology, and medical errors: Toward a national healthcare information network approach to improving patient care and reducing malpractice costs. *University of Illinois Journal of Law. Technology and Policy, 159*, 159–165.

Hill, J., Langvardt, A., Massey, A., & Rinehart, J. (2011). A proposed national health information network architecture and complementary federal preemption of state health information privacy laws. *48. American Business Law Journal*, 503. doi:10.1111/j.1744-1714.2011.01120.x

HIPAA. (2013). Retrieved from http://www.hhs.gov/ocr/privacy/

Hoepfner, G. K., & Mata, F. (1993). A multi-criteria decision analysis methodology for selection of a preferred residence based on physical attributes. *Computers & Industrial Engineering, 25*(1-4), 365–368. doi:10.1016/0360-8352(93)90297-B

Hon, C.-C., Guh, Y.-Y., Wang, K.-M., & Lee, E. S. (1996). Fuzzy multiple attributes and multiple hierarchical decision making. *Computers & Mathematics with Applications (Oxford, England), 32*(12), 109–119. doi:10.1016/S0898-1221(96)00211-8

Hoover, N. (2011). *Cloud security: Better than we think?* Retrieved from http://www.informationweek.com/government/cloud-saas/cloud-security-better-than-we-think/231902850

Hotaling, M. (2003). IDS load balancer security audit: An administrator's perspective. *SANS Institute.* Retrieved from http://it-audit.sans.org/community/papers/ids-load-balancer-security-audit-administratorsperspective_119

Hristidis, V., Farfán, F., Burke, R. P., Rossi, A. F., & White, J. A. (2007). *Information discovery on electronic medical records.* Paper presented at NSF Symposium on Next Generation of Data Mining and Cyber-Enabled Discovery for Innovation (NGDM). New York, NY. Bhaskaran, S., Suryanarayana, G., Basu, A., & Joseph, R. (2013). *Cloud-enabled search for disparate healthcare data: A case study.* Paper presented at IEEE Cloud Computing for Emerging Markets. Bangalore, India.

Hurwitz, J., Bloor, R., Kaufman, M., & Halper, F. (2012). *Cloud services for dummies.* Retrieved December 2012 from http://www.businesscloudsummit.com/sites/all/themes/bcsummit/downloads/Cloud%20Services%20for%20Dummies.pdf

Hurwitz, J., Bloor, R., Kaufman, M., & Halper, F. (2013). *Service-oriented architecture for dummies.* Retrieved March 2013 from http://www.dummies.com/Section/id-612246.html

InfoWorld. (n.d.). *Cloud computing deep dive: The journey to the private cloud.* Retrieved December 2012 from http://computerworld.com.edgesuite.net/insider/infoworld_private_cloud_insider.pdf

Interactive Computing. (n.d.). Retrieved December 2012 from http://pdp-1.computerhistory.org/pdp-1/index.php?f=theme&s=2&ss=1

ISO 27001: An Introduction to ISO 27001 (ISO27001). (n.d.). Retrieved April 2013 from http://www.27000.org/iso-27001.htm

ISO/IEC Certification Standards. (2013). Retrieved from http://www.iso27001security.com/html/27001.html

Jacob, P., & Davie, B. (2005). Technical challenges in the delivery of interprovider QoS. *IEEE Communications Magazine, 43*(6), 112. doi:10.1109/MCOM.2005.1452839

Jakobsson, M., Shi, E., Golle, P., & Chow, R. (2009). Implicit authentication for mobile devices. In *Proceedings of the 4th USENIX Workshop on Hot Topics in Security (HotSec).* USENIX.

Jansen, W., & Grance, T. (2011). *Guidelines on security and privacy in public cloud computing (NIST Special Publication 800-144).* Washington, DC: NIST.

Jennings, R. (2011). *Cloud computing with the Windows Azure platform*. Indianapolis, IN: Wiley.

JetBlue Airways (JetBlue) on Twitter. (n.d.). Retrieved March 2013 from https://twitter.com/jetblue

Johnson, M. E. (2009). Data hemorrhages in the health-care sector. In *Financial cryptography and data security*. Berlin: Springer-Verlag. doi:10.1007/978-3-642-03549-4_5

Jung, S., Hundewale, N., & Zelikovsky, A. (2005). *Energy efficiency of load balancing in MANET routing protocols*. Paper presented at the Software Engineering, Artificial Intelligence, Networking and Parallel/Distributed Computing, 2005 and First ACIS International Workshop on Self-Assembling Wireless Networks. SNPD/SAWN 2005. New York, NY.

Kamara, S., & Lauter, K. (2010). Cryptographic cloud storage. In *Proceedings of the 1st Workshop on RealLife Cryptographic Protocols and Standardization*. Academic Press.

Kamiyama, N. (2013). Designing data center network by analytic hierarchy process. *Computer Networks, 57*(3), 658–667. doi:10.1016/j.comnet.2012.10.009

Kaplan, D., & Glass, L. (1995). *Understanding nonlinear dynamics*. New York: Springer-Verlag. doi:10.1007/978-1-4612-0823-5

Karki, K. C., & Patankar, S. V. (2006). Airflow distribution through perforated tiles in raised-floor data centers. *Building and Environment, 41*(6), 734–744. doi:10.1016/j.buildenv.2005.03.005

Kauffman, S. A. (1993). *The origins of order: Self-organization and selection in evolution*. Oxford, UK: Oxford University Press.

Kaufman, L. M. (2009). Data security in the world of cloud computing. *IEEE Security and Privacy, 7*(4), 61–64. doi:10.1109/MSP.2009.87

Khajeh-Hosseini, A., Sommerville, I., & Sriram, I. (2010). Research challenges for enterprise cloud computing. *CoRR, abs/1001.3257*.

Khan, A., Kiah, M., Khan, S., & Madani, S. (2013). Towards secure mobile cloud computing: A survey. *Future Generation Computer Systems, 29*(5), 1278–1299. doi:10.1016/j.future.2012.08.003

Kim, I., Pervez, Z., Khattak, A., & Lee, S. (2010). Chord based identity management for e-healthcare cloud applications. In *Proceedings of the 10th IEEE/IPSJ Annual International Symposium on Applications and the Internet*. IEEE.

King, S. T., Chen, P. M., Wang, Y., Verbowski, C., Wang, H., & Lorch, R. (2006). SubVirt: Implementing malware with virtual machines. In *Proceedings of the 2006 IEEE Symposium on Security and Privacy*, (pp. 314–327). IEEE. Retrieved from http://web.eecs.umich.edu/~pmchen/papers/king06.pdf

Kizza, J. M. (2013). *Guide to computer network security* (2nd ed.). Berlin: Springer. doi:10.1007/978-1-4471-4543-1

Klems, M., Nimis, J., & Tai, S. (2009). Do clouds compute? A framework for estimating the value of cloud computing. *Designing E-Business Systems: Markets, Services, &. Networks, 22*, 110–123.

Knipp, E., et al. (2009). *Predicts 2010: Application infrastructure for cloud computing*. Retrieved from http://www.gartner.com/DisplayDocument?doc_cd=172072&ref=g_BETAnoreg

Knorr, E. (2012, February). Shaking up the data center: 2011-a year of surging private cloud and public cloud build-outs, cloud computing deep dive. *InfoWorld Special Report*.

Ko, R., Lee, B., & Pearson, S. (2011). Towards achieving accountability, auditability and trust in cloud computing. *Advances in Computing and Communications: Communications in Computer and Information Science, 444*(193).

Kodali, R. R. (2005). *What is service-oriented architecture? An introduction to SOA*. Retrieved March 2013 from http://www.javaworld.com/javaworld/jw-06-2005/jw-0613-soa.html

Kondo, D., Javadi, B., Malecot, P., Cappello, F., & Anderson, D. (2009). Cost-benefit analysis of cloud computing versus desktop grids. In *Proceedings of IEEE Int. Symp. on Parallel & Distributed Processing*. Washington, DC: IEEE Computer Society.

Kremer, U., Hicks, J., & Rehg, J. (2001). A compilation framework for power and energy management on mobile computers. In *Proceedings of the 14th International Conference on Languages and Compilers for Parallel Computing* (LCPC'01). LCPC.

Krigsman, M. (2012). *Cloud research: Cost matters most and confusion remains*. Retrieved December 2012 from http://www.zdnet.com/cloud-research-cost-matters-most-and-confusion-remains-7000009136/

La, H., & Kim, S. (2009). A systematic process for developing high quality SaaS cloud services. In *Proceedings of 1st Int. Conf. on Cloud Computing* (pp. 278–289). Beijing, China: IEEE.

Laprie, J.-C. (1995). Dependable computing and fault tolerance: Concepts and terminology. In *Proceedings of 25th International Symp. Fault-Tolerant Computing* (pp. 27–30). Pasadena, CA: IEEE.

Lawson, N., Orr, J., & Klar, D. (2003). The HIPAA privacy rule: An overview of compliance initiatives and requirements. *Defense Counsel Journal, 70*, 127–149.

Lawton, G. (2011). *Cloud computing crime poses unique forensics challenges*. Retrieved from http://searchcloudcomputing.techtarget.com/feature/Cloud-computing-crime-poses-unique-forensics-challenges

Lee, C., Lehoczky, J., Rajkumar, R., & Siewiorek, D. (1999). On quality of service optimization with discrete QoS options. In *Proceedings of 5th IEEE Real-Time Technology and Applications Symp.* (pp. 276-286). Washington, DC: IEEE Computer Society.

Lee, Y.-H., & Kim, S. (1993). Neural network applications for scheduling jobs on parallel machines. *Proceedings of the 21st International Conference on Computers and Industrial Engineering, 25*(1-4), 227.

Lehner, W., & Sattler, K. (2010). Database as a service (DBaaS). In *Proceedings of the International Conference on Data Engineering* (ICDE), (pp. 1216-1217). Long Beach, CA: ICDE.

Lenk, P. J., & Rao, A. G. (1993). Nonstationary conditional trend analysis: An application to scanner panel data. *JMR, Journal of Marketing Research, 30*(3), 288. doi:10.2307/3172882

Lent, R. (2012). A model for network server performance and power consumption. *Sustainable Computing: Informatics and Systems*. http://dx.doi.org/10.1016/j.suscom.2012.03.004

Li, L., Li, X., Youxia, S., & Wen, L. (2010). Research on mobile multimedia broadcasting service integration based on cloud computing. In *Proceedings of the IEEE International Conference on Multimedia Technology* (ICMT). IEEE.

Liang, G.-S., & Wang, M.-J. J. (1993). Evaluating human reliability using fuzzy relation. *Microelectronics and Reliability, 33*(1), 63–80. doi:10.1016/0026-2714(93)90046-2

Limam, N., & Boutaba, R. (2010). Assessing software service quality and trustworthiness at selection time. *IEEE Transactions on Software Engineering, 36*(4), 559–574. doi:10.1109/TSE.2010.2

Limitations of IPV4. (n.d.). Retrieved April 2013 from http://www.omnisecu.com/tcpip/ipv6/limitations-of-ipv4.htm

LogRhythm. (2011). *PCI and PA DSS compliance with LogRhythm*. Author.

Loper, J., & Parr, S. (2007). Energy efficiency in data centers: A new policy frontier. *Environmental Quality Management, 16*(4), 83–97. doi:10.1002/tqem.20144

Love, R., Morris, J., & Wesolowsky, G. (1988). *Facility location: Models and methods*. Amsterdam: North-Holland.

MacDonald, N. (2011). Yes, hypervisors are vulnerable. *Gartner Blog Network*. Retrieved from http://blogs.gartner.com/neil_macdonald/2011/01/26/yes-hypervisors-are-vulnerable/

Marko, K. (2012). *State of storage 2012*. Retrieved December 2012 from http://reports.informationweek.com/abstract/24/8697/Storage-Server/Research:-State-of-Storage-2012.html

Matthews, J., Garfinkel, T., Hoff, C., & Wheeler, J. (2009). Virtual machine contracts for datacenter and cloud computing environments. In *Proceedings of the 1st Workshop on Automated Control for Datacenters and Clouds* (ACDC 09), (pp. 25-30). ACDC.

McAfee. (2013). *PCI DSS compliance/McAfee compliances solution*. Retrieved from http://www.mcafee.com/us/solutions/compliance/pci-compliance.aspx

McKendrick, J. (2010). *NASA's nebula: A stellar example of private clouds in government*. Retrieved December 2012 from http://www.zdnet.com/blog/service-oriented/nasas-nebula-a-stellar-example-of-private-clouds-in-government/5267

Mell, P., & Grance, T. (2011). *The NIST definition of cloud computing*. Retrieved December 2012 from http://csrc.nist.gov/publications/nistpubs/800-145/SP800-145.pdf

Mell, P., & Grance, T. (2011). *The NIST definition of cloud computing, September 2011 (NIST Special Publication 800-145)*. Washington, DC: NIST.

Menascé, D., & Casalicchio, E., & Vinod. (2010). On optimal service selection in service oriented architectures. *Journal of Performance Evaluation, 67*(8). doi:10.1016/j.peva.2009.07.001

Merhi, M. I., & Ahluwalia, P. (2013). Information security policies compliance: The role of organizational punishment. In *Proceedings of the Nineteenth Americas Conference on Information Systems*. Chicago, IL: ACM.

Metzler, J., & Taylor, S. (2011). The data center network transition: Wide area networking alert. *Network World*. Retrieved from http://www.networkworld.com/newsletters/frame/2011/080811wan1.html?source=nww_rss

Microsoft. (2012). *Guiding principles and architecture for addressing life science compliance in the cloud*. Redmond, WA: Microsoft.

Minar, N., & Hedlund, M. (2001). A network of peers: Peer-to-peer models through the history of the internet. In *Peer-to-peer: Harnessing the power of disruptive technologies*. Retrieved December 2012 from http://oreilly.com/catalog/peertopeer/chapter/ch01.html

MIT. (2006). Inter-provider quality of service. Cambridge, MA: MIT Communications Futures Program (CFP) Quality of Service Working Group.

Moon-Kyu, L. (2012). A storage assignment policy in a man-on-board automated storage retrieval system. *International Journal of Production Research, 30*(10), 2281.

Moore, T. (2010). The economics of cybersecurity: Principles and policy options. *International Journal of Critical Infrastructure Protection, 3*(3-4), 103–117. doi:10.1016/j.ijcip.2010.10.002

Mulazzani, M., Schrittwieser, S., Leithner, M., Huber, M., & Weippl, E. (2011). *Dark clouds on the horizon: Using cloud storage as attack vector and online slack space*. USENIX Security.

NDB Accounts and Consults. (2008). *Introduction to SAS 70 audits*. Retrieved from http://www.sas70.us.com/SAS70TrainingvideoI.php

Nelson, P., & Steuart, C. (2009). *Guide to computer forensics and investigations* (4th ed.). Boston, MA: Course Technology.

Network as a Service. (n.d.). Retrieved December 2012 from http://en.wikipedia.org/wiki/Network_as_a_service

NetWrix. (2012). *FISMA compliance*. Retrieved from http://www.netwrix.com/FISMA_Compliance.html

Newton, D. (2011). *Dropbox authentication: Insecure by design*. Retrieved from http://dereknewton.com/2011/04/dropbox-authentication-static-host-ids/

NIST SP-800-66. (2008). *An introductory resource guide for implementing the health insurance portability and accountability act (HIPAA) security rule*. National Institute of Standards and Technology. Retrieved from http://csrc.nist.gov/publications/nistpubs/800-66-Rev1/SP-800-66-Revision1.pdf

NIST. (1995). *An introduction to computer security: The NIST handbook (Special Publication 800-12)*. Gaithersburg, MD: National Institute of Technology.

NIST. (2006). *Guide for developing security plans for federal information systems*. Gaithersburg, MD: National Institute for Standards and Technology.

Nunez, D., Agudo, I., & Lopez, J. (2012). Integrating OpenID with proxy re-encryption to enhance privacy in cloud-based identity services. In *Proceedings of IEEE 4th International Conference on Cloud Computing Technology and Science* (CloudCom). IEEE.

O'Dell, J. (2012). *Adobe acquires behance to bring more community into creative cloud.* Retrieved December 2012 from http://venturebeat.com/2012/12/20/adobe-acquires-behance/

O'Reilly, T. (2008). *Web 2.0 and cloud computing.* Retrieved March 2013 from http://radar.oreilly.com/2008/10/web-20-and-cloud-computing.html

OASIS. (2005). *SAML V2.0 executive overview.* Retrieved from https://www.oasis-open.org/

OAuthSite. (2007). Retrieved from http://oauth.net/

OAuthwiki. (2012). Retrieved from http://en.wikipedia.org/wiki/OAuth

Oberheide, J., Veeraraghavan, K., Cooke, E., Flinn, J., & Jahanian, F. (2008). Virtualized in-cloud security services for mobile devices. In *Proceedings of the 1st Workshop on Virtualization in Mobile Computing* (MobiVirt). MobiVirt.

OECD. (2013). *OECD guidelines on the protection of privacy and transborder flows of personal data.* Retrieved from http://www.oecd.org/document/18/0,2340,en_2649_34255_1815186_1_1_1_1,00.html

Ohm, P. (2011). Massive hard drives, general warrants and the power of magistrate judges. *Virginia Law Review in Brief, 1*(8), 97.

OMB. (2012). *FISMA compliance report to US congress for 2011.* Washington, DC: Office of Management and Budget.

Önüt, S., Efendigil, T., & Soner Kara, S. (2010). A combined fuzzy MCDM approach for selecting shopping center site: An example from Istanbul, Turkey. *Expert Systems with Applications, 37*(3), 1973–1980. doi:10.1016/j.eswa.2009.06.080

OpenIdwiki. (2005). Retrieved from http://en.wikipedia.org/wiki/OpenID

Oracle. (2010). *Identity federation whitepaper.* Retrieved from http://www.oracle.com/technetwork/middleware/id-mgmt/overview/idm-tech-wp-11g-r1-154356.pdf

Ostermark, R. (1997). Temporal interdependence in fuzzy MCDM problems. *Fuzzy Sets and Systems, 88*(1), 69–79. doi:10.1016/S0165-0114(96)00046-2

Patel, P., Ranabahu, A., & Sheth, A. (2009). Service level agreement in cloud computing. In *Proceedings of Cloud Workshops at OOPSLA09.* Retrieved from http://knoesis.wright.edu/library/download/OOPSLA_cloud_wsla_v3.pdf

Pathan, M., Broberg, J., & Buyya, R. (2009). Maximizing utility for content delivery clouds. In *Proceedings of 10th Int. Conf. on Web Information Systems Engineering* (pp. 13-28). Berlin: Springer-Verlag.

Pauley, W. (2010). Cloud provider transparency: An empirical evaluation. *IEEE Security and Privacy, 8*(6), 32–39. doi:10.1109/MSP.2010.140

PCI Security Standards Council. (2010). *Requirements and security assessment procedures.* Retrieved from https://www.pcisecuritystandards.org/documents/pci_dss_v2.pdf

PCI Security Standards Council. (2011). *Information supplement: PCI DSS virtualization guidelines.* PCI.

PCI. (2013). Retrieved from https://www.pcisecuritystandards.org/security_standards

Pennell, J. (2011). *Defining best practices in cloud computing.* IOActive, Inc. Retrieved from http://www.ioactive.com/cloud-computing.html

Perry, G. (2008). *How cloud and utility computing are different.* Retrieved December 2012 from http://gigaom.com/2008/02/28/how-cloud-utility-computing-are-different/

Phil Ins. (2011). *Network security & privacy liability coverage supplement.* Philadelphia Insurance Companies. Retrieved from www.phly.com/products/forms/MiscForms/NetworkSecurityCoverageSupplement.pdf

PingIdentity. (n.d.). Retrieved from https://www.pingidentity.com/resource-center/oauth-essentials.cfm

Ponemon Institute. (2011). *Security of cloud computing providers study.* Ponemon Institute.

Ponemon Institute. (2012). *The 2011 cost of data breach study: Global.* Symantec.

Ponemon. (2013). *Security of cloud computing users.* Ponemon Institute Study.

PriceWaterhouseCoopers. (2007). *Healthcare in India: Emerging market report 2007*. Retrieved from http://www. pwc.com/en_GX/gx/healthcare/pdf/emerging-market-report-hc-in-india.pdf

Public Cloud Examples and Case Studies. (n.d.). Retrieved December 2012 from http://www.cloudpro.co.uk/cloud-essentials/public-cloud/case-studies

RackSpace. (2011). *Understanding the cloud computing stack SaaS, PaaS, IaaS*. Retrieved from http://broadcast. rackspace.com/hosting_knowledge/whitepapers/Understanding-the-Cloud-Computing-Stack.pdf

Rahman, R. M., Alhajj, R., & Barker, K. (2008). Replica selection strategies in data grid. *Journal of Parallel and Distributed Computing, 68*(12), 1561–1574. doi:10.1016/j.jpdc.2008.07.013

Rajabi, S., Hipel, K. W., & Kilgour, D. M. (1995). *Multiple criteria decision making under interdependence of actions - Systems, man and cybernetics*. Paper presented at the IEEE International Conference on Systems, Man and Cybernetics --Intelligent Systems for the 21st Century. New York, NY.

Raman, T. V. (2009). Toward 2w, beyond web 2.0. *Communications of the ACM, 52*(2), 52–59. doi:10.1145/1461928.1461945

Ramasastry, A. (2009). *The EU-US safe harbor does not protect US companies with unsafe privacy practices*. Retrieved from http://writ.news.findlaw.com/ramasastry/20091117.html

Recker, J., Rosemann, M., & Gohar, E. R. (2011). *Measuring the carbon footprint of business processes*. Paper presented at the Business Process Management Workshops. New York, NY.

Reed, G. B. (2010). *Silver clouds, dark linings: A concise guide to cloud computing*. Upper Saddle River, NJ: Prentice Hall.

Reese, G. (2009). *Cloud application architectures: Building applications and infrastructure in the cloud*. Sebastopol, CA: O'Reilly.

Ren, W., Yu, L., Gao, R., & Xiong, F. (2011). Lightweight and compromise resilient storage outsourcing with distributed secure accessibility in mobile cloud computing. *Tsinghua Science & Technology Report, 16*(5), 520–528. doi:10.1016/S1007-0214(11)70070-0

Rhoton, J., & Haukioja, R. (2011). *Cloud computing architected: Solution design handbook*. Recursive Press.

Ristenpart, T., Tromer, E., Schacham, H., & Savage, S. (2009). Hey, you, get off of my cloud: Exploring information leakage in third-party compute clouds. In *Proceedings of the 16th ACM Conference on Computer and Communications Security*, (pp. 199-212). ACM.

Ritchey, T. (2006). Problem structuring using computer-aided morphological analysis. *The Journal of the Operational Research Society, 57*(7), 792–801. doi:10.1057/palgrave.jors.2602177

Rivoire, S., Shah, M. A., Ranganatban, P., Kozyrakis, C., & Meza, J. (2007). Models and metrics to enable energy-efficiency optimizations. *Computer, 40*(12), 39–48. doi:10.1109/MC.2007.436

Robinson, N., Valeri, L., Cave, J., Starkey, T., Grauz, H., Creese, S., & Hopkins, P. (2010). *The cloud: Understanding the security, privacy and trust challenges*. Brussels: Directorate-General Information Society and Media, European Commission. doi:10.1017/CBO9780511564765.012

Rodero-Merino, L., Vaquero, L. M., Gil, V., Galán, F., Fontán, J., Montero, R.S., & Llorente, I. M. (2010). From infrastructure delivery to service management in clouds. *Future Generation Computer System, 26*(8), 1226-1240. DOI=10.1016/j.future.2010.02.013

Rouse, M. (2010). *Hybrid cloud*. Retrieved December 2012 from http://searchcloudcomputing.techtarget.com/definition/hybrid-cloud

Rouse, M. (2012). *Community cloud*. Retrieved December 2012 from http://searchcloudstorage.techtarget.com/definition/community-cloud

Rudenko, A., Reiher, P., Popek, G., & Kuenning, G. (1998). Saving portable computer battery power through remote process execution. *ACM SIGMOBILE Mobile Computing and Communications Review, 2*(1), 19–26. doi:10.1145/584007.584008

Sacharen, C., & Hunter, J. (2008, February 5). IBM and European Union launch joint research initiative for cloud computing. *IBM News Room*. Retrieved March 2013 from http://www-03.ibm.com/press/us/en/pressrelease/23448.wss

Salama, M., Shawish, A., & Kouta, M. (2011). *Generic ontology-based QoS model for cloud computing*. Paper presented at the International Conference on Computer and Information Technology (ICCIT 2011). Amsterdam, The Netherlands.

Salama, M., Shawish, A., Zeid, A., & Kouta, M. (2012). Integrated QoS utility-based model for cloud computing service provider selection. In *Proceedings of 36th Annual IEEE Computer Software and Applications Conference (COMPSAC 2012)*. IEEE.

Salesforce. (2013). Retrieved from http://www.salesforce.com

Santos, N., Gummadi, K. P., & Rodrigues, R. (2009). Towards trusted cloud computing. In *Proceedings of HotCloud*. San Diego, CA: USENIX. Retrieved from http://www.usenix.org/event/hotcloud09/tech/full_papers/santos.pdf

Sarna, D. E. Y. (2011). *Implementing and developing cloud computing applications*. Boca Raton, FL: CRC Press, Taylor & Francis Group.

Scardino, S. (2005). *Spreadsheet/personal computing kills off time sharing*. Retrieved December 2012 from http://corphist.computerhistory.org/corphist/view.php?s=stories&id=46

Scarfone, K., Souppaya, M., & Hoffman, P. (2011). *Guide to security for full virtualization technologies* (Special Publication 800-125). National Institute of Standards and Technology. Retrieved March 2013 from http://csrc.nist.gov/publications/nistpubs/800-125/SP800-125-final.pdf

SearchSecurity Inc. (2009). *HIPAA compliance manual: Training, audit and requirement checklist*. Retrieved from http://searchsecurity.techtarget.com/tutorial/HIPAA-compliance-manual-Training-audit-and-requirement-checklist

Sengupta, S., Kaulgud, V., & Sharma, V. S. (2011). Cloud computing security – Trends and research directions. In *Proceedings of IEEE World Congress on Services*, (pp. 524-531). IEEE.

Shehabi, A., Masanet, E., Price, H., Horvath, A., & Nazaroff, W. W. (2011). Data center design and location: Consequences for electricity use and greenhouse-gas emissions. *Building and Environment*, *46*(5), 990–998. doi:10.1016/j.buildenv.2010.10.023

Shin, S. (2003). *Secure web services: The upcoming web services security schemes should help drive web services forward*. Retrieved from http://www.javaworld.com/javaworld/jw-03-2003/jw-0321-wssecurity.html

Shozu. (n.d.). Retrieved from http://www.shozu.com/portal/index.do

Sneide, G. A. (1995). A study of factors in office site selection using discrete choice models. *Transportation Research Part A, Policy and Practice*, *29*(1), 79–80. doi:10.1016/0965-8564(95)90286-4

Software Testing. (n.d.). Retrieved December 2012 from http://www.utest.com

Song, Z., Molina, J., Lee, S., Kotani, S., & Masuoka, R. (2009). TrustCube: An infrastructure that builds trust in client. In *Proceedings of the 1st International Conference on Future of Trust in Computing*, (pp. 68-79). Academic Press.

Spantzel, A., Squicciarini, A., & Bertino, E. (2005). Establishing and protecting digital identity in federation systems. In *Proceedings of the ACM Workshop on Digital Identity Management'05* (DIM'05), (pp. 11-19). ACM.

Spurzem, R. (2007). *SOX definition*. SearchCIO. Retrieved from http://searchcio.techtarget.com/definition/Sarbanes-Oxley-Act

Squicciarini, A., Sundareswaran, S., & Dan, L. (2010). *Preventing information leakage from indexing in the cloud*. Paper presented at IEEE 3rd International Conference on Cloud Computing (CLOUD). New York, NY.

Stallings, W., & Case, T. (2013). *Business data communications: Infrastructure, networking and security* (7th ed.). Upper Saddle River, NJ: Prentice Hall.

Stankov, I., Datsenka, R., & Kurbel, K. (n.d.). *Service level agreement as an instrument to enhance trust in cloud computing – An analysis of infrastructure-as-a-service providers*. Retrieved from http://aisel.aisnet.org/amcis2012/proceedings/HCIStudies/12/

Stantchev, V., & Schröpfer, C. (2009). Negotiating and enforcing QoS and SLAs in grid and cloud computing. *Advances in Grid and Pervasive Computing, 5529,* 25–35. doi:10.1007/978-3-642-01671-4_3

Stewart, T. J. (1992). A critical survey on the status of multiple criteria decision making theory and practice. *Omega, 20*(5-6), 569–586. doi:10.1016/0305-0483(92)90003-P

Strickland, J. (2008). *How GoogleDocs works*. Retrieved from http://computer.howstuffworks.com/internet/basics/google-docs.htm

Strickland, J. (2008). *How utility computing works*. Retrieved December 2012 from http://computer.howstuffworks.com/utility-computing.htm

Subashini, S., & Kavitha, V. (2011). A survey on security issues in service delivery models of cloud computing. *Journal of Network and Computer Applications.* doi:10.1016/j.jnca.2010.07.006

Szefer, J., & Lee, R. B. (2011). A case for hardware protection of guest VMs from compromised hypervisors in cloud computing. In *Proceedings of Distributed Computing Systems Workshops (ICDCSW)*. IEEE.

Taheri, J., & Zomaya, A. Y. (2012). Energy efficiency metrics for data centers. *Energy Efficient Distributed Computing Systems, 88,* 245. doi:10.1002/9781118342015.ch9

Takabi, H., Joshi, J., & Ahn, G. (2010). Security and privacy challenges in cloud computing environments. *IEEE Security & Privacy, 8*(6), 24–31. doi:10.1109/MSP.2010.186

Teixeira, J. C., & Antunes, A. P. (2008). A hierarchical location model for public facility planning. *European Journal of Operational Research, 185*(1), 92–104. doi:10.1016/j.ejor.2006.12.027

Telecommunications, A. D. C. (2006). *Data center standards overview. TIA-942*. Author.

Tondello, G., & Siqueira, F. (2008). The QoS-MO ontology for semantic QoS modeling. In *Proceedings of ACM Symp. Applied computing* (pp. 2336–2340). ACM.

Tran, V., & Tsuji, H. (2009). A survey and analysis on semantics in QoS for web services. In *Proceedings of Inter. Conf. on Advanced Information Networking and Applications* (pp. 379–385). IEEE.

Trevino, L. K. (1992). The social effects of punishment in organizations: A justice perspective. *Academy of Management Review, 17*(4), 647–676.

USA Patriot Act. (2001). Retrieved from http://www.fincen.gov/statutes_regs/patriot/index.html

Vaidya, O. S., & Kumar, S. (2006). Analytic hierarchy process: An overview of applications. *European Journal of Operational Research, 169,* 1–29. doi:10.1016/j.ejor.2004.04.028

Vanderster, D., Dimopoulos, N. R. P.-H., & Sobie, R. (2009). Resource allocation on computational grids using a utility model and the knapsack problem. *Future Generation Computer Systems, 25*(1). doi:10.1016/j.future.2008.07.006 PMID:21308003

Varia, J. (2011). *Architecting for the cloud: Best practices*. Retrieved from media.amazonwebservices.com/Whitepaper_Security_Best_Practices_2010.pdf

Vascellaro, J. E. (2010). *Article*. Retrieved from http://blogs.wsj.com/digits/2009/03/08/1214/

Violino, B. (2010). Five cloud security trends experts see for 2011. *CSO: Security and Risk*. Retrieved from http://www.csoonline.com/article/647128/five-cloud-security-trends-experts-see-for-2011

WatchGuard. (2009). *How to meet PCI DSS requirements*. Retrieved from http://www.watchguard.com/docs/whitepaper/wg_pci-summary_wp.pdf

Wei, J., Zhang, X., Ammons, G., Bala, V., & Ning, P. (2009). Managing security of virtual machine images in a cloud environment. In *Proceedings of 2009 ACM Workshop on Cloud Computing Security*. ACM.

Wen, M., & Kang, R. (2011). Some optimal models for facility location–allocation problem with random fuzzy demands. *Applied Soft Computing, 11*(1), 1202–1207. doi:10.1016/j.asoc.2010.02.018

Willcocks, L., Venters, W., Whitley, E., & Hindle, J. (2012). *Cloud on the landscape: Problems and challenges in the new IT outsourcing landscape: From innovation to cloud services*. London: Palgrave Macmillan Publisher.

Worldwide LHC Computing Grid. (n.d.). Retrieved December 2012 from http://wlcg.web.cern.ch/

Xifeng, T., Ji, Z., & Peng, X. (2013). A multi-objective optimization model for sustainable logistics facility location. *Transportation Research Part D, Transport and Environment, 22*, 45–48. doi:10.1016/j.trd.2013.03.003

Xiong, K., & Perros, H. (2009). Service performance and analysis in cloud computing. In *Proceedings of 2009 Congress on Services – I (SERVICES 09)* (pp. 693-700). Washington, DC: IEEE Computer Society.

Yang, B., Tan, F., Dai, Y., & Guo, S. (2009). Performance evaluation of cloud service considering fault recovery. In *Proceedings of 1st International Conference on Cloud Computing* (CloudCom 09) (pp. 571–576). Beijing, China: IEEE.

Yang, H., & Tate, M. (2012). A descriptive literature review and classification of cloud computing research. *Communications of AIS, 31*(2), 35–60.

Yin, B., & Yang, H., P., F., & Chen, X. (2010). A semantic web services discovery algorithm based on QoS ontology. *Active Media Technology, 6335*, 166–173. doi:10.1007/978-3-642-15470-6_18

Yu, L., Tasi, W., Chen, X., Liu, L., Zhao, Y., Tang, L., & Zhao, W. (2010). Testing as a service over cloud. In *Proceedings of the 5th International Symposium on Service Oriented System Engineering* (SOSE), (pp. 181-188). SOSE.

Yu, T., Zhang, Y., & Lin, K. (2007). Efficient algorithms for web services selection with end-to-end QoS constraints. *ACM Trans. on the Web, 1*(1).

Yuan, D., Yang, Y., Liu, X., & Chen, J. (2010). A data placement strategy in scientific cloud workflows. *Future Generation Computer Systems, 26*(8), 1200–1214. doi:10.1016/j.future.2010.02.004

Zeng, L., Benatallah, B., Ngu, A., Dumas, M., & Kalag, J. (2004). QoS-aware middleware for web services composition. *IEEE Transactions on Software Engineering, 30*(5), 311–327. doi:10.1109/TSE.2004.11

Zhao, Z., Lage, N., & Crespi, N. (2011). User-centric service selection, integration and management through daily events. In *Proceedings of 2011 IEEE Inter. Conf. Pervasive Computing and Communications* (pp. 94-99). IEEE.

Zhou, M., Zhang, R., Zeng, D., & Qian, W. (2010). Services in the cloud computing era: A survey. In *Proceedings of the 4th International Universal Communication Symposium*, (pp. 40-46). Beijing, China: Academic Press.

Zhu, R., Sun, Z., & Hu, J. (2012). Special section: Green computing. *Future Generation Computer Systems, 28*(2), 368–370. doi:10.1016/j.future.2011.06.011

Zikopoulos, P., Eaton, C., Deutsch, T., Deroos, D., & Lapis, G. (2012). *Understanding big data: Analytics for enterprise class Hadoop and streaming data*. New York: McGraw-Hill.

Zissis, D., & Lekkas, D. (2012). Addressing cloud computing security issues. *Future Generation Computer Systems, 28*(3), 583–592. doi:10.1016/j.future.2010.12.006

About the Contributors

S. Srinivasan (nickname Srini) joined Texas Southern University (TSU) on August 1, 2013 as Associate Dean for Academic Affairs and Research as well as Distinguished Professor of Business Administration. Prior to coming to TSU, he was Chairman of the Division of International Business and Technology Studies at Texas A&M International University's A.R. Sanchez School of Business in Laredo, TX. Before coming to Laredo, he spent 23 years at the University of Louisville (UofL) in Louisville, Kentucky. At UofL, he held joint appointments in the Computer Information Systems Department in the College of Business and the Computer Science Department in the Speed School of Engineering. During the time there, he started the Information Security Program as a collaborative effort of multiple colleges. He was Director of the InfoSec program until 2010 when he left for Laredo. The program was designated a National Center of Academic Excellence in Information Assurance Education by the National Security Agency (NSA) and the Department of Homeland Security (DHS). He successfully wrote several grant proposals in support of the InfoSec Program. He is currently completing two books on Cloud Computing. One of them will be published in March 2014 and the other in July 2014. His area of research is Information Security. He has taught the Management of Information Systems course at the MBA level at UofL, in El Salvador and Greece, Texas A&M International University (TAMIU) as well as at Texas Southern University. At TAMIU, he taught the Business Intelligence course as an online course for MBA students. He used the Tableau software for students to have firsthand experience with Business Intelligence processing. He spent his sabbatical leaves from UofL in Siemens at their R&D facility in Munich, Germany; UPS Air Group in Louisville, KY; and GE Appliance Park in Louisville, KY. Besides these industry experiences, he has done consulting work for US Army, IBM and a major hospital company in Louisville, KY. He was the Conference Chair for the 21st Annual Southwestern Business Administration Teaching Conference held at the Jesse H. Jones School of Business at Texas Southern University from October 31 to November 1, 2013. He has been the Category Editor for *ACM Computing Reviews* since 1985 and is on the Editorial Boards of other journals as well. He volunteers his time extensively for public education causes.

* * *

Amarnath Basu heads the Technology Innovation Projects at Siemens Corporate Research and Technologies, India. His work focuses on exploring how disruptive technology can serve to fill the existing gaps in healthcare delivery in the Indian rural context. Amarnath has over a decade of experience in the healthcare domain and has made key contributions in developing solutions for prominent customers including Cleveland Clinic, USA.

Sabishaw Bhaskaran is currently a technology manager at Siemens Corporate Research and Technologies, India, and his work involves application research in the areas of distributed computing, cloud, and BigData. Sabishaw joined Siemens in 1999, as a software developer for its medical imaging products division and later served as one of its architects. His interests are in furthering the capabilities of conventional IT by leveraging upcoming technologies.

D. Boopathy is a Research Scholar doing his Ph.D in Computer Science in the Department of Information Technology at Bharathiar University. He is pursuing his research in the field of Information Security area. He did his Bachelor of Science in Computer Science, Master of Science in Information Technology and Master of Computer Application in Bharathiar University. He did his Master of Philosophy in Computer Science at Dr. G R D College of Science, Coimbatore. He has published research papers on Data Warehousing and Mining, Cloud Computing, and Cloud Security. His areas of interests are Information Security, Data Security and Privacy, Data Warehousing and Mining, Cloud Computing, Mobile Computing. He is a Life Member of Computer Society of India and Indian Science Congress Association.

Dipankar Dasgupta is a Professor of Computer Science at the University of Memphis, Tennessee, USA. His research interests are broadly in the area of scientific computing, design and development of intelligent software solutions inspired by biological processes. His areas of special interests include Artificial Immune Systems, Genetic Algorithms, Neural Networks, multi-agent systems and their applications in cyber security. He received research funding from various federal organizations including the U.S. Navy, NSF, DARPA, DoD, ONR, DHS, and IARPA. Dasgupta has more than 200 publications, which are being cited widely. He is the Founding Director of Center for Information Assurance at the University of Memphis. The University of Memphis is designated as a National Center of Academic Excellence in Information Assurance and Research. He was a program Co-Chair on Nature Inspired Cyber Health at the National Cyber Leap Year Summit in 2009. Dasgupta was the Principal Investigator of the DHS/FEMA-funded Adaptive Cyber Security Training Program, a multi-track, multi-level cyber-security training program. It utilizes a state-of-the-art learning technology for more effective online cyber security education and has been used nationwide through FEMA Website. These materials are now being updated and tailored to the needs of individual companies (e.g., a current project involves creating a Web-based Cyber Security Training Suite targeting a major organization's employees, vendors, and customers). Dasgupta has delivered over 150 lectures at leading conferences and at other universities. He has been involved in the program organization and review structure of more than 85 international academic conferences, also serving as a speaker and panelist at many of these conferences. Dasgupta is a senior member of IEEE and Life Member of ACM, and is the chair of IEEE Task Force on Artificial Immune Systems.

Mario A. Garcia is a Professor of Computer Science at Texas A&M University-Corpus Christi. Dr. Garcia received his Ph.D. in Computer Science from Texas A&M University in1997. He completed a Post-doc on Information Assurance at the University of Maryland University College in 2007. He has received Information Assurance training from Carnegie Mellon University, Purdue University, University of California at Berkeley, Rochester Institute of Technology, and Stanford University. His areas of Interest are Artificial Intelligence, Software Engineering, Information Assurance, Computer Forensics, and Network Security.

Bing He received his Ph.D. degree in Computer Science from University of Cincinnati in 2010, under the direction of Professor Dharma Agrawal. His research interests include network topology and architecture design, performance analysis and optimization, security and authentication mechanisms in distributed systems and wireless networks (e.g., wireless mesh networks, wireless sensor networks, wireless ad hoc networks, etc.). Currently, he is working on end-to-end QoS optimization for large scale networks in Cisco Systems. He has rich professional experience in design and development of wireless service gateway in 4G/WiMAX networks. He received his B.S. degree in communication engineering and M.S. degree in signal and information processing from Northern Jiaotong University of China. Before joining Cisco, he was with Aviat Networks, Bosch Research and Technology Center, and Honeywell Technology Solutions Lab.

Da Huo received a Ph. D in International Business Degree from College of Business Administration at Texas A&M International University. He did his intern research in the United Nations Conference of Trade and Development in 2008, and he received the first prize of Texas A&M Research Symposium in 2006. He is good at statistical programming such as SAS, STATA, Eviews, AMOS. He is currently an assistant professor of School of International Trade and Economics, at Central University of Finance and Economics, Beijing, China. He teaches International Business and International Marketing. His research is focused on international business area, including globalization of multinational companies, competitiveness of emerging markets, and corporate strategies and decisions. He is now a co-researcher in joint-research programs sponsored by National Natural Science Foundation of China and Ministry of Education of China. He has publications in academic journals and conferences such as Competitiveness Review, ICSSE, and ISM.

Roshan Joseph is a member of technical staff at Siemens Corporate Research and Technologies, India, with 17 years of experience in object oriented designing, modeling, implementation, and delivery of customer centric business applications. His expertise includes architecture analysis, designing, development, and deployment of cloud based, e-commerce, client/server, and Web applications in different operating systems and virtualized environments.

Joseph Migga Kizza received his B.S. in Mathematics and Computer Science in 1975 from Makerere University, Kampala, Uganda, M.S. in Computer Science in 1980 from California State University, USA, MA in Mathematics from University of Toledo, Ohio, USA in 1985, and a PhD in Computer Science in 1989 from The University of Nebraska-Lincoln, Nebraska, USA. Kizza has been with the department of Computer Science at the University of Tennessee at Chattanooga, Tennessee from 1989 where he is doing teaching and research in Social Computing, Operating Systems, Computer Network Security, and Computer Forensics. Dr. Kizza has organized a number of workshops and conferences on Computer Ethics, producing proceedings and has published several books on computer ethics and network security and cyberethics. He was appointed a UNESCO expert in Information Technology in 1994.

Sathish A. Kumar (Sathish) received his PhD in Computer Science and Engineering from University of Louisville in 2007. He also completed MBA from University of Louisville in 2001. He worked in IT industry for about 15 years in various roles. He is currently an Assistant Professor of Computer Science and Information Systems at the Coastal Carolina University, Conway, SC, USA. Dr. Kumar's research interests are in the area of information and cyber security, specifically in cloud security as well as applying cloud computing and big data for scientific and business applications. He has published several papers in conference proceedings and journals. He has been a member of program committee in many conferences and editorial board member of the journals.

Anita Lee-Post is Associate Professor of Marketing and Supply Chain, C. M. Gatton College of Business and Economics, University of Kentucky. She received the Ph.D. in Business Administration from the University of Iowa. Her research interests include sustainability, supply chain management, e-learning, Web mining, knowledge management, and group technology. She has published extensively in journals such as *OMEGA*, *Decision Sciences Journal of Innovative Education*, *Computers and Industrial Engineering*, and *International Journal of Production Research*. She is the author of *Knowledge-Based FMS Scheduling: An Artificial Intelligence Perspective*. She is an Editorial Board Member of *Production Planning and Control*, *International Journal of Business Information Systems*, *International Journal of Data Mining, Modeling and Management*, and *Journal of Managerial Issues*. She is the recipient of the Human Innovative Teaching Award in 2011, Teaching and Technology Innovation Program Award in 2006, and Kentucky Science and Engineering Foundation's Research and Development Excellence Program grant in 2003.

Michael Martin Losavio teaches in the Department of Justice Administration and the Department of Computer Engineering and Computer Science at the University of Louisville, Louisville, Kentucky, U.S.A. on issues of law, society, and information assurance in the computer engineering and justice administration disciplines. His focus is on law and social sciences as they relate to computer engineering and digital forensics. He holds a J.D. and a B.S. in Mathematics from Louisiana State University, Louisiana, U.S.A. He lectured on computer law and crime at Perm State University, supported by a 2013 Fulbright Specialist grant.

Durdana Naseem completed her Master's Degree in Computer Science in December 2012 from the University of Memphis. Her project work was on security issues in cloud computing. After her graduation, she moved to Santa Clara, CA, to work for a start-up company.

Ram Pakath is Professor of Finance and Quantitative Methods, C. M. Gatton College of Business and Economics, University of Kentucky. He holds a doctorate in Management (MIS) from Purdue University. Ram's research has appeared in such forums as *Decision Sciences, Decision Support Systems, European Journal of Operational Research, IEEE Transactions on Systems, Man, and Cybernetics, Information and Management, Information Systems Research*, and *Journal of Electronic Commerce Research*. Ram's contributions include chapters in: *Cases on Information Technology Management in Modern Organizations, Handbook on Decision Support Systems 1-Basic Themes, Handbook of Industrial Engineering,* and *Operations Research and Artificial Intelligence*. He is an Associate Editor of Decision Support Systems and an Editorial Board Member of *Journal of End User Computing, Management,* and *The Open Artificial Intelligence Journal*. His research has been funded by Ashland Oil, Gatton College of Business and Economics, IBM, Kentucky Science and Engineering Foundation, and University of Kentucky.

Pavel Pastukhov teaches Criminalistics and Criminal investigations in the areas of Computer Information, High Technology, and Legal means of Computer Security in the Department of Criminal Procedure and Criminalistics at Perm State University, Perm, Russia. He holds a Ph.D. and works as an Associate Professor at the Perm State University. He served as an investigator for the Ministry of Internal Affairs of Perm city and subsequently taught at the Department of Criminal Law Institute, where he became the Chair of the Criminalistics Law Institute. He retired with the rank of Colonel in 2011. The new trend of his research activities is related to proof in criminal procedure with electronic evidence. He is developing a new specialization in Computer Forensics in the investigation of computer crime. In his activity, he interacts with the law enforcement agencies and higher education institutions across the country.

Svetlana Polyakova teaches in the Department of English Language and Intercultural Communication at Perm State University, Perm, Russia. She teaches Legal English to the students of law, international law, and forensics, as well as Academic English to Ph.D. students in the Faculty of Law. Her focus is on intercultural professional communication in law, legal linguistics, ESP (English for Specific Purposes) and EAP (English for Academic Purposes). She holds a Ph.D. in Linguistics and is an Associate Professor at the Perm State National Research University. She has published in the areas of International Professional Communication in Law, Legal English, Legal Linguistics, Cognitive Linguistics, and IT in Legal Education.

Bina Ramamurthy is a faculty at University at Buffalo, Computer Science and Engineering Department. She has been involved in the STEM area research, curriculum development and instruction for the past two decades. Her current research is in data-intensive computing with emphasis on cloud infrastructures. She is the Principal Investigator on four NSF grants and a co-investigator in three IITG grants from SUNY. She has given numerous invited presentations at prominent conferences in the areas of data-intensive and big-data computing. She has been on the program committees of prestigious conferences including the High Performance Computing Conference (HPCIC2010), India, and Special Interest Group in Computer Science Education (SIGCSE). Bina Ramamurthy received the B.E. (Honors) in Electronics and Communication from Guindy Engineering College, Madras University, India, the M.S. in Computer Science from Wichita State University, KS, and the Ph.D. in Computer Engineering (1997) from the University at Buffalo, Buffalo, NY. She is a member of ACM and IEEE Computer Society.

Maria Salama received B.Sc. in Computer Science and Post-Graduate Diploma in Management Information Systems from Sadat Academy for Management Science, Cairo, Egypt, in 2001 and 2003, respectively. She received M.Sc. in Computer Science from Arab Academy for Sciences and Technology in 2011. She is now assistant lecturer in the British University in Egypt. Prior to joining the BUE, she had a solid experience in the industry, stepping from Web development to project leading. Her research interests are in software and Web engineering, Web services, and Cloud Computing.

Ahmed Shawish received the B.Sc. and M.Sc. degree from Ain Shams University, Cairo, Egypt, in 1997 and 2002, all in Computer Sciences. In 2009, he received his Ph.D. degree from Tohoku University, Japan. He is currently assistant professor in the Scientific Computing department, faculty of Computer and Information Science, Ain Shams University, Egypt. His research covers supporting VoIP applications over wired and wireless networks. Currently, he is focusing his research on the Cloud Computing areas.

M. Sundaresan is currently an Associate Professor and Head of the Department of Computer Science and Information Technology at Bharathiar University, Coimbatore, India. He did his B.Sc. (Applied Science) at Madurai Kamaraj University, MCA at Bharathidasan University, M.Phil and Ph.D in Computer Science at Bharathiar University. He is a Member of Board of Studies in Computer Science of various Universities and Autonomous Colleges. He has served as a Member of Syndicate, Senate and Standing Committee on Academic Affairs of Bharathiar University. He has contributed more than 50 research papers in different areas of Computer Science such as Image Processing, Data Compression, Natural Language Processing, Speech Processing, and Cloud Computing. He is a Senior and Life Member of Professional Bodies such as Computer Society of India, Indian Science Congress Association, Indian Society for Technical Education and IACSIT.

Girish Suryanarayana is currently a senior member of technical staff at Siemens Corporate Research and Technologies, Bangalore, India. At Siemens, he is involved in providing architectural guidance to software development teams, pursuing research in topics related to software architecture and design, and conducting internal software design and architecture training. Girish is a member of the IEEE Software Advisory Board. Girish received a PhD in information and computer science from the University of California, Irvine, in 2007. His research interests include cloud computing, software architecture, design patterns, design smells, and reputation-based trust management systems. He is an IEEE-certified Software Engineering Certified Instructor (SECI) and regularly conducts training for the IEEE SWEBOK Certificate Program (SCP) and IEEE Certified Software Development Associate (CSDA) program. He has also helped contribute course material for the IEEE's SWEBOK Certificate Program (SCP).

Tuan T. Tran received his M.S. degree from the Polytechnic University of Turin, Italy, and Ph.D. degree from Oregon State University, USA, both in Electrical and Computer Engineering, 2006 and 2010, respectively. His research interests mainly lie in the broad area of information coding and data networks with a focus on stochastic modeling, code design, and network security. He has performed significant research on the fundamental aspects of data communication networks such as network throughput optimization, code and transmission protocol design, and network security. He won a runner-up best paper award at the 19th IEEE International Conference on Computer Communication Networks (ICCCN), 2010, and is a co-recipient of Jack Neubauer Memorial Award for the best systems paper published in the IEEE Transactions on Vehicular Technology, 2012. Dr. Tran is an IEEE member. He is a workshop Co-Chairs of the 5th International Conference on Cyber-enabled Distributed Computing and Knowledge Discovery (CyberC), 2013. Dr. Tran is currently a research scientist at InfoBeyond Technology LLC. Prior to joining InfoBeyond, he has been with Arizona State University and the University of Louisville as a postdoctoral scholar.

Haibo Wang received a Ph. D. in Production Operations Management, 2004, from The University of Mississippi. He is currently associate professor of decision sciences in the Division of International Business and Technology Studies, College of Business Administration at Texas A&M International University. He has received the scholar of the year award in 2011. He is guest professor and visiting professor of a number of institutions in China and guest editors of several international journals. He has publications in such outlets as *European Journal of Operational Research, Computers and Operation*

Research, IEEE Transactions on Control System Technology, IEEE Transactions on Automation Science and Engineering, Journal of Operational Research Society, Computers and Industrial Engineering, Journal of Applied Mathematical Modeling, International Journal of Flexible Manufacturing Systems, International Journal of Production Research, Journal of Human and Ecological Risk Assessment, Journal of Heuristics, Communications in Statistics, International Journal of Information Technology and Decision Making, Journal of Combinatorial Optimization, etc.

Bin Xie received his M.Sc and Ph.D. degrees in Computer Science and Computer Engineering from the University of Louisville, Kentucky, USA, 2003 and 2006, respectively. His book titled *Handbook/Encyclopedia of Ad Hoc and Ubiquitous Computing* (World Scientific: ISBN-10: 981283348X) is one of the bestselling handbooks at World Scientific Publisher. Dr. Xie is also the author of books *Handbook of Applications and Services for Mobile Systems* (Auerbach Publication, Taylor and Francis Group, ISBN: 9781439801529, 2012) and *Heterogeneous Wireless Networks: Networking Protocol to Security* (VDM Publishing House: ISBN: 3836419270, 2007). He has published 70+ papers in the IEEE conferences, magazines, and journals. Some of papers have appeared in the most-cited journals in the areas of Telecommunication and Computer Architecture. His research interests are focused on cyber security, clouds, wireless communication, mobile computing, and user performance. In particular, he has performed substantial research works on the fundamental aspects of network deployment, intrusion detection, performance evaluation, and Internet/wireless infrastructure security. He also studied many issues of coding theory, information process, Quality of Service (QoS), clustering, and image reconstruction. Xie is the founder of InfoBeyond Technology LLC and current is the president of the InfoBeyond. InfoBeyond has delivered advanced solutions for wireless mobile ad hoc communications, network security, information process, and data protection in support of unique needs of our customers, maintaining a stable increase of business in the past few years. NXdrive (www.NXdrive.com) is a leading approach to provide secure data storage online for customers. The research works at the InfoBeyond have been broadly supported by U.S. Navy, Air Force, and Army. Dr. Xie is an IEEE senior member. He is an editor member of the *Journal of International Information Technology, Communications and Convergence* (IJITCC) and edited a special issue in 2010. He was the Guest edit chair of *Elsevier Future Generation Computer Systems* (FGCS) in a special issue on cyber-enabled knowledge discovery in 2012. Dr. Xie was invited as the program chair or TPC member of a number of international conferences.

Li Yang received her B.S. and M.S. in Finance from Jilin University, Jilin, China, and Ph.D. in Computer Science from Florida International University. She is an Associate Professor at the University of Tennessee at Chattanooga. Her research interests include mobile security, intrusion detection, network and information security, access control, and engineering techniques for complex software system design. She teaches courses in Information Assurance (IA) area including computer network security, database security, biometrics and cryptography, and system vulnerability analysis and auditing. She authored papers on these areas in refereed journal, conferences and symposiums. Her work was sponsored by National Science Foundation.

Amir Zeid is an associate professor of computer science at the American University of Kuwait (AUK). He has above 60 publications in international conferences and journals. Dr. Zeid's research interests include software engineering, cloud computing, gender-issues in computing, and using technology to promote environmental sustainability. In addition, Dr. Zeid is interested in research about creative methods in computer education. He received numerous research funding grants and international awards. Throughout his career at AUK, Dr. Zeid has been working on encouraging student innovation. He led three teams of AUK students to win the prestigious Microsoft Imagine Cup Competition for the Gulf region in two different categories. He is a member of ACM and IEEE.

Index

A

access control 19, 38, 58, 64, 71, 76, 92, 102, 107, 111, 121, 128, 130, 154, 180, 183-184, 195-197, 199, 220, 229, 239

AlternativaPlatform 159, 167

Amazon Virtual Private Cloud (VPC) 121, 146

Amazon Web Services (AWS) 94, 112, 115-122, 125, 137, 143, 148-149, 151, 154, 199, 237

authentication 12-13, 19, 38, 63, 69, 71, 74-75, 80, 89-90, 97, 102, 107, 111, 116, 118, 120-122, 124, 131, 137, 180-181, 183-184, 186-200, 229, 236-237, 239

authorization 13, 75, 89, 98-99, 112, 135, 180, 183, 185, 189, 192, 195-196, 237, 239

Automatic Data Processing (ADP) 12, 147, 173

B

big-data 115

C

cloud architecture 92, 145, 177, 182, 215, 228

cloud computing 1-2, 4-7, 9-10, 13-30, 34-37, 39-41, 43, 46, 49, 53-66, 71-74, 86-87, 89, 92, 94, 96-99, 108, 110, 112-115, 124-125, 127-128, 130, 133, 135-140, 142-147, 154-158, 160, 162, 165, 167-168, 170-178, 180-184, 190-194, 199-207, 211, 228, 232-240, 242-246

    mobile 180, 183, 191-192, 194, 199-200

cloud identity management (CIM) 140

cloud insurers 91

cloud outage 145, 151, 154

cloud provider 18-19, 26, 29-30, 41, 55, 60, 62-64, 70-71, 84, 86-87, 92, 98, 115-116, 128, 138, 141, 146, 157, 160-161, 163-167, 174, 177, 182, 184, 227, 230, 234, 238-239, 241-244

clouds 1-2, 4-9, 11, 13-22, 24-30, 34-37, 39-43, 46, 49, 54-59, 61-64, 70-76, 79, 81, 86, 91-92, 94, 97, 99-101, 108, 112-113, 115-116, 118, 121-122, 124-125, 127-128, 130, 133, 136, 138-141, 143-149, 152, 154-157, 160, 162, 164-166, 168, 170-178, 180-185, 191-192, 199-200, 202, 215, 227-240, 243-246

    community 7, 9, 20-22, 61, 170, 173, 235

    hybrid 7-9, 18, 22, 61, 151, 170, 172-173, 235

    private 7-9, 21-22, 61, 86, 121, 145-147, 151, 170, 172-173, 177, 190, 235

    public 7-9, 11, 19, 21-22, 61, 86, 89, 137, 147, 151, 170, 172-173, 198, 228, 233, 235, 238, 245

    virtual private 8, 121, 145-146

cloud security 13, 16, 18, 20, 49, 70-73, 89, 97-99, 101, 104, 112-113, 118, 122, 128, 138, 143, 146, 156, 170, 182, 184, 199, 215, 237, 245

cloud security insurance 91, 99, 112

cloud service models 91-92

cloud service providers (CSP) 8, 16, 18-19, 24-25, 28-30, 40-42, 47, 54, 64, 73-76, 80, 87, 94, 97, 99, 113, 115, 127-128, 136-140, 145, 147-148, 151-152, 154, 157, 160, 164-165, 172, 178, 180-185, 188-190, 192-193, 196, 202, 204, 207, 235-238

cloud service users (CSU) 13, 73, 145

cloud service vendors (CSV) 73

cloud storage 11, 20, 73, 76-79, 81-86, 90, 122, 145, 150, 227, 240, 245

compliance standards 91, 94, 108, 134, 141

computer forensics 162, 170, 173-174, 176-178

confidentiality, integrity and availability (CIA) model 175